D0816920

The Windows® XP Professional Cram Sheet

This Cram Sheet contains the distilled, key facts about Windows XP Professional. Review this information as the last thing you do before you enter the testing center, paying special attention to those areas where you feel that you need the most review. You can transfer any of these facts from your head onto a blank sheet of paper immediately before you begin the exam.

INSTALLATION AND DEPLOYMENT

1. Understand ACPI and APM and how to change HALs for each.

2. Know all the following processes for unattended and Remote Installation Service (RIS) installations:
   - *winnt.exe with the /u, /s, and /udf switches*—Used for unattended installations.
   - *winnt32.exe and unattend.txt*—Automate an upgrade to Windows XP.

3. **winnt32.exe** with the **checkupgradeonly** switch are used to verify hardware and software compatibility before installation.

4. **rbfg.exe** is used to create remote boot disks for RIS clients if computers don't have network adapters with Pre-boot Execution Environment (PXE) boot ROM.

5. **riprep.exe** is used to create images of Windows XP Professional and applications for an RIS server.

6. **risetup.exe** is used to configure RIS.

7. **update.exe /s** is used to apply a service pack to a distribution share in slipstream mode.

8. Know how to convert to NTFS file system after installation, as well as how to stop the conversion after it has been initialized.

9. You can rollback the old OS from Windows XP, if you have not upgraded to NTFS.

10. Know the details surrounding dynamic update for installation, as well as the critical switches: **dudisable**, **dushare**, and **duprepare**.

11. Understand the sysprep tool and the essential switches that are available: **clean**, **factory**, **nosidgen**, and **reseal**.

12. Know the two important commands used with the User State Migration Tool: **scanstate** and **loadstate**.

13. Know the differences between the different types of "updates" that can install critical files and drivers: Dynamic Update, Automatic Updates, and Windows Update.

CONFIGURING AND MANAGING RESOURCES

14. Hidden or administrative shares are share names with a dollar sign ($) appended to their names. Administrative shares are created automatically for the root of each drive letter. Hidden shares do not display in the network browse list.

15. You can allow or deny share permissions of Full Control, Change, or Read for each shared folder. The default for new shares is Everyone, Allow, Full Control. If share permissions conflict with NTFS permissions, the *most restrictive* permissions take precedence.

16. The default for new shares is Everyone, Allow, Full Control. If share permissions conflict with NTFS permissions, the most restrictive permissions take precedence.

17. When you combine NTFS permissions based on users and their group memberships, the least restrictive permissions take precedence. However, explicit Deny entries always override Allow entries.

18. To change NTFS permissions on a file or folder, you must be the owner, or have the Change Permissions permission, which itself is part of Full Control. NTFS permissions are **retained** from the source folder whenever you **move** folders or files to another folder on the **same** NTFS volume. **NTFS** permissions are inherited from the destination folder in all other move and copy operations.

19. NTFS for Windows XP supports both file compression and data encryption. Encryption is implemented via the Encrypting File System (EFS). You can compress or encrypt a file, but not both.

20. Windows XP print server computers automatically download the correct printer drivers for client computers running Windows, as long as the correct drivers have been installed on the print server machine.

21. The Internet Printing Protocol (IPP): IIS must be running on the computer you want to connect to. You can enter one of the following URLs into your Web browser:

   - http://print_server_name/printers
   - http://print_server_name/
     printer_share_name

SECURITY ACCOUNTS AND POLICIES

22. Local user and group accounts can be granted privileges and permissions to resources only on the same system.

23. Caution deleting accounts because the SID is deleted. Renaming accounts maintains all permissions and access. Copying accounts is excellent for new users with similar roles.

24. The most powerful group on a local system is the Administrators group. The Power Users group is excellent for controlling resources on the local system.

25. Organizational Units (OUs) in Active Directory create a hierarchical structure to contain users, groups, and computers.

26. Group Policy Objects apply in the order LSDOU (local, site, domain, OU). The last policy to apply controls.

27. The Resulting Set of Policies (RSoP) is the final set of policies that is applied to the user and computer. The **gpresult** tool can help determine this RSoP, as can the RSoP MMC snap-in. The **gpupdate** tool can help "refresh" the policies to ensure the correct policies are applied.

28. Incremental security templates for Windows XP can be applied to systems using the Security Configuration And Analysis snap-in.

MANAGING USER AND DESKTOP SETTINGS

29. Know the purpose and configuration of all the accessibility features: StickyKeys, FilterKeys, Narrator, Magnifier, and On-Screen Keyboard.

30. Use the MSCONFIG utility to change system startup settings, enable and disable services, and modify BOOT.ini file settings.

31. Use the Fax Console to configure the fax modem to receive faxes. By default, only an administrator can configure the fax service options. You access the Fax Console from the Printers And Faxes window available from the Control Panel.

32. Transfer data files and program settings from pre-Windows XP computers using either the User State Migration Tool (USMT) or the File Settings And Transfer (FAST) Wizard.

33. Applications can be deployed to users via a Group Policy. Applications can be either published or assigned. Install published applications via the Add and Remove Programs applet.

34. Typically, only applications compiled as an .msi file can be deployed via a Group Policy. However, non-.msi applications can use a ZAP file to tell Group Policy how to install the application.

35. To enable roaming profiles, enter the UNC path to the user's profile in the user's account properties.

36. To configure mandatory profiles, rename ntuser.dat to ntuser.man.

37. The Offline Files feature caches copies of network files locally. It is enabled by default on the client. On the server side, Manual Caching Of Documents is the default setting for shared folders. You can choose to Encrypt Offline Files To Secure Data from the Offline Files tab of the Folder Options dialog box.

38. Use the Program Compatibility Wizard to run legacy applications in Compatibility Mode for Windows 95, Windows 98/Me, Windows NT 4 SP5, or Windows 2000. No other modes are available.

MCSE™
Windows® XP
Professional

Dan Balter
Derek Melber

MCSE™ Windows® XP Professional Exam Cram

Limits of Liability and Disclaimer of Warranty

Trademarks

The Coriolis Group, LLC
14455 N. Hayden Road
Suite 220
Scottsdale, Arizona 85260

(480) 483-0192
FAX (480) 483-0193
www.coriolis.com

Library of Congress Cataloging-in-Publication Data
Balter, Dan
    MCSE Windows XP Professional / by Dan Balter and Derek Melber
       p.   cm. -- (Exam cram)
    Includes index.
    ISBN 1-578880-266-3
    1. Electronic data processing personnel--Certification.   2. Microsoft Windows XP.   3. Operating systems (Computers)   I. Melber, Derek.
II. Series.
QA76.3 .B355   2002
005.4'4769--dc21

                         2001052952
                              CIP

Printed in the United States of America
10 9 8 7 6 5 4 3 2 1

President and CEO
Roland Elgey

Publisher
Al Valvano

Associate Publisher
Katherine R. Hartlove

Acquisitions Editor
Hilary Long

Product Marketing Manager
Jeff Johnson

Project Editor
Greg Balas

Technical Reviewer
J. Peter Bruzzese

Production Coordinator
Todd Halvorsen

Cover Designer
Laura Wellander

The Coriolis Group, LLC • 14455 North Hayden Road, Suite 220 • Scottsdale, Arizona 85260

A Note from Coriolis

Our goal has always been to provide you with the best study tools on the planet to help you achieve your certification in record time. Time is so valuable these days that none of us can afford to waste a second of it, especially when it comes to exam preparation.

Over the past few years, we've created an extensive line of *Exam Cram* and *Exam Prep* study guides, practice exams, and interactive training. To help you study even better, we have now created an e-learning and certification destination called **ExamCram.com**. (You can access the site at **www.examcram.com**.) Now, with every study product you purchase from us, you'll be connected to a large community of people like yourself who are actively studying for their certifications, developing their careers, seeking advice, and sharing their insights and stories.

We believe that the future is all about collaborative learning. Our **ExamCram.com** destination is our approach to creating a highly interactive, easily accessible collaborative environment, where you can take practice exams and discuss your experiences with others, sign up for features like "Questions of the Day," plan your certifications using our interactive planners, create your own personal study pages, and keep up with all of the latest study tips and techniques.

We hope that whatever study products you purchase from us—*Exam Cram* or *Exam Prep* study guides, *Personal Trainers*, *Personal Test Centers*, or one of our interactive Web courses—will make your studying fun and productive. Our commitment is to build the kind of learning tools that will allow you to study the way you want to, whenever you want to.

Visit ExamCram.com now to enhance your study program.

Help us continue to provide the very best certification study materials possible. Write us or email us at **learn@examcram.com** and let us know how our study products have helped you study. Tell us about new features that you'd like us to add. Send us a story about how we've helped you. We're listening!

Good luck with your certification exam and your career. Thank you for allowing us to help you achieve your goals.

ExamCram.com Connects You to the Ultimate Study Center!

Look for these other products from The Coriolis Group:

MCSE Windows XP Professional Exam Prep
By Michael D. Stewart and Neall Alcott

Windows XP Professional - The Ultimate User's Guide
By Joli Ballew

Windows XP Professional Little Black Book
By Brian Proffitt

MCSA Windows 2000 Network Environment Exam Cram
By Kalani Kirk Hausman

Windows 2000 Professional On Site
By Erik Eckel and Brian Alderman

Also recently published by Coriolis Certification Insider Press:

Mac OS X Administration Basics Exam Cram
By Samuel A. Litt

CCNA Exam Cram, Third Edition
By Sheldon Barry

A+ Practice Tests Exam Cram, Second Edition
By Mike Pastore

Linux+ Exam Cram
By Michael Jang

I dedicate this book to my family—
my loving and inspiring wife of more than 11 years, Alison Balter,
my darling daughter, Alexis, and my superlative son, Brendan!
I also dedicate this book to my mother- and father-in-law,
Charlotte and Bob Roman.
—Dan Balter

❧

This book is dedicated to my two daughters, Alexa and Ashelley.
—Derek Melber

❧

About the Authors

Dan Balter is the Chief Technology Officer for InfoTechnology Partners, Inc., a Microsoft Certified Partner company. He works as an independent consultant and trainer for both corporate and government clients, and has worked with several different network operating systems throughout his 18-year career. Dan takes pride in turning complex, technical topics into easy-to-understand concepts. He has extensive experience in integrating tax and accounting software with PC networks. Dan is certified as a Microsoft Systems Engineer (MCSE), is certified on Windows XP Professional, and he had held the Certified Novell Engineer (CNE) designation for several years. He specializes in local and wide area networking, in addition to designing and implementing messaging and business solutions for large and small organizations.

Dan is a coauthor of the best-selling book, *Windows 2000 Professional Exam Cram*, also published by The Coriolis Group. Dan frequently speaks at conferences across North America, including Advisor DevCons and Windows & .NET Server Conferences. A graduate of U.S.C.'s School of Business in 1983, Dan has authored more than 300 computer training videos, including instructional titles on installing, configuring, and maintaining Windows 95, Windows 98, Windows NT, Windows 2000, and Windows XP. He is also a featured video trainer for courses on Microsoft Exchange Server, Microsoft Outlook, and Intuit's QuickBooks small business accounting software. Dan is the video trainer for *ExamBlast—Windows XP Professional* and for *QuickBooksBlast—QuickBooks 2002* training courses on video and CD-ROM. Dan Balter can be contacted at **Dan@ExamBlast.com**.

Derek Melber is an independent technical trainer, consultant, and author who specializes in Microsoft products and technologies. Derek has focused much of his attention toward education, while spending a fair amount of time on consulting. In addition to working on multiple Exam Cram books for Coriolis, including the 216 and 222 exams, Derek has recently teamed with KeyStone Learning Systems to develop a "Solutions" series for Windows 2000. The series includes topics for Migration from Windows NT to Windows 2000, Active Directory, and Group Policy/IntelliMirror. Another part of Derek's involvement in the technical industry has been speaking at national technical conferences, including MCP Magazine's TechMentor, Windows & .NET Magazine LIVE!, MIS Training

Institute's Windows 2000/.NET conference, and others. In addition, Derek has been working with some large clients to get Windows 2000 Active Directory in place, with Windows XP Professional clients. He has recently finished a 15,000-user, 400-server implementation of Windows 2000 servers, Active Directory, and Windows XP Professional.

Derek and fellow industry gurus Don Jones and Jeremy Moskowtiz are Founding Partners of BrainCore.Net, LLC, a high-end technology consulting and education firm specializing in Microsoft-centric solutions. In a world where self-proclaimed technical experts offer questionable solutions to anyone who'll listen, BrainCore.Net provides its customers with accurate technical solutions from recognized industry experts: Those you know, who know.

Derek was one of the first Windows 2000 Microsoft Certified Systems Engineers (MCSE). Although a computer guy now, he has a Masters of Civil Engineering from the University of Kansas. When he is not working on a computer, Derek is enjoying KU Jayhawk Basketball, "Rock Chalk Jayhawk!." You can catch up with Derek at **dmelber@braincore.net**.

Acknowledgments

Writing a book is never an easy task; writing a technical book for certification on a new computer operating system is especially daunting and challenging. First of all, I want to express my gratitude to my awe-inspiring wife of more than 11 years, Alison Balter, for teaching me how to really be an effective trainer, author, and consultant. I love you, honey—looking forward to our 12th anniversary in August! I also want to acknowledge my two darling kids—Alexis and Brendan, ages 5 and 2, for being so loving and fun to be around. Thanks for being so understanding of mom and dad's long hours sometimes—I love you both very, very much—time to go to Disneyland!

An incredible amount of appreciation also goes to Sonia Aguilar, her husband Hugo, and their children Claudia, Gaby, and Huguito. Thank you all for your constant love, support, and unparalleled care for our children when we're attending to business issues! Sonia, you're the best! There are several individuals who do outstanding work for my company, InfoTechnology Partners, Inc., which helps to give me an opportunity to write books like this one. These bright, hardworking souls include Bob Hess, Nikki O'Connell, Edie Swanson, Scott Barker, and Mike McClain among others. Thanks for your ongoing support, guys! All businesses need a good CPA—I love my accountant, he's the best. Thank you, David Nadel (**www.EntousNadel.com**), for all of your help, advice, and friendship!

I want to express my heartfelt gratitude to my coauthor, Derek Melber, whom I am honored to work with! I admire and appreciate your professional, no-nonsense approach to getting this book done the *right way* and *on schedule*! I could not have picked a better person to work with!

I owe much gratitude to Richard Taylor for doing a great job on writing the questions and answers for the Practice Test and Answer Key section of the book. Thanks for being on our team, Richard!

A big tip o' the hat goes to my three *previous* coauthors who collaborated with me on the *Windows 2000 Professional Exam Cram* book: Dan Holme, Todd Logan, and Laurie Salmon of trainAbility, Inc. Although this *Windows XP Professional Exam Cram* book was completely revised, updated, and virtually rewritten by Derek and myself, their *prior* work was helpful as a framework for some of the core operating system topics.

Everyone at The Coriolis Group has been great to work with. I especially want to thank Greg Balas for being so understanding as we attempted to meet all of our deadlines. I also enjoyed working with Hilary Long, who got us our contract in a timely manner so that we could start working on the book as soon as possible.

Big thanks also go out to Greggory Peck, vice president in charge of production for ExamBlast (**www.ExamBlast.com**). Thank you for giving me the opportunity to become a trainer using video-based and CD-ROM-based technology. Alan Sugano is always there whenever I have a burning question—thank you so much for all of your support and assistance through the years! To Charlotte and Bob Roman (my in-laws)—thank you both for everything that you do for us, all the time! You two are great travel companions and terrific grandparents! Finally, to my Mom and Dad—thanks for emphasizing reading and writing, among other things—those skills come in quite handy for authoring technical books!
—*Dan Balter*

This book would not be created if it weren't for my spectacular family: Yvette, Alexa, and the newest member, Ashelley. It is easy to keep things in perspective with such incredible women around me. Many thanks to my coauthor, Dan Balter, for his friendship, knowledge, and ability to always see the glass half full.

I also can't say enough about the Coriolis team: Thank you to our acquisitions editor, Hilary Long, for her great organization skills; our project editor, Greg Balas, for his ability to keep us on course; our technical reviewer, Peter Bruzzese, for his expansive knowledge of Microsoft products, and Bill McManus for his incredible vocabulary and editing skills. Also special thanks to Tiffany Taylor and Alexandra Nickerson, who proofread and indexed the book, respectively. Also, a thanks goes out to our production coordinator at Coriolis, Todd Halvorsen; our cover designer, Laura Wellander; and our Coriolis product marketing manager, Jeff Johnson.

Finally, to my business partners, Jeremy and Don, thank you for your incredible knowledge and ability to force me to think on the next level. Last and not least, to the one who allows me to stop, think, and ask the question, WWJD?
—*Derek Melber*

Table of Contents

Chapter 4
Setting Up, Managing, and Troubleshooting Security Accounts and Policies 115

Chapter 6
Installing, Configuring, and Troubleshooting Hardware Devices and Drivers 195

Introduction

Welcome to *MCSE Windows XP Professional Exam Cram*! Whether this is your first or your fifteenth *Exam Cram* book, you'll find information here and in Chapter 1 that will help ensure your success as you pursue knowledge, experience, and certification. This book aims to help you get ready to take—and pass—the Microsoft certification Exam 70-270, titled "Installing, Configuring, and Administering Microsoft Windows XP Professional." This Introduction explains Microsoft's certification programs, in general, and talks about how the *Exam Cram* series can help you prepare for Microsoft's Windows 2000 and Windows XP certification exams.

Exam Cram books help you understand and appreciate the subjects and materials you need to pass Microsoft certification exams. *Exam Cram* books are aimed strictly at test preparation and review. They do not teach you everything you need to know about a topic. Instead, we (the authors) present and dissect the questions and problems we've found that you're likely to encounter on a test. We've worked to bring together as much information as possible about Microsoft certification exams.

Nevertheless, to completely prepare yourself for any Microsoft test, we recommend that you begin by taking the Self-Assessment included in this book immediately following this Introduction. This tool will help you evaluate your knowledge base against the requirements for an MCSA or MCSE under both ideal and real circumstances.

Based on what you learn from that exercise, you might decide to begin your studies with some classroom training or some background reading. On the other hand, you might decide to pick up and read one of the many study guides available from Microsoft or third-party vendors on certain topics, including The Coriolis Group's *Exam Prep* series. We also recommend that you supplement your study program with visits to **ExamCram.com** to receive additional practice questions, get advice, and track the Windows 2000 MCSA and MCSE program.

We also strongly recommend that you install, configure, and fool around with Windows XP Professional, because nothing beats hands-on experience and familiarity when it comes to understanding the questions you're likely to encounter on a certification test. Book learning is essential, but hands-on experience is the best teacher of all!

The Microsoft Certified Professional (MCP) Program

The MCP Program currently includes the following separate tracks, each of which boasts its own special acronym (as a certification candidate, you need to have a high tolerance for alphabet soup of all kinds):

➤ *MCP (Microsoft Certified Professional)*—This is the least prestigious of all the certification tracks from Microsoft. Passing one of the major Microsoft exams qualifies an individual for the MCP credential. Individuals can demonstrate proficiency with additional Microsoft products by passing additional certification exams.

➤ *MCP+SB (Microsoft Certified Professional + Site Building)*—This certification program is designed for individuals who are planning, building, managing, and maintaining Web sites. Individuals with the MCP+SB credential will have demonstrated the ability to develop Web sites that include multimedia and searchable content and Web sites that connect to and communicate with a back-end database. It requires one MCP exam, plus two of these three exams: 70-055, "Designing and Implementing Web Sites with Microsoft FrontPage 98," 70-057, "Designing and Implementing Commerce Solutions with Microsoft Site Server 3.0, Commerce Edition," and 70-152, "Designing and Implementing Web Solutions with Microsoft Visual InterDev 6.0." Microsoft retired Exam 70-055 on June 30, 2001 and will retire the MCP+SB certification on June 30, 2002.

➤ *MCSA (Microsoft Certified Systems Administrator)*—This exam is for anyone who has a Windows NT 4 MCSE and/or possesses a high level of networking expertise with Microsoft operating systems and products. This credential is designed to prepare individuals to plan, implement, maintain, and support information systems, networks, and Internetworks built around Microsoft Windows 2000 and Windows XP.

To obtain an MCSA, you must pass three core operating system exams and one elective exam. The operating system exams are designed to test your competency over the server and client aspects of a network, as well as managing a Windows 2000 network.

Note: If you have already passed the 70-240 exam, you will only need to pass the 70-218 exam, which is the Windows 2000 network management aspect of the MCSA certification. For more information on this exam, read below in the MCSE section.

New MCSA candidates must pass four tests to meet the MCSA requirements. It's not uncommon for the entire process to take almost a year or so, and many individuals find that they must take a test more than once to pass.

Table 1   MCSA Certification Requirements.

Client OS Exams

You must pass one of the following exams:

70-210 Installing, Configuring, and Administering Microsoft Windows 2000 Professional
OR
70-270 Installing, Configuring, and Administering Microsoft Windows XP Professional

Networking System Exams

You must pass two of the following exams:

70-215 Installing, Configuring, and Administering Microsoft Windows 2000 Server
OR
70-275 Installing, Configuring, and Administering Microsoft Windows .NET Server

70-218 Managing a Microsoft Windows 2000 Network Environment
OR
70-278 Managing a Microsoft Windows .NET Server Network Environment

Elective Exams

You must pass one of the following exams:

70-086 Implementing and Supporting Microsoft Systems Management Server 2.0

70-028 Administering Microsoft SQL Server 7.0

70-228 Installing, Configuring, and Administering Microsoft SQL Server 2000 Enterprise Edition

70-081 Implementing and Supporting Microsoft Exchange Server 5.5

70-224 Installing, Configuring, and Administering Microsoft Exchange 2000 Server

70-088 Implementing and Supporting Microsoft Proxy Server 2.0

70-227 Installing, Configuring, and Administering Microsoft Internet Security and Acceleration (ISA) Server 2000, Enterprise Edition

70-216 Implementing and Administering a Microsoft Windows 2000 Network Infrastructure

70-244 Supporting and Maintaining a Microsoft Windows NT Server 4.0 Network

CompTIA A+ and CompTIA Network+
OR
CompTIA A+ and CompTIA Server+

The primary goal of the *Exam Prep* and *Exam Cram* test preparation books is to make it possible, given proper study and preparation, to pass all Microsoft certification tests on the first try. Table 1 shows the required and elective exams for the Windows 2000 MCSA certification.

➤ *MCSE (Microsoft Certified Systems Engineer)*—Anyone who has a current MCSE is warranted to possess a high level of networking expertise with Microsoft operating systems and products. This credential is designed to prepare individuals to plan, design, implement, maintain, and support information systems, networks, and Internetworks built around Microsoft Windows 2000/XP and its BackOffice Server 2000 family of products.

To obtain an MCSE, an individual must pass four core operating system exams, one core design exam, and two elective exams. The operating system exams require individuals to prove their competence with desktop and server operating systems and networking/Internetworking components.

For Windows NT 4 MCSEs, the Accelerated exam, 70-240, "Microsoft Windows 2000 Accelerated Exam for MCPs Certified on Microsoft Windows NT 4.0," was an option. This free exam covered all of the material tested in the core four exams. The hitch in this plan is that you could take the test only once. If you failed, you were required to take all four core exams to recertify. The core four exams are as follows: 70-210, "Installing, Configuring, and Administering Microsoft Windows 2000 Professional" or 70-270, "Installing, Configuring, and Administering Microsoft Windows XP Professional"; 70-215, "Installing, Configuring, and Administering Microsoft Windows 2000 Server"; 70-216, "Implementing and Administering a Microsoft Windows 2000 Network Infrastructure"; and 70-217, "Implementing and Administering a Microsoft Windows 2000 Directory Services Infrastructure."

Note: The 70-240 exam expired December 31, 2001. So, if you had received a voucher for this exam, but were not able to take this exam in time, you will need to take the four core exams to recertify.

To fulfill the fifth core exam requirement, you can choose from four design exams: 70-219, "Designing a Microsoft Windows 2000 Directory Services Infrastructure," 70-220, "Designing Security for a Microsoft Windows 2000 Network," 70-221, "Designing a Microsoft Windows 2000 Network Infrastructure," or 70-226, "Designing Highly Available Web Solutions with Microsoft Windows 2000 Server Technologies." You are also required to take two elective exams. An elective exam can fall within any number of subject or product areas, primarily BackOffice Server 2000 components. The three design exams that you don't select as your fifth core exam also qualify as electives. If you are on your way to becoming an MCSE and have already taken some exams, visit **www.microsoft.com/** for information about how to complete your MCSE certification.

New MCSE candidates must pass seven tests to meet the MCSE requirements. It's not uncommon for the entire process to take a year or so, and many individuals find that they must take a test more than once to pass. The primary goal of the *Exam Prep* and *Exam Cram* test preparation books is to make it possible, given proper study and preparation, to pass all Microsoft certification tests on the first try. Table 2 shows the required and elective exams for the Windows 2000 MCSE certification.

Table 2 MCSE Certification Requirements.

Client OS Exams

You must pass one of the following exams:

70-210 Installing, Configuring, and Administering Microsoft Windows 2000 Professional
OR
▶ **70-270** Installing, Configuring, and Administering Microsoft Windows XP Professional

(continued)

Table 2   MCSE Certification Requirements *(continued)*.

Networking System Exams

You must pass three of the following exams:

70-215 Installing, Configuring, and Administering Microsoft Windows 2000 Server
OR
70-275 Installing, Configuring, and Administering Microsoft Windows .NET Server

70-216 Implementing and Administering a Microsoft Windows 2000 Network Infrastructure
OR
70-276 Implementing and Administering a Microsoft Windows .NET Server Network Infrastructure

70-217 Implementing and Administering a Microsoft Windows 2000 Directory Services Infrastructure
OR
70-277 Implementing and Administering a Microsoft Windows .NET Server Directory Services Infrastructure

Windows 2000 Design Exams

You must pass one of the following exams:

70-219* Designing a Microsoft Windows 2000 Directory Services Infrastructure

70-220* Designing Security for a Microsoft Windows 2000 Network

70-221* Designing a Microsoft Windows 2000 Network Infrastructure

70-226* Designing Highly Available Web Solutions with Microsoft Windows 2000 Server Technologies

Elective Exams

You must pass two of the following exams:

70-085 Implementing and Supporting Microsoft SNA Server 4.0

70-086 Implementing and Supporting Microsoft Systems Management Server 2.0

70-019 Designing and Implementing Data Warehouses with Microsoft SQL Server 7.0

70-029 Designing and Implementing Databases with Microsoft SQL Server 7.0
OR
70-229 Designing and Implementing Databases with Microsoft SQL Server 2000 Enterprise Edition

70-028 Administering Microsoft SQL Server 7.0
OR
70-228 Installing, Configuring, and Administering Microsoft SQL Server 2000 Enterprise Edition

70-081 Implementing and Supporting Microsoft Exchange Server 5.5
OR
70-224 Installing, Configuring, and Administering Microsoft Exchange 2000 Server

70-088 Implementing and Supporting Microsoft Proxy Server 2.0
OR
70-227 Installing, Configuring, and Administering Microsoft Internet Security and Acceleration (ISA) Server 2000, Enterprise Edition

70-080 Implementing and Supporting Microsoft Internet Explorer 5.0 by Using the Microsoft Internet Explorer Administration Kit

70-218 Managing a Microsoft Windows 2000 Network Environment

70-222 Migrating from Microsoft Windows NT 4.0 to Microsoft Windows 2000

70-223 Installing, Configuring, and Administering Microsoft Clustering Services by Using Microsoft Windows 2000 Advanced Server

70-225 Designing and Deploying a Messaging Infrastructure with Microsoft Exchange 2000 Server

70-230 Designing and Implementing Solutions with Microsoft BizTalk Server 2000

70-232 Implementing and Maintaining Highly Available Web Solutions with Microsoft Windows 2000 Server Technologies and Microsoft Applicatin Center 2000

70-234 Designing and Implementing Solutions with Microsoft Commerce Server 2000

70-244 Supporting and Maintaining a Microsoft Windows NT Server 4.0 Network

* These exams may also be used as electives, but can only be counted once toward a certification. You cannot receive credit for an exam as both a core and an elective in the same track.

➤ *MCSD (Microsoft Certified Solution Developer)*—The MCSD credential reflects the skills required to create multitier, distributed, and COM-based solutions, in addition to desktop and Internet applications, using new technologies. To obtain an MCSD, an individual must demonstrate the ability to analyze and interpret user requirements; select and integrate products, platforms, tools, and technologies; design and implement code, and customize applications; and perform necessary software tests and quality assurance operations.

To become an MCSD, you must pass a total of four exams: three core exams and one elective exam. Each candidate must choose one of these three desktop application exams: 70-016, "Designing and Implementing Desktop Applications with Microsoft Visual C++ 6.0," 70-156, "Designing and Implementing Desktop Applications with Microsoft Visual FoxPro 6.0," or 70-176, "Designing and Implementing Desktop Applications with Microsoft Visual Basic 6.0." Additionally, each candidate must choose one of these three distributed application exams: 70-015, "Designing and Implementing Distributed Applications with Microsoft Visual C++ 6.0," 70-155, "Designing and Implementing Distributed Applications with Microsoft Visual FoxPro 6.0," or 70-175, "Designing and Implementing Distributed Applications with Microsoft Visual Basic 6.0." The third core exam is 70-100, "Analyzing Requirements and Defining Solution Architectures." Elective exams cover specific Microsoft applications and languages, including Visual Basic, C++, the Microsoft Foundation Classes, Access, SQL Server, Excel, and more.

➤ *MCDBA (Microsoft Certified Database Administrator)*—The MCDBA credential reflects the skills required to implement and administer Microsoft SQL Server databases. To obtain an MCDBA, an individual must demonstrate the ability to derive physical database designs, develop logical data models, create physical databases, create data services by using Transact-SQL, manage and maintain databases, configure and manage security, monitor and optimize databases, and install and configure Microsoft SQL Server.

To become an MCDBA, you must pass a total of three core exams and one elective exam. The required core exams are as follows: 70-028, "Administering Microsoft SQL Server 7.0" or 70-228, "Installing, Configuring, and Administering Microsoft SQL Server 2000 Enterprise Edition"; 70-029, "Designing and Implementing Databases with Microsoft SQL Server 7.0" or 70-229, "Designing and Implementing Databases with Microsoft SQL Server 2000 Enterprise Edition"; and 70-215, "Installing, Configuring, and Administering Microsoft Windows 2000 Server" or 70-240, "Microsoft Windows 2000 Accelerated Exam for MCPs Certified on Microsoft Windows NT."

The elective exams that you can choose from cover specific uses of SQL Server and include: 70-015, "Designing and Implementing Distributed Applications with Microsoft Visual C++ 6.0," 70-019, "Designing and Implementing Data Warehouses with Microsoft SQL Server 7.0," 70-155, "Designing and Implementing Distributed Applications with Microsoft Visual FoxPro 6.0," 70-175, "Designing and Implementing Distributed Applications with Microsoft Visual Basic 6.0," and two exams that relate to Windows 2000, 70-216, "Implementing and Administering a Microsoft Windows 2000 Network Infrastructure" and 70-087, "Implementing and Supporting Microsoft Internet Information Server 4.0."

If you have taken the three core Windows NT 4 exams on your path to becoming an MCSE, you qualified for the Accelerated exam (it replaced the Network Infrastructure exam requirement). The Accelerated exam covered the objectives of all four of the Windows 2000 core exams. In addition to taking the Accelerated exam, you must take only the two SQL exams—Administering and Database Design, 70-028 and 70-029, respectively.

➤ *MCT (Microsoft Certified Trainer)*—Microsoft Certified Trainers are deemed able to deliver elements of the official Microsoft curriculum, based on technical knowledge and instructional ability. Thus, it is necessary for an individual seeking MCT credentials (which are granted on a course-by-course basis) to pass the related certification exam for a course and complete the official Microsoft training in the subject area, and to demonstrate an ability to teach.

This teaching skill criterion may be satisfied by proving that you have already attained training certification from Novell, Banyan, Lotus, the Santa Cruz Operation, or Cisco, or by taking a Microsoft-sanctioned workshop on instruction. Microsoft makes it clear that MCTs are important cogs in the Microsoft training channels. Instructors must be MCTs before Microsoft will allow them to teach in any of its official training channels, including Microsoft's affiliated Certified Technical Education Centers (CTECs) and its online training partner network. As of January 1, 2001, MCT candidates must also possess a current MCSE.

Microsoft has announced that the MCP+I and MCSE+I credentials will not be continued when the MCSE exams for Windows 2000/XP are in full swing because the skill set for the Internet portion of the program has been included in the new MCSE program. Therefore, details on these tracks are not provided here; go to **www.microsoft.com/** if you need more information.

After a Microsoft product becomes obsolete, MCPs typically have to recertify on current versions. (If individuals do not recertify, their certifications become invalid.) Because technology keeps changing and new products continually supplant old ones, this should come as no surprise. This explains why Microsoft announced that MCSEs had 12 months past the scheduled retirement date for the Windows NT 4 exams to recertify on Windows 2000 topics. (Note that this means taking at least two exams, if not more.)

The best place to keep tabs on the MCP program and its related certifications is on the Web. The URL for the MCP program is **www.microsoft.com/ trainingandservices/**. But Microsoft's Web site changes often, so if this URL doesn't work, try using the Search tool on Microsoft's site with either "MCP" or the quoted phrase "Microsoft Certified Professional" as a search string. This will help you find the latest and most accurate information about Microsoft's certification programs.

Taking a Certification Exam

After you've prepared for your exam, you need to register with a testing center. Each computer-based MCP exam costs $125, and if you don't pass, you may retest for an additional $125 for each additional try. In the United States and Canada, tests are administered by Prometric and by Virtual University Enterprises (VUE). Here's how you can contact them:

➤ *Prometric*—You can sign up for a test through the company's Web site at **www.prometric.com**. Within the United States and Canada, you can register by phone at 800-755-3926. If you live outside this region, check the company's Web site for the appropriate phone number.

➤ *Virtual University Enterprises*—You can sign up for a test or get the phone numbers for local testing centers through the Web at **www.vue.com/ms/**.

To sign up for a test, you must possess a valid credit card, or contact either company for mailing instructions to send them a check (in the U.S.). Only when payment is verified, or a check has cleared, can you actually register for a test.

To schedule an exam, call the number or visit either of the Web pages at least one day in advance. To cancel or reschedule an exam, you must call before 7 P.M. pacific standard time the day before the scheduled test time (or you may be charged, even if you don't appear to take the test). When you want to schedule a test, have the following information ready:

➤ Your name, organization, and mailing address.

➤ Your Microsoft Test ID. (Inside the United States, this means your Social Security number; citizens of other nations should call ahead to find out what type of identification number is required to register for a test.)

➤ The name and number of the exam you wish to take.

➤ A method of payment. (As we've already mentioned, a credit card is the most convenient method, but alternate means can be arranged in advance, if necessary.)

After you sign up for a test, you'll be informed as to when and where the test is scheduled. Try to arrive at least 15 minutes early. You must supply two forms of identification—one of which must be a photo ID—to be admitted into the testing room.

All exams are completely closed-book. In fact, you will not be permitted to take anything with you into the testing area, but you will be furnished with a blank sheet of paper and a pen or, in some cases, an erasable plastic sheet and an erasable pen. We suggest that you immediately write down on that sheet of paper all the information you've memorized for the test. In *Exam Cram* books, this information appears on a tear-out sheet inside the front cover of each book. You will have some time to compose yourself, record this information, and take a sample orientation exam before you begin the real thing. We suggest you take the orientation test before taking your first exam, but because they're all more or less identical in layout, behavior, and controls, you probably won't need to do this more than once.

When you complete a Microsoft certification exam, the software will tell you whether you've passed or failed. If you need to retake an exam, you'll have to schedule a new test with Prometric or VUE and pay another $125.

 The first time you fail a test, you can retake the test the next day. However, if you fail a second time, you must wait 14 days before retaking that test. The 14-day waiting period remains in effect for all retakes after the second failure.

Tracking MCP Status

As soon as you pass any Microsoft exam, you'll attain Microsoft Certified Professional (MCP) status. Microsoft also generates transcripts that indicate which exams you have passed. You can view a copy of your transcript at any time by going to the MCP secured site and selecting Transcript Tool. This tool will enable you to print a copy of your current transcript and confirm your certification status.

After you pass the necessary set of exams, you'll be certified. Official certification normally takes anywhere from six to eight weeks, so don't expect to get your credentials overnight. When the package for a qualified certification arrives, it includes a Welcome Kit that contains a number of elements (see Microsoft's Web site for other benefits of specific certifications):

➤ A certificate suitable for framing, along with a wallet card and lapel pin.

➤ A license to use the MCP logo, thereby allowing you to use the logo in advertisements, promotions, and documents, and on letterhead, business cards, and so on. Along with the license comes an MCP logo sheet, which includes camera-ready artwork. (Note: Before using any of the artwork, individuals must sign and return a licensing agreement that indicates they'll abide by its terms and conditions.)

➤ A subscription to *Microsoft Certified Professional Magazine*, which provides ongoing data about testing and certification activities, requirements, and changes to the program.

Many people believe that the benefits of MCP certification go well beyond the perks that Microsoft provides to newly anointed members of this elite group. We're starting to see more job listings that request or require applicants to have an MCP, MCSE, and so on, and many individuals who complete the program can qualify for increases in pay and/or responsibility. As an official recognition of hard work and broad knowledge, one of the MCP credentials is a badge of honor in many IT organizations.

How to Prepare for an Exam

Preparing for any Windows 2000- or Windows XP-related test (including "Installing, Configuring, and Administering Microsoft Windows XP Professional") requires that you obtain and study materials designed to provide comprehensive information about the product and its capabilities that will appear on the specific exam for which you are preparing. The following list of materials will help you study and prepare:

➤ The Windows XP Professional product CD includes comprehensive online documentation and related materials; it should be a primary resource when you are preparing for the test.

➤ The exam preparation materials, practice tests, and self-assessment exams on the Microsoft Training & Services page at **www.microsoft.com/**. The Testing Innovations link offers samples of the new question types found on the Windows 2000 MCSA and MCSE exams. Find the materials, download them, and use them!

➤ The exam preparation advice, practice tests, questions of the day, and discussion groups on the **ExamCram.com** e-learning and certification destination Web site (**www.examcram.com**).

In addition, you'll probably find any or all of the following materials useful in your quest for Windows XP Professional expertise:

➤ *Microsoft training kits*—Microsoft Press offers a training kit that specifically targets Exam 70-270. For more information, visit: **http://mspress.microsoft. com/findabook/list/series_ak.htm**. This training kit contains information that you will find useful in preparing for the test.

➤ *Microsoft TechNet CD*—This monthly CD-based publication delivers numerous electronic titles that include coverage of Windows XP Professional and related topics on the Technical Information (TechNet) CD. Its offerings include product facts, technical notes, tools and utilities, and information on how to access the Seminars Online training materials for Windows XP Professional. A subscription to TechNet costs $299 per year, but it is well worth the price. Visit **www.microsoft.com/technet/** and check out the information under the "TechNet Subscription" menu entry for more details.

➤ *Study guides*—Several publishers—including The Coriolis Group—offer Windows 2000 titles. The Coriolis Group series includes the following:

  ➤ *The Exam Cram series*—These books give you information about the material you need to know to pass the tests.

  ➤ *The Exam Prep series*—These books provide a greater level of detail than the *Exam Cram* books and are designed to teach you everything you need to know from an exam perspective. Each book comes with a CD that contains interactive practice exams in a variety of testing formats.

  Together, the two series make a perfect pair.

➤ *Multimedia*—These Coriolis Group materials are designed to support learners of all types—whether you learn best by reading or doing:

  ➤ *The Exam Cram Personal Trainer*—Offers a unique, personalized self-paced training course based on the exam.

  ➤ *The Exam Cram Personal Test Center*—Features multiple test options that simulate the actual exam, including Fixed-Length, Random, Review, and Test All. Explanations of correct and incorrect answers reinforce concepts learned.

➤ *Classroom training*—CTECs, online partners, and third-party training companies (like Wave Technologies, Learning Tree, Data-Tech, and others) all offer classroom training on Windows XP. These companies aim to help you prepare to pass Exam 70-270. Although such training runs upwards of $350 per day in class, most of the individuals lucky enough to partake find it to be quite worthwhile.

➤ *Other publications*—There's no shortage of materials available about Windows XP Professional. The "Need to Know More?" resource sections at the end of each chapter give you an idea of where we think you should look for further discussion.

By far, this set of required and recommended materials represents a nonpareil collection of sources and resources for Windows XP Professional and related topics. We anticipate that you'll find that this book belongs in this company.

About this Book

Each topical *Exam Cram* chapter follows a regular structure, along with graphical cues about important or useful information. Here's the structure of a typical chapter:

➤ *Opening hotlists*—Each chapter begins with a list of the terms, tools, and techniques that you must learn and understand before you can be fully conversant with that chapter's subject matter. We follow the hotlists with one or two introductory paragraphs to set the stage for the rest of the chapter.

➤ *Topical coverage*—After the opening hotlists, each chapter covers a series of topics related to the chapter's subject title. Throughout this section, we highlight topics or concepts likely to appear on a test using a special Exam Alert layout, like this:

This is what an Exam Alert looks like. Normally, an Exam Alert stresses concepts, terms, software, or activities that are likely to relate to one or more certification test questions. For that reason, we think any information found offset in Exam Alert format is worthy of unusual attentiveness on your part. Indeed, most of the information that appears on The Cram Sheet appears as Exam Alerts within the text.

Pay close attention to material flagged as an Exam Alert; although all the information in this book pertains to what you need to know to pass the exam, we flag certain items that are really important. You'll find what appears in the meat of each chapter to be worth knowing, too, when preparing for the test. Because this book's material is very condensed, we recommend that you use this book along with other resources to achieve the maximum benefit.

In addition to the Exam Alerts, we have provided tips that will help you build a better foundation for Windows XP Professional knowledge. Although the information may not be on the exam, it is certainly related and will help you become a better test-taker.

This is how tips are formatted. Keep your eyes open for these, and you'll become a Windows XP Professional guru in no time!

➤ *Practice questions*—Although we talk about test questions and topics throughout the book, a section at the end of each chapter presents a series of mock test questions and explanations of both correct and incorrect answers.

➤ *Details and resources*—Every chapter ends with a section titled "Need to Know More?". This section provides direct pointers to Microsoft and third-party resources offering more details on the chapter's subject. In addition, this section tries to rank or at least rate the quality and thoroughness of the topic's coverage by each resource. If you find a resource you like in this collection, use it, but don't feel compelled to use all the resources. On the other hand, we recommend only resources we use on a regular basis, so none of our recommendations will be a waste of your time or money (but purchasing them all at once probably represents an expense that many network administrators and would-be MCPs and MCSEs might find hard to justify).

The bulk of the book follows this chapter structure slavishly, but we'd like to point out a few other elements. Chapter 11 includes a sample test that provides a good review of the material presented throughout the book to ensure you're ready for the exam. Chapter 12 is an answer key to the sample test that appears in Chapter 11. In addition, you'll find a handy glossary and an index.

Finally, the tear-out Cram Sheet attached next to the inside front cover of this *Exam Cram* book represents a condensed and compiled collection of facts and tips that we think you should memorize before taking the test. Because you can dump this information out of your head onto a piece of paper before taking the exam, you can master this information by brute force—you need to remember it only long enough to write it down when you walk into the test room. You might even want to look at it in the car or in the lobby of the testing center just before you walk in to take the test.

How to Use this Book

We've structured the topics in this book to build on one another. Therefore, some topics in later chapters make more sense after you've read earlier chapters. That's why we suggest you read this book from front to back for your initial test preparation. If you need to brush up on a topic or you have to bone up for a second try, use the index or table of contents to go straight to the topics and questions that you need to study. Beyond helping you prepare for the test, we think you'll find this book useful as a tightly focused reference to some of the most important aspects of Windows XP Professional.

Given all the book's elements and its specialized focus, we've tried to create a tool that will help you prepare for—and pass—Microsoft Exam 70-270. Please share your feedback on the book with us, especially if you have ideas about how we can improve it for future test-takers. We'll consider everything you say carefully, and we'll respond to all suggestions.

Send your questions or comments to us at **learn@examcram.com**. Please remember to include the title of the book in your message; otherwise, we'll be forced to guess which book you're writing about. And we don't like to guess—we want to *know*! Also, be sure to check out the Web pages at **www.examcram.com**, where you'll find information updates, commentary, and certification information.

Thanks, and enjoy the book!

Self-Assessment

The reason we included a Self-Assessment in this *Exam Cram* book is to help you evaluate your readiness to tackle MCSE certification. It should also help you understand what you need to know to master the topic of this book—namely, Exam 70-270 "Installing, Configuring, and Administering Microsoft Windows XP Professional." But before you tackle this Self-Assessment, let's talk about concerns you may face when pursuing an MCSE for Windows XP, and what an ideal MCSE candidate might look like.

MCSEs In the Real World

In the next section, we describe an ideal MCSE candidate, knowing full well that only a few real candidates will meet this ideal. In fact, our description of that ideal candidate might seem downright scary, especially with the changes that have been made to the program to support Windows 2000 and Windows XP. But take heart: Although the requirements to obtain an MCSE may seem formidable, they are by no means impossible to meet. However, be keenly aware that it does take time, involves some expense, and requires real effort to get through the process.

Increasing numbers of people are attaining Microsoft certifications, so the goal is within reach. You can get all the real-world motivation you need from knowing that many others have gone before, so you will be able to follow in their footsteps. If you're willing to tackle the process seriously and do what it takes to obtain the necessary experience and knowledge, you can take—and pass—all the certification tests involved in obtaining an MCSE. In fact, we've designed *Exam Preps*, the companion *Exam Crams*, *Exam Cram Personal Trainers*, and *Exam Cram Personal Test Centers* to make it as easy on you as possible to prepare for these exams. We've also greatly expanded our Web site, **www.examcram.com**, to provide a host of resources to help you prepare for the complexities of Windows 2000 and Windows XP.

Besides MCSE, other Microsoft certifications include the following:

➤ *MCSA (Microsoft Certified Systems Administrator)*—This is the brand new certification that Microsoft has provided for those Microsoft professionals who are not going to design networks, but rather administer networks. This certification includes three core exams (210 or 270, 215, and 218) and a single elective.

Instead of two core exams and the elective, you could have taken the 70-240 exam, which is to replace the 210/270, 215, 216, and 217 exams for those Microsoft professionals who upgraded from Windows NT to Windows 2000.

➤ *MCSD (Microsoft Certified Solution Developer)*—This is aimed at software developers and requires one specific exam, two more exams on client and distributed topics, plus a fourth, elective exam drawn from a different, but limited, pool of options.

➤ *Other Microsoft certifications*—The requirements for these certifications range from one test (MCP) to several tests (MCP+SB, MCDBA, and so on).

The Ideal Windows 2000 MCSE Candidate

Just to give you some idea of what an ideal MCSE candidate is like, here are some relevant statistics about the background and experience such an individual might have. Don't worry if you don't meet these qualifications, or don't come that close—this is a far-from-ideal world, and where you fall short is simply where you'll have more work to do.

➤ Academic or professional training in network theory, concepts, and operations. This includes everything from networking media and transmission techniques through network operating systems, services, and applications.

➤ Three-plus years of professional networking experience, including experience with Ethernet, Token Ring, modems, and other networking media. This must include installation, configuration, upgrade, and troubleshooting experience.

Note: The Windows 2000 MCSE program is much more rigorous than the previous NT MCSE program; therefore, you'll really need some hands-on experience. Some of the exams require you to solve real-world case studies and network design issues, so the more hands-on experience you have, the better.

➤ Two-plus years in a networked environment that includes hands-on experience with Windows 2000 Server, Windows 2000/XP Professional, Windows NT Server, Windows NT Workstation, and Windows 95 or Windows 98. A solid understanding of each system's architecture, installation, configuration, maintenance, and troubleshooting is also essential.

➤ Knowledge of the various methods for installing Windows 2000, including manual and unattended installations.

➤ A thorough understanding of key networking protocols, addressing, and name resolution, including TCP/IP, IPX/SPX, and NetBEUI.

➤ A thorough understanding of NetBIOS naming, browsing, and file and print services.

➤ Familiarity with key Windows 2000/XP-based TCP/IP-based services, including HTTP (Web servers), DHCP, WINS, and DNS, plus familiarity with one or more of the following: Internet Information Server (IIS), Index Server, and Proxy Server.

➤ An understanding of how to implement security for key network data in a Windows 2000/XP environment.

➤ Working knowledge of NetWare 3.x and 4.x, including IPX/SPX frame formats, NetWare file, print, and directory services, and both Novell and Microsoft client software. Working knowledge of Microsoft's Client Service For NetWare (CSNW), Gateway Service For NetWare (GSNW), the NetWare Migration Tool (NWCONV), and the NetWare Client For Windows (NT, 95, and 98) is essential.

➤ A good working understanding of Active Directory. The more you work with Windows 2000, the more you'll realize that this new operating system is quite different than Windows NT. New technologies like Active Directory have really changed the way that Windows is configured and used. We recommend that you find out as much as you can about Active Directory and acquire as much experience using this technology as possible. The time you take learning about Active Directory will be time very well spent!

Fundamentally, this boils down to a bachelor's degree in computer science, plus three years' experience working in a position involving network design, installation, configuration, and maintenance. We believe that well under half of all certification candidates meet these requirements, and that, in fact, most meet less than half of these requirements—at least, when they begin the certification process. But because all the people who already have been certified have survived this ordeal, you can survive it too—especially if you heed what our Self-Assessment can tell you about what you already know and what you need to learn.

Put Yourself to the Test

The following series of questions and observations is designed to help you figure out how much work you must do to pursue Microsoft certification and what kinds of resources you may consult on your quest. Be absolutely honest in your answers, or you'll end up wasting money on exams you're not yet ready to take. There are no right or wrong answers, only steps along the path to certification. Only you can decide where you really belong in the broad spectrum of aspiring candidates.

Two things should be clear from the outset, however:

➤ Even a modest background in computer science will be helpful.

➤ Hands-on experience with Microsoft products and technologies is an essential ingredient to certification success.

Educational Background

1. Have you ever taken any computer-related classes? [Yes or No]

   If Yes, proceed to Question 2; if No, proceed to Question 4.

2. Have you taken any classes on computer operating systems? [Yes or No]

   If Yes, you will probably be able to handle Microsoft's architecture and system component discussions. If you're rusty, brush up on basic operating system concepts, especially virtual memory, multitasking regimes, user mode versus kernel mode operation, and general computer security topics.

   If No, consider some basic reading in this area. We strongly recommend a good general operating systems book, such as *Operating System Concepts, 5th Edition*, by Abraham Silberschatz and Peter Baer Galvin (John Wiley & Sons, 1998, ISBN 0-471-36414-2). If this title doesn't appeal to you, check out reviews for other, similar titles at your favorite online bookstore.

3. Have you taken any networking concepts or technologies classes? [Yes or No]

   If Yes, you will probably be able to handle Microsoft's networking terminology, concepts, and technologies (brace yourself for frequent departures from normal usage). If you're rusty, brush up on basic networking concepts and terminology, especially networking media, transmission types, the OSI Reference Model, and networking technologies such as Ethernet, Token Ring, FDDI, and WAN links.

   If No, you might want to read one or two books in this topic area. The two best books that we know of are *Computer Networks, 3rd Edition*, by Andrew S. Tanenbaum (Prentice-Hall, 1996, ISBN 0-13-349945-6) and *Computer Networks and Internets, 2nd Edition*, by Douglas E. Comer and Ralph E. Droms (Prentice-Hall, 1998, ISBN 0-130-83617-6).

   Skip to the next section, "Hands-on Experience."

4. Have you done any reading on operating systems or networks? [Yes or No]

   If Yes, review the requirements stated in the first paragraphs after Questions 2 and 3. If you meet those requirements, move on to the next section. If No, consult the recommended reading for both topics. A strong background will help you prepare for the Microsoft exams better than just about anything else.

Hands-on Experience

The most important key to success on all of the Microsoft tests is hands-on experience, especially with Windows 2000 Server and 2000/XP Professional, plus the many add-on services and BackOffice components around which so many of the Microsoft certification exams revolve. If we leave you with only one realization after taking this Self-Assessment, it should be that there's no substitute for time spent installing, configuring, and using the various Microsoft products upon which you'll be tested repeatedly and in depth.

5. Have you installed, configured, and worked with:

➤ Windows 2000 Server? [Yes or No]

If Yes, make sure you understand basic concepts as covered in Exam 70-215. You should also study the TCP/IP interfaces, utilities, and services for Exam 70-216, plus implementing security features for Exam 70-220.

 You can download objectives, practice exams, and other data about Microsoft exams from the Training and Certification page at **www. microsoft.com/trainingandservices/default.asp?PageID=mcp**. Use the "Exams" link to obtain specific exam information.

If No, you must obtain one or two machines and a copy of Windows 2000 Server. Then, learn the operating system and whatever other software components on which you'll also be tested.

In fact, we recommend that you obtain two computers, each with a network interface, and set up a two-node network on which to practice. With decent Windows 2000-capable computers selling for about $500 to $600 apiece these days, this shouldn't be too much of a financial hardship. You may have to scrounge to come up with the necessary software, but if you scour the Microsoft Web site, you can usually find low-cost options to obtain evaluation copies of most of the software that you'll need.

➤ Windows 2000/XP Professional? [Yes or No]

If Yes, make sure you understand the concepts covered in Exam 70-210/ 70-270.

If No, you will want to obtain a copy of Windows 2000/XP Professional and learn how to install, configure, and maintain it. You can use *MCSE Windows 2000/XP Professional Exam Cram* to guide your activities and studies, or work straight from Microsoft's test objectives if you prefer.

> For any and all of these Microsoft exams, the Resource Kits for the topics involved are a good study resource. You can purchase softcover Resource Kits from Microsoft Press (search for them at **http://mspress.microsoft.com/**), but they also appear on the TechNet CDs (**www.microsoft.com/technet**). Along with *Exam Crams* and *Exam Preps*, we believe that Resource Kits are among the best tools you can use to prepare for Microsoft exams.

6. For any specific Microsoft product that is not itself an operating system (for example, SQL Server), have you installed, configured, used, and upgraded this software? [Yes or No]

If Yes, skip to the next section. If No, you must get some experience. Read on for suggestions on how to do this.

Experience is a must with any Microsoft product exam, be it something as simple as FrontPage 2000 or as challenging as SQL Server 7. For trial copies of other software, search Microsoft's Web site using the name of the product as your search term. Also, search for bundles like "BackOffice" or "Small Business Server."

> If you have the funds, or your employer will pay your way, consider taking a class at a Certified Training and Education Center (CTEC) or at an Authorized Academic Training Partner (AATP). In addition to classroom exposure to the topic of your choice, you get a copy of the software that is the focus of your course, along with a trial version of whatever operating system it needs, with the training materials for that class.

Before you even think about taking any Microsoft exam, make sure you've spent enough time with the related software to understand how it may be installed and configured, how to maintain such an installation, and how to troubleshoot that software when things go wrong. This will help you in the exam, and in real life!

Testing Your Exam-Readiness

Whether you attend a formal class on a specific topic to get ready for an exam or use written materials to study on your own, some preparation for the Microsoft certification exams is essential. At $125 a try, pass or fail, you want to do everything you can to pass on your first try. That's where studying comes in.

Microsoft has just changed the cost of a Microsoft exam to $125. This is a change from the standard $100 that has been in place for at least the past seven years.

We have included a practice exam in this book, so if you don't score that well on the test, you can study more and then tackle the test again. We also have exams that you can take online through the **ExamCram.com** Web site at **www.examcram.com**. If you still don't hit a score of at least 70 percent after these tests, you'll want to investigate the other practice test resources we mention in this section.

For any given subject, consider taking a class if you've tackled self-study materials, taken the test, and failed anyway. The opportunity to interact with an instructor and fellow students can make all the difference in the world, if you can afford that privilege. For information about Microsoft classes, visit the Training and Certification page at **www.microsoft.com/education/partners/ctec.asp** for Microsoft Certified Education Centers or **www.microsoft.com/aatp/default.htm** for Microsoft Authorized Training Providers.

If you can't afford to take a class, visit the Training and Certification page anyway, because it also includes pointers to free practice exams and to Microsoft Certified Professional Approved Study Guides and other self-study tools. And even if you can't afford to spend much at all, you should still invest in some low-cost practice exams from commercial vendors.

7. Have you taken a practice exam on your chosen test subject? [Yes or No]

   If Yes, and you scored 70 percent or better, you're probably ready to tackle the real thing. If your score isn't above that threshold, keep at it until you break that barrier.

   If No, obtain all the free and low-budget practice tests you can find and get to work. Keep at it until you can break the passing threshold comfortably.

When it comes to assessing your test readiness, there is no better way than to take a good-quality practice exam and pass with a score of 70 percent or better. When we're preparing ourselves, we shoot for 80-plus percent, just to leave room for the "weirdness factor" that sometimes shows up on Microsoft exams.

Assessing Readiness for Exam 70-270

In addition to the general exam-readiness information in the previous section, there are several things you can do to prepare for the Installing, Configuring, and Administering Microsoft Windows XP Professional exam. As you're getting ready for Exam 70-270, visit the Exam Cram Windows 2000 Resource Center at **www.examcram.com/studyresource/w2kresource/**. Another valuable resource is the Exam Cram Insider newsletter. Sign up at **www.examcram.com** or send a blank email message to **subscribe-ec@mars.coriolis.com**. We also suggest that you join an active MCSE mailing list. One of the better ones is managed by Sunbelt Software. Sign up at **www.sunbelt-software.com** (look for the Subscribe button).

You can also cruise the Web looking for "braindumps" (recollections of test topics and experiences recorded by others) to help you anticipate topics you're likely to encounter on the test. The MCSE mailing list is a good place to ask where the useful braindumps are.

 You can't be sure that a braindump's author can provide correct answers. Thus, use the questions to guide your studies, but don't rely on the answers in a braindump to lead you to the truth. Double-check everything you find in any braindump.

Microsoft exam mavens also recommend checking the Microsoft Knowledge Base (available on its own CD as part of the TechNet collection, or on the Microsoft Web site at **http://support.microsoft.com/support/**) for "meaningful technical support issues" that relate to your exam's topics. Although we're not sure exactly what the quoted phrase means, we have also noticed some overlap between technical support questions on particular products and troubleshooting questions on the exams for those products.

Onward, through the Fog!

After you've assessed your readiness, undertaken the right background studies, obtained the hands-on experience that will help you understand the products and technologies at work, and reviewed the many sources of information to help you prepare for a test, you'll be ready to take a round of practice tests. When your scores come back positive enough to get you through the exam, you're ready to go after the real thing. If you follow our assessment regime, you'll not only know what you need to study, but also when you're ready to make a test date at Prometric or VUE. Good luck!

Microsoft Certification Exams

Terms you'll need to understand:

✓ Case study
✓ Multiple-choice question formats
✓ Build-list-and-reorder question format
✓ Create-a-tree question format
✓ Drag-and-connect question format
✓ Select-and-place question format
✓ Fixed-length tests
✓ Simulations
✓ Adaptive tests
✓ Short-form tests

Techniques you'll need to master:

✓ Assessing your exam-readiness
✓ Answering Microsoft's varying question types
✓ Altering your test strategy depending on the exam format
✓ Practicing (to make perfect)
✓ Making the best use of the testing software
✓ Budgeting your time
✓ Guessing (as a last resort)

Exam taking is not something that most people anticipate eagerly, no matter how well prepared they may be. In most cases, familiarity helps offset test anxiety. In plain English, this means you probably won't be as nervous when you take your fourth or fifth Microsoft certification exam, as you'll be when you take your first one.

Whether it's your first exam or your tenth, understanding the details of taking the new exams (how much time to spend on questions, the environment you'll be in, and so on) and the new exam software will help you concentrate on the material rather than on the setting. Likewise, mastering a few basic exam-taking skills should help you recognize—and perhaps even outfox—some of the tricks and snares you're bound to find in some exam questions.

This chapter, besides explaining the exam environment and software, describes some proven exam-taking strategies that you should be able to use to your advantage.

Assessing Exam-Readiness

We strongly recommend that you read through and take the Self-Assessment included with this book (it appears just before this chapter, in fact). This will help you compare your knowledge base to the requirements for obtaining an MCSE, and it will also help you identify parts of your background or experience that may be in need of improvement, enhancement, or further learning. If you get the right set of basics under your belt, obtaining Microsoft certification will be that much easier.

After you've gone through the Self-Assessment, you can remedy those topical areas where your background or experience may not measure up to an ideal certification candidate. But you can also tackle subject matter for individual tests at the same time, so you can continue making progress while you're catching up in some areas.

After you've worked through an *Exam Cram*, have read the supplementary materials, and have taken the practice test, you'll have a pretty clear idea of when you should be ready to take the real exam. Although we strongly recommend that you keep practicing until your scores top the 75 percent mark, 80 percent would be a good goal to give yourself some margin for error in a real exam situation (where stress will play more of a role than when you practice). After you hit that point, you should be ready to go. But if you get through the practice exam in this book without attaining that score, you should keep taking practice tests and studying the materials until you get there. You'll find more pointers on how to study and prepare in the Self-Assessment. But now, on to the exam itself!

The Exam Situation

When you arrive at the testing center where you scheduled your exam, you'll need to sign in with an exam coordinator. He or she will ask you to show two forms of identification, one of which must be a photo ID. After you've signed in and your time slot arrives, you'll be asked to deposit any books, bags, or other items you brought with you. Then, you'll be escorted into a closed room.

All exams are completely closed book. In fact, you will not be permitted to take anything with you into the testing area, but you will be furnished with a blank sheet of paper and a pen or, in some cases, an erasable plastic sheet and an erasable pen. Before the exam, you should memorize as much of the important material as you can, so you can write that information on the blank sheet as soon as you are seated in front of the computer. You can refer to this piece of paper anytime you like during the test, but you'll have to surrender the sheet when you leave the room.

You will have some time to compose yourself, to record this information, and to take a sample orientation exam before you begin the real thing. We suggest you take the orientation test before taking your first exam, but because they're all more or less identical in layout, behavior, and controls, you probably won't need to do this more than once.

Typically, the room will be furnished with anywhere from one to six computers, and each workstation will be separated from the others by dividers designed to keep you from seeing what's happening on someone else's computer. Most test rooms feature a wall with a large picture window. This permits the exam coordinator to monitor the room, to prevent exam-takers from talking to one another, and to observe anything out of the ordinary that might go on. The exam coordinator will have preloaded the appropriate Microsoft certification exam—for this book, that's Exam 70-270—and you'll be permitted to start as soon as you're seated in front of the computer.

All Microsoft certification exams allow a certain maximum amount of time in which to complete your work (this time is indicated on the exam by an on-screen counter/clock, so you can check the time remaining whenever you like). All Microsoft certification exams are computer generated. In addition to multiple choice, you'll encounter select and place (drag and drop), create a tree (categorization and prioritization), drag and connect, and build list and reorder (list prioritization) on most exams. Although this may sound quite simple, the questions are constructed not only to check your mastery of basic facts and figures about Windows XP Professional, but also to require you to evaluate one or more sets of circumstances or requirements. Often, you'll be asked to give more than one answer to a question. Likewise, you might be asked to select the best or most effective solution to a problem from a range of choices, all of which technically are correct. Taking the exam is quite an adventure, and it involves real thinking. This book shows you what to expect and how to deal with the potential problems, puzzles, and predicaments.

In the next section, you'll learn more about how Microsoft test questions look and how they must be answered.

Exam Layout and Design

The format of Microsoft's Windows 2000 exams is different from that of its previous exams. For the design exams (70-219, 70-220, and 70-221), each exam consists entirely of a series of case studies, and the questions can be of six types. For the Core Four exams (70-210 or 70-270, 70-215, 70-216, and 70-217), the same six types of questions may appear, but you are not likely to encounter complex multiquestion case studies.

Note: The new Windows 2000 MCSE requirements include this Windows XP Professional exam as a possible Core Four exam. You can either take the 70-270 (Windows XP Professional) exam or the 70-210 (Windows 2000 Professional) exam. So, now when someone refers to a Core Four exam, they could mean more than just four possible exams.

For design exams, each case study or "testlet" presents a detailed problem that you must read and analyze. Figure 1.1 shows an example of what a case study looks like. You must select the different tabs in the case study to view the entire case.

Following each case study is a set of questions related to the case study; these questions can be one of six types (which are discussed next). Careful attention to details provided in the case study is the key to success. Be prepared to toggle frequently between the case study and the questions as you work. Some of the case studies also include diagrams, which are called *exhibits* that you'll need to examine closely to understand how to answer the questions.

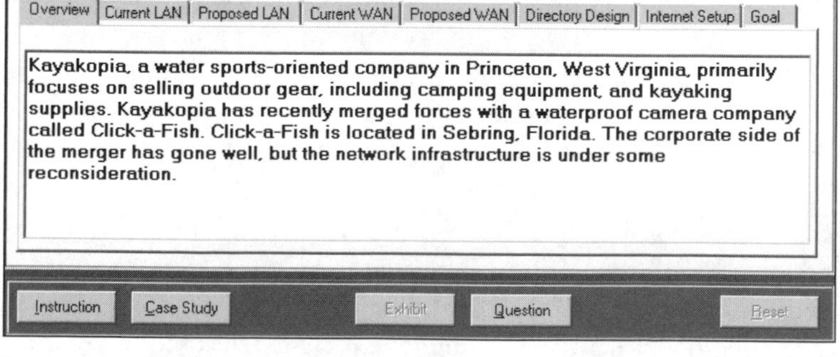

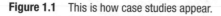

Figure 1.1 This is how case studies appear.

After you complete a case study, you can review all the questions and your answers. However, after you move on to the next case study, you may not be able to return to the previous case study and make any changes.

The six types of question formats are the following:

➤ Multiple choice, single answer

➤ Multiple choice, multiple answers

➤ Build list and reorder (list prioritization)

➤ Create a tree

➤ Drag and connect

➤ Select and place (drag and drop)

Note: Exam formats may vary by test center location. You may want to call the test center or visit ExamCram.com to see if you can find out which type of test you'll encounter.

Multiple-Choice Question Format

Some exam questions require you to select a single answer, whereas others ask you to select multiple correct answers. The following multiple-choice question requires you to select a single correct answer. Following the question is a brief summary of each potential answer and why it is either right or wrong.

Question 1

You have three domains connected to an empty root domain under one contiguous domain name: **tutu.com**. This organization is formed into a forest arrangement with a secondary domain called **frog.com**. How many Schema Masters exist for this arrangement?

○ a. 1

○ b. 2

○ c. 3

○ d. 4

The correct answer is a because only one Schema Master is necessary for a forest arrangement. The other answers (b, c, and d) are misleading because they try to make you believe that Schema Masters might be in each domain, or perhaps that you should have one for each contiguous namespace domain.

This sample question format corresponds closely to the Microsoft certification exam format—the only difference on the exam is that questions are not followed by answer keys. To select an answer, you would position the cursor over the radio button next to the answer. Then, click the mouse button to select the answer.

Let's examine a question where one or more answers are possible. This type of question provides checkboxes rather than radio buttons for marking all appropriate selections.

Question 2

How can you seize FSMO roles? [Check all correct answers]

❑ a. The Ntdsutil.exe utility

❑ b. The Replication Monitor

❑ c. The Secedit.exe utility

❑ d. Active Directory Domains and FSMOs

Answers a and b are correct. You can seize roles from a server that is still running through the Replication Monitor or, in the case of a server failure, you can seize roles with the Ntdsutil.exe utility. The Secedit.exe utility is used to force group policies into play; therefore, answer c is incorrect. Active Directory Domains and Trusts are a combination of truth and fiction; therefore, answer d is incorrect.

For this particular question, two answers are required. Microsoft sometimes gives partial credit for partially correct answers. For Question 2, you have to check the boxes next to items a and b to obtain credit for a correct answer. Notice that picking the right answers also means knowing why the other answers are wrong!

Build-List-and-Reorder Question Format

Questions in the build-list-and-reorder format present two lists of items—one on the left and one on the right. To answer the question, you must move items from the list on the right to the list on the left. The final list must then be reordered into a specific order.

These questions can best be characterized as "From the following list of choices, pick the choices that answer the question. Arrange the list in a certain order." To give you practice with this type of question, some questions of this type are included in this study guide. Here's an example of how they appear in this book; for a sample of how they appear on the test, see Figure 1.2.

Question 3

From the following list of famous people, pick those that have been elected President of the United States. Arrange the list in the order in which they served.

Thomas Jefferson

Ben Franklin

Abe Lincoln

George Washington

Andrew Jackson

Paul Revere

The correct answer is:

George Washington
Thomas Jefferson
Andrew Jackson
Abe Lincoln

On an actual exam, the entire list of famous people would initially appear in the list on the right. You would move the four correct answers to the list on the left, and then reorder the list on the left. Notice that the answer to the question did not include all items from the initial list. However, this may not always be the case.

To move an item from the right list to the left list, first select the item by clicking it, and then click the Add button (left arrow). After you move an item from one list to the other, you can move the item back by first selecting the item and then clicking the appropriate button (either the Add button or the Remove button). After items have been moved to the left list, you can reorder an item by selecting the item and clicking the up or down button.

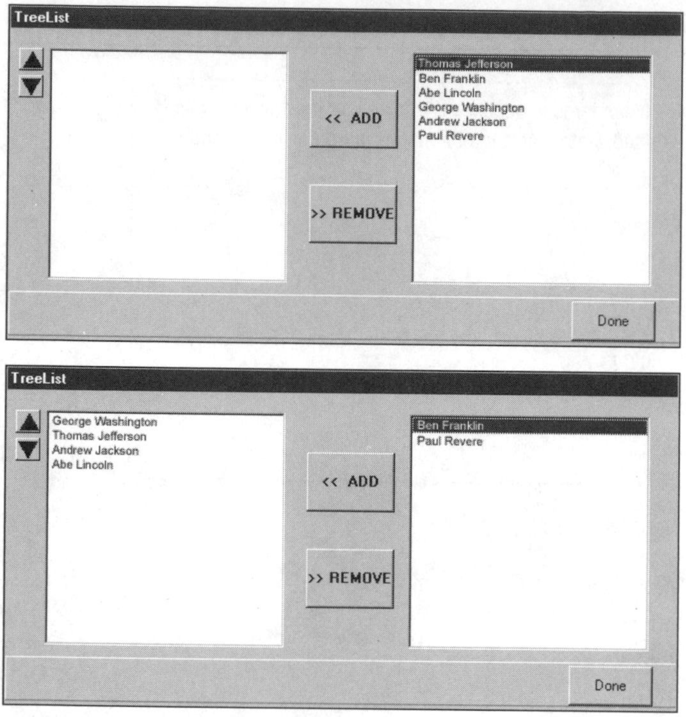

Figure 1.2 This is how build-list-and-reorder questions appear.

Create-a-Tree Question Format

Questions in the create-a-tree format also present two lists—one on the left side of the screen and one on the right side of the screen. The list on the right consists of individual items, and the list on the left consists of nodes in a tree. To answer the question, you must move items from the list on the right to the appropriate node in the tree.

These questions can best be characterized as simply a matching exercise. Items from the list on the right are placed under the appropriate category in the list on the left. Here's an example of how they appear in this book; for a sample of how they appear on the test, see Figure 1.3.

Question 4

The calendar year is divided into four seasons:

Winter

Spring

Summer

Fall

Identify the season when each of the following holidays occurs:

Christmas

Fourth of July

Labor Day

Flag Day

Memorial Day

Washington's Birthday

Thanksgiving

Easter

The correct answer is:

Winter
Christmas
Washington's Birthday

Spring
Flag Day
Memorial Day
Easter

Summer
Fourth of July
Labor Day

Fall
Thanksgiving

In this case, all the items in the list were used. However, this may not always be the case.

To move an item from the right list to its appropriate location in the tree, you must first select the appropriate tree node by clicking it. Then, you select the item to be moved and click the Add button. If one or more items have been added to a tree node, the node will be displayed with a "+" icon to the left of the node name. You can click this icon to expand the node and view the item(s) that have been added. If any item has been added to the wrong tree node, you can remove it by selecting it and clicking the Remove button.

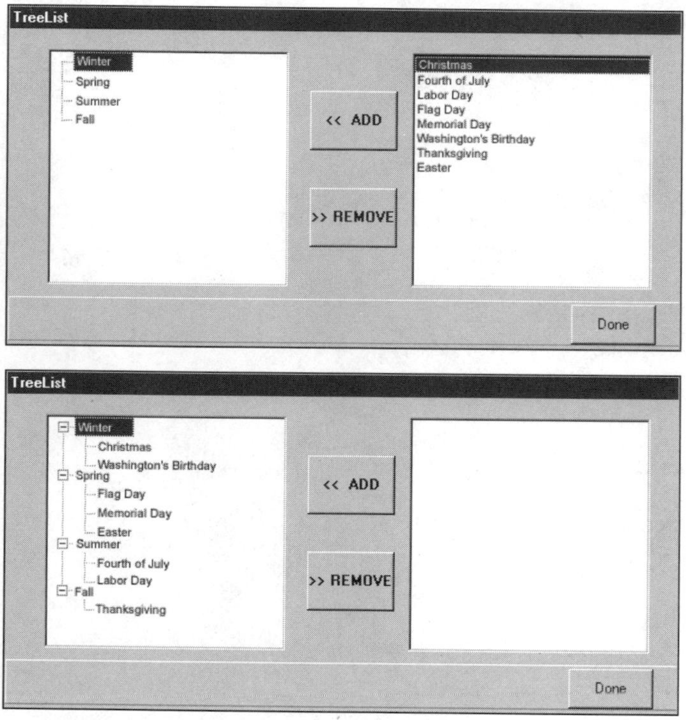

Figure 1.3 This is how create-a-tree questions appear.

Drag-and-Connect Question Format

Questions in the drag-and-connect format present a group of objects and a list of "connections." To answer the question, you must move the appropriate connections between the objects.

This type of question is best-described using graphics. Here's an example.

Question 5

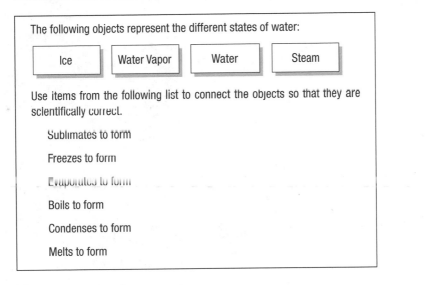

The following objects represent the different states of water:

| Ice | Water Vapor | Water | Steam |

Use items from the following list to connect the objects so that they are scientifically correct.

Sublimates to form

Freezes to form

Evaporates to form

Boils to form

Condenses to form

Melts to form

The correct answer is:

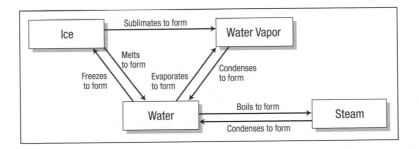

For this type of question, it's not necessary to use every object, and each connection can be used multiple times.

Select-and-Place Question Format

Questions in the select-and-place (drag-and-drop) format present a diagram with blank boxes, and a list of labels that need to be dragged to correctly fill in the blank boxes. To answer the question, you must move the labels to their appropriate positions on the diagram.

This type of question is best-described using graphics. Here's an example.

Question 6

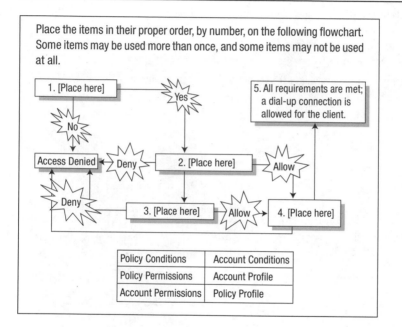

The correct answer is:

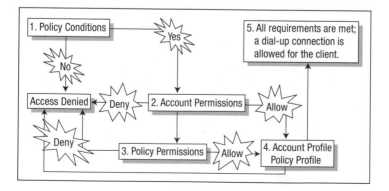

Microsoft's Testing Formats

Currently, Microsoft uses four different testing formats:

➤ Case study

➤ Fixed length

➤ Adaptive

➤ Short form

As mentioned earlier, the case study approach is used with Microsoft's design exams. These exams consist of a set of case studies that you must analyze to enable you to answer questions related to the case studies. Such exams include one or more case studies (tabbed topic areas), each of which is followed by 4 to 10 questions. The question types for design exams and for Core Four Windows 2000 exams are multiple choice, build list and reorder, create a tree, drag and connect, and select and place. Depending on the test topic, some exams are totally case-based, whereas others are not.

Other Microsoft exams employ advanced testing capabilities that might not be immediately apparent. Although the questions that appear are primarily multiple choice, the logic that drives them is more complex than older Microsoft tests, which use a fixed sequence of questions, called a *fixed-length test*. Some questions employ a sophisticated user interface, which Microsoft calls a *simulation*, to test your knowledge of the software and systems under consideration in a more or less "live" environment that behaves just like the original. The Testing Innovations link at **www.microsoft.com/trainingandservices/default.asp?PageID=mcp** includes a downloadable practice simulation.

For some exams, Microsoft has turned to a well-known technique, called *adaptive testing*, to establish a test-taker's level of knowledge and product competence. Adaptive exams look the same as fixed-length exams, but they discover the level of difficulty at which an individual test-taker can correctly answer questions. Test-takers with differing levels of knowledge or ability therefore see different sets of questions; individuals with high levels of knowledge or ability are presented with a smaller set of more difficult questions, whereas individuals with lower levels of knowledge are presented with a larger set of easier questions. Two individuals may answer the same percentage of questions correctly, but the test-taker with a higher knowledge or ability level will score higher because his or her questions are worth more.

Also, the lower-level test-taker will probably answer more questions than his or her more-knowledgeable colleague. This explains why adaptive tests use ranges of values to define the number of questions and the amount of time it takes to complete the test.

Adaptive tests work by evaluating the test-taker's most recent answer. A correct answer leads to a more difficult question (and the test software's estimate of the test-taker's knowledge and ability level is raised). An incorrect answer leads to a less difficult question (and the test software's estimate of the test-taker's knowledge and ability level is lowered). This process continues until the test targets the test-taker's true ability level. The exam ends when the test-taker's level of accuracy meets a statistically acceptable value (in other words, when his or her performance demonstrates an acceptable level of knowledge and ability), or when the maximum number of items has been presented (in which case, the test-taker is almost certain to fail).

Microsoft also introduced a short-form test for its most popular tests. This test delivers 25 to 30 questions to its takers, giving them exactly 60 minutes to complete the exam. This type of exam is similar to a fixed-length test, in that it allows readers to jump ahead or return to earlier questions, and to cycle through the questions until the test is done. Microsoft does not use adaptive logic in this test, but claims that statistical analysis of the question pool is such that the 25 to 30 questions delivered during a short-form exam conclusively measure a test-taker's knowledge of the subject matter in much the same way as an adaptive test. You can think of the short-form test as a kind of "greatest hits exam" (that is, the most important questions are covered) version of an adaptive exam on the same topic.

Note: Some of the Microsoft exams can contain a combination of adaptive and fixed-length questions.

Microsoft tests can come in any one of these forms. Whatever you encounter, you must take the test in whichever form it appears; you can't choose one form over another. If anything, it pays more to prepare thoroughly for an adaptive exam than for a fixed-length or a short-form exam: The penalties for answering incorrectly are built into the test itself on an adaptive exam, whereas the layout remains the same for a fixed-length or short-form test, no matter how many questions you answer incorrectly.

The biggest difference between an adaptive test and a fixed-length or short-form test is that on a fixed-length or short-form test, you can revisit questions after you've read them over one or more times. On an adaptive test, you must answer the question when it's presented and will have no opportunities to revisit that question thereafter.

Strategies for Different Testing Formats

Before you choose a test-taking strategy, you must know if your test is case-study based, fixed length, short form, or adaptive. When you begin your exam, you'll know right away if the test is based on case studies. The interface will consist of a tabbed window that allows you to easily navigate through the sections of the case.

If you are taking a test that is not based on case studies, the software will tell you that the test is adaptive, if in fact the version you're taking is an adaptive test. If your introductory materials fail to mention this, you're probably taking a fixed-length test (50 to 70 questions). If the total number of questions involved is 25 to 30, you're taking a short-form test. Some tests announce themselves by indicating that they will start with a set of adaptive questions, followed by fixed-length questions.

You'll be able to tell for sure if you are taking an adaptive, fixed-length, or short-form test by the first question. If it includes a checkbox that lets you mark the question for later review, you're taking a fixed-length or short-form test. If the total number of questions is 25 to 30, it's a short-form test; if more than 30, it's a fixed-length test. Adaptive test questions can be visited (and answered) only once, and they include no such checkbox.

The Case Study Exam Strategy

Most test-takers find that the case study type of test used for the design exams (70-219, 70-220, and 70-221) is the most difficult to master. When it comes to studying for a case study test, your best bet is to approach each case study as a standalone test. The biggest challenge you'll encounter is that you'll feel that you won't have enough time to get through all of the cases that are presented.

Each case provides a lot of material that you'll need to read and study before you can effectively answer the questions that follow. The trick to taking a case study exam is to first scan the case study to get the highlights. Make sure you read the overview section of the case so that you understand the context of the problem at hand. Then, quickly move on and scan the questions.

As you are scanning the questions, make mental notes to yourself so that you'll remember which sections of the case study you should focus on. Some case studies may provide a fair amount of extra information that you don't really need to answer the questions. The goal with this scanning approach is to avoid having to study and analyze material that is not completely relevant.

When studying a case, carefully read the tabbed information. It is important to answer each and every question. You will be able to toggle back and forth from case to questions, and from question to question within a case testlet. However, once you leave the case and move on, you may not be able to return to it. You may want to take notes while reading useful information so you can refer to them when you tackle the test questions. It's hard to go wrong with this strategy when taking any kind of Microsoft certification test.

The Fixed-Length and Short-Form Exam Strategy

A well-known principle when taking fixed-length or short-form exams is to first read over the entire exam from start to finish while answering only those questions you feel absolutely sure of. On subsequent passes, you can dive into more complex questions more deeply, knowing how many such questions you have left.

Fortunately, the Microsoft exam software for fixed-length and short-form tests makes the multiple-visit approach easy to implement. At the top-left corner of each question is a checkbox that permits you to mark that question for a later visit.

Note: Marking questions makes review easier, but you can return to any question by clicking the Forward or Back button repeatedly.

As you read each question, if you answer only those you're sure of and mark for review those that you're not sure of, you can keep working through a decreasing list of questions as you answer the trickier ones in order.

> Reading the exam over completely before answering the trickier questions has at least one potential benefit: Sometimes, information supplied in later questions sheds more light on earlier questions. At other times, information you read in later questions might jog your memory about Windows XP Professional facts, figures, or behavior that helps you answer earlier questions. Either way, you'll come out ahead if you defer those questions about which you're not absolutely sure.

Here are some question-handling strategies that apply to fixed-length and short-form tests. Use them if you have the chance:

➤ When returning to a question after your initial read-through, read every word again—otherwise, your mind can fall quickly into a rut. Sometimes, revisiting a question after turning your attention elsewhere lets you see something you missed, but the strong tendency is to see what you've seen before. Try to avoid that tendency at all costs.

➤ If you return to a question more than twice, try to articulate to yourself what you don't understand about the question, why answers don't appear to make sense, or what appears to be missing. If you chew on the subject awhile, your subconscious might provide the details you lack, or you might notice a "trick" that points to the right answer.

As you work your way through the exam, another counter that Microsoft provides will come in handy—the number of questions completed and questions outstanding. For fixed-length and short-form tests, it's wise to budget your time by making sure that you've completed one-quarter of the questions one-quarter of the way through the exam period, and three-quarters of the questions three-quarters of the way through.

If you're not finished when only five minutes remain, use that time to guess your way through any remaining questions. Remember, guessing is potentially more valuable than not answering, because blank answers are always wrong, but a guess may turn out to be right. If you don't have a clue about any of the remaining questions, pick answers at random, or choose all a's, b's, and so on. The important thing is to submit an exam for scoring that has an answer for every question.

 At the very end of your exam period, you're better off guessing than leaving questions unanswered.

The Adaptive Exam Strategy

If there's one principle that applies to taking an adaptive test, it could be summed up as "Get it right the first time." You cannot elect to skip a question and move on to the next one when taking an adaptive test, because the testing software uses your answer to the current question to select whatever question it plans to present next. Nor can you return to a question after you've moved on, because the software gives you only one chance to answer the question. You can, however, take notes, because sometimes information supplied in earlier questions will shed more light on later questions.

Also, when you answer a question correctly, you are presented with a more difficult question next, to help the software gauge your level of skill and ability. When you answer a question incorrectly, you are presented with a less difficult question, and the software lowers its current estimate of your skill and ability. This continues until the program settles into a reasonably accurate estimate of what you know and can do, and takes you on average through somewhere between 15 and 30 questions as you complete the test.

The good news is that if you know your stuff, you'll probably finish most adaptive tests in 30 minutes or so. The bad news is that you must really, really know your stuff to do your best on an adaptive test. That's because some questions are so convoluted, complex, or hard to follow that you're bound to miss one or two, at a minimum, even if you do know your stuff. So the more you know, the better you'll do on an adaptive test, even accounting for the occasionally weird or unfathomable questions that appear on these exams.

Because you can't always tell in advance if a test is fixed length, short form, or adaptive, you will be best served by preparing for the exam as if it were adaptive. That way, you should be prepared to pass no matter what kind of test you take. But if you do take a fixed-length or short-form test, remember the tips from the preceding section. They should help you improve on what you could do on an adaptive test.

If you encounter a question on an adaptive test that you can't answer, you must guess an answer immediately. Because of how the software works, you may suffer for your guess on the next question if you guess right, because you'll get a more difficult question next!

Question-Handling Strategies

For those questions that take only a single answer, usually two or three of the answers will be obviously incorrect, and two of the answers will be plausible—of course, only one can be correct. Unless the answer leaps out at you (if it does, reread the question to look for a trick; sometimes those are the ones you're most likely to get wrong), begin the process of answering by eliminating those answers that are most obviously wrong.

Almost always, at least one answer out of the possible choices for a question can be eliminated immediately because it matches one of these conditions:

➤ The answer does not apply to the situation.

➤ The answer describes a nonexistent issue, an invalid option, or an imaginary state.

After you eliminate all answers that are obviously wrong, you can apply your retained knowledge to eliminate further answers. Look for items that sound correct but refer to actions, commands, or features that are not present or not available in the situation that the question describes.

If you're still faced with a blind guess among two or more potentially correct answers, reread the question. Try to picture how each of the possible remaining answers would alter the situation. Be especially sensitive to terminology; sometimes the choice of words ("remove" instead of "disable") can make the difference between a right answer and a wrong one.

Only when you've exhausted your ability to eliminate answers, but remain unclear about which of the remaining possibilities is correct, should you guess at an answer. An unanswered question offers you no points, but guessing gives you at least some chance of getting a question right; just don't be too hasty when making a blind guess.

Note: If you're taking a fixed-length or a short-form test, you can wait until the last round of reviewing marked questions (just as you're about to run out of time, or out of unanswered questions) before you start making guesses. You will have the same option within each case study testlet (but once you leave a testlet, you may not be allowed to return to it). If you're taking an adaptive test, you'll have to guess to move on to the next question if you can't figure out an answer some other way. Either way, guessing should be your technique of last resort!

Numerous questions assume that the default behavior of a particular utility is in effect. If you know the defaults and understand what they mean, this knowledge will help you cut through many Gordian knots

Mastering the Inner Game

In the final analysis, knowledge breeds confidence, and confidence breeds success. If you study the materials in this book carefully and review all the practice questions at the end of each chapter, you should become aware of those areas where additional learning and study are required.

After you've worked your way through the book, take the practice exam in the back of the book. Taking this test will provide a reality check and help you identify areas to study further. Make sure you follow up and review materials related to the questions you miss on the practice exam before scheduling a real exam. Only when you've covered that ground and feel comfortable with the whole scope of the practice exam should you set an exam appointment. Only if you score 80 percent or better should you proceed to the real thing (otherwise, obtain some additional practice tests so you can keep trying until you hit this magic number).

If you take a practice exam and don't score at least 80 to 85 percent correct, you'll want to practice further. Microsoft provides links to practice exam providers and also offers self-assessment exams at **www.microsoft.com/trainingandservices/**. You should also check out **ExamCram.com** for downloadable practice questions.

Armed with the information in this book and with the determination to augment your knowledge, you should be able to pass the certification exam. However, you need to work at it, or you'll spend the exam fee more than once before you finally pass. If you prepare seriously, you should do well. We are confident that you can do it!

The next section covers other sources you can use to prepare for the Microsoft certification exams.

Additional Resources

A good source of information about Microsoft certification exams comes from Microsoft itself. Because its products and technologies—and the exams that go with them—change frequently, the best place to go for exam-related information is online.

If you haven't already visited the Microsoft Certified Professional site, do so right now. The MCP home page resides at **www.microsoft.com/trainingandservices** (see Figure 1.4).

Note: This page might not be there by the time you read this, or may be replaced by something new and different, because things change regularly on the Microsoft site. Should this happen, please read the sidebar titled "Coping with Change on the Web."

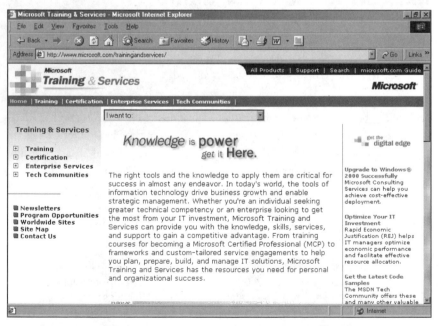

Figure 1.4 The Microsoft Certified Professional home page.

Coping with Change on the Web

Sooner or later, all the information we've shared with you about the Microsoft Certified Professional pages and the other Web-based resources mentioned throughout the rest of this book will go stale or be replaced by newer information. In some cases, the URLs you find here might lead you to their replacements; in other cases, the URLs will go nowhere, leaving you with the dreaded "404 File not found" error message. When that happens, don't give up.

There's always a way to find what you want on the Web if you're willing to invest some time and energy. Most large or complex Web sites—and Microsoft's qualifies on both counts—offer a search engine. On all of Microsoft's Web pages, a Search button appears along the top edge of the page. As long as you can get to Microsoft's site (it should stay at **www.microsoft.com** for a long time), use this tool to help you find what you need.

The more focused you can make a search request, the more likely the results will include information you can use. For example, you can search for the string

    "training and certification"

to produce a lot of data about the subject in general, but if you're looking for the preparation guide for Exam 70-058, "Networking Essentials," you'll be more likely to get there quickly if you use a search string similar to the following:

    "Exam 70-058" AND "preparation guide"

Likewise, if you want to find the Training and Certification downloads, try a search string such as this:

    "training and certification" AND "download page"

Finally, feel free to use general search tools—such as **www.search.com**, **www.altavista.com**, and **www.excite.com**—to look for related information. Although Microsoft offers great information about its certification exams online, there are plenty of third-party sources of information and assistance that need not follow Microsoft's party line. Therefore, if you can't find something where the book says it lives, intensify your search.

Installing and Deploying Windows XP Professional

Terms you'll need to understand:

- ✓ FAT, FAT32, and NTFS
- ✓ Unattended installation
- ✓ Setup Manager
- ✓ Answer file
- ✓ System Preparation Tool (Sysprep.exe)
- ✓ Remote Installation Services (RIS)
- ✓ Risetup.exe
- ✓ Riprep.exe
- ✓ Automatic Updates
- ✓ Dynamic Updates
- ✓ Windows Update
- ✓ User State Migration Tool (USMT)
- ✓ FAST Wizard

Techniques you'll need to master:

- ✓ Understanding installation advantages and disadvantages of using FAT, FAT32, and NTFS
- ✓ Creating an answer file using Setup Manager
- ✓ Creating an image using Sysprep
- ✓ Configuring the RIS server
- ✓ Creating an image for the RIS server using Riprep
- ✓ Scanning and loading user data using the USMT
- ✓ Troubleshooting installation failures

Planning for the installation of Windows XP is an essential part of getting the job done right. If an attempt is made to install XP without taking a look at your current environment and hardware, the installation will most likely fail and it will be hard to determine why. With all of this in mind, let's take a look at some of the requirements and items to consider during the planning phase of your installation.

Hardware Requirements

The following are the minimum hardware requirements for installing Windows XP Professional:

➤ 233MHz Pentium or higher central processing unit (CPU)

➤ 64MB of memory (Microsoft recommends 128MB)

➤ A 1.5GB hard drive with a minimum of 650MB of free space

➤ Super VGA (800×600) or higher-resolution video adapter and monitor

➤ Keyboard

➤ Mouse

➤ CD-ROM or DVD drive

Another important aspect to consider before installing Windows XP Professional is the BIOS version and features of your system. It is best to install the latest BIOS from your hardware vendor before tackling the XP Professional installation. Features such as Plug and Play and Advanced Configuration and Power Interface (ACPI) are important for the full functionality of XP.

ACPI allows the OS to control power management and drives the core Plug and Play functions in Windows XP. If you install Windows XP on a system that does not support ACPI, then upgrade the system to support ACPI, you will most likely see a Blue Screen of Death. This is because the Hardware Abstraction Layer (HAL) for ACPI is not the same as that of Advanced Power Management (APM), which is used if ACPI is not supported.

After you've verified that the computer meets these minimum hardware requirements, you should check to see whether devices such as the video adapter and the network adapter are compatible. To do this, check the Hardware Compatibility List (HCL), which every Windows XP CD-ROM contains. However, this file is out of date rather quickly, with all of the new additions to the HCL that occur after the burning of your CD. To view the most current HCL, visit **www.microsoft.com/hcl**.

Setup Disks

Microsoft feels that the hardware that is required to run Windows XP Professional needs to be bigger and better than the hardware required by any previous OS. With newer hardware, you will get all of the great new features, such as Plug and Play, ACPI, bootable CD-ROMs, and so on. Because of these robust features, Microsoft has removed the need or ability to create or use the setup disk sets that were available with Windows NT and 2000 Professional.

Upgrading to Windows XP Professional

Windows NT 4 supported upgrades only from previous Windows NT operating systems, whereas Windows 2000 would upgrade from almost anything. Windows XP, on the other hand, allows for many upgrade paths, but does have some limitations. The following is a list of Windows operating systems that you can directly upgrade to Windows XP Professional:

➤ Windows 2000

➤ Windows NT 4 (Service Pack 6)

➤ Windows 98 (all editions)

➤ Windows ME

All other OS versions must first get to one of these levels before an upgrade to XP can be performed.

The easiest operating system to upgrade from is Windows 2000. This operating system shares a lot of features with Windows XP, including its Registry. You can upgrade Windows 98 and NT quite smoothly as well, but you need to take some precautions, which are detailed in the next section.

Preupgrade Checklist

Before you upgrade to Windows XP Professional, you need to check the current operating system configuration for any of the following areas that could cause conflicts during and after the upgrade process:

➤ *Hardware and software compatibility*—The Windows XP Professional CD-ROM contains a utility called Chkupgrd.exe, which scans the current OS and hardware to see whether any known items are incompatible with Windows XP Professional. You can run the utility using various methods. One of the most common methods is to place the Windows XP CD-ROM in the computer and click the Upgrade option. The utility runs before the upgrade to alert you about any incompatibilities. However, if you are not prepared to perform an upgrade on the computer, you can run the utility by placing the Windows XP Professional CD-ROM in the computer, selecting Start|Run, and then typing "D:\I386\winnt32.exe /checkupgradeonly" (where D: is the drive letter your CD-ROM drive uses). The utility scans the system and creates a text file of the results, which you can save to the computer or print. The Chkupgrd.exe tool is also referred to as the Readiness Analyzer.

 If you are attempting to install Windows XP Professional on a system that has third-party SCSI or RAID controllers, you will need to select F6 during the initial blue screen of the setup process. If you miss this selection and setup proceeds, you will most likely end up with an error specifying that the boot device is not accessible, and you will need to start the installation again.

➤ *Update packs*—Due to the major differences between the Windows XP Registry and those of Windows 95 and 98, some applications may not work after the upgrade. Software vendors may supply an update pack (also called *migration dynamic link libraries*, or DLLs) that you can use during the upgrade process. Obtain an upgrade pack and place it on the local hard drive. During the upgrade process, the installer asks whether any upgrade packs should be used. Select Yes and then type in the file path to the upgrade pack to continue the installation process.

➤ *File system selection*—Windows XP has three options from which to choose for a file system: the old stand-by, FAT; the newer option, FAT32; and the best option for the systems that support it, NT File System (NTFS). NTFS is the best option because it supports compression, disk quotas, encryption, mount points, and remote storage.

➤ *Disk utilities*—Windows XP Professional uses a new version of NTFS that causes conflicts with antivirus software and disk defragmenting software. You should remove such applications before you upgrade.

➤ *Drive compression*—Before upgrading, you should uncompress any drives that you have compressed with DriveSpace or DoubleSpace. These Windows 95 and 98 drive compression utilities are incompatible with Windows XP.

➤ *BIOS*—Ensure you have the latest BIOS that will support Windows XP.

➤ *Backup*—The only true way to recover from a failed installation or OS is with a good backup.

➤ *Compression*—Windows XP supports compression when NTFS is installed. However, Windows XP does not support any other third-party compression utilities in an upgrade scenario. Always uncompress files before upgrading to ensure a clean and successful path.

➤ *Virus scan software*—It is always best to disable, and in some instances remove, virus scan software before an upgrade. These programs may have files open and limit the access to system resources during an upgrade.

➤ *Incompatible software*—This is a rather vague item, but it is better to be safe than sorry in an upgrade. Programs such as third-party protocols and clients, virus scanners, and ACPI/APM tools can cause serious problems with an upgrade. Always try to eliminate these programs from interfering with your upgrade.

File System Considerations

During the upgrade to Windows XP, Microsoft makes some assumptions about which file system you are running, based on your current OS. If you are running Windows 9*x*, Microsoft assumes you are running FAT32 or, in some instances, FAT. If you are running Windows NT or 2000, Microsoft assumes you are running NTFS.

If you are upgrading from Windows NT or 2000, you will simply keep the existing file system, NTFS, as you move into Windows XP. If you are upgrading from Windows 98, then you will have more choices. Remember, you are running FAT32, so for security reasons, you probably want to run NTFS in XP. However, for compatibility reasons and functionality, you might want to stick with your FAT32 file system, at least for a little while. One main reason is the new uninstall feature, discussed next.

 If you want to take advantage of both uninstall and NTFS, do your file system configuration in phases. First, keep FAT32 until your XP Professional box has proved itself to be stable. Then, convert your system to NTFS using the **convert** command to get the benefits of the better security, compression, and encryption features.

Windows XP Uninstall Feature for Windows 98 and Windows ME Upgrades

Microsoft has built in an uninstall feature to Windows XP Professional, but it has serious limitations. The main reason that the option was built in was to accommodate those who want to move from Windows 98 to Windows XP Professional.

Of course, many of these installations will be for those who work in a small office or home environment. Those who work in a medium to large corporate environment will be better off installing Windows XP Professional fresh, to eliminate some of the potential Registry, security, and folder structure differences that occur with an upgrade.

Some of the limitations that come with the uninstall feature include the following:

➤ You cannot uninstall if you have converted the file system from FAT to NTFS.

➤ You do not have the uninstall option if you have upgraded from Windows NT or Windows 2000.

➤ Applications that have been removed while running XP will behave strangely. For example, although the Start menu icons will be present, the executables will have been removed.

➤ Applications that were added while running XP will behave strangely. This occurs because the restored image does not have the correct Registry values for these applications.

To successfully remove Windows XP Professional, you simply need to go to the Add/Remove Programs applet in the Control Panel. Then, select the Add/Remove button associated with the Windows XP option that is under the list of installed software. This enables you to uninstall Windows XP and return to the version of Windows 98/ME that you were running previously.

Installation Options for Windows XP Professional

Microsoft understands that many different installation needs exist, and thus supplies many methods. Windows XP keeps that tradition by offering multiple options for fresh installations.

Installation Methods

Windows XP Professional has many different installation methods, which are listed here. Some of these methods are manual in nature, requiring human intervention during the installation process. Other methods require only minimal initial human intervention, and are considered to be automated installation methods:

➤ Manual CD method

➤ Network attended installations

➤ Network unattended installations using an answer file

➤ Sysprep installation

➤ Sysprep unattended installation using an answer file

➤ Remote Installation Services (RIS)—using a CD image

➤ RIS—CD image unattended installation using an answer file

➤ RIS—Riprep image

➤ RIS—Riprep image unattended installation using an answer file

CD-ROM Installation

One of the easiest methods for installing Windows XP Professional is simply to put the Windows XP Professional CD-ROM in the computer and boot the computer. The computer boots from the CD-ROM and starts the first phase of the installation, copying the installation files to the local hard drive. Then, the computer reboots and starts the graphical user interface (GUI) phase of the installation. You can install Windows XP Professional in this fashion if your computer's BIOS supports the option to boot from a CD-ROM drive and the system has El-Torito No Emulation support for bootable CD-ROMs. The El-Torito No Emulation is the standard for bootable CD-ROM support.

This form of installation is an attended installation of Windows XP Professional that requires someone to sit in front of the target computer and answer all the installation prompts, such as the End User License Agreement (EULA). Before you start the installation process, you need to ensure that the computer meets the minimum hardware requirements of Windows XP Professional. Unlike Windows NT, Windows XP supports only Intel-based computers.

Installing Over a Network

Another installation method is to place the contents of the Windows XP Professional CD-ROM in a folder on a network server and then share the folder. This network server is referred to as a *distribution server*. Establish a network connection to the distribution server to start the installation. If Windows 95, 98, NT, or 2000 is on the target computer, connect to the share point and execute winnt32.exe to start the installation process. If DOS is on the target computer, use a network boot disk to connect to the source files and use winnt.exe to start the installation. You use winnt32.exe in a 32-bit environment, whereas you use winnt.exe in a 16-bit/DOS environment.

Automating the Installation of Windows XP Professional

When performing an attended installation option, someone must be in front of the computer to answer all the installation prompts. If you need to install hundreds, maybe thousands, of computers, this is a very inefficient method. This section discusses how to use Setup Manager, the System Preparation (Sysprep) Tool, and Remote Installation Service (RIS) for automating the installation process.

Creating Unattended Answer Files and Uniqueness Database Files by Using Setup Manager

The Setup Manager utility answers the installation prompts and saves the answer results in an answer file called Unattend.txt. Windows XP can then use Unattend.txt during the installation to configure the screen resolution and other typical hardware and OS settings. This tool is much improved in Windows XP and adds more options and greater flexibility than its predecessor. Setup Manager can now do the following:

➤ Agree to the EULA

➤ Input the Product ID for installation

➤ Create a distribution share point

➤ Create a listing of unique computer names for a Uniqueness Database File (UDF)

➤ Add third-party Plug and Play drivers and other resources

➤ Add printers, scripts, batch files, and other commands to the distribution share

You must extract Setup Manager from a CAB file on the Windows XP Professional CD-ROM to create Unattend.txt. To extract Setup Manager, perform the following steps:

1. Insert the Windows XP Professional CD-ROM into the computer and select the Deploy.cab file, located in the Support\Tools folder.

2. Double-click the Deploy.cab file to view the contents.

3. Right-click Setupmgr.exe and select Extract. Choose a location from the Explorer menu to extract the file.

You can now create the answer file. Double-click the Setupmgr.exe icon to launch the wizard. The Setupmgr.exe utility is a multipurpose tool because you can use it to create answer files for several types of unattended installations. We will concentrate on a Windows XP unattended installation. Perform the following steps to create an answer file:

1. Double-click the Setupmgr.exe icon to start the utility.

2. Click Next to pass the welcome page.

3. Select the Create A New Answer File radio button (it is selected by default) and click Next.

4. The next page displays which product the answer file installs. The three choices are Windows XP Unattended Installation, Sysprep Install, and RIS. Select the Windows XP Unattended Installation radio button and click Next.

5. Choose the Windows XP Professional radio button and click Next.

6. The next page displays several options regarding user interaction. Typically, no user interaction is required. If, however, you want the installation to stop so you can enter the computer name, select Hide Pages. This option hides all pages in which answers were provided but stops at any areas that you have left blank. Select the Fully Automated radio button and click Next.

7. Next, you will determine whether you will use this answer file with the CD or a distribution folder. For the purposes of this example, select Yes, Create Or Modify A Distribution Folder.

8. The next window ask where the installation files will be obtained—copied from the CD or from the file system. Select Copy The Files From CD.

9. After selecting the source, you need to determine the destination folder. The next page offers suggested locations and folder names for the distribution share point. If you have already created the distribution share, select Modify An Existing Distribution Folder. If you select this option, just the answer file is created. Accept the default by clicking the Next button.

10. Select the checkbox to agree to the EULA, and click Next.

11. Type in a name and an organization and click Next.

12. Select display settings such as Color, Screen Area, and Refresh Frequency. Unless all computers have identical video cards with identical monitors, you should set these fields to Use Windows Default. Click Next to continue.

13. The Time Zone page appears next. Simply choose the correct time zone the computer is located in and click Next.

14. Input the Product ID that matches the CD-ROM contents that you will be using for the installation.

15. Type in the computer names or import a comma-delimited file that contains all computer names that should be used for the installation of new computers. Optionally, you can select the Automatically Generate Computer Names Based On Organization Name checkbox. Checking this results in a combination of the organization name that you typed in the dialog box and a unique

alphanumeric combination (for example, coriol-1AD2RT). Use either method and click the Next button.

16. Enter a password that the local administrator of the computer will use. You also have an option to encrypt the administrator password, which will be stored in the answer file. This is a good option, to ensure security of the installed system.

Note: The password can be up to 127 characters long.

Enter a password and click Next.

17. This page provides two options for Network Settings—Typical and Custom. If you select Typical, Microsoft Client, File, and Print Sharing as well as the Transmission Control Protocol/Internet Protocol (TCP/IP) are installed. Additionally, the client will be configured as a Dynamic Host Configuration Protocol (DHCP) client. If you need to enter a static IP address or add or subtract network services, use the Custom option. Select Typical or Custom and click Next.

18. The Workgroup or a Domain page appears next. If the computer is to join a domain during the installation, you must type in the name of the domain as well as enter a username and password of a user who has the right to add workstations to a domain. Fill in the appropriate fields and click Next.

19. You've reached the end of creating a basic answer file. If you need to add other drivers or scripts, select the Yes, Edit The Additional Settings radio button. For the purposes of this discussion, select No, Do Not Edit The Additional Settings, and click Next.

20. The files are copied to the distribution share; the last page displayed is a summary page of the files that you created. Click Finish.

Piecing Together an Unattended Network Install

Now that you have created the answer file and the distribution share, let's put it all together to see how to launch an unattended installation of Windows XP Professional. To master this task, you must understand a few switches that are involved. The **winnt.exe** command has multiple switches to control its functionality. The following is a list of switches that relate to unattended installs:

➤ /u:answer *<file>*—Used for an unattended installation from a DOS-based client (which will use the **winnt.exe** command). The file contains answers to the installation prompts.

➤ /s:sourcepath—Points to the location of the Windows XP installation files.

➤ **/udf:id**—Used in conjunction with a UDF file, which overrides the values of the answer file. You typically use this file to provide unique configuration parameters during the installation process. The ID designates which settings contained in the UDF file should be used.

If you are upgrading or installing from a Windows 98/ME or Windows NT/ 2000 client, you need to use the **winnt32.exe** command to perform the installation. For this case, you will have some different switches available. The following are the more important switches that differ from those in the preceding list:

➤ **/unattend**—Used with **winnt32.exe** to create an unattended upgrade or install to Windows XP from a Windows 98/ME or Windows NT/2000 client.

➤ **/makelocalsource**—Copies the contents of the CD-based installation to the local hard drive for future reference, when the CD is not available.

➤ **/dudisable**—Turns off the Dynamic Updates function on the client that is being installed.

➤ **/duprepare:***pathname*—Prepares a folder for the distribution of Windows Update files and device drivers. This folder will then be used by subsequent installations to obtain these files.

➤ **/dushare:***pathname*—Specifies the shared folder where the installation will point during the dynamic update portion of installation.

These switches are new to Windows XP and are emphasized for installations. Memorize them so you can distinguish between the right and wrong answers, if you get these on your exam.

You use these switches in combination to launch an unattended installation of Windows XP Professional using Setup Manager. To launch an unattended install, follow these steps:

1. Use a network boot disk to connect the target computer to the network.

2. Next, use the **net use** command to map to the distribution share point using an available drive letter.

3. Switch the command prompt to the mapped drive letter (such as I) and use the following as an example to launch an unattended install for a computer called computer1:

```
I:\WINNT.EXE /s:I:\i386 /u:unattend.txt
   /udf:computer1,unattend.udfb
```

Investigate all the options that are available with the Setup Manager by running through the file creation process several times while choosing different options each time to see how the results vary. Remember that you can use this Setup Manager utility to also create answer files for System Preparation Tool installs and RIS installs, which are both discussed in this chapter.

Creating and Deploying a Windows 2000 XP Image Using the System Preparation Tool

The System Preparation Tool (Sysprep) prepares a master image of a computer that contains Windows XP Professional and any software applications that users might need. The concept is to use Sysprep in conjunction with third-party disk-imaging software. Disk-imaging software makes an exact mirror image of whatever is on the computer, including all the unique parameters of Windows XP. Each Windows XP computer has its own unique Security Identifier (SID) and its own unique computer name. Multiple computers on the network can't duplicate these settings. If you were to apply an image that contained these unique settings to several computers, they would all have the same computer name and the same SID. Sysprep removes all the unique parameters from a Windows XP computer before the computer is imaged. It is a very easy tool to use, but you must follow several specific steps to use it. The first step is to create a folder called sysprep in %systemdrive% (for example, c:\sysprep).

To use Sysprep, you must extract it from the Deploy.cab file and place it in the sysprep folder. Perform the following steps to extract Sysprep.exe and a helper file called Setupcl.exe:

1. Insert the Windows XP Professional CD-ROM into the computer and select the Deploy.cab file, located in the Support\Tools folder.

2. Double-click the Deploy.cab file to view the contents.

3. Right-click Sysprep.exe and select Extract. Use the Explorer menu to extract the file to the sysprep folder that you created. Right-click Setupcl.exe and extract it to the sysprep folder.

The next step is to install and configure all applications that must be in the disk image. After you have accomplished this, run **sysprep.exe** in the sysprep folder. Using the **sysprep.exe** command removes all unique parameters from the computer and then shuts down the computer. Reboot the computer with a disk image boot disk and create an image of the computer.

After you have applied an image to a computer, a Mini-Setup Wizard runs. It prompts you to put back the unique parameters that you took out. The SID is generated automatically at this point. However, you'll have to input the following settings:

> Computer Name

> User Name

> Regional Settings

> Company Name

> Network Settings

> Time Zone

> Place Computer In A Workgroup Or Join A Domain

As you can see, you need to enter a fair amount of information for every computer you apply the image to. You can use Setup Manager, discussed earlier in this chapter, to create an answer file called Sysprep.inf. This file provides the preceding settings to the Mini-Setup Wizard to answer all the installation prompts. The end result is an unattended install of the image.

Note: You must place Sysprep.inf in the sysprep folder or on a floppy disk, which are the default locations where the Mini-Setup Wizard looks for the answer file (it checks the sysprep folder first) after you have applied the image. Another point to note is that you should apply the image to computers with similar hardware. When you apply the image, Sysprep.exe triggers Plug and Play to resolve the differences in hardware. However, if the hard disk controller or the HAL on the image is different than its counterpart on the computer to which you are applying the image, the image installation will fail (for example, if you create the image on a computer that contains a HAL for a computer with multiple processors, but you are applying the image to a uniprocessor computer).

Windows XP has incorporated another new feature that is great for OEMs and might just be great for you too: new switches that control the installation of a system that will be used for redistribution. These options, listed next, allow for a cleaner and more efficient manipulation of the images that are created with Sysprep:

> *Audit*—Reboots the computer into factory mode, not generating a new SID or running any applications located in the Run Once portion of the setup files.

> *Clean*—Clears the critical devices database that is used by the SysprepMassStorage section in the Sysprep.inf file.

> *Factory*—Boots the system into a special mode that will allow for automated customization of a preinstallation on the factory floor. This will be done by using a Bill of Materials file to automate software installations and updates to software, drivers, the file system, and the Registry.

The Factory.exe file must be located in the %systemdrive%\sysprep folder to utilize the factory switch.

➤ *Nosidgen*—Runs Sysprep without generating a new SID for the computer. This is an excellent option if you are preinstalling domain controllers.

➤ *Reseal*—This option is run after the OEM has run Sysprep in factory mode and configured the system to be delivered to the customer.

Deploying Windows XP Professional by Using Remote Installation Services (RIS)

You can use RIS to deploy Windows XP Professional over a network from a remote installation server. RIS integrates a few of the installation methods discussed thus far into one tight bundle. You can use it to install Windows XP Professional to a computer with a blank hard drive or to reinstall Windows XP Professional to repair a corrupted system.

The main goal of RIS is to reduce total cost of ownership (TCO) by having one central location for either the end users or administrators to install Windows XP Professional. To install Windows XP Professional using RIS, a user presses the F12 key during the boot process to find a RIS server and start the installation. Three steps are involved in making RIS work:

1. Configure the client.

2. Configure network servers for RIS.

3. Create a Windows XP Professional image.

The next few sections uncover the details of these areas.

Configuring Network Services and Hard Drive Space Requirements

Before you can install and configure RIS, several prerequisites must be in place on the network. The following is a list of the RIS requirements you must meet before you install it:

➤ *DHCP server*—The client will obtain an IP address from a DHCP server during the boot process. You cannot use RIS until a DHCP server is available. A Windows XP DHCP server cannot give IP addresses to clients unless it is authorized to do so. Authorization is done through the DHCP Manager snap-in.

➤ *Domain Name Service (DNS)*—After the network adapter has an IP address, it needs to find a RIS server. The client finds RIS by querying a DNS server to find where an Active Directory server or domain controller (DC) is located.

➤ *Active Directory*—Active Directory informs the client where a RIS server can be found.

➤ *Nonsystem partition*—RIS demands its own partition. You cannot install RIS on a system or boot partition, which is usually the C partition.

Note: The reason for the separate partition is the Single Instance Storage (SIS) groveler service, which will create pointers to existing duplicate files, thereby saving disk space. The service won't use system files that are active.

It is recommended to reserve at least 2GB for a RIS partition.

Installing and Configuring the RIS Service

You can install the RIS service on a Windows 2000 DC or member server after you have met all the prerequisites. After you have installed the service, you must configure it. Perform the following steps to install the RIS service:

1. Log on to the server as Administrator

2. Open the Control Panel (select Start|Settings|Control Panel) and double-click Add/Remove Programs.

3. Click the Add/Remove Windows Components button and select the Remote Installation Services checkbox.

4. Insert the Windows 2000 Server CD-ROM. The service is copied to the server and you are prompted to reboot the server after the service has been installed.

Now that you have installed RIS, you must run **risetup.exe** to copy the initial CD-based image of Windows XP Professional on the RIS server and configure the RIS server to respond to clients' requests. The initial image is simply a copy of the I386 folder found on the Windows XP Professional CD-ROM. Perform the following steps to configure RIS:

1. Select Start|Run, type "risetup.exe" in the Run dialog box, and click OK.

2. The Remote Installation Services Setup Wizard presents a welcome page that reminds you of some of the RIS prerequisites. Click the Next button.

3. By default, the wizard offers to create the RIS folder structure and files on the C partition (even though the wizard itself reminds you that this can't be done). Choose a drive letter for a non-system partition to place the files into and then click the Next button.

4. The next dialog box asks whether the RIS server should respond immediately to client requests before you have even finished the configuration. Leave the checkbox deselected. You can select it after you have configured the RIS server in Active Directory Users and Computers.

5. The next dialog box asks where the system should look for the Windows XP Professional installation files. Type the drive letter for the CD-ROM drive and the path to the installation files (for example, D:\I386). Click Next.

6. The next dialog box suggests a folder name for the initial image. Each image that is created has its own folder. Use the default name provided or type in a different name, and then click Next.

7. The next dialog box asks you to provide a descriptive name for this image. Use the default or type in a different name. Click the Next button to get to the finish line.

8. You're finished. The final dialog box summarizes the parameters that you selected. Click the Finish button. Risetup.exe now copies the contents of the I386 folder to the folder structure that you just created and completes the installation process.

When the installation is finished, you need to configure the RIS server to respond to RIS clients. You have to log on as a domain administrator to complete this final step. Launch the Active Directory Users and Computers console by selecting Start|Programs|Administrative Tools|Active Directory Users and Computers. Next, right-click the RIS Server Computer object and select Properties. Click the Remote Install tab from the Properties page. On this tab, select the Respond To Client Computers Requesting Service option, shown in Figure 2.1.

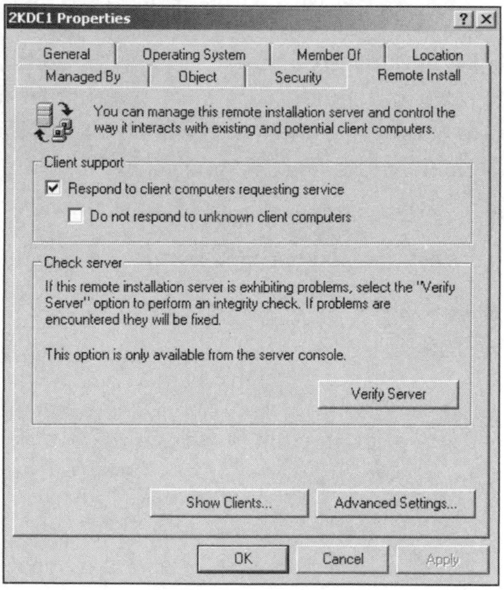

Figure 2.1 The Remote Install tab.

Creating Additional Images

The Risetup.exe wizard created the first image of Windows XP Professional for you. However, that image provides only an attended installation of the OS. You can create additional images in a few different ways:

➤ Use Setup Manager to create an answer file for your CD-based image. This allows for custom and unattended installations. The answer file will simply be attached to the CD-based image by using the Remote Install tab from the RIS server properties page. Here, you will add another image by attaching the answer file to the existing image.

 When locking down the security to images, it is best to control the ACL to the answer file, not the image folder. This will still allow users or administrators access to the installation files, but not the answer file that controls the listing of the additional images.

➤ Install another CD-based image to the RIS server. This will be important if you will be supporting multiple OSs, such as Windows 2000 and XP Professional.

➤ Create additional images that contain the OS as well as any necessary applications and configuration. RIS installs a utility called Riprep.exe that you can use to create images of the OS and any installed applications.

The functionality of Riprep.exe is similar to that of a third-party disk-imaging application. The major benefit of using a Riprep image is that you can include software in the image, instead of having to wait for SMS or GPO software deployment to install the applications. However, Riprep.exe has some limitations. It can only make an image of the C partition of a computer. If a computer contains C and D partitions, only the C partition will be part of the image. Also, when you apply the image to a computer via RIS, any existing partitions are deleted. The entire hard drive is repartitioned as a single partition and then is formatted with NTFS. If you can work within those limits, you can easily configure and deploy Riprep.exe images. Perform the following steps to create a Riprep.exe image:

1. Connect the computer that you are imaging to the network.

2. Install Windows XP Professional and any applications that users may need. Connect to the REMINST share point on the RIS server. Run **riprep.exe** from \RIS Server\REMINST\Admin\I386\riprep.exe.

3. The Remote Installation Preparation Wizard is launched. It asks you on which RIS server the image should be placed and the name of the folder to which the image should be copied.

4. The last task is to provide a user-friendly name for the image (such as Marketing or Sales).

After you complete these steps, Riprep.exe copies the image to the designated RIS server. However, Riprep.exe acts a lot like Sysprep.exe. In addition to creating an image, Riprep.exe removes the unique attributes, such as the SIDs and the computer name. When the RIS client downloads the image, the Mini-Setup Wizard asks you to put back what was taken out. The creation of the Riprep image contains an answer file, which is located in the i386\Templates folder of the image on the RIS server. This answer file, Risetup.sif, can be modified to automate and customize the installation of the Risetup image.

Because the Riprep process takes everything from the disk and puts it into the image, you could store virtually anything in the image for future reference. You could place the critical drivers for printers, NICs, and video adapters from the XP Professional CD. You could place custom settings in the image as well, such as critical help files for a business application, custom drivers, and business files.

Configuring Clients

The client computer can connect to a RIS server in two ways. The first method is to install a peripheral connection interface (PCI) network adapter that contains a Preboot Execution Environment (PXE) boot ROM. You then have to configure the computer's BIOS to boot from the PXE network adapter. When the computer boots from the PXE network adapter, it attempts to get an IP address from a DHCP server. After the network adapter has an IP address, the user is prompted to press the F12 key to locate a RIS server.

The second method is when the network adapter does not have the PXE boot ROM on board. In this case, you can use a RIS boot disk, which supports multiple network adapter manufacturers' NICs, such as 3Com and Intel. Use the rbfg.exe utility to create a RIS boot disk. After you have installed RIS, you can find the utility in RemoteInstall\Admin\i386\rbfg.exe.

Downloading an Image

After you have configured a RIS server with several images, users can boot their computers from the network adapter and press F12 to find a RIS server. The server then displays a welcome screen; simply press Enter to bypass this screen. Next, users must log on to the domain.

The person installing the system must have the ability to add computers to the domain. Within Windows 2000 and XP, this is done by giving the user the permission to add child objects to the domain, typically at the OU level.

After the users are logged on, they see a list of images to choose from. The users select an image from the list, and RIS reformats the entire drive and downloads the image to the target computer. After about 30 to 40 minutes, users have a clean installation of the operating system and applications.

Joining a Workgroup

When you are installing your Windows XP Professional client, you will be asked whether you want to be a member of a workgroup or domain. This is a very important issue, but one that can be addressed easily to help you decide. A workgroup is a great option for a small company or a home office environment. In a workgroup, the usernames are kept locally, in a decentralized manner. So, for example, if Derek needs to gain access to Dan's PC, Dan will need to add Derek to his list of users, which is located on his local PC. Of course, you can see that this arrangement can get out of hand very quickly, and become too much overhead for even a small environment.

To join a domain, you need to right click My Computer and select Properties. Then, select the Computer Name tab. Here, you can select either the manual option, the Change button, or the automated wizard option, the Network ID button. Figure 2.2 illustrates the interface.

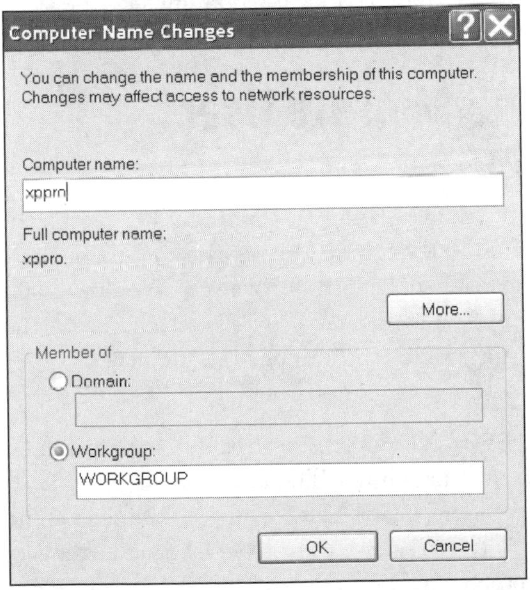

Figure 2.2 Interface to change between a workgroup and domain.

Joining a Domain

For most environments that will be using Windows XP Professional, it will be better to have the computer join a domain. Unlike the workgroup option, the domain option keeps the list of users centrally, on the domain controllers. This allows for easier tracking and access to resources, because a single username exists for each user in the entire domain. The domains that you can join include Windows NT and Windows 2000 (soon to include Windows .NET). To join a domain, you still need to have the credentials that you did in previous Microsoft OSs:

➤ Local administrator privileges to the Windows XP Professional computer

➤ Username and password of a domain type administrator with permission to Create Computer Accounts in the OU or domain

➤ Account operators

➤ Domain Admins

➤ Enterprise Admins

If you want to add the computer to the domain after the installation, you would use the interface that is shown in Figure 2.2. If you want to join the domain during the installation of the OS, you need to supply the credentials for the domain administrative account that meets the criteria in the preceding list. Both attended and unattended installations can have the computer join the domain during the installation.

Using the USMT to Migrate User Settings and Files

If you have decided to perform a fresh installation of Windows XP Professional, you have made a good choice. However, you have also decided that the settings that were on the computer OS before will be lost, or have you? Windows 2000 launched with a tool that allowed administrators to copy user settings before the old OS was removed. These settings were then reapplied to the new OS after installation. The tool was the User State Migration Tool (USMT).

Microsoft has included this tool with XP directly so that user settings can be gracefully migrated from one system to another. The idea is to allow for fresh installations, but also to achieve a lower TCO. The following is a sampling of the different settings, folders, and file types that are transferred by default (the settings are for both the OS and certain Microsoft applications):

Accessibility options:

➤ Fonts

➤ Network printers and mapped network driver

Browser and mail settings:

➤ Folder and taskbar options

Mouse and keyboard options:

➤ Regional settings

➤ Microsoft Office, Outlook, Word, Excel, PowerPoint settings

➤ Stored mail and contacts

Folders:

➤ My Documents, My Pictures

➤ Desktop

➤ Favorites

File types:

➤ CH3, CSV, DIF, DOC, DOT, DQY, IQY, MEW, OQY, POT, PPA, PPS, PPT, PRE, RQY, RTF, SCD, SH3, TXT, WPD, WPS, WQ1, WRI, XLS

Files and Settings Transfer (FAST) Wizard

The FAST Wizard is designed to accommodate the transfer of settings from a single computer or an upgrade to the same system. The data that is going to be saved can be stored on the local system, a server, or removable media. After the user data has been saved to a UNC file, it can then be backed up or burned to a CD-ROM for more permanent storage.

To get the transfer of the user data to work, you need to mine the information from the existing, or old, system. If this is a pre-XP box, you need to obtain a Wizard Disk, or use the Windows XP Professional CD to access the Fastwiz.exe tool. To create the Wizard Disk, you need to run the Files and Settings Transfer Wizard, located under Start|All Programs|Accessories|System Tools. Figure 2.3 shows the portion of the tool that creates the Wizard Disk.

To start the process of saving data, you need to be logged on as the user that will be migrated. During the archiving of the old system, you will have an opportunity to customize exactly which portion of the system, files, and settings you want saved. Figure 2.4 shows the interface for customizing the settings, files/folders, and file types.

After you have the old system archived, you can install the new Windows XP Professional computer. After the computer is installed, you simply need to start up the FAST Wizard and download the information to the new XP system.

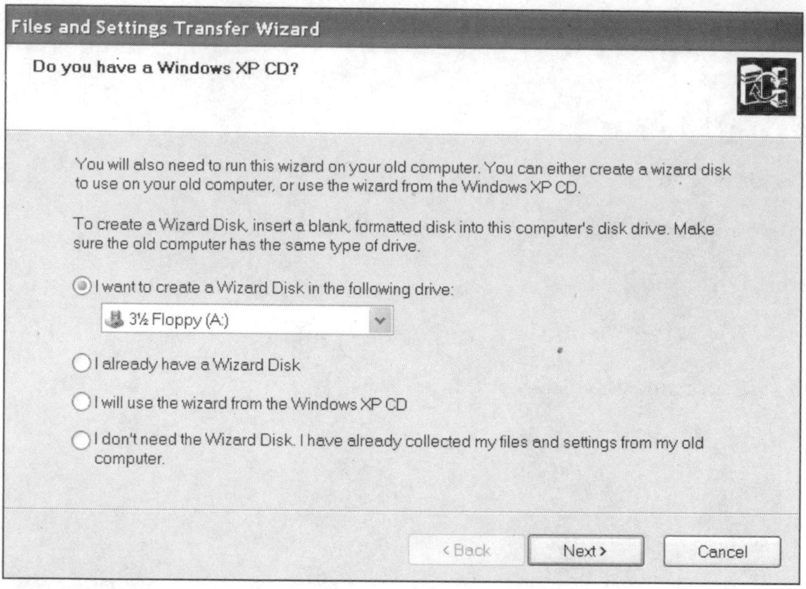

Figure 2.3 The FAST Wizard interface that allows for the creation of the Wizard Disk.

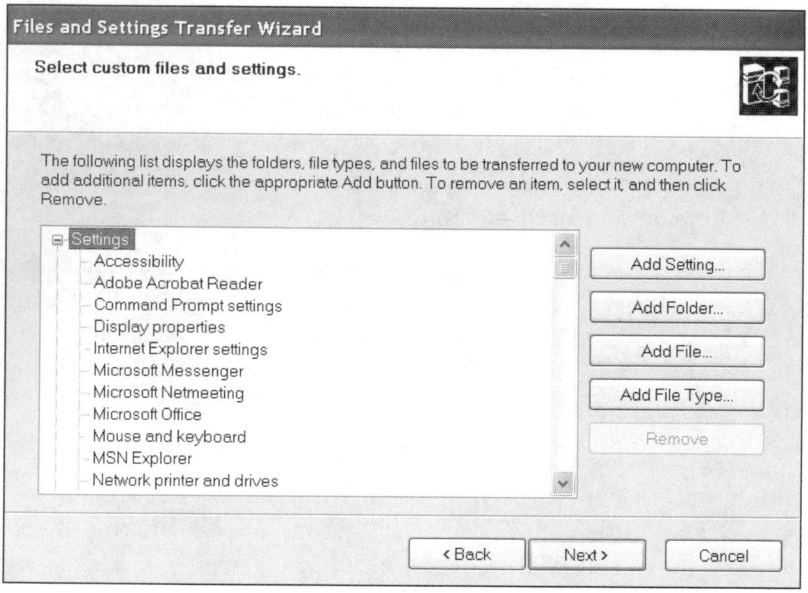

Figure 2.4 Customization of the FAST Wizard files and settings.

Note: If you want to run the FAST Wizard for multiple users, you need to perform these steps multiple times.

USMT from the Command Line

If you work for a large corporation, you will certainly need a more robust tool than the FAST Wizard. That is where the USMT command-line options come into play. These options are fully customizable to migrate multiple user settings. However, you will need to have the following requirements in place to use this option:

➤ A server to which both source and target computers can gain access.

➤ Adequate space for migrating all users' data.

➤ Source computers containing the users' accounts to be transferred.

➤ A target computer running Windows XP Professional that does not contain a profile for the user whose state you will be transferring.

➤ An account with administrative privilege on the target computer. The account cannot have the same name as the migrating user account.

➤ The account name and password of the users whose settings and files are to be transferred.

After you have acquired all of this information, you are ready to start the migration. The migration will occur in three phases.

Phase I: Prepare the Server

The server share needs to be created to house the users' data. A standard configuration needs to have a large amount of disk space with a shared folder to house the users' data. For purposes of this discussion, suppose that folder is named USMT_DATA. Then, you need two distinct folders to house the USMT migration files and executables. It might be best to make two different folders, to keep each portion separate. You will need one folder to house the scanning portion and another folder to handle the loading portion of the process. In the scanning folder, copy the following files from the ValueAdd\MSFT\USMT folder off of the Windows XP Professional CD:

➤ Scanstate.exe

➤ *.dll

➤ *.inf

In the loading folder, copy the following files from the same location:

➤ Loadstate.exe

➤ *.dll

➤ MigUser.inf

Phase II: Scan the Source Computer

Next, you need to scan the user state on the source computer. This is an easy phase that consists of multiple steps. First, map a drive to the scanning folder that you have on the server. Then, run the following command, while logged in as the user that will be migrated:

```
Scanstate /I .\migapp.inf /I .\migsys.inf /I .\migfiles.inf
/I .\sysfiles.inf \\<server>\USMT_DATA
```

The INF files in the command are fully customizable to incorporate different applications, files, and settings.

Phase III: Load the Target Computer

Finally, you are ready to load the target computer. To successfully install the user settings, you need to be logged in with administrative rights and confirm that the users whose data that you are migrating does not have an existing account on the target computer. When all of these items are taken care of, you can map a drive to the loading folder that you have on the server and run the following command:

```
Loadstate /I .\miguser.inf \\<server>\\UMT_DATA
```

Deploying Service Packs (SPs) Using Group Policy and Slipstreaming

Installing SPs in Windows NT is a very time-consuming process. First, you have to install the OS, and then you must apply the SP. Windows XP allows you to incorporate a SP with the installation files. Combining the latest SP with the Windows XP installation files enables you to install them as one. In Windows NT, however, if you installed a new service after applying an SP, you had to reapply the SP for the new service to gain any benefits the SP might have to offer. Additionally, you had to reinstall some services after you applied an SP. Thankfully, you don't have to contend with these situations in Windows XP.

Group Policy Deployments of SPs

One great feature of Windows 2000 and XP is the ability to control the computing environment via Group Policy. One control method is the deployment of software through Group Policy Objects (GPOs). A new option is provided for deploying service packs through MSI files and GPOs. This option works best when you assign the service pack to computers in the environment. This way, you get a consistent installation of the SP regardless of which user logs on to the computer.

Slipstreaming SPs

The process of combining the Windows XP installation files with an SP is called *slipstreaming*. You apply an SP to a distribution share of the installation files by executing **update.exe /s**.

If you install Windows XP using the slipstreamed distribution, the installations contain the SP. Using this method can save you a lot of time and helps you to avoid having to apply an SP after each installation.

Applying SPs Manually

If you didn't have the opportunity or ability to create a slipstreamed distribution share, you can apply an SP simply by running **update.exe** on the local machine. If you install any new services after applying the SP, Windows XP gets any files it needs for those services from the installation files or the SP. This process updates a service or an application without requiring you to continually reapply the SP whenever you add something new.

Installing Hotfixes

A few common ways exist to deploy hotfixes to Windows XP Professional clients. The first way is to deploy the hotfixes during the installation of the OS itself. To accomplish this form of installation, you need to create and configure the following items:

1. Create a distribution folder. This will be named i386 and contain a folder named OEM. The installation process will refer to this folder for the inclusion of additional files and content.

2. Create an answer file. This will instruct the installation on how to interact with the distribution folder that you have created in the first step.

3. Create a Cmdlines.txt file. This file will contain specific lines of code that install each hotfix separately.

4. Copy files to the distribution folder. After all the files are created, you will then copy the answer file, Cmdlines.txt file, and hotfix executables to the distribution folder.

5. Start the installation. The final step is to install the OS, which will in turn install the hotfixes from the entries that were placed in the Cmdlines.txt file. The two installation commands for XP are **winnt.exe** and **winnt32.exe**.

Another option to install hotfixes with ease is to use the Qchain.exe tool from Microsoft. This tool allows multiple hotfixes to be installed without a reboot. Of course, if you attempt to install hotfixes normally, without a reboot, you could cause serious damage to your system, even corruption and complete failure.

Automatic Updates

Automatic Updates is the new look and feel for the Critical Update Notification feature that was available in the Windows 9*x* series and Windows 2000. This feature automatically contacts the Windows Update site at Microsoft to detect any critical updates for the system. This is an excellent service that is built in; but for some environments, usually corporations, the service can be a problem, not knowing which updates have been installed on the client computers. However, by selecting Control Panel|System and then selecting the Automatic Updates tab, the administrator can control how these critical updates are handled, as shown in Figure 2.5. The three configurations are as follows:

➤ *Download the updates automatically and notify me when they are ready to be installed*—Downloads the update in the background, and then prompts the user for the installation of the update

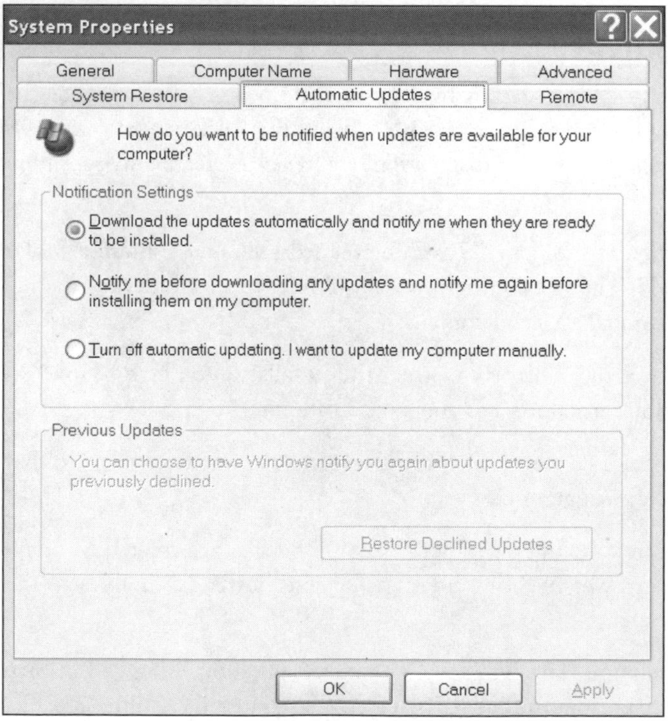

Figure 2.5 Automatic Updates tab of the System Properties dialog box.

➤ *Notify me before downloading any updates and notify me again before installing them on my computer*—First prompts the user to download the update, and then prompts the user for the installation of the update after it is downloaded

➤ *Turn off automatic updating. I want to update my computer manually*—Disables the automatic update feature, forcing manual installation of the updates or the use of Start|Windows Update to obtain the new updates

Dynamic Update

Dynamic Updates allows Windows XP Professional Setup to function with the built-in Windows Update feature. Dynamic Update will allow the download of critical fixes and drivers needed during the setup process. This feature is designed to help reduce difficulties during setup. One way that the difficulties are minimized is to make the device drivers that are not included on the Windows XP Professional CD-ROM available through Dynamic Update. Dynamic Update cannot overwrite any device drivers that are located on the OS CD-ROM by default. It only allows for new device drivers. If a new device driver is available from Microsoft, it can be obtained after the installation by using the Windows Update feature.

Two types of files are downloaded by Dynamic Update:

➤ *Replacement files*—Files that are typically DLLs that replace the errant files located on the CD-ROM. These replacement files are flagged to replace files that need critical fixes or updates.

➤ *Device drivers*—These files are new device drivers that were not available on the CD-ROM. Any updates to existing device drivers are not available through Dynamic Update.

For clients to take advantage of Dynamic Update, the following criteria must be met:

➤ A connection must exist to the location of the files and drivers. This can be either the Internet or a network share containing the updates, which were downloaded by a network administrator earlier.

➤ The client needs to be running Internet Explorer 4.1 or later versions of the following two files: Winenet.dll and Shlwapi.dll.

During a manual installation, the user will be prompted to connect to the Internet and download the updates from the Microsoft Web site. In an unattended installation, Dynamic Updates are enabled by default, which will have the installation attempt to connect to the Internet or shared folder. If Dynamic Updates need to be disabled for an unattended installation, the **DUDisable=yes** switch must be used. This will typically be located in the answer file that is generated.

Creating a Network Share for Dynamic Updates

Many compelling reasons exist to not want users accessing the Internet to download Windows Updates during the installation of the OS or even after the OS is installed. One method to eliminate this access is to create a network share that contains the files and drivers that the administrator feels are important for the company environment.

To create the shared folder, the administrator first needs to access the corporate site for the Windows Update and download the essential files for the computers in the enterprise, including updates and device drivers. This establishes a controlled environment for these updates and device drivers, ensuring that users cannot simply connect and download files that could cause compatibility issues. After the files have been downloaded to the correct share point on the server, the **DUPrepare:pathname** switch needs to be used against the path to prepare it for delivery to the clients. To point the installation, either attended or unattended, to this new share point, add the **DUShare:pathname** switch to the installation command or the answer file.

Product Activation

Product activation is an attempt to reduce the piracy of the Windows XP Professional product. Every system that is installed needs to be activated within 30 days or the system will no longer function until it is activated.

Note: Those enterprises, both large and small, that have an open license agreement for Windows XP do not have to activate the installations of XP Professional. This is to allow for the disperse methods of installation and optimize the installation process.

The activation of your OS is based on the Product ID as well as hardware that is located within the system. For those of you who change hardware on your systems, this can cause some issues. However, if you "significantly overhaul" your hardware, you will need to reactivate your system. Activation can be done over the Internet or via a phone call to Microsoft. In either case, the process is rather painless and takes only a few minutes.

In the latest release from Microsoft, Windows Product Activation (WPA) will be tied solely to the BIOS. This means that any hardware device can be swapped and the product will not need to be reactivated. However, if the motherboard manufacturer changes, the system will require a reactivation. Don't expect to see this information detailed on the exam for some time, because it was released after the exam went to beta. If you upgrade your system, the same rules apply, which means that if you "significantly overhaul" your hardware, you will need to reactivate.

Troubleshooting Failed Installations

Windows XP Professional should install on most new computers without too much difficulty. However, there are some common reasons why it may not install properly. The following is a list of typical installation problems:

➤ *Media errors*—These are problems you encounter with the distribution CD-ROM. Make sure the problem exists with the media itself, not access to the media. If you place the Windows XP Professional CD-ROM in a shared drive for installation, too many people could be using the drive at one time. This may generate some errors. However, if only one person is connected to the shared drive and errors persist, get a replacement for the distribution CD-ROM. In addition, always restart failed installations caused by media errors.

➤ *Incompatible CD-ROM drive*—Many specifications exist for CD-ROM drives. You can install Windows XP from most drives, but there are always exceptions. If the CD-ROM drive is not compliant, replace it or place the distribution files on the network. Also, as mentioned earlier in this chapter, the Windows XP CD-ROM is bootable and can be installed from El-Torito-compatible drives. If the CD-ROM can't boot, ensure that the drive is compliant and that the boot order in the BIOS has been set to the CD-ROM drive. Ensure that the level of BIOS that you are running supports bootable CD-ROMs. Also, the controller card for the CD-ROM drive could be failing, or the drive itself could be bad.

➤ *Installation halts or errors*—If a STOP error occurs during the installation, it is typically the result of incorrect or incompatible drivers. Obtain the correct and current drivers and restart the installation process. Also, the installation may stop just after the copy or text phase, with a warning that the master boot record has a virus. This warning typically results when the BIOS has the virus warning option enabled. Turn this option off and restart the installation. As a final measure, ensure that all devices are on the HCL.

➤ *Lack of drive space*—Windows XP needs much more free space compared to its predecessors. Ensure that at least 650MB of free space is available, at a minimum.

➤ *Dependency failures*—For the installation to be completed successfully, all services must be able to start when needed. Some services depend on others to complete a task. For example, if the drivers for the network adapter could not load, that will affect all services that depend on the network adapter's successful installation. As a result, the computer won't be able to join the domain.

➤ *Problems joining the domain*—If the network adapter has initialized but the computer still can't join the domain, verify that the DNS server is online and that you are using the correct IP address of the DNS server. Also, verify that you typed the domain name correctly. If problems persist, install the computer to a workgroup to complete the installation.

Practice Questions

Question 1

You are the network administrator for the East branch of the ACME publishing company. You have a Windows 2000 domain that contains Windows 95, Windows 98, Windows NT 4, and Windows 2000 clients. Your network has four locations, each configured as an Active Directory site.

You want to upgrade all of the clients to Windows XP to take advantage of the Remote Assistance capability. You upgrade the Windows 98, NT, and 2000 clients, but are having trouble upgrading the Windows 95 clients. What should you do to the Windows 95 clients?

- ○ a. Run the Readiness Analyzer
- ○ b. Run **winnt32 /checkupgradeonly**
- ○ c. Run **winnt /checkupgradeonly**
- ○ d. Upgrade them to Windows 98

Answer d is correct. It is not possible to upgrade Windows 95 clients directly to Windows XP Professional. You must first upgrade them to Windows 98, and then you can make the upgrade to Windows XP. Answer a is incorrect because this is a tool that is used to determine if your system will be compatible with Windows XP. Answers b and c are incorrect because the **/checkupgradeonly** switch will determine if the existing system is compatible with Windows XP. In addition, the **/checkupgradeonly** switch is not compatible with the **winnt** command.

Question 2

You are the network administrator at the AllMine talent company. You are looking to upgrade your Windows NT domain to Windows 2000. You want to take advantage of the new Group Policy Objects that can control desktop settings, security, and software installation. You want to use the DFS service to create a load-balanced and fault-tolerant environment for the software deployment and maintenance via Group Policy.

To prepare your environment for the Windows 2000 domain, you want to install Windows XP on all the clients before the Windows 2000 domain is installed. You want to create the most efficient installation for your 10,000 client computers. You currently use a third-party cloning and distribution package and need to continue to use this package for the distribution of Windows XP Professional. You want the installation to be completely automated.

Which options should you use? [Check all correct answers]

❑ a. Create an answer file using Setup Manager.

❑ b. Create a uniqueness database file using Setup Manager.

❑ c. Use the CD-based image using RIS.

❑ d. Create an image using Riprep.

❑ e. Create an image using Sysprep.

Answers a and e are correct. To optimize the installation of Windows XP Professional using a third-party cloning and distribution package, you need to use Sysprep.exe. Sysprep allows for the creation of images that use a minisetup program to make the system unique on the network. In addition to using the Sysprep tool, you need to make an answer file to answer the minisetup questions automatically. This will make the installation automated. Answer b is incorrect because the uniqueness database file is used for network installations, not for Sysprep installations. Answers c and d are incorrect because they are referring to the use of RIS. RIS is not used with third-party cloning tools.

Question 3

As the administrator for the CertCore consulting group, you are responsible for 50 consultants and 100 office personnel. CertCore has four offices within the major metropolitan area that the consultants work out of. Domain controllers are in each of the four locations.

At this time, the budget is insufficient to have a quality lab, so the consultants are using their own desktop systems to troubleshoot client issues. You need to enable a technology that will enable the consultants in the company to quickly reinstall their Windows XP Professional desktop in case they corrupt their system while troubleshooting client issues. The consultants need to have the ability to boot their system without any floppy disk. After the installation, the computer account needs to be located in the same OU that it was before, to obtain the correct Group Policies. Finally, the installation needs to include a core set of applications that can then be controlled after the OS is installed via Group Policy.

How should you proceed?

○ a.   Save the contents of the i386 folder from the Windows XP Professional CD to the network, giving the consultants permissions to the winnt32 command.

○ b.   Install a RIS server, which contains the CD-based image for Windows XP Professional.

○ c.   Create a Riprep image.

○ d.   Create a Sysprep image.

Answer c is correct. Riprep is a tool that is used with RIS servers. Riprep enables not only the core OS to be imaged, but also the applications that are currently installed. The image is stored on the RIS server and is made available to clients that have a PXE boot ROM NIC or can support a PXE boot ROM floppy disk. The system that is created can have the applications installed via Group Policy software deployment. Then, when the Riprep image is created, the applications and software are both included and the software will be maintained and controlled via Group Policy. Answer a is incorrect because the i386 folder from the CD will not give the application requirements in the image, nor the ability to boot without a floppy, in the case that the existing OS is corrupt. Answer b is incorrect because a CD-based image through RIS will not include the applications that are required in the scenario. Answer d is incorrect because Sysprep is not capable of producing an image that will work without some form of third-party client, which would require an OS running or a boot disk.

Question 4

You are in charge of the deployment of Windows XP for all 25,000 users at ACME computer sales. The current network consists of Windows 2000 Professional systems and a Windows 2000 domain. Most of the users are located at the main production plant, but others are located at sales offices throughout the United States.

You do not want to upgrade the systems, because most of them were upgraded from Windows NT 4 Workstation in the last rollout. However, you want to save as much of the user-based settings and files as possible to minimize both calls to the Help Desk and user complaints. You decide to use the File and Settings Transfer Wizard to migrate the user settings and files. What will you need to do to get the settings from the Windows 2000 Professional systems?

- ○ a. Run the **scanstate** command from the Windows 2000 domain controller.
- ○ b. Run the **loadstate** command from the client computer.
- ○ c. Create a Wizard Disk to run on the Windows 2000 Professional computers.
- ○ d. Run the FAST Wizard from the Windows XP client to save the user settings.

Answer c is correct. To save the settings and files from a Windows 2000 Professional system, you need to have a Wizard Disk or the Fastwiz.exe tool from the Windows XP Professional CD-ROM. This will start the FAST Wizard and allow the user settings to be saved to the hard disk, removable media, or network share. Answers a and b are incorrect because they would be used in the command line method, not with the FAST Wizard. Answer d is incorrect because you can't run the FAST Wizard on a client to save files from another system.

Question 5

You are the chief technology officer for the ACME Web development company. Your company develops high-end Web sites and Web applets for e-commerce companies. You have more than 1,000 developers in the company who code in many different languages, including C#, ASP, VB, and XML. Each developer computer is running Windows XP Professional, and the user is not a Power User or Administrator on their local system.

The current infrastructure is a Windows 2000 domain running Active Directory. You had to implement Active Directory to control each type of developer through Group Policy and to delegate control to the head developer in each discipline. Each type of developer, user account, and computer account is located in a separate OU. You have had issues with some service packs overwriting critical system files that were needed to develop and test certain applications that were developed. You need to develop a strategy to roll out future service packs to each discipline only after the service pack has been tested and shown that it does not cause any damage to the developer computer.

What should you do?

- ○ a. Create a logon script that runs a batch file to install the service pack when the computer is rebooted.

- ○ b. Save the service pack to a network share and allow the developer access to the share to install the service pack at their own leisure.

- ○ c. Use the **QCHAIN** command to install the service pack through a logon script, based on the group that the developer is a member of.

- ○ d. Configure a Group Policy at each developer OU that will apply the service pack after it has been tested for that type of developer.

Answer d is correct. For this deployment, it will be ideal to create a Group Policy that will apply the service pack through the use of MSI packages. After the service pack has been thoroughly tested for a developer type, it can be quickly installed through the use of software deployment using Group Policy. Answer a is incorrect because the ability to control the installation is too limiting through a batch file. Also, it would be extremely difficult to control the batch file application to computers, where through GPOs it would be very easy. Answer b is incorrect because there would be no control over who actually had the service pack or not. There could also be a problem if the developer uses someone else's machine and incorrectly installs the service pack there. Answer c is incorrect because this tool is used to install hotfixes without rebooting, not service packs.

Question 6

> As the administrator for The Coriolis Group, you are planning to install 1,000 Windows XP Professional computers in the next month. You are currently running Windows 95 on these clients and will use a network unattended installation to install the new OS.
>
> Security is an important facet for your industry, because the users need to use the Internet so much to do research. You are aware of at least four security hotfixes that you want installed during the installation of the initial OS. You want to use the new Dynamic Update feature to install these up- dates, as well as some of the other updates that you have tested to be safe and stable for your environment. However, you do not want the client to access the Internet during the installation to receive these updates.
>
> What should you do? [Check all correct answers]
>
> ❑ a. Create a Group Policy to point the client to the share that contains the hotfixes and updates.
>
> ❑ b. Create a share on the network and download the hotfixes and updates to it.
>
> ❑ c. When installing the client, be sure to use the **dushare** switch with the installation command.
>
> ❑ d. When installing the client, be sure to use the **duprepare** switch with the installation comamnd.

Answers b and c are correct. First, you need to create a share that contains the hotfixes and updates. You need to connect to the corporate site located on the Windows Update site to select which files you want to include in your share. Then, the client needs to be redirected to the correct share, by using the **dushare** switch during the installation. Answer a is incorrect because GPOs can't be used to install from the Dynamic Update share; this is available at installation only. Answer d is incorrect because the **duprepare** switch prepares the Dynamic Up- date share, not used on the client portion of the installation.

Question 7

You are in charge of the Web developers in your company. Your company creates e-commerce Web sites and applications for small businesses. The developers' computers run Windows XP Professional and Internet Information Services (IIS).

The company has 150 developers. The developers need to have stable environments to work in, to ensure that they are productive. During the installation process of Windows XP Professional, the OS is installed, service packs are applied, applications are installed, and any Microsoft hotfixes or updates are installed. However, sometimes additional hotfixes and updates need to be applied to support security and functionality of the development environment. The developer must automatically be made aware of any update and then must be in control of the update being downloaded and installed.

Which option should you configure?

○ a. Windows Update

○ b. Automatic Updates

○ c. Dynamic Update

○ d. Configure a server and share with the contents of the updates and use the **dushare** command on the client

Answer b is correct. When a user needs to be automatically updated about new hotfixes and updates, the Automatic Updates option needs to be configured. This tool can be set up to trigger when there is an update, to then allow the user to download and also install the update. This option also has settings that can always download the updates, but then prompt for installation and, of course, completely disable the automatic updates. If you disable the automatic updates, you will need to manually use the Windows Update feature. Answer a is incorrect because this option is a manual process. Answer c is incorrect because this option is available only during the installation of the product. Answer d is incorrect because the **dushare** switch is used with Dynamic Update and is available only during the installation of the product.

Question 8

> You are the network administrator in charge of the Windows XP Professional rollout for your company. You have been planning for your 1,500-user rollout for the past three months. You have a Windows 2000 Active Directory–based domain and only two locations.
>
> You have eight phases to your overall deployment plan, which will last for two months. You are half way through the phases when trouble hits. You have users complaining that they can no longer access their Windows XP Professional computer.
>
> What should you do?
>
> ○ a. Have the user restart their computer and press F12.
>
> ○ b. Activate the Windows XP Professional computers.
>
> ○ c. Boot the computers to the Recovery Console.
>
> ○ d. Boot the computers and press F8.

Answer b is correct. If you are installing your Windows XP Professional computers from a nonvolume license CD, you need to activate your computers. This requires that the computer communicate with the clearinghouse located on the Internet, or via a phone call to the clearinghouse to activate the installation of XP. By default, you have 30 days to use the product before it will become inoperable from not having activated your system. Answer a is incorrect because this is used for a RIS installation. You have a good installation; you just need to activate what is installed. Answer c is incorrect because the Recovery Console won't be available without activating the system. Answer d is incorrect because the F8 menu option won't be available until you activate the product.

Need to Know More?

 Microsoft Corporation. *Microsoft Windows 2000 Professional Resource Kit Documentation.* Redmond, WA: Microsoft Press, 2000. ISBN 1-57231-808-2. This book reviews the core aspects of installation preparations and the installation options.

 Search the TechNet CD (or its online version through **www.microsoft.com**) and the *Windows 2000 Professional Resource Kit* CD using the keywords "sysprep", "RIS", "Remote Installation Services", "Windows Product Activation (WPA)", "Setup Manger", and "Automatic Updates".

Establishing, Configuring, and Managing Resources

Terms you'll need to understand:

✓ Shared folders

✓ Hidden shares

✓ Simple file sharing

✓ Offline files/client-side caching

✓ Share permissions

✓ NT File System (NTFS)

✓ NTFS permissions

✓ User rights

✓ Built-in security principals

✓ Access control list (ACL)

✓ Access control entry (ACE)

✓ Taking ownership of objects

✓ Auditing

✓ Internet Information Server (IIS)

✓ Internet Printing Protocol (IPP)

Techniques you'll need to master:

✓ Creating network shares

✓ Configuring share permissions

✓ Configuring options for offline files

✓ Setting basic and advanced NTFS permissions

✓ Viewing effective permissions

✓ Learning how to turn on auditing

✓ Installing and managing Internet Information Server

✓ Connecting to printers over the Internet

Why do we have computer networks anyway? Well, they empower us to collaborate on projects and share information with others, whether they're around the corner or across the globe. If you're working on a Windows XP Professional system that is connected to a network, you can share one or more of that system's folders with other computers and users on that network. Drive volumes and folders are not automatically shared for all users in Windows XP Professional. Members of the Administrators group and the Power Users group, discussed later in this chapter, are the only users who retain the rights to create shared network folders.

Managing Access to Shared Folders

Windows XP Professional implements a new feature called Simple File Sharing, which is *enabled* by default when the computer is standalone or a member of a network workgroup. Simple File Sharing is *disabled* when the computer is a member of a Windows domain. Simple File Sharing creates a Shared Documents folder, inside of which it creates two subfolders, Shared Pictures and Shared Music. Remote users who access a shared folder over the network *always* authenticate as the Guest user account when Simple File Sharing is enabled. The Properties sheet for a shared folder under Simple File Sharing configures both share permissions and NTFS permissions (if the shared folder is stored on an NTFS volume) simultaneously—you are not allowed to configure the two permissions separately. For example, you cannot make a shared folder private, under Simple File Sharing, unless the folder resides on an NTFS volume.

To turn off Simple File Sharing for a standalone system, or for a computer that is a member of a workgroup, perform the following steps:

1. Open a window in either My Computer or Windows Explorer.

2. Click Tools|Folder Options from the menu.

3. Click the View tab.

4. Clear the Use Simple File Sharing (Recommended) checkbox under the Advanced Settings section.

5. Click OK.

Note: The Shared Documents, Shared Pictures, and Shared Music folders are not available if the Windows XP Professional computer is a member of a Windows domain.

Creating Shared Folders from My Computer or Windows Explorer

To share a folder with the network with Simple File Sharing disabled, you can use My Computer or Windows Explorer and follow these steps:

1. Open a window in either My Computer or Windows Explorer.

2. Right-click the folder that you want to share and then select Sharing And Security from the pop-up menu.

3. Click the Share This Folder button.

4. Type in a Share Name or accept the default name. Windows XP uses the actual folder name as the default Share Name.

5. Type in a Comment, if you desire. Comments appear in the Browse list when users search for network resources. Comments can help users to locate the proper network shares.

6. Specify the User Limit: Maximum Allowed or Allow This Number Of Users. Windows XP Professional permits a maximum of 10 concurrent network connections per share. Specify the Allow This Number Of Users option only if you need to limit the number of concurrent users for this share to fewer than 10.

7. Click OK to create the shared folder. The folder now becomes available to others on your network.

Note: To remove a network share, right-click the shared folder and choose the Sharing And Security option. Click the Do Not Share This Folder option button and click OK. The folder will no longer be shared with the network

 The Security tab of an NTFS folder's properties dialog box is *not* displayed when Simple File Sharing is enabled and the computer is not a member of a Windows domain. To display the Security tab so that you can view and work with NTFS permissions for folders and files, open a window in My Computer or Windows Explorer and select Tools|Folder Options. Click the View tab and clear the checkbox entitled Use Simple File Sharing (Recommended).

Creating Shared Folders from the Shared Folders MMC Snap-in

To share a folder with the network with Simple File Sharing disabled, you may use the Shared Folders MMC snap-in from a custom console, or you can use the Shared Folders snap-in as part of the Computer Management Console by following these steps:

1. Right-click the My Computer icon and select Manage, or open an empty Microsoft Management Console window and add the Shared Folders snap-in for the local computer.

2. Expand the Shared Folders node and click Shares.

3. Right-click the Shares subnode and select New File Share.

4. Type the path and folder name in the Folder To Share box, or click Browse to locate it.

5. Type a name for the share in the Share Name box, and optionally, type in a Share Description.

6. Click Next.

7. Select one of the basic share permissions listed, or click Customize Share And Folder Permissions to define your own share permissions. The default selection is All Users Have Full Control. Remember, these are share permissions that apply only to users accessing this share remotely over the network—not NTFS security permissions!

8. Click Finish and then click Yes or No when prompted to create another shared folder.

 Generally, if you are working with shared folders residing on NTFS volumes, it is a good idea to leave all share permissions at their default setting: Everyone–Full Control. Use NTFS security permissions to specify access control levels for both users and groups. By having only one set of permissions to manage, security access levels are less confusing, and you avoid possible conflicts with share permissions. In addition, NTFS security permissions apply to both remote network users and local users, so users cannot circumvent security permissions by logging on to the local computer.

To remove a shared folder from the Shared Folders snap-in, simply right-click the shared folder and select Stop Sharing. Click Yes and the folder will no longer be shared on the network.

Using Automatically Generated Hidden Shares

Windows XP Professional automatically creates shared folders by default each and every time the computer is started. These default shares are often referred to as *hidden* or *administrative* shares because a dollar sign ($) is appended to their share names, which prevents the shared folder from being displayed on the network Browse list; users cannot easily discover that these shares exist. When users browse through the My Network Places window, for example, they cannot see that such hidden shares even exist; Microsoft Windows Networking does not allow hidden shares to be displayed. The default hidden network shares include the following:

➤ *C$, D$, E$, and so on*—One share gets created for the root of each available hard drive volume on the system.

➤ *ADMIN$*—This shares the %systemroot% folder with the network (for example, C:\Windows).

➤ *IPC$*—This share is used for interprocess communications (IPCs). IPCs support communications between objects on different computers over a network by manipulating the low-level details of network transport protocols. IPCs enable the use of distributed application programs that combine multiple processes working together to accomplish a single task.

➤ *print$*—This share holds the printer drivers for the printers installed on the local machine. When a remote computer connects to a printer over the network, the appropriate printer driver is downloaded to the remote PC.

Although you can temporarily disable hidden shares, you cannot delete them without modifying the Registry (which is not recommended), because they get re-created each time the computer restarts. You can connect to a hidden share, but only if you provide a user account with administrative privileges along with the appropriate password for that user account. Administrators can create their own custom administrative (hidden) shares simply by adding a dollar sign to the share name of any shared folder. Administrators can view all the hidden shares that exist on a Windows XP Professional system from the Shared Folders MMC snap-in.

Connecting to Shared Resources on a Windows Network

Users and network administrators have several options available to them for connecting to shared network resources. These options include the following:

➤ Type in a Universal Naming Convention (UNC) path from the Start|Run dialog box in the format \\servername\sharename.

➤ Navigate to the share from the My Network Places window.

➤ Employ the **net use** command from a command prompt window.

If you want to connect to a shared folder named "samples" that resides on a Windows computer named SALES7, click Start|Run, type "\\SALES7\samples", and click OK. At this point, you are connected to that shared resource, provided that you possess the proper user ID, password, and security permissions needed to access the shared folder.

Connecting to Network Resources with the My Network Places Window

You can connect to a network share from My Network Places. To use the My Network Places window, perform the following steps:

1. Click Start|My Network Places.

2. In the right-hand Network Tasks section, click the Add A Network Place link, which reveals the Add Network Place Wizard.

3. Click Next, click Choose Another Network Location, and then click Next again.

4. Enter the Internet Or Network Address, or click Browse to locate the network share by viewing the available network resources. You can connect to one of the following types of resources:

    ➤ A shared folder using the following syntax: \\server\share

    ➤ A Web folder using the following syntax: **http://webserver/share**

    ➤ An FTP site using the following syntax: **ftp://ftp.domain.name**

5. Click Next to enter a name for the network place or accept the default name.

6. Click Next again to view a summary of the Network Place that you are adding.

7. Click Finish to establish the connection to the shared folder, provided that you have the proper permissions. A list of network resources to which you have already connected is then displayed within the My Network Places window.

For Command-Line Junkies: The **Net Share** and **Net Use** Commands

You can create and delete shared folders from the command line instead of using the GUI. Windows XP offers several **Net** commands that you use from the command line. You can view all of the available **Net** commands by typing "Net /?" at a command prompt window. To create a new shared folder, you simply type "Net Share share_name=x:\folder_name", where **share_name** represents the name you want to assign to the shared folder, x: represents the drive letter where the folder resides, and **folder_name** represents the actual name of the folder. For help with the various options and syntax of the **Net Share** command, type "Net Share /?" at the command prompt.

You also have the option of connecting to network shares via the **Net Use** command. For help with the various options and syntax of the **Net Use** command, type "net use /?" at the command prompt. To connect to a remote resource from the command line, follow these steps:

1. Open a command prompt window (click Start|All Programs|Accessories| Command Prompt, or click Start|Run, type CMD, and click OK).

2. At the command prompt, type "net use X: \\servername\sharename" and press Enter, where X: is a drive letter that you designate (for example, net use M: \\sales7\samples). If you possess the appropriate permissions for that network share, you should see the message The Command Completed Successfully displayed in your command prompt window.

Controlling Access to Shared Folders

When you, as a network administrator, grant access to shared resources over the network, the shared data files become very vulnerable to unintentional, as well as intentional destruction or deletion by others. This is why network administrators must be vigilant in controlling data access security permissions. If access permissions to shared folders are too lenient, shared data may become compromised. On the other hand, if access permissions are set too stringently, the users who need to access and manipulate the data may not be able to do their jobs. Managing access control for shared resources can be quite challenging.

Shared Folder Properties: Configuring Client-Side Caching (Offline Files)

By right-clicking a shared folder and selecting Sharing, you can modify some of the shared folder's properties. You can specify whether network users can cache shared data files on their local workstations. To configure offline access settings for the shared folder, click the Caching button to display the Cache Settings dialog box. The default is to allow caching of files whenever you create a new shared folder. To disable this feature, you must clear the Allow Caching Of Files In This Shared Folder checkbox in the Cache Settings dialog box. If you allow caching of files for a shared folder, you must choose from three options in the Caching Settings dialog box:

➤ *Automatic Caching Of Documents*—This option relies on the workstation and server computers to automatically download and make available offline any opened files from the shared folder. Older copies of files are automatically deleted to make room for newer and more recently accessed files. To ensure proper file sharing, the server version of the file is always opened.

➤ *Automatic Caching Of Programs And Documents*—This setting is recommended for folders that contain read-only data, or for application programs that have been configured to be run from the network. This option is not designed for sharing data files, and file sharing in this mode is not guaranteed. Older copies of files are automatically deleted to make room for newer and more recently accessed files.

➤ *Manual Caching Of Documents*—This is the *default* caching setting. This setting requires network users to manually specify any files that they want available when working offline. This setting is recommended for folders that contain user documents. To ensure proper file sharing, the server version of the file is always opened.

Click OK in the Caching Settings dialog box after making any configuration changes for offline access to the shared folder.

Note: The default cache size is configured as 10 percent of the client computer's available disk space. You can change this setting by selecting Tools\Folder Options from the menu bar of any My Computer or Windows Explorer window. The Offline Files tab of the Folder Options dialog box displays the system's offline files settings, as shown in Figure 3.1.

The Offline Files feature is also known as Client-Side Caching (CSC). The default location on Windows XP computers for storage of offline files is %systemroot%\CSC (for example, C:\Windows\CSC). You can use the Cachemov.exe tool from the Windows 2000 Professional Resource Kit, or the Windows 2000 Server Resource Kit to relocate the CSC folder onto a different drive volume. The Cachemov.exe utility moves the CSC folder to the root of the drive volume that is specified. After the CSC folder has been moved from its default location, all subsequent moves place it in the root of the drive volume—Cachemov.exe never returns the folder to its original default location.

Shared Folder Permissions

In addition to the Caching button, located at the bottom of the Sharing tab of a shared folder's Properties dialog box, is the Permissions button. The caption next to this button reads To Set Permissions For Users Who Access This Folder Over The Network, Click Permissions. However, these "share" permissions are intended solely for backward-compatibility purposes; you should actually avoid changing the default settings on share permissions (Everyone:Allow Full Control) unless a share resides on a file allocation table (FAT) or FAT32 drive volume, which provides no file system security. In most circumstances, you should store all data and applications on NT File System (NTFS) drive volumes. In fact, as a general rule, you should format (or convert) all system drive volumes as NTFS. With the availability of third-party tools, as well as the native Windows XP Recovery Console, which permit command-line access to NTFS drives (even if the system won't boot), it's difficult to argue against NTFS for all drives in Windows XP.

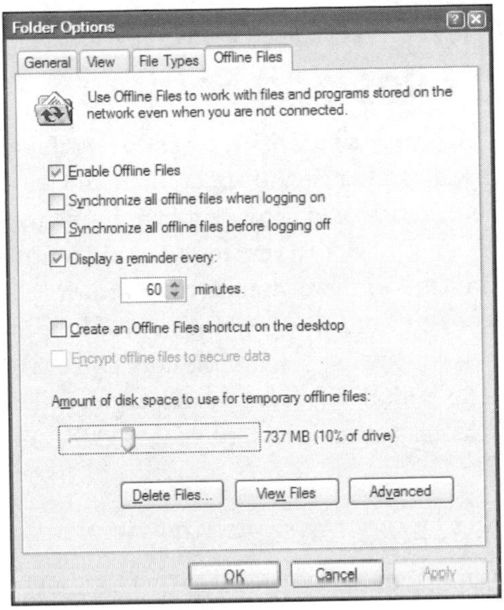
Folder Options
General
View
File Types
Offline Files
Use Offline Files to work with files and programs stored on the network even when you are not connected.
Enable Offline Files
Synchronize all offline files when logging on
Synchronize all offline files before logging off
Display a reminder every:
60
minutes.
Create an Offline Files shortcut on the desktop
Encrypt offline files to secure data
Amount of disk space to use for temporary offline files:
737 MB (10% of drive)
Delete Files...
View Files
Advanced
OK
Cancel
Apply

Figure 3.1 The Offline Files tab of the Folder Options dialog box.

TIP: Microsoft has positioned the NTFS file system as the preferred file system for Windows XP by making features such as security permissions, auditing, data compression, data encryption, reparse points, multiple named data streams, and Volume Shadow Copy Technology available only on NTFS drive volumes.

Network share permissions have their roots back in the days of Windows for Workgroups 3.11, before Windows NT and NTFS. Share permissions provided a way for administrators to control access to files for network users. Only three permissions are available: Full Control, Change, and Read. These three permissions can be explicitly allowed or denied. The default is Allow Full Control for the Everyone group. For shared folders that reside on FAT or FAT32 drives, share permissions do offer some degree of access control for network users. However, they provide *no security for local access*! Share permissions apply only to access over the network; these permissions have absolutely nothing to do with the underlying file system, which is why NTFS permissions are preferred. If you have a mixture of share permissions and NTFS permissions on the same folder, troubleshooting access control issues becomes more difficult—use either share permissions or NTFS permissions, not both.

Monitoring, Managing, and Troubleshooting Access to Files and Folders

The NTFS file system for Windows XP Professional offers several accessibility features that help administrators maintain and safeguard applications and data. Although you can somewhat control access to shared network folders by managing share permissions, Windows XP NTFS provides a very robust access control solution. In addition to offering administrators more granularity of security access control over files and folders than network share permissions, NTFS permissions reside at the file system level, which allows administrators to manage only one set of access control settings for both network users and local users. For troubleshooting resource access, you can enable auditing for folders and files residing on NTFS volumes.

NTFS Security: Users and Groups

You can apply NTFS security permissions to resources like files, folders, and printers for specific users or groups of users. Windows XP Professional installs four local users by default: Administrator, HelpAssistant, SUPPORT_xxxxxxxx (the x's represent a unique number for your Windows XP system), and Guest. The Guest user account and the SUPPORT_xxxxxxxx account are disabled by default. The Administrator user account is all powerful on the local machine and cannot be deleted, although it can be renamed.

Nine local groups are installed automatically: Administrators, Backup Operators, Guests, HelpServicesGroup, Network Configuration Operators, Power Users, Remote Desktop Users, Replicator, and Users. The Power Users group is not present in any edition of Windows 2000 Server or Windows .NET Server; it exists only as a Local group in Windows XP Professional. The Administrators account is all powerful because it is a member of the Administrators group, and you cannot remove the Administrator user account from membership in the Administrators group. Table 3.1 outlines the Local groups that are installed by default when you first install Windows XP Professional.

Special Built-in Security Principals

Special built-in security principal entities apply to any user account that happens to be using a Windows XP computer in a particular manner at a given point in time. For example, when a user logs on to a Remote Desktop session, the security principal Terminal Server User gets applied to his user account for the duration of the Remote Desktop session until he logs off. When a user logs on to a computer remotely over the network, that user's account gets the Network security principal

Table 3.1   Local groups installed by default in Windows XP Professional.

Local Group	Role
Administrators	Group members possess full administrative control for managing the local system, local users, and Local groups.
Backup Operators	Group members have the rights to back up and restore files and folders on the local system.
Guests	Group members can't make permanent alterations to their desktop settings. The default Guest account is automatically a member of this group. By default, group members possess no specific rights or permissions on objects. If the local computer joins a Windows domain, the Global Domain Guests group automatically becomes a member of the Local Guests group.
HelpServicesGroup	Members of this group can log on to the system and use helper applications to diagnose system problems. This group is used in conjunction with the HelpAssistant and SUPPORT_xxxxxxxx user accounts.
Network Configuration Operators	Members in this group can have some administrative privileges to manage configuration of networking features.
Power Users	Group members can add new local user accounts and change existing local user accounts. Members can also create shared folders and shared printers on the network. Power Users retain administrative powers with some restrictions. Thus, Power Users can run legacy applications in addition to certified applications.
Remote Desktop Users	Members in this group are granted the right to log on using the Remote Desktop or Terminal Services client software.
Replicator	This group supports file replication within a Windows domain.
Users	Group members can perform tasks only after an administrator has specifically granted them rights to do so. They can access resources on only those objects for which an administrator has granted them permissions. When user accounts get created, each new user automatically becomes a member of the Local Users group. If the local computer becomes a member of a Windows domain, the Global Domain Users group automatically becomes a member of the Local Users group.

applied to it until he disconnects from that network connection. Table 3.2 outlines the various user-related built-in security principals for Windows XP Professional. Figure 3.2 displays both user-related and computer-, process-, and service-related built-in security principals for a Windows XP domain member computer.

Built-in Security Principal	Role
Table 3.2	**Built-in security principals installed by default under Windows XP Professional.**
Everyone	Includes all users who access the computer. The best practice is to avoid using this group. If you enable the Guest account, any user can become authorized to access the system, and the user inherits the rights and permissions assigned to the Everyone group.
Authenticated Users	These users have valid user accounts on the local system, or they possess a valid user account within the domain of which the system is a member. It is preferable that you use this group over the Everyone group for preventing anonymous access to resources. The Guest account is never considered as an Authenticated User.
Creator Owner	A user who creates or takes ownership of a resource. Whenever a member of the Administrators group creates an object, the Administrators group is listed as the owner of that resource in lieu of the actual name of the user who created it.
Creator Group	A placeholder for an access control entry (ACE) that can be inherited.
Network	Any user accounts from a remote computer that access the local computer via a current network connection.
Interactive	Any user accounts who are logged on locally.
Anonymous Logon	Any user accounts that Windows XP did not validate or authorize. Users cannot log on to the system both as an Interactive user and an Anonymous Logon User at the same time.
Dialup	Any user accounts that are currently connected via dial-up networking.
Remote Interactive Logon	Any user who logs on to the computer using a Remote Desktop (Terminal Services) client connection.
Terminal Server User	Any user who accesses the computer using a Remote Desktop (Terminal Services) client connection.

NTFS Security: Basic and Advanced Permissions

NTFS security permissions can be assigned to both users and groups and are applied to resources such as folders, files, printers, and other objects. NTFS permissions are broken down into access control list (ACL) settings and access control entries (ACEs). The ACL details "who" (user or group) is granted access to an object. ACEs detail the specific permission entries (read, write, and so on) for each specific object (folder or file, for example). NTFS permissions for Windows XP can be very complex and granular when you use advanced permissions. Basic permissions are much more simple; they enable you to allow or deny access to

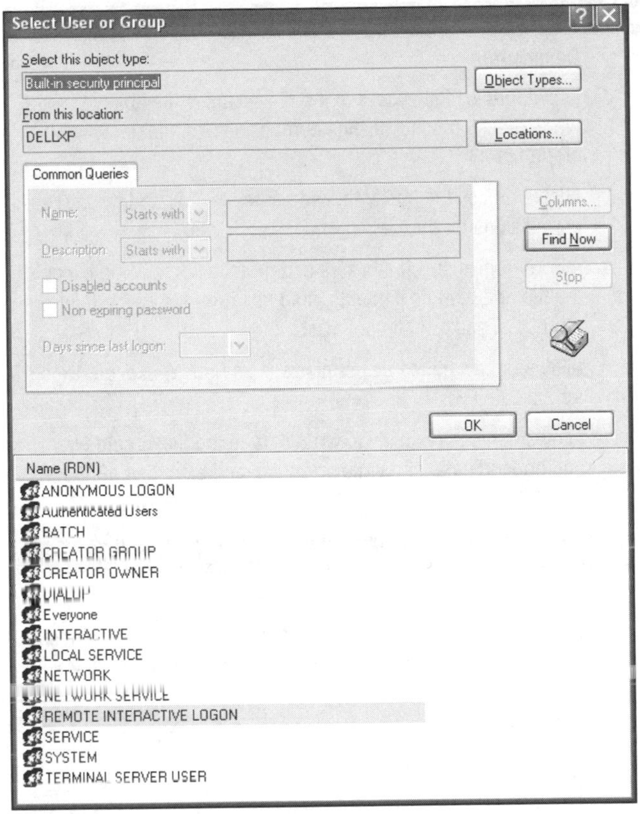

Figure 3.2 Windows XP built-in security prinicipals can be displayed from the Select User Or Group dialog box.

resources based on six fundamental levels: Read, Read and Execute, List Folder Contents (applies to folders only), Write, Modify, and Full Control. Advanced (or special) permissions enable you to fine-tune permission settings for allowing or denying such activities as reading or writing extended objcct attributes.

Basic NTFS Permissions

Basic permissions are actually comprised of predefined advanced NTFS permissions and are applied per user and per group. Individual file permissions differ slightly from the permissions that apply to folders. Table 3.3 highlights the basic permissions available for files, whereas Table 3.4 outlines the basic permissions available for folders.

Table 3.3 Basic NTFS security permissions applicable to files.	
Permission	**Description**
Full Control	Allows/denies full access to the file. Includes the ability to read, write, delete, modify, change permissions, and take ownership of the file.
Modify	Allows/denies the ability to read, write, delete, modify, and read permissions for the file.
Read & Execute	Allows/denies specified users and groups the ability to execute the file and read its contents, read its attributes and extended attributes, and read its permissions.
Read	Allows/denies the same permissions as Read & Execute except for Execute File.
Write	Allows/denies the ability to write data to the file, create files and append data, and write attributes and extended attributes.

Table 3.4 Basic NTFS security permissions applicable to folders.	
Permission	**Description**
Full Control	Allows/denies full access to objects within the folder. Includes the ability to read, write, delete, modify, change permissions, and take ownership of the folder.
Modify	Allows/denies the ability to read, write, delete, modify, and read permissions for the folder.
Read & Execute	Allows/denies specified users and groups the ability to traverse the folder, execute files within the folder, list its contents, read its contents, read its attributes and extended attributes, and read its permissions.
List Folder Contents	Allows/denies essentially the same permissions as Read & Execute. Allows/denies the ability to display files and subfolders, but this permission does not affect a user's ability to run (execute) an application program as the Read & Execute permission does.
Read	Allows/denies the same permissions as List Folder Contents except for Traverse Folder and Execute File.
Write	Allows/denies the ability to create files and write data, create folders and append data, and write attributes and extended attributes.

The List Folder Contents permission is inherited by folders, but not by files, and it should appear only when you view folder permissions. Read & Execute is inherited by both files and folders, and is always present when you view file or folder permissions. By default, NTFS security permissions are inherited from an object's parent. An administrator can manually override the default inheritance and can explicitly configure permission settings.

Advanced NTFS Permissions

NTFS advanced permissions are the building blocks for basic permissions. In Windows XP, advanced permissions allow administrators to have very granular control over exactly what types of access users can have over files and folders. Advanced permissions are somewhat hidden from view. They allow administrators to fine-tune ACE (security) settings. The Security tab in a file or folder's Properties dialog box notifies you when advanced permissions are present. Click the Advanced button to view, add, modify, or remove advanced permissions. At the bottom of the Security tab, Windows XP displays a notification just to the right of the Advanced button that says For Special Permissions Or For Advanced Settings, Click Advanced.

After you click Advanced, you see the Advanced Security Settings dialog box, which shows each access control setting that has been applied per user and per group. To view individual advanced permission entries, click one of the users or groups listed and then click the Edit button. The Permission Entry dialog box, shown in Figure 3.3, appears. It gives administrators very fine control over the ability of individual users and groups to manipulate data and program files that are stored on NTFS drive volumes. Table 3.5 shows the list of advanced NTFS permissions available under Windows XP.

From this dialog box, you can perform the following:

➤ Change the Name so that this permission entry applies to some other user or group.

➤ Modify the Apply Onto drop-down list to specify exactly where these advanced permissions should apply.

➤ Alter the actual permission entries themselves by marking or clearing the Allow or Deny checkbox for each permission that you want to affect.

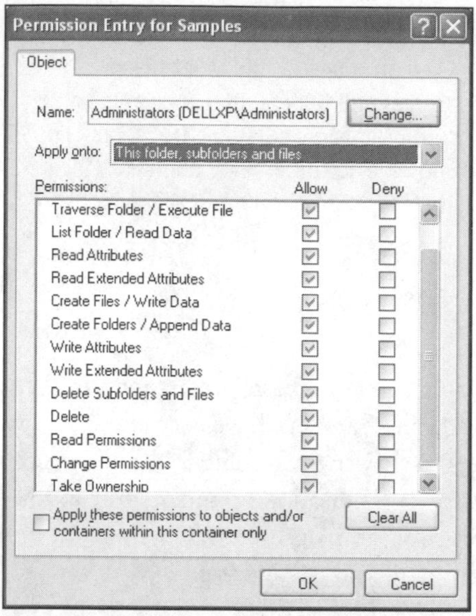

Figure 3.3 The Permission Entry dialog box for the Samples NTFS folder.

To change NTFS security permissions, you must be the owner of the file or folder whose permissions you want to modify, or the owner must grant you permission to make modifications to the object's security settings. Groups or users who are granted Full Control on a folder can delete files and subfolders *within* that folder *regardless* of the permissions protecting those files and subfolders. If the checkboxes for the Security tab under Permissions are *shaded*, the file or folder has *inherited* the permissions from the parent folder. By clearing the Inherit From Parent The Permission Entries That Apply To Child Objects checkbox, you can copy those inherited permissions and turn them into explicit permissions, or you can remove them entirely and manually establish new explicit permissions. This checkbox is located at the bottom of the Advanced Security Settings dialog box.

Table 3.5   Advanced NTFS security permissions for both files and folders.

Permission	Description
Full Control	Grants the Allow setting for all basic and advanced NTFS security permissions including the entries for Change Permissions and Take Ownership.

(continued)

Table 3.5	Advanced NTFS security permissions for both files and folders *(continued)*.
Permission	**Description**
Traverse Folder/Execute File	Allows or denies moving through folders to reach other files or folders, even if the user has no permissions for the traversed folders (applies to folders only). Traverse Folder takes effect only when the group or user is not granted the Bypass Traverse Checking user right in the Group Policy snap-in. (By default, the Everyone group is given the Bypass Traverse Checking user right). The Execute File permission allows or denies running application program files.
List Folder/Read Data	Allows or denies viewing file names and subfolder names within the folder, and allows or denies viewing data in files.
Read Attributes	Allows or denies viewing the attributes—such as read-only, hidden, and archive—of a file or folder.
Read Extended Attributes	Allows or denies viewing the extended attributes of a file or folder. Some extended attributes are defined by application programs and can vary by application.
Create Files/Write Data	Allows or denies creating files within a folder, and allows or denies making changes to a file and overwriting the existing data.
Create Folders/Append Data	Allows or denies creating folders within a folder, and allows or denies making changes to the end of a file, but not changing, deleting, or overwriting existing data.
Write Attributes	Allows or denies changing the attributes—such as read-only or hidden—of a file or folder.
Write Extended Attributes	Allows or denies changing the extended attributes of a file or folder. Extended attributes are defined by programs and may vary by program. Some extended attributes are defined by application programs and can vary by application.
Delete Subfolders and Files	Allows or denies deleting subfolders and files, even if the Delete permission has not been granted on the subfolder or file.
Delete	Allows or denies deleting the file or folder. If you don't have the Delete permission on a file or folder, you can still delete it if you have been granted Delete Subfolders And Files permission on the parent folder.
Read Permissions	Allows or denies reading the permissions that exist on a file or folder.
Change Permissions	Allows or denies changing permissions—such as Full Control, Read, and Modify—on the file or folder.
Take Ownership	Allows or denies taking ownership of a file or folder. The owner of a file or folder can always change permissions on it, even if other permissions have been assigned to safeguard the file or folder.

NTFS security permissions are *cumulative*. Users obtain permissions by having them assigned directly to their user accounts, in addition to obtaining permissions via group memberships. Users retain all permissions as they are assigned. If a user named Dan has the Allow Read permission for the Graphics folder, and if Dan is a member of the Users group, which has been assigned Allow Write permission for the same folder, Dan has both the Allow Read and Allow Write permissions. Permissions continue to accumulate. However, Deny entries always override Allow entries for the same permission type (Read, Modify, Write, and so on).

Default NTFS Security Permissions

Under Windows XP, by default, all NTFS-formatted drive volumes are assigned Allow Read and Execute as special permissions for the Everyone group for the root of each drive volume. Folders and subfolders within each drive volume *do not* automatically inherit this default permission setting. These defaults are different than the defaults for previous versions of Windows. When you install Windows XP Professional on an NTFS volume, the %systemroot% folder (for example, C:\Windows) is automatically assigned special default security permissions for the following groups: Administrators, System, and Creator Owner.

 If you upgrade from Windows NT 4 Workstation to Windows XP Professional, all existing users become members of the Local Power Users group under Windows XP. This default upgrade behavior ensures that existing users can run noncertified applications under Windows XP, because Windows XP permissions for members of the Users group are more restrictive than under Windows NT 4.

More stringent NTFS security permissions now get applied to the root of all NTFS drive volumes whenever you upgrade to Windows XP, format a drive volume as NTFS under Windows XP, or use the **convert.exe** command on a drive volume under Windows XP. The new default NTFS security permissions are outlined here and illustrated in Figure 3.4:

➤ *System*—Full Control with inherited permissions from parent folder

➤ *Administrators*—Full Control with inherited permissions from parent folder

➤ *Creator Owner*—Full Control with inherited permissions from parent folder

➤ *Everyone*—Read and Execute with no inherited permissions from parent folder

➤ *Users*—Read and Execute with inherited permissions from parent folder

Advanced Security Settings for XP_PRO (F:)

Permissions | Auditing | Owner | Effective Permissions

To view more information about Special permissions, select a permission entry, and then click Edit.

Permission entries:

Type	Name	Permission	Inherited From	Apply To
Allow	Administrators (DELL...	Full Control	<not inherited>	This folder, subfolders and files
Allow	SYSTEM	Full Control	<not inherited>	This folder, subfolders and files
Allow	CREATOR OWNER	Full Control	<not inherited>	Subfolders and files only
Allow	Users (DELLXP\Users)	Read & Execute	<not inherited>	This folder, subfolders and files
Allow	Everyone	Read & Execute	<not inherited>	This folder only

[Add...]   [Edit...]   [Remove]

☐ Replace permission entries on all child objects with entries shown here that apply to child objects

[OK]   [Cancel]   [Apply]

Figure 3.4   The Advanced Security Settings dialog box showing the default NTFS permissions for the root of a drive volume converted to NTFS.

You should not change the default security settings for the %systemroot% folder and its subfolders. Modifying the default permissions for the Windows XP Professional system files can have very adverse effects on the system. In addition to not changing its default permissions, you should never attempt to compress or encrypt the %systemroot% folder or any of its subfolders. Compression or encryption placed on the system folders can render Windows XP Professional unstable or possibly unbootable.

NTFS Permission Conflicts

Obviously, a user may be a member of several different groups. You can apply NTFS permissions to both users and groups for access control over resources such as files and folders. For security permissions assigned to a user that conflict with other security permissions that have been granted to groups, of which the user is also a member, the most *liberal* permissions take precedence for that user. The one *overriding* exception is any explicit Deny permission entry. Deny permissions always take precedence over Allow permissions.

Just as Deny permissions always take precedence over Allow permissions, explicit permissions always override inherited permissions.

NTFS Permissions vs. Share Permissions

Because share permissions apply to network access only, they can serve only to complicate and possibly confuse access control settings when you apply them on top of NTFS security permissions, which take effect at the file system level. If share permissions and NTFS permissions conflict, the *most restrictive* permissions apply. For example, suppose that you have set share permissions on the shared folder named C:\Samples, and have set the share permissions for the Users group to Allow Read. At the same time, suppose that you also have NTFS permissions set on that folder, and have applied the Allow Change permission for the Users group on that folder in NTFS. Now you have conflicting permissions: Allow Read at the share level and Allow Change at the NTFS level. The net result is that members of the Users group are granted the ability only to read the files within that folder when accessing it over the network; they cannot make any changes to those files, because the most restrictive permissions always win.

As you can see, conflicting permissions may make it difficult to decipher which permissions users are granted when they are accessing files over the network. Therefore, the best practice is to place all shared network data and applications on NTFS drive volumes and set the appropriate security permissions for users and groups at the NTFS level. Do not change the default shared folder permissions; leave them at Full Control for the Everyone group. The most restrictive permissions apply, so all NTFS permissions "flow through" the network share. NTFS security settings can then apply equally to both local users and network users, and administrators have to manage only one set of permissions.

Users and Groups: Local Accounts vs. Domain Accounts

In Windows networking environments, user accounts and group accounts always participate in one of two security contexts: workgroup security (also known as *peer-to-peer networking*) and domain security. Workgroup security is the default security context for individual and networked Windows 2000 Professional and Windows XP Professional computers that *are not members* of a Windows domain. Workgroups are logical groupings of computers that do *not* share a centrally managed user and group database. Local users and groups are managed from each computer's Local Users And Groups folder within the Computer Management Console. You must maintain users and groups separately on each computer. No centralized management scheme exists within a workgroup environment; duplicate user and group accounts must exist on each computer to grant and control access permissions on each workstation's individual resources. User and group accounts are stored within a local database on each Windows XP Professional computer.

In a Windows domain network environment, on the other hand, the domain acts as a central administration point for managing users, groups, and security permissions. A *domain* is simply a logical grouping of computers that share a centrally managed database. Duplicate user and group accounts are unnecessary and unwarranted within the domain security context. Users simply log on to the domain from any domain member computer, and their Domain group memberships, along with their user rights, follow them wherever they travel throughout the domain.

A Windows Active Directory domain maintains a domain-wide database of users and groups that is referred to as the *directory*. The Active Directory database is physically stored on domain controller computers. The Active Directory database can contain much detailed information about its users. The Active Directory database is *replicated* and *synchronized* with all the other domain controllers within a domain. Under Windows Active Directory domains, group memberships travel with users throughout the entire forest.

Windows XP User Permissions vs. User Rights

In Windows XP, users are granted two types of access control settings:

➤ *Permissions*—Windows XP permissions pertain to what the user can do to objects (for example, permissions for reading, creating, modifying, or deleting files, folders, or printers). Windows XP objects include a wide variety of items in addition to files, folders, and printers, including processes, threads, ports, devices, and Registry keys.

➤ *Rights*—Windows XP user rights determine what privileges the user has to interact with the operating system (for example, shut down the system, install software, log on locally, log on over the network, and so on). Administrators for Windows XP Professional computers can modify the default rights for users through the Local Security Settings snap-in of the Microsoft Management Console (MMC).

Controlling Access to Files and Folders by Using Permissions

Users gain access to NTFS files and folders by virtue of being granted explicit or implicit (inherited) permissions for those resources directly to their user account, or through access permissions granted to groups to which the users belong. To assign Read Only security permissions to a user or a group for a specific folder, follow these steps:

1. Right-click the folder on which you wish to apply permissions and select either the Sharing And Security option or the Properties option.

2. Click the Security tab.

3. If the permissions checkboxes for the user or group are grayed out, this means that those permissions are being inherited from a parent folder. To set your own permissions and not allow permissions to be inherited, click the user and/or group that you want to work with and click the Advanced button. Clear the checkbox labeled Inherit From Parent The Permission Entries That Apply To Child Objects. Include These With Entries Explicitly Defined Here. As soon as you clear that checkbox, a Security message box will appear, shown in Figure 3.5.

4. For permissions that are not being inherited, skip this step. Click Copy to copy the permissions that were being applied to the file or folder through inheritance and make the permission explicit, click Remove to completely remove all the permissions that were being applied through inheritance, or click Cancel to leave the inherited permissions in place. Click OK to close the Advanced Security Settings dialog box and return to the Security tab of the object's properties sheet.

5. If the user(s) or group(s) to which you want to assign permissions do not currently appear, click the Add button.

6. From the Select Users Or Groups dialog box, shown in Figure 3.6, type the group or user to which you want to assign permissions in the Enter The Object Names To Select text box. Click the Check Names button to verify

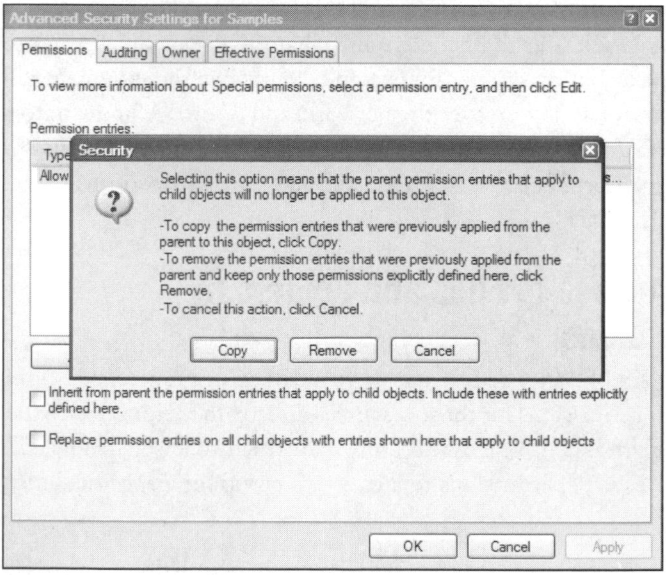

Figure 3.5 The Security message box for disallowing inherited NTFS permissions.

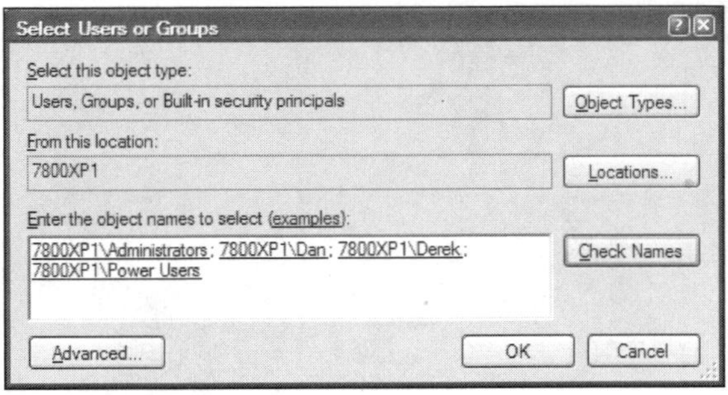

Figure 3.6   The Select Users Or Groups basic dialog box.

that you have entered the correct names for the users or groups. Optionally, you may click the Advanced button to generate a list of users and groups from which to choose, as shown in Figure 3.7. Click the Find Now button to generate the list of users and groups. Select the users and/or groups you want to apply permissions to. Click OK for the advanced Select Users Or Groups dialog box.

7. Click OK for the basic Select Users Or Groups dialog box.

8. Verify that the Allow checkboxes are marked for the Read & Execute, List Folder Contents, and Read permissions, as shown in Figure 3.8.

9. Click OK to accept your settings.

Denying Access to a Resource

Deny permissions always override Allow permissions, so you can be assured that after you establish Deny permissions for a particular user or group on a resource, no other combination of Allow permissions through group memberships can circumvent the Deny permission. To assign Deny security permissions to a user or a group for a specific folder, follow these steps:

1. Right-click the folder on which you wish to apply permissions and select Properties.

2. Click the Security tab.

3. If permissions are being inherited for the user and/or group that you want to work with, click the Advanced button and clear the checkbox labeled Inherit From Parent The Permission Entries That Apply To Child Objects. Include These With Entries Explicitly Defined Here. Click Copy or Remove for the inherited permission entries, and click OK for the Advanced Security Settings dialog box.

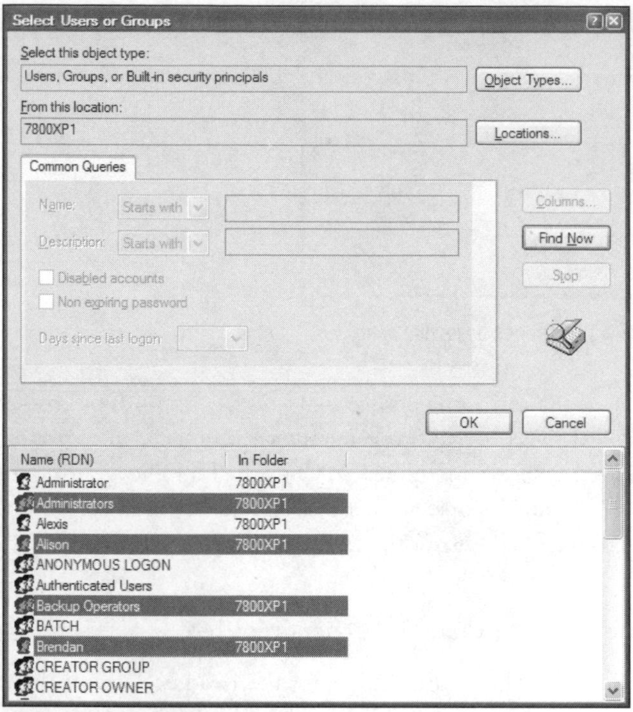

Figure 3.7 The Select Users Or Groups advanced dialog box.

Figure 3.8 The Security tab of an NTFS folder showing permissions for users and groups.

4. If the user(s) or group(s) to which you want to assign permissions do not currently appear, click the Add button.

5. Type in the group(s) or user(s) that you want to assign permissions to from the Select Users Or Groups dialog box.

6. Click OK.

7. Click the Deny checkbox for each permission entry that you wish to explicitly disallow.

8. Click OK to accept your settings.

If you deny the Read permission for a group on a particular folder, any member of that group is denied the ability to read the contents of that folder. When you assign Deny permissions for a user or a group on a file or folder, as soon as you click OK in the Properties dialog box, a Security message box, shown in Figure 3.9, appears. It reminds you that Deny permissions take precedence over Allow permissions.

Click Yes in the Security message box to have the new Deny permissions take effect. When users who are members of a group that is assigned Deny permissions for reading a folder attempt to gain access to that folder, they are greeted by an Access Is Denied message box, shown in Figure 3.10.

Optimizing Access to Files and Folders

The best practice is to always assign NTFS security permissions to groups rather than to individual users. You should place users into appropriate groups and set NTFS permissions on those groups. In this manner, permissions are easier to assign and maintain.

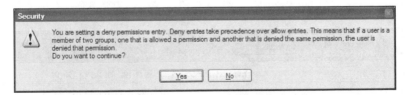

Figure 3.9   A Security message box requests confirmation that you want to set a Deny permissions entry.

Figure 3.10   The Access Is Denied message box.

NTFS Permissions: Moving and Copying Files and Folders

Moving or copying files and folders from an NTFS drive volume to network drives or other media that are non-NTFS volumes results in the *loss of all NTFS security permission settings* for the objects moved or copied. The result of moving or copying NTFS files and folders to different NTFS folders varies depending upon whether the objects are being moved or copied, and depending upon the destination drive volume. Table 3.6 shows the different effects on NTFS permissions when copying files and folders versus moving files and folders.

The standard Windows XP Xcopy.exe command-line utility offers /O and /X options that retain an object's NTFS permissions, in addition to inheriting the destination folder's permissions. The /X switch also retains any auditing settings (which are discussed later in this chapter). To retain only an object's source permissions without inheriting any permissions from the destination folder, use the Scopy.exe tool or the Robocopy.exe tool from the Windows 2000 Professional Resource Kit, or the Windows 2000 Server Resource Kit.

Viewing Effective Permissions

Prior to Windows XP, there was no simple way to determine quickly which *effective* permissions a user actually had by evaluating implicit permissions against explicit permissions, and by comparing a user's own assigned permissions to his or her inherited permissions from his or her group memberships. Now, under Windows XP, an easy method exists for determining effective NTFS permissions right from the Advanced Security Settings dialog box. To display effective permissions for a user or a group, perform the following steps:

1. Right-click an NTFS folder and select Sharing And Security.

2. Click the Security tab and then click the Advanced button.

Table 3.6	NTFS permissions that are retained or inherited when you move and copy files and folders.
Type of Transfer	**Effective Permissions after Move or Copy**
Moving within the same NTFS volume	Files and folders that are moved retain their permissions from the source folder.
Moving to a different NTFS volume	Files and folders that are moved inherit their permissions from the destination folder.
Copying within the same NTFS volume	Files and folders that are copied inherit their permissions from the destination folder.
Copying to a different NTFS volume	Files and folders that are copied inherit their permissions from the destination folder.

3. From the Advanced Security Settings dialog box, click the Effective Permissions tab.

4. Click the Select button to choose a user or a group to display effective permissions for. Type in the user, group, or security principal name and click OK.

5. View the effective permissions for the user, group, or security principal that you selected, as shown in Figure 3.11.

Taking Ownership of Files and Folders

A user who has ownership of a file or folder can transfer ownership of it to a different user or to a group. Administrators can grant users the ability to take ownership of specified files and folders. In addition, administrators have the authority to take ownership of any file or folder for themselves. Object ownership cannot be assigned to others; a user must have permission to take ownership of an object.

Changing ownership of files and folders can become necessary when someone who is responsible for certain files and folders leaves an organization without granting any other users permissions to them. To take ownership of a folder as an administrator, follow these steps:

1. Log on to the system as the administrator or an equivalent user.

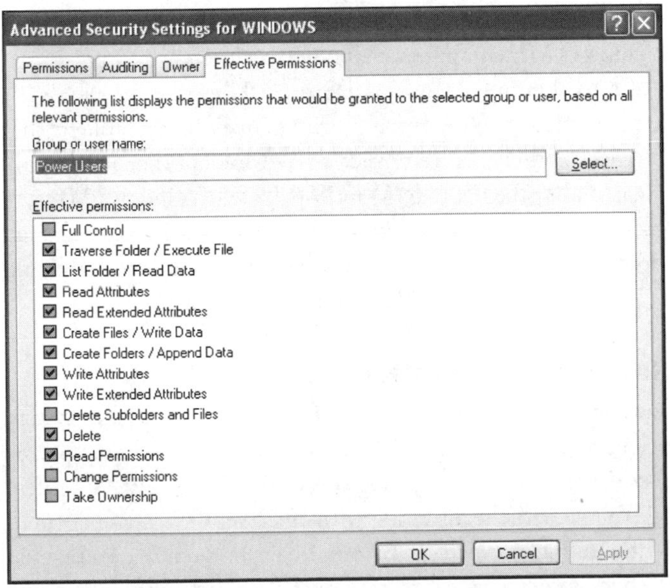

Figure 3.11   The Effective Permissions tab displays effective NTFS security permissions for users and groups for specific folders and files.

2. Right-click the folder from Windows Explorer or My Computer and select Properties.

3. Click the Security tab.

4. Click the Advanced button.

5. Click the Owner tab in the Advanced Security Settings dialog box.

6. Click the name of the person in the Change Owner To section to change the folder's ownership.

7. If you also want the ownership to change for the subfolders and files, mark the Replace Owner On Subcontainers And Objects checkbox.

8. Click OK for the Advanced Security Settings dialog box.

9. Click OK for the Properties dialog box.

How Upgrading to Windows XP Affects File Sharing Behavior

Windows NT 4 Workstation computers and Windows 2000 Professional computers, whether members of a workgroup or a domain, maintain their workgroup or domain membership, respectively, and retain the classic file sharing and security user interface when they are upgraded to Windows XP Professional. Simple File Sharing *is disabled*. NTFS security permissions and shared folder permissions are not changed after the upgrade.

Windows 98 and Windows ME computers that have "per share" sharing permissions as members of a workgroup always have Simple File Sharing *enabled by default* after they are upgraded to Windows XP Professional. Shared folders that have passwords assigned to them are removed; shared folders that have blank passwords remain shared after the upgrade. Windows 98 and Windows ME systems that are logged on to a Windows domain with share-level access enabled are joined to that domain when they are upgraded using the Windows XP Setup program, and Simple File Sharing is disabled after the upgrade.

Auditing System and Network Events

Windows XP Professional enables administrators to audit both user and system events enabling various auditing policies. When auditing is enabled for specific events, the occurrence of the events triggers a log entry in the Windows XP Professional Security Log. You view the security log with the Event Viewer snap-in of the MMC. By default, auditing is turned off. Before you enable auditing, you should formulate an audit policy to determine which workstations will employ auditing and which events will be audited on those systems. When planning the events to audit, you also need to decide whether you will audit successes and/or failures for each event.

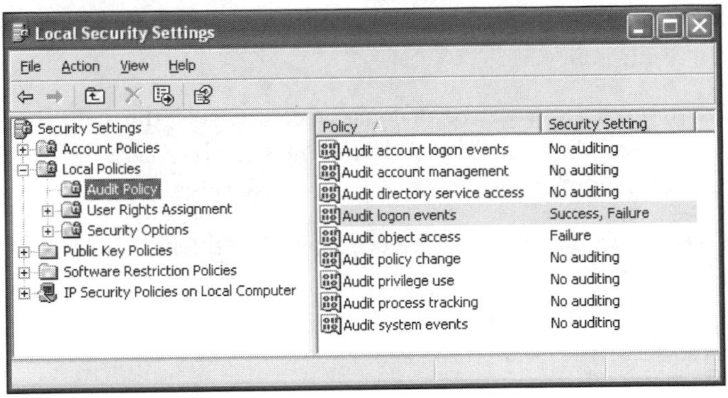

Figure 3.12 The Local Security Settings Console.

Auditing for the local Windows XP system is enabled through the Local Security Settings snap-in of the MMC, shown in Figure 3.12. You must initially turn on auditing from the Local Security Settings Console for each type of event that you want to monitor.

You can audit several types of events, such as the following:

➤ File and folder access

➤ Logons and logoffs

➤ System shutdowns and restarts

➤ Changes to user and group accounts

➤ Changes attempted on Active Directory objects if the Windows XP Professional computer is a member of a Windows Active Directory domain

When you track successful events, you can gauge how often different resources are used. This information can be useful when you are planning for future resource allocation. By tracking failed events, you can become aware of possible security intrusions. Unsuccessful logon attempts, attempts to change security permissions, or efforts to take ownership of files or folders may all point to someone trying to gain unauthorized access to the system or to the network. If such attempts occur at odd hours, these events take on an even more suspicious tone. You must be a member of the Administrators group to turn on audit policies; if your computer is connected to a network, network policy settings may prohibit you from configuring audit settings. To enable auditing on a Windows XP Professional system, follow these steps:

1. Launch the Local Security Policy MMC snap-in from the Start|All Programs| Administrative Tools folder.

2. At the Local Security Settings Console, expand the Local Policies folder and then click Audit Policy.

3. Double-click the audit policy setting that you want to enable; the dialog box for the audit event will display, as shown in Figure 3.13. To enable auditing of object access, double-click the Audit Object Access policy.

4. Click the Success checkbox, the Failure checkbox, or both checkboxes.

5. Click OK.

6. Close the Local Security Settings Console.

After you have turned on audit tracking for object access events, you need to specify which files, folders, or other objects you want to audit. You should be fairly selective about which ones you choose to audit. If you have enabled auditing for successes as well as failures, the system's Security Event log may become filled very quickly if you are auditing heavily used files and folders. You can only audit object access for *files and folders* that are stored on *NTFS* volumes. To enable audit logging for specific files, folders, or other objects (such as printers), follow these steps:

1. Log on to the system as the administrator or an equivalent user.

2. Right-click the object from Windows Explorer, My Computer, or Printers And Faxes, and select Properties.

3. Click the Security tab.

4. Click the Advanced button.

5. Click the Auditing tab in the Advanced Security Settings dialog box.

6. Click the Add button.

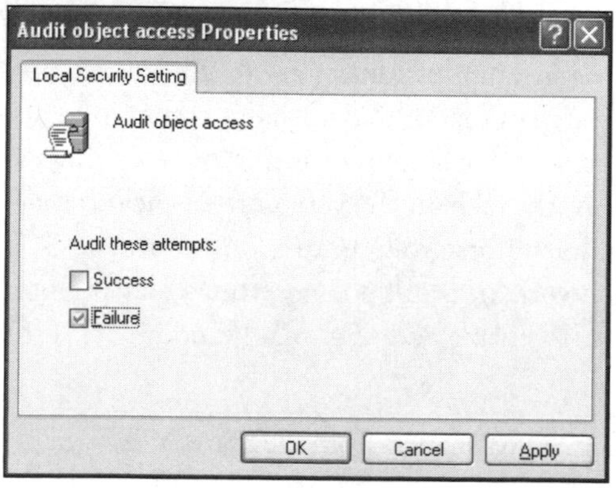

Figure 3.13   The Audit Object Access Properties dialog box.

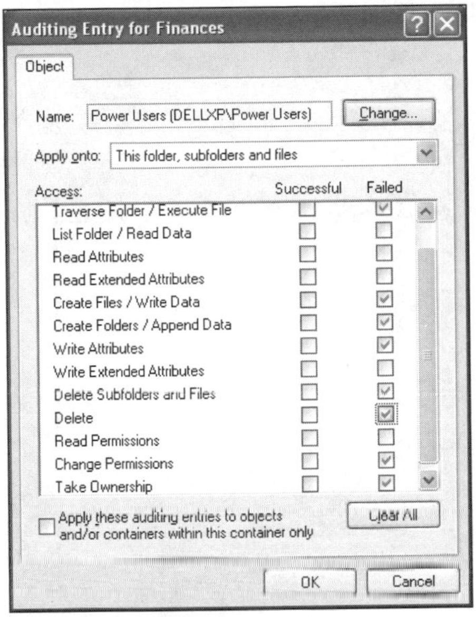

Figure 3.14   The Auditing Entry dialog box.

7. Type in the user or group that you want to track for accessing the object and then click OK. The Auditing Entry dialog box, shown in Figure 3.14, appears.

8. Select each access event that you want to track by marking each event's associated Successful checkbox, Failed checkbox, or both checkboxes.

9. By default, audit settings apply to the current folder, subfolders, and files. You can change this behavior by clicking the Apply Onto drop-down list.

10. Click OK for the Auditing Entry dialog box.

11. Click OK for the Advanced Security Settings dialog box.

12. Click OK for the object's Properties dialog box.

After you have properly set up auditing, all events that meet your auditing criteria are logged into the system's Event Viewer Security Log. You access the Event Viewer Console from Start|Administrative Tools|Event Viewer or by right-clicking the My Computer desktop icon and selecting Manage. You'll find the Event Viewer beneath the System Tools folder in the Computer Management Console. By selecting the Security Log, you can view all of the auditing events that the system has recorded based on the parameters you have set. If a user deletes an object, for example, that event is listed with all the pertinent information in the security log, shown in Figure 3.15. Double-clicking an event in the log displays the detailed information.

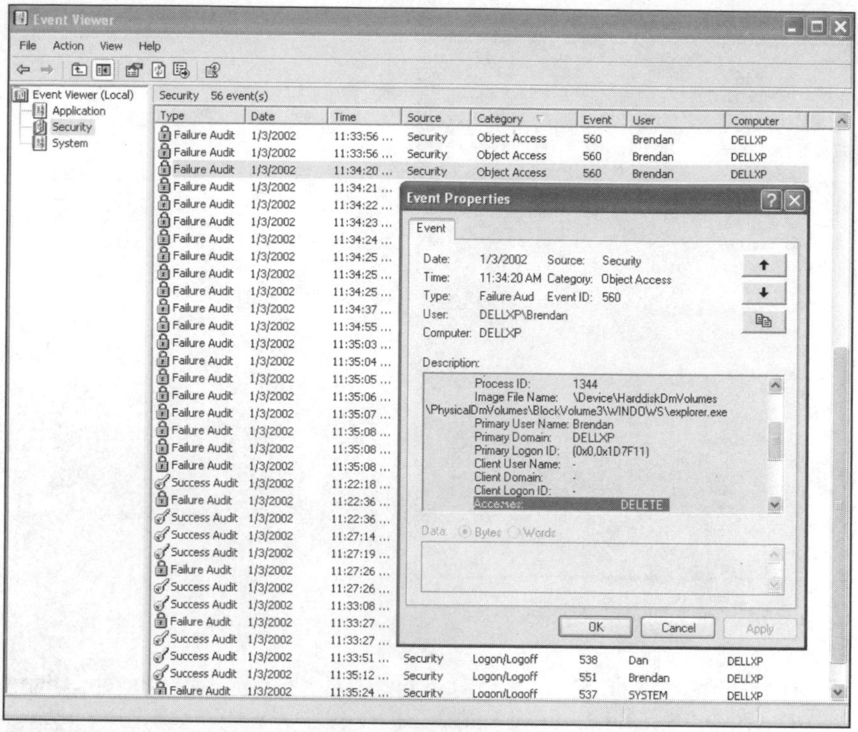

Figure 3.15 An Event Properties window from the Event Viewer security log.

Managing and Troubleshooting Web Server Resources

Unlike Windows 2000 Server and Windows .NET Server, Windows XP Professional is designed for the desktop, and therefore, Internet Information Services (IIS) is not installed by default. IIS version 5.1 ships with Windows XP Professional. You must manually install IIS by going to the Control Panel, double-clicking the Add Or Remove Programs icon, and clicking the Add/Remove Windows Components button. Mark the checkbox for Internet Information Services (IIS). After you select Internet Information Services (IIS), you can click the Details button to add or remove selective IIS components before you proceed with the installation. Click Next to have the Windows Components Wizard install the Web server resources for you. If you upgrade your computer from Windows NT 4 Workstation (or from Windows 2000 Professional) to Windows XP Professional, IIS 5.1 is installed automatically, provided that you had installed Peer Web Services (or IIS 5) on your previous version of Windows.

Before you can install IIS, your computer must already have the Transmission Control Protocol/Internet Protocol (TCP/IP) network protocol and its related connectivity utilities installed. In addition, Microsoft recommends that you have a Domain Name System (DNS) server available on your network for hostname to IP address resolution. For very small networks, you may use a HOSTS file or a LMHOSTS file in lieu of a DNS server. A HOSTS file maps DNS host computer names to IP addresses. A LMHOSTS file maps NetBIOS computer names to IP addresses. Windows XP Professional looks for these two text files in the %systemroot%\system32\drivers\etc folder. Sample HOSTS and LMHOSTS files are also installed by default into this folder.

After you have installed IIS, you manage the services from the Internet Information Services snap-in of the MMC. You can launch the IIS Console by clicking Start|All Programs|Administrative Tools|Internet Information Services. From the IIS Console, you can administer the default FTP site (not installed by default), default Web site, and the default Simple Mail Transfer Protocol (SMTP) virtual server for the Windows XP Professional computer, as shown in Figure 3.16.

Additional, HTML-based documentation on IIS administration is available by pointing to http://localhost/ in your Web browser, as shown in Figure 3.17.

IIS Console: Administering the Default Web and FTP Sites

You can view and modify the settings for each IIS service through the IIS Console by right-clicking the root folder for a service (such as Default Web Site) in the left-hand pane of the console window and selecting Properties. Unlike IIS 5, there are no Master Properties that you can modify that control both Web and FTP settings. You must configure each site separately. IIS stores all of its configuration information for its Web site(s), FTP site(s), and so forth in its metabase.

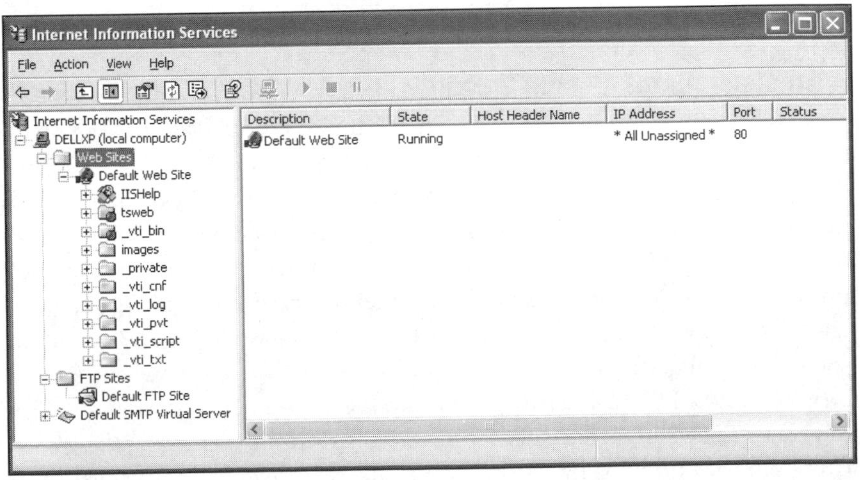

Figure 3.16   The Internet Information Services Console.

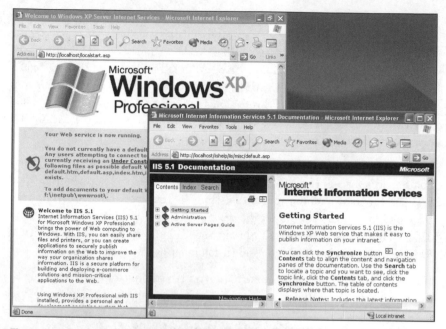

Figure 3.17 The Getting Started Web page for IIS HTML-based help documentation.

If the IIS metabase gets damaged or deleted, an administrator must reconfigure all of the IIS sites and services. To avoid such a catastrophe, be sure to back up the metabase on a regular basis by right-clicking the computer name root container and selecting All Tasks|Backup/Restore Configuration. The backup gets stored as a file with the .md0 extension, and the default backup location is %systemroot%\system32\inetsrv\metaback. You should copy the metabase backups to removable media or to another computer over the network to preserve the backups in case of a hard drive failure on the IIS computer.

Administering the Default Web Site

At any time, an administrator can modify the settings for the default Web site by right-clicking the site name and selecting Properties from the Internet Information Services (IIS) MMC snap-in. The Default Web Site Properties window, shown in Figure 3.18, enables you to work with settings for the home directory, directory security, HTTP, ISAPI filters, and other configurations. You can change the settings for a virtual directory by right-clicking the directory name and selecting Properties. The Properties dialog box for a virtual directory, shown in Figure 3.19, enables you to configure settings for the virtual directory, for its Web documents, for directory security, for HTTP headers, and for working with custom error messages. You can create a new virtual directory for the default Web site by right-clicking <Default Web Site> from the IIS MMC snap-in and selecting New|Virtual Directory.

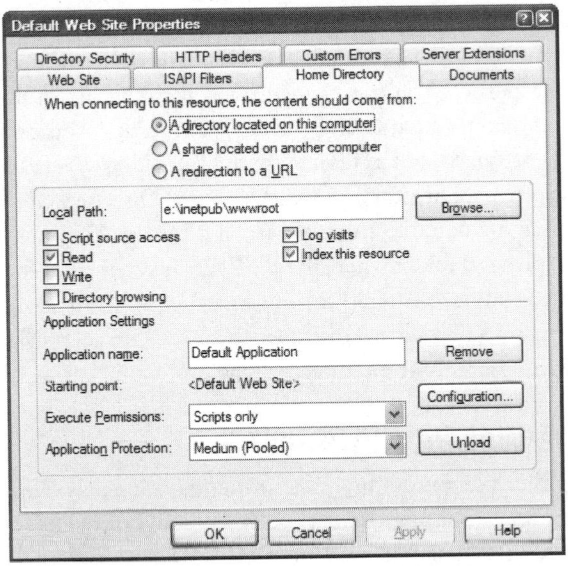

Figure 3.18   The Home Directory tab for the IIS Default Web Site Properties dialog box.

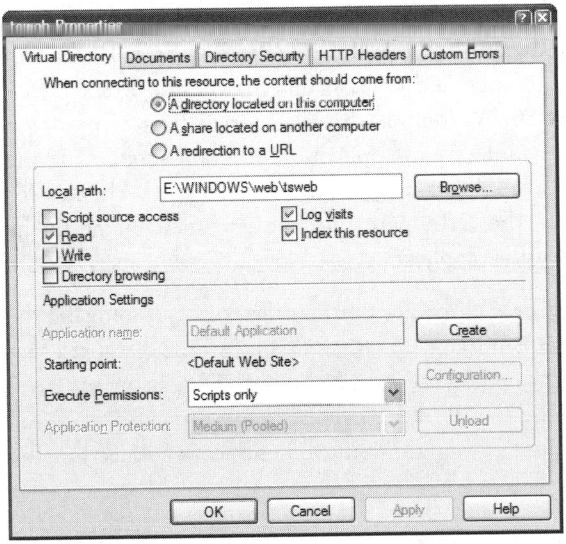

Figure 3.19   The Properties dialog box for a virtual directory under IIS.

When the Virtual Directory Creation Wizard launches, you assign a name to the new virtual directory. You must also designate the path for the physical folder where the Web files are stored for the new virtual directory. After you have entered this information, you can complete the wizard, thereby setting up a new virtual directory that users can access via the **http://computer_name/virtual_directory_name** Uniform Resource Locator (URL), also known simply as a Web address.

Administering the Default FTP Site

An administrator can modify the settings for the default FTP site by right-clicking the site name and selecting Properties. You can change the settings for a virtual directory by right-clicking the directory name and selecting Properties. You can create a new virtual directory for the default FTP site by right-clicking <Default FTP Site> and selecting New|Virtual Directory. When the Virtual Directory Creation Wizard launches, you assign a name to the new virtual directory. You must also designate the path for the physical folder where the FTP files will be stored for the new virtual directory. After you have entered this information, you can complete the wizard, thereby setting up a new virtual directory that users can access via the FTP address **ftp://computer_name/virtual_directory_name**.

Web Folders and the WebDAV Protocol

You can share folders with other computers by making them available as Web Folders instead of, or in addition to, sharing them as network shared folders. To share a folder on a Windows XP Professional system as a Web Folder, right-click the folder, select Properties, and click the Web Sharing tab. Click the Add button to assign an Alias name for the Web Folder, specify the permissions for the Web Folder, and click OK to create the Web Folder on the default Web site. The WebDAV (Web Distributed Authoring and Versioning) protocol acts as a redirector that enables users to open and save documents via Hypertext Transport Protocol (HTTP) port 80. As long as the Web server host computer is running IIS 5 or above, and as long as an application program supports saving and retrieving documents via HTTP, you can take advantage of WebDAV. To use WebDAV, simply type in the URL path plus the document name in the Open or Save As dialog box for an application.

Users can encrypt files stored in Web Folders without fear of compromising the data whenever the files are transmitted across the network wire. Encrypted files are always encrypted and decrypted on the local computer before being sent over the network. Encrypted files are transferred in cybertext over the network—even if encrypted files get intercepted as they are sent over a network connection, the encrypted files cannot be interpreted.

Troubleshooting Internet Information Services

If users are experiencing problems connecting to the default Web site, to the default FTP site, or to a new virtual directory that you have created, you can follow the steps listed in the next few sections to attempt to rectify the problem(s).

Internet Web Site

To isolate problems that may be preventing users from connecting to the Internet Web site:

➤ Check that the Web server contains HTML files in the drive_letter:\inetpub\ wwwroot folder.

➤ Attempt to connect to the Web server's home directory using a browser on a computer that has a live connection to the Internet. Your Web site must have a public IP address that is registered with the InterNIC, and that public IP address must be registered with the Internet's DNS servers. For example, if your registered domain name is ExamCram.com and you want to view a virtual directory on that Web site named "aboutus", you would type "www.ExamCram.com/aboutus" in the Address line of your Web browser. The Web page that you requested should appear within your Web browser's window.

Intranet Web Site

To isolate problems that may be preventing users from connecting to an intranet Web site:

➤ Check that the Web server and the client computers have active network connections.

➤ Verify that a Windows Internet Naming Service (WINS) and/or DNS server is available and functioning on your network for computer name to IP address name resolution.

➤ Go to a client computer, launch a Web browser, and type in a valid URL for the Web server computer. Intranet URLs can take the format of **http://computer_name/home_page_name.htm** or **http://computer_name/virtual_directory_alias_name**. Examples of this syntax are **http://computer1/myhomepage.htm** and **http://computer1/myvirtualdirectory**.

Managing Local and Network Print Devices

You manage print devices in Windows XP Professional from the Printers And Faxes folder, which is accessible from the Control Panel, or by clicking Start|Printers And Faxes. When working with printing in Windows XP, you need to fully understand the following printing terminology as defined by Microsoft:

➤ *Printer*—A software interface between the operating system and a print device. It defines ports through which print jobs get routed. Printer names direct print jobs to one or more print devices.

➤ *Print device*—A piece of equipment (hardware) that physically produces printed documents. A print device may be attached to a local computer or connected via a network interface.

➤ *Printer port*—A software interface through which print jobs get directed to either a locally attached print device, or a network-connected print device. Windows XP supports local line printer terminal (LPT), COM (serial), and Universal Serial Bus (USB) ports. It also supports network-connected printer port devices such as the Intel NetPort and the Hewlett-Packard (HP) JetDirect.

➤ *Print server*—A computer that serves as the host for printers that are associated with print devices.

➤ *Printer driver*—Software specific to each print device (designed to run in Windows XP) that translates printing commands into printer language codes for each print device. PCL5 and PostScript are examples of two types of printer languages.

➤ *Print job*—The actual document to be printed along with the necessary print processing command.

➤ *Print resolution*—What determines the quality and smoothness of the text or images that the print device will render. This specification is expressed in dots per inch (dpi). Higher dpi numbers generally result in better print quality.

➤ *Print spooler*—The process (service) that runs in the background of Windows XP that initiates, processes, and distributes print jobs. The spooler saves print jobs into a temporary physical file on disk. Print jobs are then despooled and transferred to the appropriate print device.

➤ *Print queue*—A logical "waiting area" where print jobs are temporarily stored until the print device is available and ready to process each job according to the job's priority level, and according to its order within the queue.

Connecting to Local and Network Printers

After you add a local printer to a Windows XP Professional computer, you have the option of sharing it with other users on the network. To add a local printer to your system, perform these steps:

1. Log on as an administrator or a member of the Administrators group.

2. Click Start|Printers And Faxes to open the Printers And Faxes window.

3. Click the Add A Printer link from the Printer Tasks pane. The Add Printer Wizard appears. Click Next to continue.

4. Click the Local Printer button. If the printer that you are adding is not Plug and Play compatible, you may clear the Automatically Detect And Install My Plug And Play Printer checkbox. If the printer is Plug and Play compliant, Windows XP Professional automatically installs and properly configures it for you.

5. If the printer is not Plug and Play, the Select A Printer Port dialog box appears. Click the port you want to use from the Use The Following Port drop-down list, or click the Create A New Port button and choose the type of port to create from the drop-down list.

6. Click Next.

7. Select the printer Manufacturer and Model. Click the Have Disk button if you have a DVD-ROM, CD-ROM, or diskette with the proper printer drivers from the manufacturer. Click the Windows Update button to download the latest drivers available from Microsoft's Web site. You should strive to use only drivers that have been digitally signed by Microsoft, for compatibility.

8. Click Next.

9. Enter a name for the printer. The name should not exceed 31 characters, and best practice dictates that the printer name should not contain any spaces or special characters. Specify whether this printer will be designated as the system's default printer.

10. Click Next.

11. In the Printer Sharing dialog box, click the Share Name button if you want to share this printer with the network. Enter a share name for the printer; it's a good idea to limit the share name to 14 or fewer characters, and to place no spaces within the share name.

12. Click Next.

13. Enter an optional Location name and Comment.

14. Click Next.

15. Click Yes and then click Next when prompted to print a test page; it's always a good idea to make sure that the printer has been set up and is working properly.

16. Click Finish to exit the Add Printer Wizard.

To connect to a network printer, you also use the Add Printer Wizard from the Printers folder. Simply follow these steps:

1. Log on as an administrator or a member of the Administrators group.

2. Click Start|Printers And Faxes to open the Printers And Faxes window.

3. Click the Add A Printer link from the Printer Tasks pane. The Add Printer Wizard appears. Click Next to continue.

4. Click the option button labeled A Network Printer, Or A Printer Attached To Another Computer.

5. Click Next.

6. Follow one of these options:

   ➤ Select Browse For A Printer, and then click Next.

   ➤ Select Connect To This Printer, type in the UNC path for the printer, and then click Next.

   ➤ Select Connect To A Printer On the Internet Or On A Home Or Office Network, type in the URL address for the printer, and then click Next.

7. If you choose to browse for a printer, locate the printer from the Browse For Printer dialog box and then click Next.

8. Click Yes or No when prompted to make the printer the system's default, and click Next.

9. Click Finish to exit the Add Printer Wizard.

Connecting to Network Printers via the Command Line

As mentioned earlier in this chapter, you can use the **net use** command to connect to network drive shares. You can also use this command to connect to remote printers from a command prompt window. The syntax is as follows:

```
net use lptx: \\print_server_name\printer_share_name
```

Printer ports lpt1, lpt2, and lpt3 are represented by **lptx**. The **net use** command is the only way to connect client computers that are running MS-DOS to network printers.

Managing Printers and Print Jobs

From the Printers And Faxes folder, you manage print jobs by double-clicking the printer icon that you want to work with. After you have opened the printer's print queue window, you can pause printing or cancel all documents from the Printer menu. You can also take the printer offline from the Printer menu. If you select an individual print job that is listed, you can Pause, Resume, Start, or Cancel that job by selecting one of these options from the Documents menu. The print queue window itself displays the document name, the status, the document owner, the number of pages for each print job, the size of the job, the time and date that the job was submitted, and the port used.

Members of the Administrators group and members of the Power Users group have permissions to manage print jobs that are listed in the print queue. At the time that users print one or more documents, they get the built-in security principal Creator Owner applied to their user accounts so that they are granted permission to manage documents as well. Users may manage only their own print jobs, unless they are members of the Administrators group or the Power Users group (if the computer is standalone or a member of a workgroup), or members of the Print Operators group or the Server Operators group (if the Windows XP print server is a member of a Windows domain). Users can also manage other users' print jobs if they have been granted the Allow Manage Documents permission.

Windows XP has dropped support for the Data Link Control (DLC) protocol, which is used by some older Hewlett-Packard (HP) Jet Direct cards and Jet Direct print server devices. These older devices should be upgraded to newer HP network interface cards and print devices that support TCP/IP and the standard port monitor.

Configuring Print Server and Printer Properties

A Windows XP Professional computer becomes a print server when you physically connect a printer to the system and then share that printer with the network. You can easily configure many of the properties of your Windows XP Professional system as a print server by selecting File|Server Properties from the Printers And Faxes window. You can configure many print server settings—such as changing the location of the Spool folder—from the Print Server Properties dialog box. Using this dialog box means that you don't have to edit the Registry directly to make changes to your Windows XP print server configuration settings.

By right-clicking one of the available printer icons in the Printers And Faxes folder and choosing Properties, you can configure that printer's settings and options. The printer Properties dialog box contains six tabs (seven tabs for a color printer): General, Sharing, Ports, Advanced, Security, Device Settings, and Color Management (for a color printer).

The General Tab

From the General tab, you can work with the following settings:

➤ Add or modify printer location and comment information.

➤ Set printing preferences such as portrait or landscape orientation.

➤ Select paper source and quality.

➤ Print a test page.

The Sharing Tab

The Sharing tab displays the following options:

➤ Share the printer, change the network share name, or stop sharing the printer.

➤ Install additional printer drivers for client computers that use different operating systems or different Windows NT CPU platforms.

 Windows XP print server computers automatically download the correct printer drivers for client computers running Windows 95, Windows 98/Me, Windows NT, Windows 2000, and Windows XP that connect to the print server, as long as the correct drivers have been installed on the print server.

The Ports Tab

On the Ports tab, you have these configuration options:

➤ Select a port to print to.

➤ Add, configure, and delete ports.

➤ Enable bidirectional printing support.

➤ Enable printer pooling, which enables you to select two or more identical print devices that are configured as one logical printer; print jobs are directed to the first available print device.

The Advanced Tab

On the Advanced tab, you work with scheduling and spooling settings, like these:

➤ Set time availability limits.

➤ Set print job priority.

➤ Change the printer driver or add a new driver.

➤ Spool print jobs and start printing immediately, or start printing after the last page has spooled.

➤ Print directly to the printer; do not spool print jobs.

➤ Hold mismatched documents.

➤ Print spooled documents first.

➤ Retain documents after they have been printed.

➤ Enable advanced printing features (such as metafile spooling) and enable advanced options (such as Page Order, Booklet Printing, and Pages Per Sheet); advanced options vary depending upon printer capabilities.

➤ Set printing defaults.

➤ Select a different print processor: RAW, EMF, or Text.

➤ Specify a separator page.

The Security Tab

You can configure the following security settings with the Security tab:

➤ Set permissions for users and groups (similar to NTFS file and folder permissions): Allow or Deny the Print, Manage Printers, and Manage Documents.

➤ Set up printer auditing (similar to NTFS file and folder access auditing) via the Auditing tab by clicking the Advanced button.

➤ Take ownership of the printer (similar to taking ownership of NTFS files and folders) via the Owner tab by clicking the Advanced button.

➤ View the effective permissions for the printer (similar to viewing the effective permissions for NTFS files and folders) via the Effective Permissions tab by clicking the Advanced button.

 For a Windows XP computer that is not a domain member, the default security permissions for printers are as follows: Administrators–Allow Print, Allow Manage Printers, and Allow Manage Documents; Creator Owner–Allow Manage Documents; Everyone–Allow Print; Power Users–Allow Print, Allow Manage Printers, and Allow Manage Documents. For a Windows XP computer that is joined to a domain, the default security permissions for printers are as follows: Administrators–Allow Print, Allow Manage Printers, and Allow Manage Documents; Creator Owner–Allow Manage Documents; Everyone–Allow Print; Print Operators and Server Operators–Allow Print, Allow Manage Printers, and Allow Manage Documents.

The Device Settings Tab

The Device Settings tab enables you to configure printer-specific settings. The available settings on this tab vary depending on the manufacturer and the model of the printer that you are working with. For example, many printers enable you to configure paper tray assignments, font cartridge settings, and any installable options such as printer memory settings.

Using the Internet Printing Protocol (IPP)

Windows XP Professional computers can connect to printers that are attached to Windows XP, Windows 2000, or Windows .NET Server print servers by using a Web browser and a URL, instead of connecting via the GUI or via the command line using a UNC path. IPP works over a corporate intranet or through an Internet connection. IPP gives users the ability to print over an Internet connection. IIS version 5 or later must be running on the print server computer. You can enter one of two available URLs into your Web browser:

➤ *http://print_server_name/printers*—This address connects you to the Web page for the Printers And Faxes folder on the Windows XP print server computer (however, fax devices are not displayed in the browser window).

➤ *http://print_server_name/printer_share_name*—This address connects you to the Web page for the print queue folder for the printer that you specify, as shown in Figure 3.20.

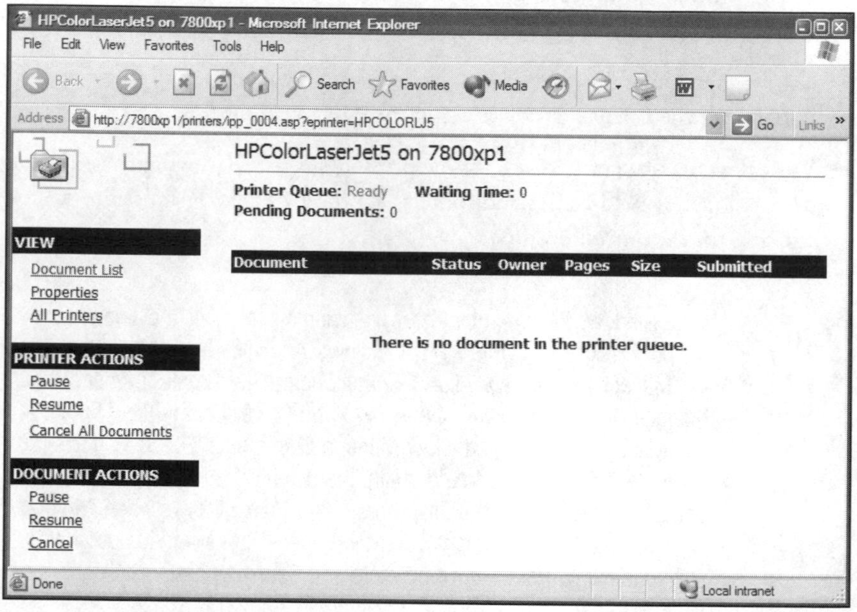

Figure 3.20   The Web browser interface for a network printer that uses IPP.

Practice Questions

Question 1

Greggory has just installed Windows XP Professional on a new computer that is a member of a workgroup named Sales. When he goes to create a network shared folder by right-clicking a folder and selecting Sharing And Security, the Properties dialog box for the folder displays only four tabs: General, Sharing, Web Sharing, and Customize. The Sharing tab is divided into two sections: Local Sharing, and Network Sharing And Security. No Security tab exists for NTFS permissions, nor does any way exist to set Share permissions. Even when Greggory right-clicks a folder and selects Properties, he still gets the same tabbed dialog box with the same four tabs. The folder resides on an NTFS drive volume. How can Greggory fix this problem?

- ○ a. Go to Control Panel|Administrative Tools|Local Security Policy and enable the policy for Network Access: Sharing And Security Model For Local Accounts.

- ○ b. Open My Computer or Windows Explorer, click Tools|Folder Options, click the View tab, and clear the checkbox for Use Simple File Sharing.

- ○ c. Open the Computer Management Console, expand Services And Applications, and click the Services node. Right-click the Workstation service and select Start. Double-click the Workstation service and set the Startup Type to Automatic.

- ○ d. Open Control Panel and double-click Network Connections. Right-click the Local Area Connection and select Properties. Mark the checkbox for File And Printer Sharing For Microsoft Networks and click OK.

Answer b is correct. Simple File Sharing is enabled by default for standalone and workgroup-member computers. Simple File Sharing is disabled by default for domain-member computers. The Folder Options menu is the only way to enable or disable Simple File Sharing. Answer a is incorrect because the policy for Network Access: Sharing And Security Model For Local Accounts does not deal with Simple File Sharing. Answer c is incorrect because the Workstation service is enabled by default. Answer d is incorrect because File And Printer Sharing For Microsoft Networks is enabled by default.

Question 2

> Which of the following methods enable you to create shared network folders?
> [Check all correct answers]
>
> ❑ a. Right-click a folder in either My Computer or Windows Explorer, select Sharing And Security, click the option button Share This Folder, and click OK.
>
> ❑ b. Right-click a folder in either My Computer or Windows Explorer, select Properties, click the Sharing tab, click the option button Share This Folder, and click OK.
>
> ❑ c. Open the Computer Management Console, expand Shared Folders, right-click the Shares node, and click New File Share. Follow the on-screen instructions for the Create Shared Folder Wizard.
>
> ❑ d. Open a command prompt window. Type "Net Share share_name=x:\folder_name", where share_name represents the name you want to assign to the shared folder, x: represents the drive letter where the folder resides, and folder_name represents the actual name of the folder.

Answers a, b, c, and d are all correct. All of these methods are valid ways to create shared network folders.

Question 3

> What is the default setting for offline files under Windows XP Professional when acting as a "server" for other client computers?
>
> ○ a. Manual caching of documents.
>
> ○ b. Automatic caching of documents.
>
> ○ c. Caching is disabled.
>
> ○ d. Automatic caching of programs and documents.

Answer a is correct because manual caching of documents is the default setting for Windows XP Professional. Answer b is incorrect because automatic caching of documents is not the default setting; however, it is an option. Answer c is incorrect because the caching of offline files is enabled by default. Answer d is incorrect because automatic caching of programs and documents is not the default setting; however, it is an option.

Question 4

> Which of the following Local groups are installed automatically by Windows XP Professional? [Check all correct answers]
>
> ❑ a. Network Configuration Operators
>
> ❑ b. Replicator
>
> ❑ c. Authenticated Users
>
> ❑ d. HelpServicesGroup
>
> ❑ e. Remote Desktop Users
>
> ❑ f. Creator Group

Answers a, b, d, and e are all correct. Answer c is incorrect because Authenticated Users is considered to be a built-in security principal, not a Local group. Answer f is incorrect because Creator Group is also considered to be a built-in security principal, not a Local group.

Question 5

> How can you determine the actual, effective NTFS permissions on a file or a folder for a user or a group with the least amount of administrative effort?
>
> ○ a. Log on as the specific user and test the user's permissions by attempting to read, write, modify, delete, change permissions, and take ownership of specific files and folders.
>
> ○ b. Log on as an administrative user, right-click a folder or file in question, choose Properties, click Security, click the Advanced button, and click the Effective Permissions tab. Select a user or group to view the effective permissions for that user or group on the specific file or folder.
>
> ○ c. Open the Computer Management Console, click Shared Folders, and then click Effective Permissions.
>
> ○ d. Open the Control Panel and double-click Component Services. Right-click the NTFS Permissions node and select Effective Permissions.

Answer b is correct. The Effective Permissions tab is a new feature in Windows XP Professional. Answer a is incorrect because it requires more administrative effort than using the Effective Permissions tab. Answer c is incorrect because no Effective Permissions tab exists for the Shared Folders snap-in. Answer d is incorrect because no Effective Permissions feature exists in the Component Services snap-in.

Question 6

> If you use Windows Explorer to move seven subfolders containing 152 files from e:\docs to e:\letters on Server3, what will happen to their NTFS permissions?
>
> ○ a. The folders and files moved will retain their same NTFS permissions.
>
> ○ b. The folders and files moved will inherit their NTFS permissions from the target (destination) folder.
>
> ○ c. The folders and files moved will have their NTFS permissions reset to the default settings for drive volumes, such as Allow Everyone Read and Execute, and Administrators Full Control.
>
> ○ d. You will be prompted by a message box asking whether you want the folders and files moved to retain their permissions, or if you want them to inherit their permissions from the target (destination) folder.

Answer a is correct. Folders and files that are moved within the same NTFS drive volume always retain their permissions from the source folder. Answer b is incorrect because folders and files moved to a different NTFS drive volume inherit their permissions from the target (destination) folder. Answer c is incorrect because folders and files that are moved never have their NTFS permissions reset to drive volume defaults. Answer d is incorrect because Windows Explorer does not prompt the user about retaining or inheriting NTFS permissions when moving or copying files.

Question 7

As a network administrator, how can you ensure that members of the Interns group are allowed only to print documents on Printer4, and that they can print only those documents during nonbusiness hours. In addition, how can you make sure that their print jobs have a higher priority than other print jobs from members of other groups?

○ a. Configure the printer properties for Printer4 on each computer for each member of all the other network groups. In the Printers And Faxes window, right-click Printer4, select Properties, click the Advanced tab, click the Available From button, and specify the business hours that the printer will be unavailable for the Interns group. Decrement the Priority counter so that each member of the other groups will have a lower printing priority for Printer4 than members from the Interns groups.

○ b. For each user in the Interns group, open the Printers And Faxes window, right click Printer4, select Properties, and click the Security tab. Grant the permissions Allow Print, Allow Manage Printers, and Allow Manage Documents to the Interns group.

○ c. Configure the printer properties for Printer4 on each computer for each member of the Interns group. In the Printers And Faxes window, right-click Printer4, select Properties, click the Advanced tab, click the Available From button, and specify the nonbusiness hours that the printer will be available. Increment the Priority counter so that each member of the Interns group will have a higher printing priority for Printer4 than members from other groups.

○ d. For each user in the Interns group, open the Printers And Faxes window, right-click Printer4, select Properties, and click the Security tab. Click the Advanced button, click the Owner tab, and change the owner to the Interns group.

Answer c is correct. If you set up each computer for each user who belongs to the Interns group, you can specify during which time period the printer is available, and you can specify a higher priority than the default, which is 1. Answer a is incorrect because you do not need to configure computers for the users in groups other than the Interns group, and you cannot specify a priority setting lower than 1 (the default). Answer b is incorrect because printer permissions do not modify printer availability or printer priority settings. Answer d is incorrect because the printer ownership setting does not modify printer availability or printer priority settings.

Question 8

Which of the following statements are true about using the Internet Printing Protocol (IPP)? [Check all correct answers]

❑ a. The print server computer must be running IIS 4 or later.

❑ b. The print server computer may be running Windows 2000 Professional.

❑ c. You can view all available printers and faxes by typing the following URL into a Web browser: "http://print_server_name/printers".

❑ d. You can connect to specific printer by typing the following URL into a Web browser: "http://print_server_name/printer_share_name".

Answers b and d are correct. IPP is supported on Windows 2000 (all editions) and later Microsoft operating systems. You can connect directly to printer by typing the URL "http://print_server_name/printer_share_name" into a Web browser. Answer a is incorrect because a print server computer must be running IIS 5 or later to support IPP. Answer c is incorrect because IPP displays only print devices, not fax devices. However, the URL is correct.

Need to Know More?

 Bott, Ed and Carl Siechert. *Microsoft Windows XP Inside Out*. Redmond, WA: Microsoft Press, 2001. ISBN 0-73561-382-6. This book offers timesaving tips, troubleshooting techniques, and workarounds. It focuses on techniques such as taking advantage of the rich integration of devices, applications, and Web services in Windows XP.

 Microsoft Corporation. *Microsoft Windows XP Professional Resource Kit Documentation*. Redmond, WA: Microsoft Press, 2001. ISBN 0-73561-485-7. This all-in-one reference is a compilation of technical documentation and valuable insider information that computer-support professionals and administrators can reference to install, customize, and support Windows XP.

Minasi, Mark. *Mastering Windows XP Professional*. Alameda, CA: Sybex, Inc., 2001. ISBN 0-78212-981-1. This book provides in-depth coverage of installing, configuring, and administering Windows XP Professional.

Search the Microsoft TechNet CD (or its online version through **www.microsoft.com**) using keywords such as "Backup", "System Restore", "Automated System Recovery", "Safe Mode", and "Performance".

Setting Up, Managing, and Troubleshooting Security Accounts and Policies

Terms you'll need to understand:

✓ Local user account

✓ Local group

✓ Complex password

✓ Domain user account

✓ Global, Universal, and Domain Local groups

✓ Security Identifier (SID)

✓ Authentication

✓ Local Group Policy

✓ Group Policy Object (GPO)

✓ Resulting Set of Policies (RSoP)

✓ Software Restriction Policy

✓ Microsoft Passport

Techniques you'll need to master:

✓ Adding and configuring new local user accounts

✓ Adding users and groups from a Domain to a Local group

✓ Properly renaming user accounts to maintain resource access

✓ Configuring the Local Security Policy and the Local Group Policy

✓ Understanding the order in which Group Policies apply to a user and computer, when the computer is a member of the domain

✓ Analyzing and configuring computers with the security templates

✓ Using and configuring a Microsoft Passport

The Local Users and Groups snap-in enables you to manage local users and groups. You can get to the snap-in by choosing Start|Control Panel|Performance And Maintenance Category|Administrative Tools|Computer Management and then by expanding the tree pane of the Computer Management Console until you see the snap-in. In this snap-in, you can create, modify, duplicate, and delete users (in the Users folder) and groups (in the Groups folder).

Built-in User and Group Accounts

The three primary built-in user accounts are Administrator, Guest, and HelpAssistant. The Administrator account is a critical account for your computer and has some essential characteristics, including the following:

➤ Cannot be disabled, locked out, or deleted

➤ Has, through its membership in the Administrators group, all privileges required to perform system administration duties

➤ Can be renamed

The Guest account is on your system for rare and infrequent use and should be kept securely disabled. This account also has some distinct characteristics, including the following:

➤ Is disabled by default. Only an administrator can enable the account. If it is enabled, it should be given a password, and User Cannot Change Password should be set if multiple users will log on with the account

➤ Cannot be deleted

➤ Can be locked out

➤ Does not save user preferences or settings

The HelpAssistant account is on your system for use when the Remote Desktop Assistance functions are used. This account's characteristics include the following:

➤ Disabled by default

➤ Is automatically enabled when an invitation is created for Remote Assistance

➤ Can be deleted

➤ Can be renamed

Built-in Local groups have assigned to them specific privileges (also called user rights) that enable them to perform specific sets of tasks on a system. The default local group accounts on a Windows XP Professional system are the following:

➤ *Administrators*—Users in this group have all built-in system privileges assigned They can create and modify user and group accounts, manage security policies, create printers, and manage permissions to resources on the system. The local Administrator account is the default member and cannot be removed. Other accounts can be added and removed. When a system joins a domain, the Domain Admins group is added to this group, but it can be removed

➤ *Backup Operators*—Users in this group can back up and restore files and folders regardless of security permissions assigned to those resources. They can log on and shut down a system, but cannot change security settings

➤ *Power Users*—Users in this group can share resources and create user and group accounts. They cannot modify user accounts they did not create, nor can they modify the Administrators or Backup Operators groups. They cannot take ownership of files, back up or restore directories, load or unload device drivers, or manage the security and auditing logs. They can run all Windows XP-compatible applications, as well as legacy applications, some of which members of the Users group cannot execute

If you want certain users to have broad system administration capabilities, but do not want them to be able to access all system resources, consider putting them in Backup Operators and Power Users rather than Administrators.

➤ *Users*—Users in this group can log on, shut down a system, use local and network printers, create local groups, and manage the groups they create. They cannot create a local printer or share a folder. Some down-level applications do not run for members of the Users group because security settings are tighter for the Users group in Windows XP than in Windows NT 4. By default, all local user accounts you create are added to the Users group. In addition, when a system joins a domain, the Domain Users group is made a member of that system's local Users group

➤ *Guests*—Users in this group have limited privileges but can log on to a system and shut it down. Members cannot make permanent changes to their desktop or profile. By default, the Built-in Local Guest account is a member. When a system joins a domain, the Domain Guests group is added to the Local Guests group

➤ *Network Configuration Operators*—Users in this group have administrative privileges to manage the configuration of networking features

➤ *Remote Desktop Users*—Users in this group have the added privilege of logging on through Terminal Services, which in Windows XP is established through a Remote Desktop connection

Built-in System groups also exist, which you do not see in the user interface while managing other group accounts. Membership of system groups changes based on how the computer is accessed, not on who accesses the computer. Built-in System groups include the following:

➤ *Everyone*—Includes all users who access the computer, including the Guest account.

➤ *Authenticated Users*—Includes all users with a valid user account in the local security database or (in the case of domain members) in Active Directory's directory services. You use the Authenticated Users group rather than the Everyone group to assign privileges and group permissions, because doing so prevents anonymous access to resources.

➤ *Creator Owner*—Contains the user account that created or took ownership of a resource. If the user is a member of the Administrators group, the group is the owner of the resource.

➤ *Network*—Contains any user with a connection from a remote system.

➤ *Interactive*—Contains the user account for the user logged on locally at the system.

➤ *Anonymous Logon*—Includes any user account that Windows XP did not authenticate.

➤ *Dial-up*—Contains all users that currently use a dial-up connection.

Creating Local User and Group Accounts

To create a local user or group account, right-click the appropriate folder (Users or Groups) and choose New User (or New Group), enter the appropriate attributes, and then click Create.

User account names:

➤ Must be unique

➤ Are recognized only up to their 20th character, although the name itself can be longer

➤ Cannot contain the following characters: " / \ [ ] ; : | = + * ? < >

➤ Are not case sensitive, although the user account's name property displays the case as entered

User account passwords:

➤ Are recommended

➤ Are case sensitive

➤ Can be up to 127 characters, although down-level operating systems like Windows NT 4 and Windows 9x support only 14-character passwords

➤ Should be a minimum of seven to eight characters

➤ Should be difficult to guess and, preferably, should mix uppercase and lower-case letters, numerals, and nonalphanumeric characters

➤ Can be set by the administrator (who can then determine whether users must, can, or cannot change their password) or the user (if the administrator has not specified otherwise)

Select the option User Must Change Password At Next Logon to ensure that the user is the only one who knows the account's password. Select User Cannot Change Password when more than one person (such as Guest) uses the account.

Note: The User Cannot Change Password option is not available when User Must Change Password At Next Logon is selected.

The Password Never Expires option is helpful when a program or a service uses an account. To avoid having to reconfigure the service with a new password, you can simply set the service account to retain its password indefinitely.

Configuring Account Properties

The information you can specify when creating an account is limited in Windows XP. Therefore, after creating an account, you often need to go to the account's Properties dialog box, which you can access by right-clicking the account and choosing Properties. After the creation of a user, you can specify the groups the user belongs to and the profile settings for the user, as shown in Figure 4.1.

Managing Local Group Membership

To manage the membership of a Local group, right-click the group and choose Properties. To remove a member, select the account and click Remove. To add a member, click Add and select or enter the name of the account, as shown in Figure 4.2.

In a workgroup, Local groups can contain only accounts defined in the same machine's local security database. When a system belongs to a domain, its Local groups can also include domain accounts, including user accounts, Universal groups, and Global groups from the enterprise's Active Directory, as well as Domain Local groups from within the system's domain.

Figure 4.1   The Properties dialog box of a typical user.

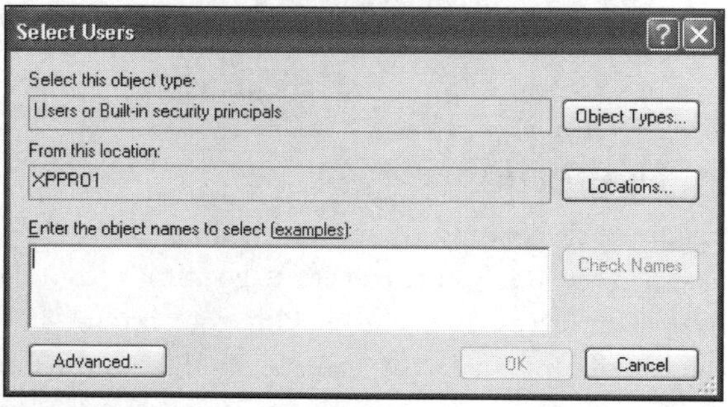

Figure 4.2   Interface for adding a user or group to a Local group.

Note: Universal groups and Domain Local groups are available to add as members only when the domain is in native mode, meaning that it can contain only Windows 2000 domain controllers and no legacy backup domain controllers.

Renaming Accounts

To rename an account, right-click the account and choose Rename. Type the new name and press Enter. Each user and group account is represented in the local security database by a long, unique string called a *Security Identifier (SID)*, which is generated when the account is created. It is the SID that is assigned permissions and privileges. The user or group name is just a user-friendly interface name for humans to interact with the computer. Therefore, when you rename an account, the account's SID remains the same and the account retains all of its group memberships, permissions, and privileges.

Two situations mandate renaming an account. The first occurs when one user stops using a system and a new user requires the same access as the first. Rather than creating a new local user account for the new user, simply rename the old user account. The account's SID remains the same, so its group memberships, privileges, and permissions are retained. You should also specify a new password in the account's Properties dialog box and select the User Must Change Password At Next Logon option.

Note: One thing to keep in mind is that the users' Home Directory name will not change along with renaming the user. The administrator will need to change the reference in the user properties and within the directory structure where the folder resides.

The second situation that warrants renaming a user account is the security practice of renaming the built-in Administrator and Guest accounts. You cannot delete these accounts, nor can you disable or remove the Administrator account from the Local Administrators group, so renaming the accounts is a recommended practice for hindering malicious access to a system.

 A Group Policy exists to modify the Administrator and Guest name. You can either create this at the local computer level or at the site, domain, or organizational unit (OU) level within Active Directory.

Disabling or Enabling User Accounts

To disable or enable a user account, open its Properties dialog box and select or clear the Account Is Disabled checkbox. If an account is disabled, a user cannot log on to the system using that account. The Administrator account cannot be disabled, and only Administrators can enable the Guest account.

Deleting Accounts

You can delete a local user or group account (but not built-in accounts such as Administrator, Guest, or Backup Operators) by right-clicking the account and choosing Delete. When you delete a group, you delete the group account only, not the members of the group. A group is a membership list, not a container.

Note: When you delete an account, you are deleting its SID. Therefore, if you delete an account by accident and re-create the account, even with the same name, it will not have the same permissions, privileges, or group memberships—you will have to regenerate them. For that reason, and to facilitate auditing, it is recommended that you disable, not delete, any user that leaves an organization.

Using the User Accounts Tool

Another tool for administering local user accounts is the User Accounts tool in Control Panel, shown in Figure 4.3. This tool enables you to create and remove user accounts, as well as specify specific configurations for those users. It is wizard-driven and is useful for novice administrators and home users.

The User Account tool changes functions as the computer joins a domain from a workgroup. These changes are to control the access to the computer from other domain users. The following is a list of configurations that can be completed after the computer has become a member of a domain:

➤ Manage the users that can access the local computer.

➤ Modify the type of access a user has on the computer. This would include Standard user, Limited user, or a custom type of user, such as an Administrator.

➤ Manage passwords that are stored on the local computer.

➤ Manage .NET Passport.

➤ Access advanced user and computer settings.

➤ Change the local administrator password.

➤ Modify the secure logon preferences; basically, whether or not a user is required to press Ctrl+Alt+Delete to log on.

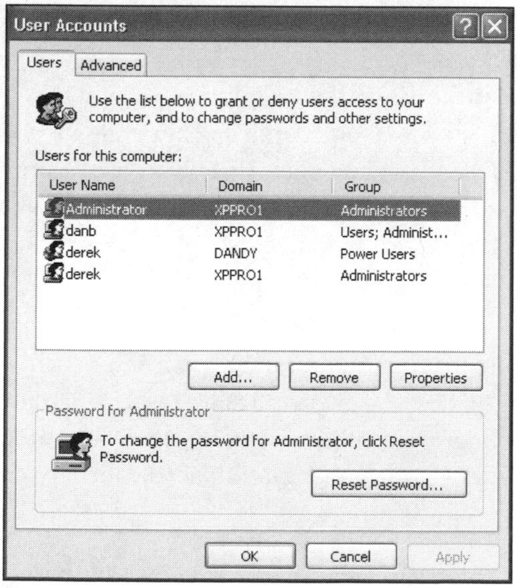

Figure 4.3   User Accounts tool for administering local users.

For machines that do not participate in a domain in Windows XP, two categories of user accounts exist: Limited and Administrator. By default, the person installing the operating system is an administrator. An account that is an administrator can perform any and all functions on the computer. By contrast, an account designated as Limited cannot create shares or install software. Table 4.1 lists several of the differences between the accounts.

Passwords

Passwords are not required, but are highly recommended. If your system has accounts that don't require any form of password, virtually anyone will be able to access your files and folders, even if you don't want them to. It is always recommended to have a password; even a simple password is better than no password at all.

Forgotten Passwords

If you forget your password, you can recover your settings and user account with the Forgotten Password Wizard. The wizard enables you to create a Password Reset Disk to help you open your account and create a new password. The Password Reset Wizard also enables you to change your password.

To protect user accounts in the event that the user forgets the password, every local user can make a Password Reset Disk and keep it in a safe place. Then, if the user forgets his or her password, the password can be reset using the Password Reset Disk, enabling the user to access the local user account again.

Table 4.1 Account types.		
Function	Limited	Administrator
Create shares		X
Create printers		X
Install software		X
Create other accounts		X
Change network settings		X
Change passwords	X	X
Change account picture	X	X
Set up .NET Passport	X	X
Access programs	X	X
Change background	X	X
Request Remote Assistance	X	X

If you already made a Password Reset Disk for your local user account through the Forgotten Password Wizard, you can use it to access the computer, even if you have forgotten your password.

Fast User Switching

Fast User Switching is another new feature of Windows XP Professional. Don't be fooled with this option, though, because it is available only when the computer is in a workgroup, not joined to a domain. This function makes it possible for users to switch quickly between other users without actually logging off from the computer. Multiple users can share a computer and use it simultaneously, switching back and forth without closing the programs they are running. To switch to another user, click Start, click Log Off, click Switch User, and then click the user account you would like to switch to. The following caveats apply when using Fast User Switching:

➤ It will not appear if it has not been turned on in User Accounts in Control Panel.

➤ It is not available on computers that are members of a network domain.

➤ It can be turned on or off only by users with a computer administrator account on a computer.

➤ It cannot be turned off while multiple users are logged on to the computer.

➤ When it is not turned on, programs shut down when you log off, and the computer runs faster for the next user who logs on.

Authentication

When a user wants to access resources on a machine, that user's identity must first be verified through a process called *authentication*. For example, when a user logs on, the security subsystem evaluates the user's username and password. If they match, the user is authenticated. The process of logging on to a machine where you are physically sitting is called an *interactive logon*. Authentication also happens when you access resources on a remote system. For example, when you open a shared folder on a server, you are being authenticated as well, only this time, the process is called a *remote* or *network logon*, because you are not *physically* at the server.

The Security Dialog Box

The *Security dialog* box allows for interactive logon to a Windows XP system. You can access the Security dialog box shortly after a system has started, and at any time after logon, by pressing Ctrl+Alt+Delete. If you are not currently logged on, you can enter a username and password. If the system belongs to a domain, you need to be certain that the domain in which your account exists is selected in the Log On To text box. You can either select the domain from the drop-down list or enter your User Principal Name (UPN). The UPN is an attribute of an Active Directory user object and, by default, is of the form *username@domain.name*, where *domain.name* is the Windows 2000 domain for which your user account resides (for example, braincore.net). The suffix, following the @ symbol, indicates the domain against which to authenticate the user.

If you are currently logged on to a system, pressing Ctrl+Alt+Delete takes you to the Windows XP Security dialog, at which point you can do the following:

➤ Log off the system, which closes all programs and ends the instance of the session.

➤ Lock the system, which allows programs to continue running but prevents access to the system. When a system is locked, you may unlock it by pressing Ctrl+Alt+Delete and entering the username and password of the user who locked the system, or an administrator's username and password.

➤ Shut down the system.

➤ Change your password

➤ Access Task Manager.

Managing Domain User Accounts

Domain user accounts are managed with the Active Directory Users and Computers snap-in. To access it, choose Start|Settings|Control Panel|Administrative Tools|Active Directory Users And Computers. When you open the tool, you connect to an available domain controller. If you want to specify which domain controller or domain you wish to modify, right-click the Active Directory Users And Computers node and choose Connect To Domain or Connect To Domain Controller.

Unlike the local security database, which is a flat list of users and groups, Active Directory has containers and OUs, which collect database objects such as users, computers, printers, and other OUs. Therefore, to manage domain user accounts in Windows 2000, you need to access the correct container or OU that houses your user object.

Creating Domain User Accounts

You create domain user accounts by right-clicking the container or OU that will contain the user account and then selecting New|User. A wizard prompts you for basic account properties, including the following:

➤ First name and last name

➤ Full name (by default, the combination of the first and last names)

➤ User logon name and User Principal Name (UPN) suffix

➤ User logon name (pre-Windows 2000)

➤ Password

Creating Template User Accounts

When you expect to create multiple user objects with similar properties, you can create a "template" account that, when copied, initiates the new accounts with predefined attributes. One thing to keep in mind when working with templates is to *disable the template account*. This will ensure that a real user can't access the network as the template user. Of course, when copying the template account to create a new user, make sure to enable the new account.

Disabling and Deleting User Accounts

The process for disabling and deleting domain user accounts is the same as for local user accounts, except that you use the Active Directory Users and Computers snap-in to perform the tasks. The checkbox for disabling an account is on the user's Property sheet, or you can disable the account by right-clicking the user object and selecting the Disable Account menu option.

Understanding and Implementing Group Policy

One of the most powerful aspects of Windows XP Professional and Windows 2000 Active Directory is the implementation of Group Policy. Group Policy is the ability to control finite details of a computer or user quickly and easily. These policies can either be configured at the local level or within the Active Directory structure. Regardless of the location of implementation, these settings are extremely powerful and can change the way normal control and administration is done within a company.

Local Group Policy

Actually, you can administer Local Policies from two different locations: a Local Group Policy and a Local Security Policy. The Local Group Policy can be accessed by opening the Group Policy snap-in within a Microsoft Management Console, and then selecting the Local Computer option. You can configure security-related settings using the Local Security Policy, which contains the Security

Settings snap-in. Simply choose Start|Administrative Tools|Local Security Policy. Each of the nodes in the Local Security Policy Console is a security area or scope, within which you will find dozens of security-related settings. The Local Security Policy is nothing more than a subset of the Local Group Policy. So, when you open the Local Group Policy, you are also accessing the Local Security Policy.

Managing Local Group Policies

The Local Group Policy and the Local Security Policy tools are most helpful on standalone systems and laptops that roam away from the network environment. The Local Group Policy controls the configuration of the local computer and user. These local settings will override any other settings that might be made to the local system. The policy-based settings will apply to a computer at startup and to a user at logon. Also, these policy settings are applied at a refresh interval, which does not require a reboot or logging off.

In a workgroup environment, you will need to access each computer and make the desired settings on each computer individually. Methods exist to make this more efficient, by using security templates, but the process is still a manual one that requires decentralized administration of the policy settings. The solution to this decentralized administration is to implement Active Directory and apply the desired settings to a grouping of computers or users by using Group Policy Objects within Active Directory.

Group Policy Objects

Group Policy Objects (GPOs) take the concept of policy-enforced configurations and applies it to multiple computers or users. Unlike Local Group Policy, GPOs provide a centralized enumeration of configuration settings. You can apply, or *link*, GPOs to the following:

➤ *A site*—This is an Active Directory object that represents a portion of your network topology with good connectivity—a local area network (LAN), for example.

➤ *A domain*—This causes the configuration specified by the policy to be applied to every user or computer in the domain.

➤ *An OU*—This applies policies to users or computers in the OU or any child OUs.

To access Group Policy, you must go to the properties of a site, domain, or OU (SDOU), and click the Group Policy tab. Therefore, to work with group policy for a site, you use the Active Directory Sites and Services Console, whereas to work with group policy for a domain or OU, you use Active Directory Users and Computers.

In the case of an individual machine, it can only have one Local Group Policy, whereas an SDOU can have multiple GPOs. In the Group Policy Properties dialog box, you can create a new GPO by clicking New, or link an existing GPO to the SDOU by clicking Add. If you select a group policy and click Edit, you expose the GPO in the Group Policy Editor.

Application of Group Policy Objects

GPOs are divided into the Computer Configuration and User Configuration nodes. The computer settings apply to every computer in the SDOU to which the policy is linked, and, by default, to all child OUs. Computer settings take effect at startup and every refresh interval, which by default is 90 minutes. User settings affect every user in the SDOU and its children at logon, and after each refresh interval.

 When configuring GPOs, ensure that the computers and/or users lie within the path of the GPO SDOU to receive the policy settings. For example, if you want to control a Web server named IIS_Apps, you would need to move this computer object to the proper OU in order to have the GPO for that OU apply to the IIS_Apps computer.

When a computer starts, its current settings are modified first by any configuration specified by the Local Group Policy. Then, the configurations for the SDOU GPOs are applied. The SDOU policies are applied in order. First, the policies linked to the computer's site, and then the policies for its domain, and finally the policies for each OU in the branch that leads to the object's OU. The policy settings from the Local Group Policy and the SDOU will append to each other. If there is ever a conflict in a particular configuration setting, the last setting applied controls. Therefore, the policies that are "closest" to the computer—the policies linked to its OU, for example—take precedence if a conflict arises. The same application of policies applies to a user at logon: local policy, site policy, domain policy, and OU policy.

User Rights Assignment

User rights, also called privileges, enable a user or group to perform system functions such as changing the system time, backing up or restoring files, and formatting a disk volume. Some rights are assigned to Built-in groups. For example, the Administrators group can format a disk volume. You cannot deny that right to the members of the Administrators group, nor can you assign that right to a user or group you create. Other rights are assignable. For example, the right to back up files and folders is given by default to Administrators and Backup Operators, but you can remove the right for those groups or assign the right to other users or groups. You can modify the rights that are visible in the Local Security Policy Console. You do not see the "hard wired" rights in this interface.

User rights, because they are system-oriented, override object permissions when the two are in conflict with each other. For example, a user may be denied permission to read a folder on a disk volume. However, if the user has been given the privilege to back up files and folders, a backup of the folder succeeds, even though the user cannot actually read the folder.

Security Options

In the *Security Options* node are a number of useful security settings. This node highlights one of the advantages of policies, because while many of these settings are accessible elsewhere in the user interface (for example, you can specify driver signing in the System applet), a policy enables you to configure all of those settings, from all the tools and applets, into a centralized location.

Some particularly useful options to be familiar with are the following:

➤ *Clear the Virtual Memory Pagefile when the system shuts down*—By default, the pagefile is not cleared and could allow unauthorized access to sensitive information that remains in the pagefile.

➤ *Do not display last username in logon screen*—This option forces users to enter both their username and password at logon. By default, the policy is disabled and the name of the previously logged-on user is displayed.

➤ *Number of previous logons to cache*—This policy will limit the number of cached profiles that are on a system. Not only will this clean up the hard drive space on a system, but also if there are no cached profiles, users will be forced to access a domain controller when logging on to the domain, instead of using cached credentials.

Account Policies

Account policies control the password requirements and how the system responds to invalid logon attempts. The policies you can specify include the following:

➤ *Maximum password age*—Specifies the period of time after which a password must be changed.

➤ *Minimum password length*—Specifies the number of characters in a password. Passwords can contain up to 127 characters; however, most passwords should not exceed 14 characters.

➤ *Passwords must meet complexity requirements*—This policy, if in effect, does not allow a password change unless the new password contains at least three of four character types: uppercase (A through Z), lowercase (a through z), numeric (0 through 9), and nonalphanumeric (such as !).

➤ *Enforce password history*—The system can remember a specified number of previous passwords. When a user attempts to change his or her password, the new password is compared against the history; if the new password is unique, the change is allowed.

➤ *Minimum password age*—Specifies the number of days that a new password must be used before it can be changed again.

➤ *Account lockout threshold*—Specifies the number of denied logon attempts after which an account is locked out. For example, if this is set to 3, a lockout occurs if a user enters the wrong password three times; any further logon attempt will be denied. If this is set to 0, there is no lockout threshold.

➤ *Reset account lockout counter after*—Specifies the number of minutes after which the counter that applies to the lockout threshold is reset. For example, if the counter is reset after five minutes and the account lockout threshold is three, a user can log on twice with the incorrect password. After five minutes, the counter is reset, so the user can log on twice more. A third invalid logon during a five-minute period locks out the account.

➤ *Account lockout duration*—Specifies how long logon attempts are denied after a lockout. During this period, a logon with the locked out username is not authenticated.

Audit Policies

Audit policies specify what types of events are entered into the Security Log. The most important policies to understand include those in the following list.

➤ *Logon events*—Authentication of users logging on or off locally and making connections to the computer from remote systems.

➤ *Account management*—Any change to account properties, including password changes and additions, deletions, or modifications to users or groups.

➤ *Object access*—Access to objects on which auditing has been specified. Auditing object access, for example, enables auditing of files and folders on an NT File System (NTFS) volume, but you must also configure auditing on those files and folders. Refer to Chapter 2 for a detailed discussion of auditing.

➤ *Privilege use*—Use of any user rights, now called *privileges*. For example, this policy audits a user who changes the system time, because changing the system time is a privilege.

For each policy, you can specify to audit successes, failures, or both. As events are logged, they appear in the Security Log, which can be viewed, by default, only by administrators. Other logs can be viewed by anyone.

Resultant Set of Policy (RSoP)

As you become more familiar with Group Policy, both at the local and Active Directory levels, you will quickly see that they can be very complex. The complexity results not only from the numerous settings that are available within a single Group Policy, but also from the fact that many policies can be applied, and at many different areas within the enterprise. When these settings finally apply to the computer and user on a Windows XP Professional computer, it can be very difficult to determine the final policies that are applied. Microsoft has gone to great lengths with Windows XP Professional to help decipher the complex array of GPOs and security settings that are possible. Microsoft has done this with three fantastic tools: Group Policy Result (**gpresult**), Group Policy Update (**gpupdate**), and the RSoP snap-in.

Group Policy Result

The first tool, *Group Policy Result*, is a command-line tool. This tool will give you the Resulting Set of Policies (RSoP) that apply to your computer and user accounts. The tool is extremely simple to run and is easy to read when it spits the results back to you. All you need to do is start a command prompt and enter **gpresult**, as shown in Figure 4.4.

Group Policy Update

It is well known that Group Policies automatically refresh by default. The default refresh time is 90 minutes. So, when you configure any new setting in the Local or Active Directory Group Policies, the settings will automatically refresh for both the computer and user. For some instances, this is not sufficient, though. You might be testing out new policies and want to see the results immediately, or want to force a new policy to a department of users immediately. If you need to force a policy immediately, you only need to run the command-line tool Group Policy Update. This tool will investigate the Local and Active Directory–based Group Policies and apply them immediately to both the computer and user. You do not need to run any switches with the tool, but if you want better control, you can use the primary switches listed here:

➤ /**target:** (*Computer*|*User*)—Allows explicit refreshing of either the computer or user portions of the policies that need to be applied.

➤ /**force**—Reapplies all settings in the policies, whereas if no switches are used, only the changed policies will apply.

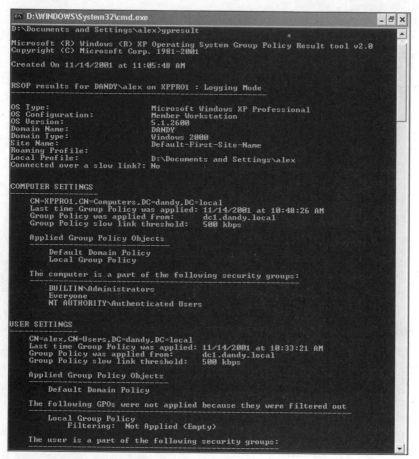

Figure 4.4 Group Policy Result output for the RSoP.

➤ **/logoff**—Some user-based Group Policy settings exist (such as Folder Redirection) that do not apply until the user logs off and back on. With this switch, the user will automatically be logged off after the other policies refresh.

➤ **/boot**—Like the user settings, some computer settings require a reboot (such as software deployment). With this switch, the computer will automatically reboot after the other policies refresh.

RSoP Snap-in

The final tool for determining the RSoP is the new *RSoP snap-in*. This tool enables you to investigate the policies in a GUI interface, which can then be saved to a file or Web site for archiving. To open this tool, open up a new MMC and add the Resulting Set of Policy snap-in. When you open the tool, you will have the following options for your Windows XP Professional computer:

➤ *Computer scope*—You will have the choice of selecting either your computer or another computer on the network (as long as you have administrative credentials on the remote computer). You will also be able to eliminate the computer portion of the RSoP, if you only want to see user-based settings.

➤ *User scope*—You can select the currently logged on user or another user that can access the local computer. Again, you must have the correct privileges to view another user's RSoP. You can also eliminate the user portion of the RSoP, if you only want to see the computer-based settings.

Note: For Windows XP Professional, you can only view Logging mode. Planning mode will be available only on Windows .NET servers or XP Professional client computers that have the administrative pack installed from the future release of Windows .NET Server.

When the tool is run and finishes, it gives you the results in the MMC that you initially opened. Figure 4.5 show the resulting RSoP format, which is the same format as the original Group Policy Editor.

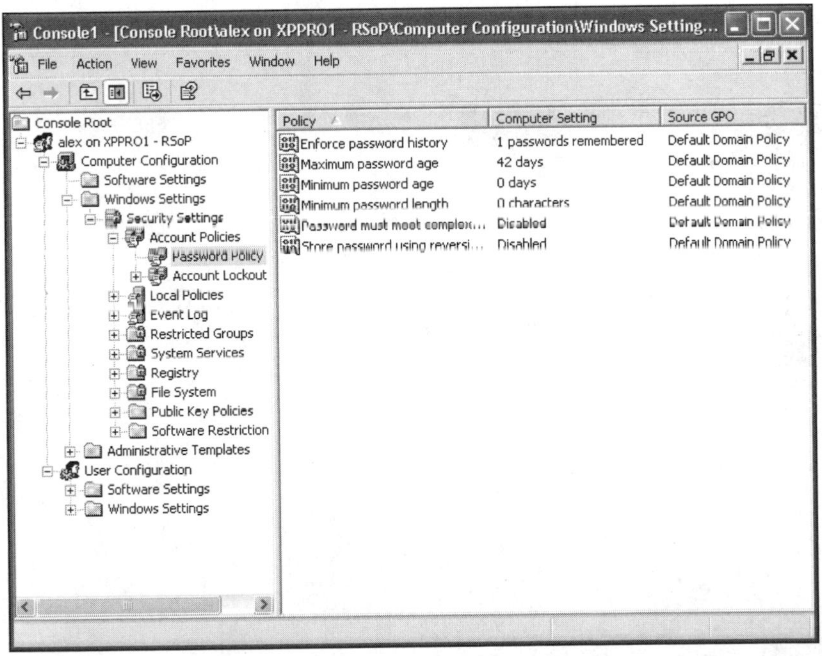

Figure 4.5   RSoP snap-in results for both the local computer and currently logged on user.

Security Configuration and Analysis

It was back in the late days of Windows NT 4 that Microsoft introduced the security templates and the ability to lock down the security of a system with a centralized group of settings. The tool has evolved over time and has now come to be known as the *Security Configuration and Analysis tool.* The tool is a snap-in that is used on a computer-by-computer basis. The tool allows for security analysis and configuration, as well as development of security templates.

 The **secedit** command can also be used to analyze and configure security settings to a computer.

After the tool is opened in an MMC, as shown in Figure 4.6, you need to open one of the security templates into a database. The idea is that you will bring the security template settings into the database for further analysis of the existing computer settings. With the security template settings in a database, you can easily run an analysis against the computer settings to see if the existing settings are in compliance with what the database has recorded. Figure 4.6 is a result of one analysis. Note that some settings are equal to or better than the database, but some settings are not as secure as what the database indicates, which are shown with a red x by them.

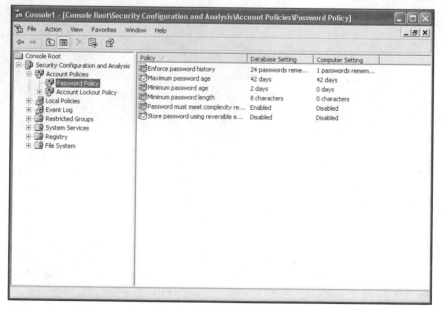

Figure 4.6   Security Configuration and Analysis tool.

Security Templates

Multiple security templates are available that can be used to analyze your computers' security settings. Some are related to the security levels of the system, and others are related to compatibility of a system with legacy applications. Here is a listing of the different types of security templates that are available:

➤ *Basicwk.inf*—This template contains the default settings for a typical installation of Windows XP Professional.

➤ *Securews.inf*—This template is designed to boost the security of a Windows XP system with regard to Auditing, Account Policy, and some well-known Registry subkeys.

➤ *Hisecws.inf*—The settings in this security template will significantly increase the security of the system. You should use this template with caution, because the settings might cause the computer to drop communication with the network due to the lack of security on other computers on the network.

➤ *Compatws.inf*—This template is designed to reduce the security settings on your computer, basically the Users group, so that they can run legacy applications more easily.

Software Restriction Policies

A *Software Restriction Policy* can help to control users running untrusted applications and code. It is clear that most viruses are introduced into the computing environment when users run unauthorized applications and open email attachments. With software restrictions, these undesired applications and code can be eliminated. The following is a listing of some of the control that these policies provide:

➤ Untrusted code is prevented from sending email, accessing files, or performing other normal computing functions until verified as safe.

➤ Protection is provided against infected email attachments. This includes file attachments that are saved to a temporary folder as well as embedded objects and scripts.

➤ ActiveX controls downloaded from the Web are monitored, and neutralized if necessary.

➤ Software restriction policies can be used on a standalone computer by configuring the Local Security Policy.

Two Types of Software Restriction Policies

Software restriction policies can be applied at the two security levels:

➤ *Unrestricted*—Only let trusted code run. If all trusted code can be identified, the administrator can effectively lock down the system. The following are examples of where to apply an "only let trusted code run" policy:

  ➤ Application station

  ➤ Task station

  ➤ Kiosk

➤ *Disallowed*—Prevent unwanted code from running. In some cases, an administrator cannot predict the entire list of software that users will need to run. In these cases, the administrator can only react and identify undesirable code as it is encountered. Companies with loosely managed clients would fall into this model. The following scenarios are examples of this case:

  ➤ Lightly managed personal computers

  ➤ Moderately managed personal computers

Software Identification Rules

An administrator identifies software through one of the following rules:

➤ *Hash rule*—A Software Restriction Policy's MMC snap-in allows an administrator to browse to a file and identify that program by calculating its hash. A *hash* is a digital fingerprint that uniquely identifies a program or file. A file can be renamed or moved to another folder or computer and it will still have the same hash.

➤ *Path rule*—A path rule can identify software by a full path name, such as C:\Program Files\Microsoft Office\Office\excel.exe; or by the path name leading to the containing folder, such as C:\Windows\System32. (This would refer to all programs in that directory and its subdirectories.) Path rules can also use environment variables, such as %userprofile%\Local Settings\Temp.

➤ *Certificate rule*—A certificate rule identifies software by the publisher certificate used to digitally sign the software. For example, an administrator can configure a certificate rule that allows only software signed by Microsoft or its IT organization to be installed.

➤ *Zone rule*—A zone rule identifies software that comes from the Internet, local intranet, trusted sites, or restricted sites zones.

Integration with Microsoft Passport via the Internet

A *.NET Passport* (also referred to as a Microsoft Passport) provides you with personalized access to Passport-enabled services and Web sites by using your email address. Passport implements a single sign-in service that enables you to create a single username and password. You can obtain a .NET Passport through the .NET Passport Wizard in User Accounts, shown in Figure 4.7. The .NET Passport Wizard helps you to obtain a .NET Passport or sign in with a Passport you already have. You will be required to configure a .NET Passport when you attempt to use the Windows Messenger application.

> Those companies that don't have access to the Internet or don't allow users to use a Microsoft Passport for Windows Messenger, but still want users to take advantage of the Windows Messenger capabilities, can take advantage of the Windows Messenger functionality that is built into Exchange 2000. With Exchange 2000, a user can use their Active Directory credentials to open a Windows Messenger session and talk to other users on the network who also have an Exchange 2000 Windows Messenger account.

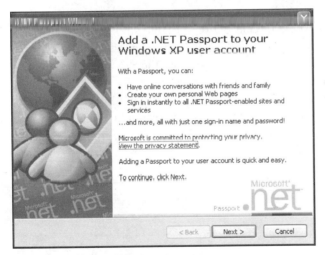

Figure 4.7 Microsoft .NET Passport Wizard.

Practice Questions

Question 1

You are the administrator for a large company. You have a group of Windows XP Professional computers in a workgroup and want to enable your users to create user and group accounts without giving them excessive rights. How should you configure the users' accounts?

○ a. Assign your users to the Local Administrators group on the local machine.

○ b. Assign your users to the Server Operators group on the local machine.

○ c. Assign your users to the Domain Administrators group in the domain.

○ d. Assign your users to the Power Users group on the local machine.

Answer d is correct. Power Users have the right to create user and group accounts, but they do not have total control over the computer, as an administrator does. Answer a is incorrect because making the users administrators would give them excessive rights. Answer b is incorrect because the Server Operators group does not exist on a Windows XP Professional machine, nor is this group given any privileges on the local system after joining the domain. Answer c is incorrect because, like answer a, it would give the users excessive rights; also, because the machines are in a workgroup, putting them in the Domain Administrators group would have no effect on their abilities to create users and groups on the local machine.

Question 2

> Bob took over Mary's duties when Mary retired. You created Bob's user account and put him in the same groups as Mary, and changed the ACLS on the resources to allow Bob access. You then deleted Mary's account. Later, Bob comes to you and reports that he can't get access to some resources that he needs that Mary had access to. You give him access, and later he reports the same problem on different resources. How should you have configured Bob's account to avoid the problems you are now facing, without giving Bob unnecessary access?
>
> ○ a. You should have renamed Mary's account to Bob.
>
> ○ b. You should have made Bob an administrator in the domain.
>
> ○ c. You should have made Bob a Server Operator.
>
> ○ d. You should have changed the dACLS on all resources in the domain to give Bob access.

Answer a is correct. Renaming the account would have ensured that Bob had all the access to resources that Mary had. Answer b is incorrect because you would have given Bob more access than was necessary, plus it does not ensure that Bob has access to all resources that Mary had. Answer c is incorrect because making Bob a Server Operator does not ensure that Bob has access to all resources that Mary had. Answer d is incorrect because that would have given Bob unnecessary access.

Question 3

> You successfully set the Local Security Policy to enable you to shut down your Windows XP Professional computer without logging on. After joining your computer to the domain, you attempt to shut down your computer without logging on, but the option is not available. Why is the option not available?
>
> ○ a. The Shutdown Without Logging On option is not available to computers that have joined a domain.
>
> ○ b. The option in the Local Group Policy no longer applies, because the computer is in the domain.
>
> ○ c. The user needs to be placed in the Local Administrators group for the Local Group Policy to apply.
>
> ○ d. The Domain Group Policy to Shutdown Without Logging On option is set to disabled.

Answer d is correct. Local Group Policies are the first to apply of all policies and are overridden by conflicting policy settings that are located at the Active Directory levels. Answer a is incorrect because the option is available at all GPO levels. Answer b is incorrect because Local Group Policies still apply when computers join domains, although they have lower priority. Answer c is incorrect because users don't need to be placed in the Local Administrators group to apply policies after a computer has joined the domain.

Question 4

You have enabled auditing on your company's laptops. You want to configure your remote users' laptops to shut down if they are unable to log security events and log all attempts to change Local Group Policies. How should you configure the systems? [Check all correct answers]

❑ a. Use Security Options in the Local Security settings to set the option to shut down the system if it's unable to log security audits.

❑ b. Configure the Audit Policy Change setting to monitor failed changes.

❑ c. Configure the Audit Policy Change setting to monitor successful changes.

❑ d. Configure the Audit Object Access setting to monitor successful changes.

Answers a, b, and c are correct. You will need to set the option in the Local Security settings to shut down the system if the computer is unable to log security audits, as well as set the Audit Policy Change policy for both success and failure. Answer d is incorrect because auditing object access logs users' access to resources, but not changes to policies.

Question 5

You have 250 Windows XP Professional computers in various OUs in your domain. You want to find out which computer GPOs are being applied to your computers, specifically policies that have been applied in multiple places with a precedence of 1 or higher. What would be the correct syntax to determine this?

○ a. **gpresult /scope user /z**

○ b. **gpresult /scope computer /z**

○ c. **gpresult /scope user /v**

○ d. **gpresult /scope computer /v**

Answer b is correct. The Group Policy Result tool will display the Resultant Set of Policy (RSoP) for a target user and computer. The /Scope switch specifies whether the user or the computer settings need to be displayed. The /z switch specifies that the super-verbose information is to be displayed, which enables you to see whether a setting was set in multiple places. Answer a is incorrect because the scope specified in the syntax is **user** and you wanted to see computer settings. Answer c is incorrect because the switch /v is used, which will not let you see whether a setting was set in multiple places. This requires super-verbose mode. Answer d is incorrect because of the switch used, as well.

Question 6

You make changes to the local policy on a Windows XP Professional work-station named WKSTN1. You want to refresh only the policy settings that have changed for the computer. What command will you run to accomplish this?

- ○ a. **gpupdate /target:computer**
- ○ b. **gpupdate /target:computer /force**
- ○ c. **gpresult /scope computer**
- ○ d. **gpresult /scope computer /z**

Answer a is correct. The Group Policy Update tool refreshes Group Policy settings and has a number of different switches. The /target: switch has two options: Computer or User. By default, both User and Computer policy settings are refreshed if no switch is specified. Therefore, because you want to refresh only the settings for the computer, you need to specify the option Computer. Answer b is incorrect because the /force switch reapplies all policy settings and you only want the settings that have changed to be refreshed. Answers c and d are incorrect because the gpresult command only gives the Resulting Set of Policies, it does not refresh them in any manner.

Question 7

> You have made changes to group policy and need to import the new template. What are some different ways to apply these new security template settings to the computers in the enterprise? [Check all correct answers]
>
> ❑ a. Use the **secedit** command.
>
> ❑ b. Use an Active Directory–based Group Policy Object.
>
> ❑ c. Use the Local Group Policy.
>
> ❑ d. Use the **gpupdate** command.

Answers a, b, and c are correct. The **secedit** command as well as the Group Policy options at the local and Active Directory level can apply the security templates to a computer. The **secedit** command is manual, whereas the other two options are more automated, because they will automatically refresh for the computer. Answer d is incorrect because **gpupdate** will update an existing Group Policy, but not apply the security templates themselves.

Question 8

> You are the administrator of a multidivisional company's network and some of your users are using network applications from a server that may not be approved for their division. All applications are in the same folder. Which software restriction rule would you apply?
>
> ○ a. Hash rule
>
> ○ b. Certificate rule
>
> ○ c. Zone rule
>
> ○ d. Path rule

Answer d is correct. A path rule can identify software by a full path name, such as C:\Program Files\Microsoft Office\Office\excel.exe, or by the path name leading to the containing folder, such as C:\Windows\System32. Answer a is incorrect because a hash is a digital fingerprint that uniquely identifies a program or file. You would have to identify all the applications' hash. Answer b is incorrect because a certificate rule identifies software by the publisher certificate used to digitally sign the software. The applications may be by different publishers, and you don't want to restrict users' ability to run approved applications. Answer c is incorrect because a zone rule identifies software that comes from the Internet, local intranet, trusted sites, or restricted sites zones. These applications are from a local file server.

Need to Know More?

 Microsoft Corporation. *Microsoft Windows XP Professional Resource Kit Documentation.* Redmond, WA: Microsoft Press, 2001. ISBN 0-73561-485-7. This all-in-one reference is a compilation of technical documentation and valuable insider information that computer-support professionals and administrators can reference to install, customize, and support Windows XP.

 Mark Minasi. *Mastering Windows XP Professional.* Alameda, CA: Sybex, Inc., 2001. ISBN 0-78212-981-1. This text will give you all the insider information for the creation of users and groups, and how they interact with a domain. The book also gives a good description of how Group Policies should be used for your XP Professional computer.

Search the TechNet CD (or its online version through **www.microsoft. com**) and the *Windows 2000 Professional Resource Kit* CD using the keywords "local user", "SID", "Group Policy Objects", "Local Security Policy", "SDOU", "GPRESULT", "GPUPDATE", and "Microsoft Passport".

Implementing and Managing User and Desktop Settings

5

Terms you'll need to understand:

✓ User profiles

✓ Fast user switching

✓ Offline Files and Folders

✓ MSCONFIG utility

✓ Windows Installer Service

✓ MSI files

✓ ZAP files

✓ Multilingual User Interface Pack

✓ File Settings and Transfer Wizard

✓ StickyKeys

✓ MouseKeys

✓ Narrator

✓ ClearType

✓ Dualview

✓ Utility Manager

✓ Fax Console

✓ Scheduled Tasks

Techniques you'll need to master:

✓ Configuring Offline Files and Folders options

✓ Implementing Windows Installer Packages

✓ Understanding the functionality of various Control Panel applets

✓ Configuring system startup settings

✓ Implementing software Group Policies

✓ Configuring support for multiple languages

✓ Transferring files and settings between computers

✓ Configuring accessibility options

✓ Setting up Dualview and ClearType display options

✓ Implementing and configuring the Fax service

✓ Configuring and managing tasks with Task Scheduler

Windows XP Professional supports the mobile user community more than ever before. Microsoft addressed several complaints that many users had with Windows NT Workstation 4 under Windows 2000 Professional. Windows XP Professional enhances the mobile user's experience even further. Mobile users of Windows NT Workstation 4 had a difficult job of keeping files on a network file server synchronized with copies they kept on their mobile computer. Windows XP Professional goes a long way toward fixing this age-old problem and other problems such as Dynamic Link Library (DLL) conflicts, application repair, and software updates. Also, the user environment has been enhanced and made even more robust in Windows XP Professional by using various control applets.

Configuring and Managing User Profiles

A *user profile* is the look and feel of the user's desktop environment. A profile is a combination of folders, data, shortcuts, application settings, and personal data. For example, users can configure their computer with the screen saver they prefer along with their favorite desktop wallpaper. These settings are independent of other users' settings for a specific local computer. When users log on to their computer for the very first time, a new profile is created for those users from a default user profile. So, when Joe logs on, a profile is created just for Joe. This type of profile is known as a *local profile* and is stored on the computer on which it was created. If Joe logged on to a different computer, his profile would not follow him to the computer he just logged on to. However, you can have a user's profile follow the user around the network if you so choose. This type of profile is called a *roaming user profile*. These profiles are stored on a network server. A local copy of the roaming profile is also found on the client computer.

User Profiles

User profiles in Windows XP employ a similar folder structure as introduced under Windows 2000. This structure is different than the one used with Windows NT 4. One of the folders found within a user's profile is called Local Settings. The Local Settings folder is local to the machine it resides on and does not roam from workstation to workstation. Also, a folder called My Documents is contained within a profile. This folder resides in the default location where users' files are saved to disk. The My Documents folder does have the capability to follow users around the network (roam) as they log on to different workstations.

Local Profiles

Windows XP Professional and Windows 2000 Professional local profiles are found in a different location than those in Windows NT 4 Workstation—possibly. If you perform a clean install of Windows XP Professional, a user profile is stored in the root of the system volume in a folder called Documents and Settings\

user_logon_name (for example, C:\Documents and Settings\Joe_User). If, however, you upgrade a Windows NT 4 Workstation to Windows XP Professional, the local profile is stored in the same location as it always was: %SystemRoot%\Profiles*user_logon_name*.

Logon Scripts, Home Folders

When a user logs on to a Windows NT domain or to a Windows Active Directory domain from Windows XP Professional, a *logon script* may execute and a *home folder* may be assigned to the user. Logon scripts are often used to map network drives or to execute some type of batch file. To configure a logon script for a user, perform the following steps on a Windows 2000 server or on a Windows .NET Server Active Directory domain controller:

1. Place the logon script in %SystemRoot%\sysvol\domain\scripts (this is the location for logon scripts for Windows servers acting as domain controllers).

2. Run the Active Directory Users and Computers MMC snap-in, right-click the name of the user, and select Properties. Go to the Profile tab and simply type the name of the logon script in the Logon Script box.

A home folder is a central location on a network server where users can store their files. All users can have their own home folders to store data. This way, if their workstation fails, they don't lose all of their data. Home folders also provide one central location in which users can back up all of their data. To create a home folder, perform the following steps on a Windows 2000 server or on a Windows .NET server:

1. Create a shared folder on the network server to enable home folders

2. Run the Active Directory Users and Computers MMC snap-in, right-click the name of the user, and select Properties. Go to the Profile tab and click the Connect radio button.

3. Click the drop-down arrow and choose an available drive letter.

4. Type in the Uniform Naming Convention (UNC) path to the user's home folder (for example, \\server1\homedir\dan).

 Microsoft suggests that users store their data in My Documents instead of home folders. You can then enable a Group Policy under Active Directory to redirect My Documents from the local computer to a network file server. The Group Policy also activates offline caching of My Documents to the user's local computer. Group Policy as well as Offline Files and Folders are covered later in this chapter.

Roaming User Profiles

If you have users who move from computer to computer, you can configure their profiles to move with them. A roaming profile is stored on a network server so that the profile is accessible regardless of which computer a user logs on to anywhere within the domain. You can put the profile on the server in two ways. You can copy a profile that is stored locally on a client computer to the profile server the next time the user logs on to the computer. Or, you can create on a client computer a profile that you will use as a company standard and then manually copy it to the profile server.

 Roaming user profiles behave differently in Windows XP and Windows 2000 than in Windows NT 4 Workstation. When a user logs on to a computer for the first time, the roaming profile is copied to the client computer. From that point forward, whenever a user logs on to a computer, the locally cached copy of the profile is compared to the roaming user profile. If the local profile and the roaming profile are the same, the local copy is used. Windows XP copies only files that have changed, not the entire profile, as was the case in Windows NT 4.

Use the following steps to configure a roaming profile:

1. Create a shared folder on a server for the profiles.

2. On a Windows XP Professional computer, open the Control Panel, select Performance And Maintenance, and then open the System icon to view the System Properties dialog box.

3. Click the Advanced tab.

4. From the User Profiles section, click the Settings button.

5. Select the user's profile you wish to use as a roaming profile and select Copy To. Then, type in the UNC path to the shared folder that was created (for example, \\server1\profiles\Dan or \\server1\profiles\%username%).

6. In the Active Directory Users and Computers MMC, select the account properties for the user. Then, select the Profile tab and enter the UNC path to the profile server in the Profile Path field.

7. The first time that the roaming user successfully logs on and then subsequently logs off from a Windows XP workstation, the user's profile is uploaded to the profile server and stored. The next time that the user logs on to the network, their roaming profile is compared with their local profile and the most recent profile is used (see Figure 5.1).

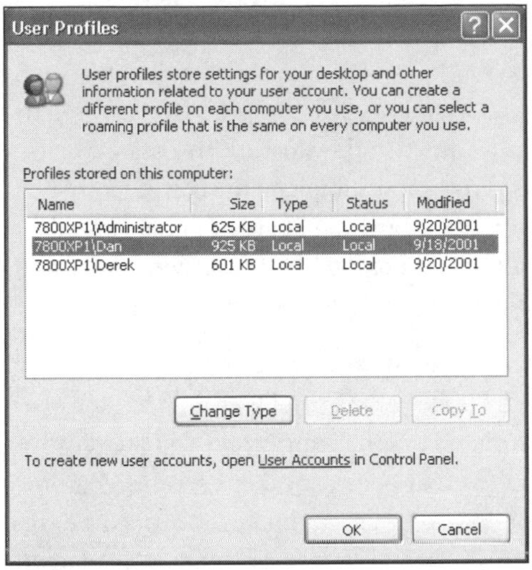

Figure 5.1   The User Profiles dialog box.

In Windows XP, if you create a roaming profile on an NTFS drive volume by using the **%username%** variable, the user and the built-in local Administrators group are assigned Full Control permission of that directory.

Note: Local or roaming profiles are protected from permanent change by renaming NTUSER.DAT to NTUSER.MAN. By renaming the file, you have effectively made the profile read-only, meaning that Windows XP does not save any changes made to the profile when the user logs off. NTUSER.DAT is found in the root of a profile and is hidden by default. This file is responsible for the user portion of the Registry and contains all the user settings.

Managing User Profiles Behavior through Group Policy

Windows XP offers several useful Group Policy settings for working with User Profiles. When you load the Group Policy snap-in for the MMC, expand Computer Configuration|Administrative Templates|System and click User Profiles. The settings for User Profiles include Delete Cached Copies of Roaming Profiles so that they won't be stored on the local computer. The Log Users Off When Roaming Profile Fails setting prohibits users from logging on unless their roaming profile is available. Another setting, Prevent Roaming Profile Changes From Propagating To The Server, will not allow any changes to roaming profiles centrally stored on a server. This setting is an excellent option for computers that have multiple users sharing the same profile.

Fast User Switching

Fast User Switching is a new feature in Windows XP. This feature supports switching between multiple users on the same Windows XP computer *without* requiring each user to exit from their applications when they log off. In a standalone or workgroup environment, Windows XP Professional implements Fast User Switching by default. Windows XP Professional computers that are members of a Windows network domain cannot use Fast User Switching. Only users whose accounts have been granted administrator status may enable or disable this feature.

When Fast User Switching is turned on, users may click Start|Log Off and they are presented with two options: Switch User or Log Off. If you click Switch User, any applications that are currently running remain running and you are returned to the Windows XP Welcome Screen. At that point, another user may log on to the system to work. Multiple users can log on to the computer, one at a time. The application programs that were running when each user is "switched out" continue to execute while another user works on the computer. To enable or disable Fast User Switching, click Start|Control Panel|User Accounts and select the option Change The Way Users Log On Or Off. You must enable Use The Welcome Screen if you want to turn on Fast User Switching.

Using Offline Files

Windows XP offers an improved Offline Files feature as compared to Windows 2000. Also known as *Client-side Caching (CSC)*, Offline Files under Windows XP addresses several file access problems that plagued Windows NT, such as if the file server is down and users need to access files on the file server, or when users are not connected to the network and they cannot get access to the files they may need. By using Offline Files, users can select files on a network file server and mark them for offline usage. This means that users now have a cached copy of the file on their local computer and can work on the file just as if they were connected to the network. Any offline files that have been changed on a local computer are synchronized with the network file server when the users reconnect to the network.

Setting Up Offline Files and Folders

In Windows XP, the Offline Files feature cannot be turned on if Fast User Switching is enabled, as shown in Figure 5.2. You must go to User Accounts in the Windows XP Control Panel and choose the option Change The Way Users Log On Or Off. After Fast User Switching has been disabled, two steps are involved in configuring Offline Files. The first is to configure the share point for offline usage. The second is to cache the files to the client computer.

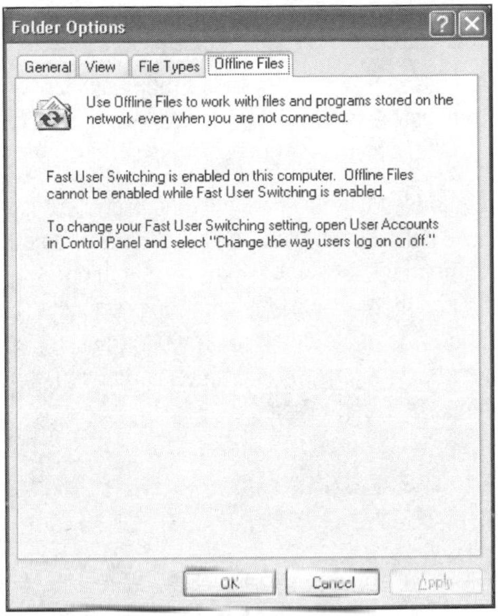

Figure 5.2   The Folder Options dialog box.

Configuring Share Points on a Windows 2000 Server or on a Windows .NET Server

Use the following steps to configure a network shared folder for Offline Files:

1. Share the folder(s) that you want to make available offline.

2. From the Sharing tab, select the Caching button.

3. Select the Allow Caching Of Files In This Shared Folder option (this option is selected by default).

4. Select one of the following three options from the Settings drop-down list and then click OK:

   ➤ *Manual Caching For Documents*—Requires users to select the files they want available for offline usage. This is the default setting.

   ➤ *Automatic Caching For Documents*—Caches all files that users have opened to their local disk for offline usage. Any older files that are out of synchronization are automatically deleted and replaced by a newer version of the same file.

   ➤ *Automatic Caching For Programs*—Provides the same capabilities as Automatic Caching For Documents but also caches applications that are run from the network.

5. Click OK to close the Sharing dialog box and to accept the options that you selected.

By default, Windows XP does not allow you to cache files with the .slm, .ldb, .mdw, .mdb, .mde, .pst, and .db extensions. However, you can override this setting through a Group Policy. Create a Group Policy for Computer Configuration\Administrative templates\Network\Offline Files\Files not cached.

This policy is meant to exclude files with specific file extensions from being cached. However, if the policy is enabled *and no file extensions are added,* all file types can be made available offline. This setting overrides the default configuration; it allows files with the previously listed extensions to be cached. You must log off and then log back on for the new settings to take effect. Microsoft recommends that you do not modify the default settings for Offline Files.

Configuring Shared Network Folders for Offline Use

Use the following steps under Windows XP to configure a network-shared folder for making files available offline for remote users:

1. From the My Computer window, select Tools|Folder Options and click the Offline Files tab to enable Offline Files.

2. Mark the Enable Offline Files checkbox.

3. Select or deselect any of the other options as you deem appropriate.

4. For increased security of offline data, mark the Encrypt Offline Files To Secure Data checkbox as shown in Figure 5.3. This is a new feature of

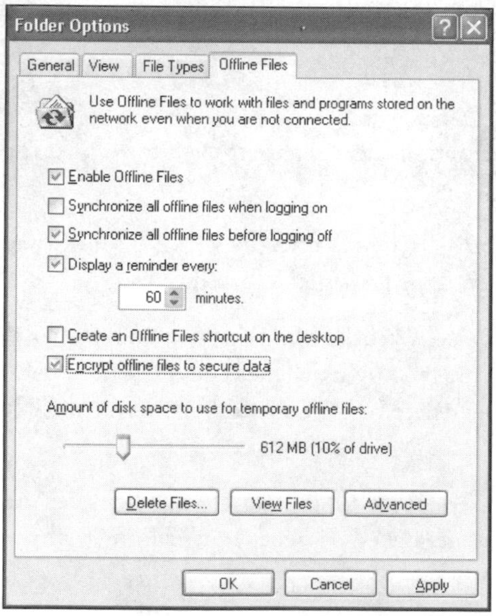

Folder Options

General | View | File Types | Offline Files

Use Offline Files to work with files and programs stored on the network even when you are not connected.

☑ Enable Offline Files
☐ Synchronize all offline files when logging on
☑ Synchronize all offline files before logging off
☑ Display a reminder every:

    60 ⬍ minutes.

☐ Create an Offline Files shortcut on the desktop
☑ Encrypt offline files to secure data

Amount of disk space to use for temporary offline files:

    612 MB (10% of drive)

[Delete Files...] [View Files] [Advanced]

[OK] [Cancel] [Apply]

Figure 5.3 The Folder Options dialog box displaying the Offline Files options.

Windows XP. Enabling Offline Files encryption is considered a best practice by Microsoft.

5. Share each folder that you want to make available offline.

6. From the Sharing tab, select the Caching button.

7. Select the Allow Caching Of Files In This Shared Folder option (this option is selected by default).

8. Select one of the three options from the Settings drop-down list, as outlined previously, and then click OK.

> The Offline Files feature cannot be turned on if Fast User Switching is enabled, as shown previously in Figure 5.2. You must go to User Accounts in the Windows XP Control Panel and choose the option Change The Way Users Log On Or Off.

Making Files and Folders Available Offline

By default, a Windows XP Professional computer is configured for offline file and folder usage. Use the following steps to make a file or folder available offline:

1. Connect to a share point on a domain or workgroup file server. Right click a file that you want to use offline and select Make Available Offline (see Figure 5.4).

2. A wizard appears if you are using this feature for the first time, asking whether offline files should be synchronized during logon and logoff. Click Next to accept the default. (Additional options are available after the wizard is finished.)

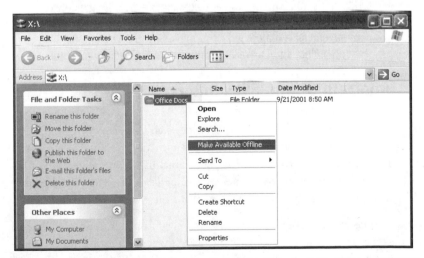

Figure 5.4   The right-click menu for a file displays the Make Available Offline option when Offline File Caching is enabled.

3. If you want the operating system to remind you that you are not connected to the network, click the Finish button to accept the default option, Enable Reminders. If you accept this option, a computer icon appears in the system tray. Whenever you are disconnected from the network, a balloon appears, notifying you that offline files are available.

After you have completed these steps, a little double-arrow icon appears on the file or folder that you have selected for offline usage. This is simply a graphic indicator to inform users that the file is located on the network and that a local cached copy of the file is located on their computer.

Note: A Windows NT 4 client cannot use the offline feature of Windows 2000 or Windows .NET servers. However, a Windows XP Professional client can make files available for offline usage from a Windows NT 4 server share. When using a Windows XP computer, you can make network files available offline from any remote computer that supports Server Message Block (SMB)-based file sharing, such as Windows 9x, Windows NT 4, Windows 2000, and Windows XP computers.

To view offline files after you are disconnected from the network, open My Network Places. Yes, that is correct. Offline files maintain their original location even though the computer is offline. Go to My Network Places and select the file server that contains the files. You can see only the files that you made available while offline. Users don't see the "network" while they are offline (see Figure 5.5).

Under the Windows 2000 Server and Windows .NET Server family of network operating systems, *when used as a workstation*, the Offline Files feature is not available if the server has Terminal Services installed. This holds true whether you are working directly from the console of the Terminal Server or through a Terminal Services session. However, clients can still connect to any Terminal Server and make the files stored on that server available offline from their local workstations.

Synchronizing Offline Files and Folders

After you have worked on one or more offline files while you have been away or disconnected from your network, you can re-establish a network connection and log on to the network. Any changes that you made to the file(s) while you were offline are then synchronized with the original file(s) on the network. One caveat: if you have logged on to the network from a slow dial-up connection, it could take a long time to synchronize your offline files while you are logging on.

Several options are available to customize the synchronization process to deal with this type of problem. To customize the process when offline files are synchronized, open a Windows Explorer window and select Tools|Synchronize. The first dialog box displays the files and folders that are available offline. To configure

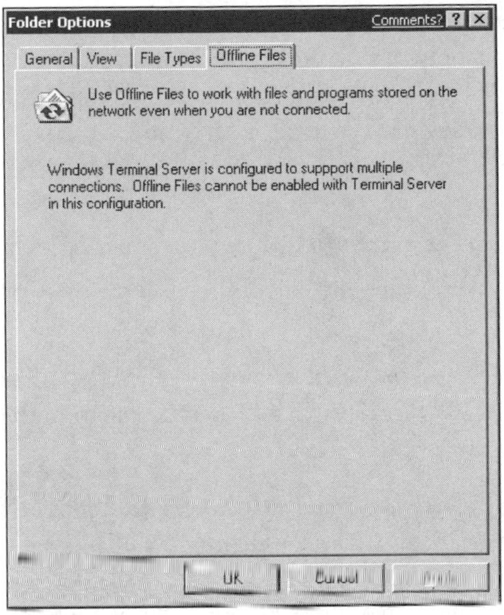

Figure 5.5   The Offline Files tab of the Folder Options dialog box from a Windows Terminal Server computer.

synchronization, click the Setup button, which opens the Synchronization Settings dialog box, shown in Figure 5.6.

This dialog box offers three tabs that help you determine when you should synchronize offline files: Logon/Logoff, On Idle, and Scheduled. However, you can

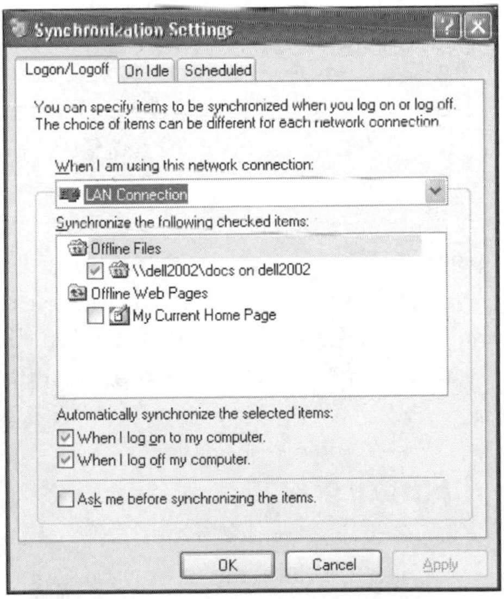

Figure 5.6   The Synchronization Settings dialog box.

also select over what network connection synchronization takes place. For example, to have synchronization occur only when you are connected to the network (versus when you have a slow dial-up connection), select LAN Connection in the When I Am Using This Network Connection drop-down list.

Synchronization Details

Now that you have configured synchronization, you are probably wondering what actually happens during this process. Well, that depends. The following are several synchronization scenarios:

➤ *An offline file has been deleted and the original network version of the file has not changed.* If this happens, Windows XP Professional removes the file from the network file server during synchronization.

➤ *A network file has been deleted and the offline version of the file has not changed.* If this happens, Windows XP Professional presents a dialog box of this state and gives you the option to either remove the file from the local computer during synchronization or keep the local version.

➤ *The offline file has changed and the network version has changed.* If this happens, you are presented with a dialog box during the synchronization; it asks you what should be done. The options are: keep the network version, keep the local version, and keep both and rename the local version.

➤ *Only files that have changed are synchronized.* If no changes have occurred, the locally cached copied is used before the network version of the offline file.

Accessing Offline Files and Folders

To access offline files, use My Network Places; however, that is not where the files are actually kept. Offline files are kept in %SystemRoot%\CSC (CSC is hidden by default). This directory contains a database of the offline files. You cannot view or edit individual files from this location. However, if the CSC directory gets quite large and if you use offline files frequently, it is advisable to move this directory from the system partition to a different partition or drive. However, you can't move this directory using Windows Explorer. To move the CSC directory from one partition to another, use the Windows XP Resource Kit utility named Cachemov.exe. You may also use the Cachemov.exe tool from the Windows 2000 Resource Kit as an alternative.

Managing Offline Files and Folders

To manage offline files, open a Windows Explorer window and select Tools|Folder Options and then select the Offline Files tab. The key options for managing offline folders are: turn off the Offline Files feature, delete offline files, and view all the offline files in one window. You can also use a sliding bar to control the amount of disk space made available for files that have been automatically cached to the local drive. The default disk space made available for automatically cached files is 10 percent.

Configuring and Troubleshooting Desktop Settings

The Windows XP Professional desktop combines the best features of Windows 98, Windows ME, and Windows 2000. In general, a regular local or domain user account can configure very few changes on a Windows XP Professional computer. The options that users can configure to customize their desktop are the following Control Panel applets and customization options (see Figure 5.7):

➤ Keyboard

➤ Display

➤ Mouse

➤ Sounds and Audio Devices

➤ Scanners and Cameras

➤ Speech

➤ Taskbar and Start Menu

➤ Wireless Link

Figure 5.7 The Windows XP Professional Control Panel.

Keyboard Applet

The Keyboard applet adjusts the cursor blink rate, the speed at which a character repeats when you hold down a key, the time lapse before a character repeats, and the input locale for different language groups of keyboard hardware. For example, you can use several language locales with a U.S. keyboard layout so that you can add foreign accent marks to documents that are written in French, Spanish, Italian, and so on. The Regional applet can also be used to configure Input Locales.

Display Applet

The Display applet has changed a bit from Windows 2000. You can now choose from five tabs to affect various aspects of the display:

➤ *Themes*—Enables the user to choose from various Windows XP desktop themes to customize the graphical user experience. Themes comprise a background for the desktop plus a set of sounds, icons, and associated other elements that serve to personalize a Windows XP computer.

➤ *Desktop*—Enables the user to select a background wallpaper or a background color for the Windows XP desktop. By clicking the Customize Desktop button, you can choose which icons are displayed on the desktop (the default is Recycle Bin only), modify the graphic for each icon, and run or schedule the Desktop Cleanup Wizard to move unused desktop items to a folder that you select.

➤ *Screen Saver*—Selects a screen saver but is also a shortcut to the Power Options applet. The Power button on the Screen Saver tab enables you to adjust power schemes and configure Standby and Hibernate modes.

➤ *Appearance*—Adjusts the window and button styles along with the color and font schemes that are displayed in all dialog boxes and windows. The Effects button gives the user the ability to turn on or off various effects such as menu and tooltip transitions, menu shadowing, and showing window contents while dragging. The Advanced button enables you to highly customize the color and fonts for the Windows XP environment.

➤ *Settings*—Enables the user to set the screen resolution and the color quality for the display adapter. If you encounter problems with the video display, you can click the Troubleshoot button to invoke the Video Display Troubleshooter. If Windows XP doesn't detect a Plug and Play monitor, it assigns default color depths and resolutions. By clicking the Advanced button, you can adjust several properties for the video display and the display adapter, such as whether to apply new settings without restarting, adjusting the display mode, changing the refresh rate, altering hardware acceleration, and working with color management.

Mouse Applet

The Mouse applet adjusts for left-handed or right-handed use. It also adjusts the double-click speed and the rate at which the cursor moves across the screen.

Sounds and Audio Devices Applet

The Sounds and Audio Devices applet controls sounds for startup, logoff, and other Windows events. It also controls what WAV files are used for critical error alerts and general alerts. You can modify the default devices for voice playback and voice recording as well as work with the properties of various sound and audio hardware that may be installed on a particular PC.

Scanners and Cameras Applet

The Scanners and Cameras applet enables you to manage scanned and photographic images. It also can help you to install a digital camera, scanner, or other image device that Windows XP Plug and Play may have been unable to detect. To install an image device you must be an administrative user.

Speech Applet

The Speech applet invokes the Speech Properties dialog box in which you can control the text-to-speech voice selection, preview the voice selection, and specify the voice speed. You can also click the Audio Output button to specify the preferred audio output device and volume level.

Taskbar and Start Menu Applet

The Taskbar and Start Menu applet gives you control over the appearance and behavior of both the taskbar and the Windows XP Start menu. Launching the Taskbar and Start Menu icon from the Control Panel invokes the Taskbar and Start Menu Properties dialog box, illustrated in Figure 5.8. You can also access the Taskbar and Start Menu Properties dialog box by right-clicking a blank area on the taskbar and selecting Properties or by right-clicking a blank area on the Start menu itself and selecting Properties.

Windows XP follows in the footsteps of Windows 2000 by making it much easier to arrange and customize the Start menu items than under previous versions of Windows. You can very easily sort menu items by dragging and dropping them. You can drag a menu item from one submenu to another. Also, you can open pop-up menus by right-clicking them. Windows XP automatically adjusts menu items as well. Windows XP does not attempt to clean up the Start menu by displaying only those items that are used most frequently, as is the case with Windows 2000. However, if you select Classic Start Menu, then Use Personalized Menus is enabled by default and items on the Start menu that are not used

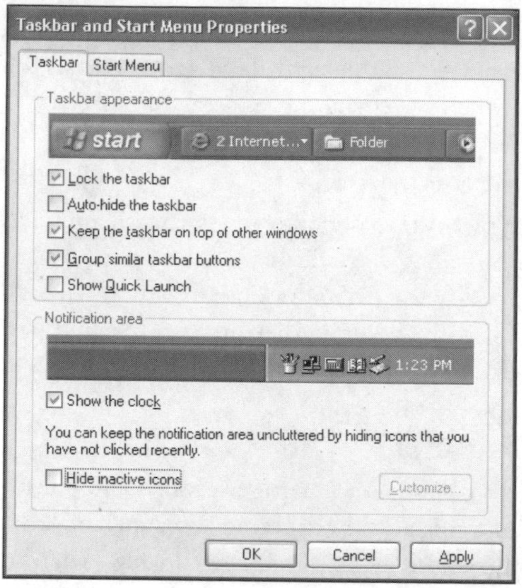

Figure 5.8   The Taskbar and Start Menu Properties dialog box.

often are hidden. You can turn off this feature quite easily: Right-click a blank area on the Start menu and select the Properties option. Doing so displays the Start Menu tab of the Taskbar and Start Menu Properties dialog box. Click the Customize button for the Classic Start Menu option to display the Customize Classic Start Menu dialog box. Deselect the option for Use Personalized Menus.

You can find even more customization options when you click the Customize button for either the Start Menu or the Classic Start Menu on the Start Menu tab of the Taskbar and Start Menu Properties dialog box, as shown in Figure 5.9. On the Advanced tab of the Customize Start Menu dialog box, available options include having submenus open when you pause the mouse pointer over a parent menu item, and having newly installed programs highlighted on the Start menu.

The following is a list of the Start menu features and items that you can customize from the Advanced tab of the Customize Start Menu dialog box:

➤ Control Panel

➤ Drag and drop

➤ Favorites menu

➤ Help and Support

➤ My Computer

➤ My Documents

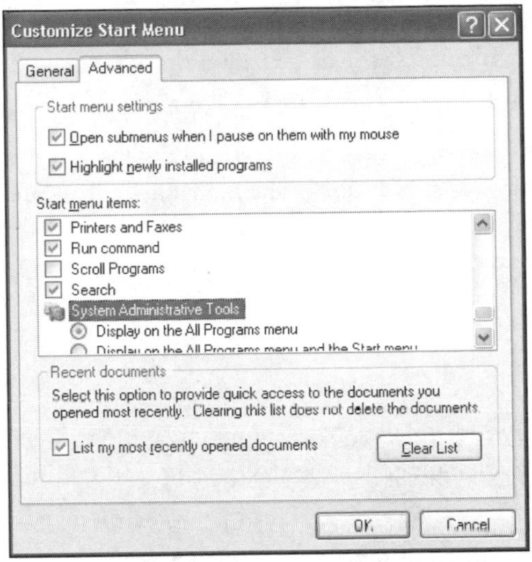

Figure 6.0   The Advanced tab of the Customize Start Menu dialog box.

➤ My Music

➤ My Network Places

➤ My Pictures

➤ Network Connections

➤ Printers and Faxes

➤ Run command

➤ Scroll Programs

➤ Search

➤ System Administrative Tools

Other Taskbar Options

The taskbar serves as a multipurpose tool to help make navigating the interface more efficient. The taskbar in Windows XP, similar to that in Windows 2000, offers several customization options. One of the new options for the taskbar is the Group Similar Taskbar Buttons checkbox, located on the Taskbar tab of the Taskbar and Start Menu Properties dialog box. This option keeps similar opened documents and files together on the taskbar while you are working on them. In addition, if the taskbar becomes too crowded with buttons, this option will automatically group all the same applications into a single button on the taskbar. When you click a grouped taskbar button, you can choose from a pop-up list of all the currently open documents for that group. When you right-click a blank area on the taskbar, you can view many customization choices. One of the available selections is Lock The Taskbar. If you select Lock The Taskbar, you cannot move or size it—it remains stationary.

The Toolbars option enables you to add one or more toolbars to the taskbar for quick access to frequently used features or applications. The available toolbars are the following:

➤ *Address*—Adds an Address box for entering URLs on the taskbar.

➤ *Links*—Adds the default Links for Internet Explorer 6 that ships with Windows XP as well as any custom links that you create.

➤ *Desktop*—Adds icons such as My Documents, My Computer, and My Network Places to the taskbar that by default appear on the desktop under Windows 2000 and Windows 9x.

➤ *Quick Launch*—Adds three icons (by default) that contain shortcuts to programs that you use most frequently. Under Windows XP, the default Quick Launch toolbar places the Show Desktop (minimizes all windows, even modal dialog boxes), Internet Explorer, and Windows Media shortcuts onto the Quick Launch Pad. You can add or remove shortcuts simply by dragging and dropping them on or off the Quick Launch toolbar.

➤ *New Toolbar*—Enables you to add your own items to a custom toolbar for placement on the taskbar.

Wireless Link

The *Wireless Link applet* enables you to control infrared, image transfer, and wireless hardware settings for your computer's infrared port, if available.

Troubleshooting and System Settings

Windows XP sports several new and enhanced troubleshooting and system configuration utilities. By combining the best of Windows 9x and Windows NT/2000, Microsoft now integrates into one product, tools that had only been available under Windows 9x and other utilities that had only been available under Windows NT/2000.

The MSCONFIG.EXE Utiilty

The MSCONFIG.EXE tool has been available under Windows 98 and Windows ME, but never under Windows NT/2000. MSCONFIG can be a very useful tool, because it combines several important configuration settings into one central utility. By default, no preconfigured icon exists for this tool. You can launch it from a command window or from the Start|Run box simply by typing

"MSCONFIG" and clicking OK. The file itself is located in %SystemRoot%\ windows\pchealth\helpctr\binaries. *A user does not need administrative privileges to run this program.* The System Configuration Utility is divided into six tabs (as shown in Figure 5.10):

➤ *General*—Enables you to work with system startup settings, the Boot.ini file, and the System Restore feature, and enables you to expand Windows XP setup files from compressed cabinet files.

➤ *SYSTEM.INI*—Enables you to directly edit the System.ini file instead of using Notepad or the SYSEDIT utility.

➤ *WIN.INI*—Enables you to directly edit the Win.ini file instead of using Notepad or the SYSEDIT utility.

➤ *BOOT.INI*—Enables you to manipulate the system's Boot.ini file, *but does not allow you to actually edit the line-item entries.* You can change the default operating system, modify the Timeout setting, verify all boot paths, and select from several predefined boot options, such as /SAFEBOOT, /NOGUIBOOT, /BOOTLOG, /BASEVIDEO (standard VGA), and /SOS (display system device drivers as they load into memory). You also have the ability to set advanced options such as /MAXMEM, /NUMPROC, /PCILOCK, and /DEBUG (see Figure 5.11).

➤ *Services*—Displays a listing of all installed services and their current status (stopped or running) on the Windows XP computer. You can enable or disable each service for the next time the computer is restarted.

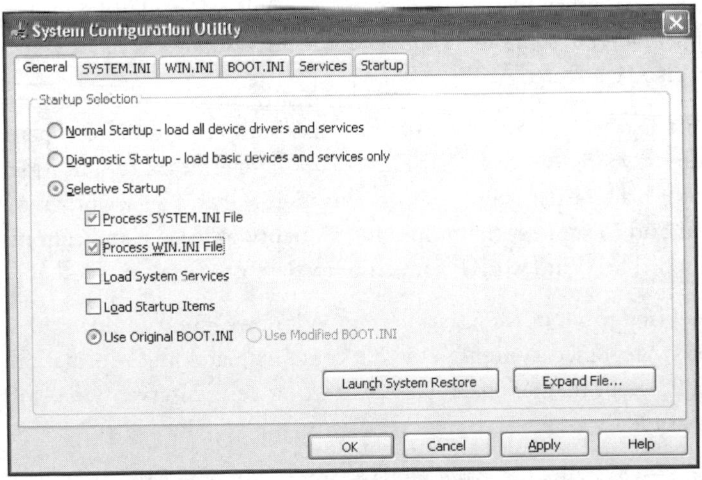

Figure 5.10   The General tab of the MSCONFIG utility.

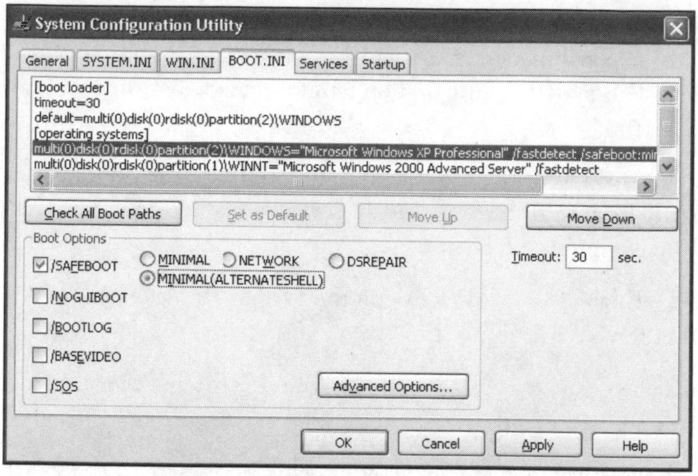

Figure 5.11 The BOOT.INI tab of the MSCONFIG Utility.

➤ *Startup*—Lists the programs and utilities that are configured to run at system startup. You can enable or disable each startup item to take effect at the next system restart.

Application Program Compatibility Support

Applications that worked under earlier versions of Windows may fail to operate properly under Windows XP for any one of a number of reasons: A program may expect older formats of Windows data, or it may expect user information, such as that in personal and temporary folders, to be in specific locations or formats. These types of compatibility issues mostly concern applications developed for Windows 95, 98, or ME, but some applications written for Windows NT 4 or Windows 2000 may also be affected.

To better support legacy applications, Microsoft has built application compatibility support directly into Windows XP. The OS uses a set of legacy application database files both to alert users about compatibility issues when a legacy program is being installed and to support the proper functionality of legacy applications when they are used. The Windows XP compatibility database files are as follows:

➤ *MigDB.inf*—Used to support migration from Windows 95–, Windows 98–, and Windows Me–based systems. This file contains matching information and flags applications that are incompatible or require user intervention prior to system upgrade.

➤ *NTCompat.inf*—Contains the same kinds of information as MigDB, but is used to support upgrades from Windows NT 4 and Windows 2000 systems (see Figure 5.12).

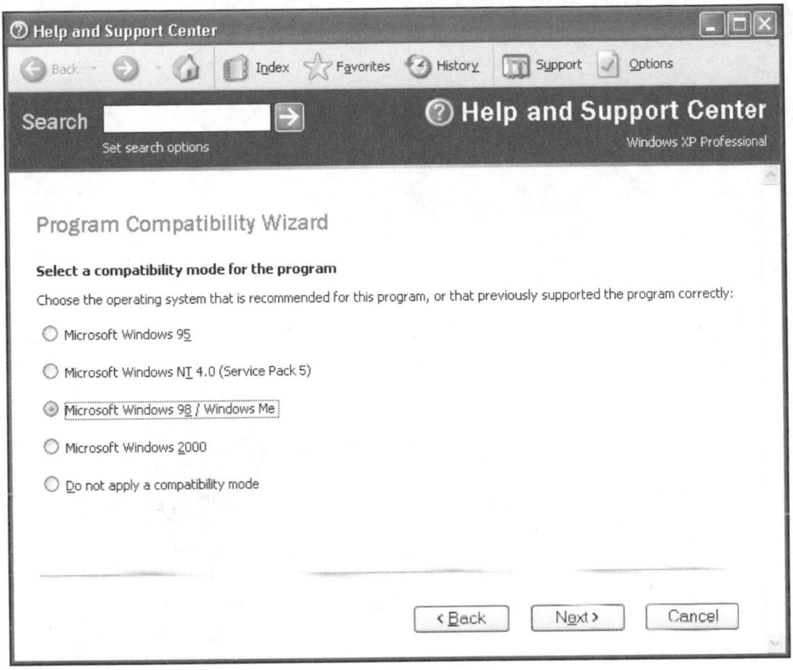

Figure 5.12 The Program Compatibility Wizard.

➤ *SysMain.sdb*—Contains both matching information and compatibility fixes. It can be found in the %Windir%\AppPatch folder.

➤ *AppHelp.sdb*—Stores only the Help messages that prompt users for patches, provides them with a URL from which to download non-Microsoft patches, or tells them where to find further information. This file is also found in the %Windir%\AppPatch folder.

A compatibility check is performed during the installation of Windows XP Professional. This check serves to warn the user of any serious compatibility problems *before* the setup routine is complete. Problematic applications are listed along with hardware compatibility information in the upgrade report generated by the setup program. Windows XP compatibility support consists of three different modes:

➤ *End-user modes*—Accessible via the Compatibility tab on the Properties dialog box for an application program shortcut or from the Program Compatibility Wizard. You can access the Program Compatibility Wizard by clicking Start|All Programs|Accessories|Program Compatibility Wizard. Users can access six basic modes through the GUI: Windows 95, Windows 98/Windows Me, Windows NT 4 with Service Pack 5, Windows 2000, Run in 256 Colors, and Run in 640×480 Screen Resolution (see Figure 5.13).

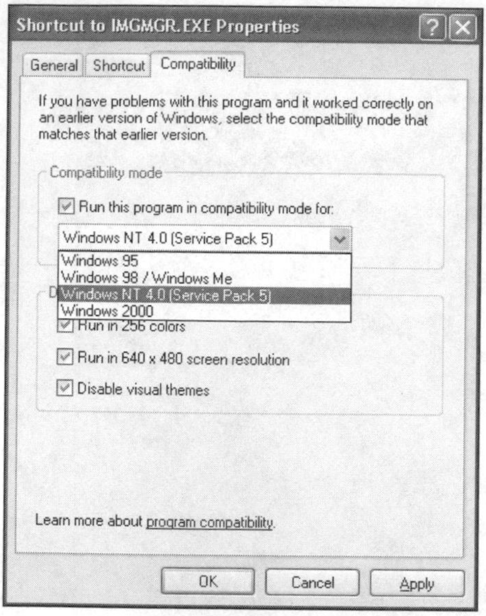

Figure 5.13 The Compatibility tab for a program shortcut's Properties dialog box.

➤ *System modes*—These include all the end-user modes listed plus a few other options that independent software vendors (ISVs), system administrators, and other IT professionals can use to control the behavior of their applications. These include the Limited User Account security mode and the Profiles mode. The Limited User Account mode is used when an application must operate under a limited security context for a particular user. The Profiles mode can be used to assist an application in determining how to interact with Windows XP user profiles. They can all be accessed and set using either the QFixApp or CompatAdmin tool, which are available from Microsoft.

➤ *Custom modes*—These modes can be created by a system administrator for a particular application or set of applications using the CompatAdmin tool. Once created, custom modes can apply only to the specific application that the user is installing, and can use any specific fix in that package.

Configuring Application Compatibility Settings

You can work with application compatibility settings from the GUI in one of two ways—use the Compatibility tab on the properties sheet for a program's executable file or its shortcut icon, or, run the Program Compatibility Wizard. Click Start|All Programs|Accessories|Program Compatibility Wizard to launch this tool. The wizard leads you through all the option settings for running an older application under Windows XP. The wizard even prompts you to test the application so that you can verify that it runs correctly. When you complete the wizard, it saves the compatibility settings as part of the program's properties, which you can access by right-clicking the program's executable file, selecting Properties, and clicking the Compatibility tab.

Windows Installer Service

Microsoft created a new method for installing applications under Windows 2000 called *Windows Installer Service Packages*. This software installation service is integrated into Windows XP. Windows Installer Service actually installs packages on a computer.

Windows Installer Service has two essential functions:

➤ It is an operating system service that is responsible for installing, removing, and updating software by asking the Windows Installer Service Package for instructions on how the application should be installed, removed, modified, or repaired.

➤ To create a standard for installing, removing, or modifying applications, you use an application programming interface (API) to communicate with Windows Installer Service about how a package should be modified after an application is installed.

After an application has been installed, Windows Installer Service checks the state of the application while it is being launched. This service provides "self-healing" capabilities to applications if they were installed as a Windows Installer Service Package. The service is always checking to see if the application needs to be repaired.

The service also helps to resolve DLL conflicts. Windows XP has devised a way to allow an application to alter the location from which DLLs are loaded, instead of having all DLLs located in the system32 directory. This helps to protect DLLs from being overwritten and from other conflicts.

Key parts of an application have a protected tag on them. A Windows Installer Service Package lists critical files that you would need to replace if they were deleted or missing. For example, executables are listed as critical files. If, for example, App1.exe were deleted, Windows Installer Service would locate App1.exe from a network server or ask the user to insert the CD-ROM that contains App1.exe. After locating App1.exe, it would be installed and the application would launch.

Windows Installer Service does a much better job of removing applications compared to previous versions of Windows. During the installation of an application, Windows Installer Service sits in the background looking at everything that is installed, where everything is installed, and what has been changed during the installation. When it comes time to uninstall an application, Windows Installer

Service knows exactly where every last component of the application is, thereby successfully uninstalling the application.

If during the installation of an application something happens and the install fails, Windows Installer Service can restart the installation from the point of failure. That may not always be the best solution, though. Windows Installer Service can also roll back everything that was installed up to the point of failure, enabling the user to start the install from scratch.

Installing Packages

A Windows Installer Package (MSI file) contains all the information necessary to tell Windows Installer Service how the application should be installed. To take advantage of the features that Windows Installer Service offers, you must install an application as an MSI file. Applications such as Microsoft Office 2000 and Office XP have their own MSI files. Software developers must design their applications to use this new service. However, existing applications can still gain some of the functionality that MSI files have to offer.

An application can repackage existing applications using third-party tools such as WinInstall LE, which is available on the Windows 2000 Professional CD-ROM but does not ship on the Windows XP Professional CD-ROM. The full-featured version, WinInstall, is published by Veritas Software. This application tracks the installation process and notes all the files that were installed, their locations, and modifications they made to the Registry. You can then customize this information and turn it into an MSI file.

A Windows Install Transform file (MST) can be used to modify and customize a Windows Installer Package (MSI file) using tools such as those found in the Microsoft Office Resource Kit. Transform files contain the customizations; MSI files themselves should never be altered. An MSP file is a Windows Installer patch file used for deploying bug fixes or service releases of a software product. Patch files cannot remove components or features, change product codes, or remove or change the names of shortcuts, files, or Registry keys. Application assignment scripts (AAS files) contain instructions associated with the publication or assignment of a Windows Installer Package.

You may be wondering what to do if you don't have an MSI file or if you can't repackage the file. Non-Windows Installer–based applications such as Install.exe and Setup.exe must use a ZAP file to publish a package. A ZAP file is just a text file with a .zap extension. The file provides information about how to install a program and the application's properties. ZAP files can only be published, *not* assigned. ZAP files cannot utilize the advanced features of using MSI files. ZAP file installations cannot use elevated installation privileges, take advantage of the unsuccessful installation rollback feature, or implement the Install On First Use Feature. The following is a basic example of how to create a ZAP file:

```
[application]
FriendlyName= "WinZip Version 7.0"
SetupCommand= \\server1\apps\winzip\WinZip70.EXE
DisplayVersion = 7.0
[ext]
ZIP =
```

Publishing MSI Packages

You typically install MSI files over the network or locally on the client computer. A common method for installing MSI files in a Windows Active Directory domain environment is to *publish* or *assign* applications to *users* through Active Directory. Users (and computers) in Active Directory can be grouped into containers called organizational units (OUs). You can create a Group Policy Object (GPO) for an OU that either publishes or assigns MSI files to users. Any users in the OU would then receive the software when they log on to their Windows XP Professional computers.

Using Group Policy to Publish or Assign Windows Installer Packages

Network administrators use Group Policy Objects (GPOs) to publish or assign application programs. When you *publish* a software application using a GPO, you are making it available to one or more *users* and the published application will follow the user(s) from workstation to workstation within an Active Directory domain. Users install a published application from the Add/Remove Programs icon in the Windows Control Panel. You may only publish an application to users. When you *assign* a software application using a GPO, you are placing an icon for that application on the Start menu and associating its file extensions. You may assign applications to both *computers* and *users*. An assigned application actually gets installed the first time that a user opens the assigned program or attempts to open a file with a file extension that is registered to that application (such as sheet1.xls, which would be associated with Microsoft Excel).

Windows Installer Packages are published or assigned to users through an Active Directory–based Group Policy. Perform the following steps to create a software installation Group Policy:

1. On an Active Directory domain controller, open Active Directory Users and Computers.

2. Select the domain to deploy the software to all users in the domain, or select a specific OU to deploy software to users just in that OU.

3. Right-click the domain or OU and choose Properties.

4. Select the Group Policy tab.

5. Click the New button to create a new Group Policy. Type a name for the Group Policy and press Enter.

6. Select the policy and then click Edit.

7. Under User Configuration, expand Software Settings. Next, right-click Software Installation and select New|Package.

8. Type the UNC path to the .MSI package on the network (for example, \\server1\ officeXP\proplus.msi, the MSI file for Microsoft Office XP Professional with Front Page).

9. Select either Published or Assigned from the Deploy Software dialog box and then click OK.

Note: If you are using a transform, you must select Advanced Published Or Assigned. (You can create a transform to install only specific applications from a software suite of applications or to customize the installation.)

10. Close the Group Policy console and click the Close button for the OU Properties dialog box.

The software Group Policy will take effect when the users of the domain or the OU log on to the network. The users can then install the software.

Publishing Applications

A software package is typically published to users when it is not mandatory that they have a particular application installed on their computer. This is a means to make the applications available for users if they decide they want to use them. Once you have created a GPO to publish a software package, you can log on to your computer and find any applications that were published from the Add or Remove Programs applet in the Windows XP Control Panel.

Select the Add New Programs button to see which applications have been published. Users can install a published application with user credentials. Windows Installer Service installs the published application with elevated privileges on behalf of users. This method provides a central location for users to install applications. This saves users from having to search for network-shared folders that contain applications they want to install.

Assigning Applications

Assigning an application is very similar to publishing one. When an application has been assigned, you can install it from Add or Remove Programs. Additionally, a shortcut for the application that has been assigned is placed on the Start|All Programs menu when users log on to their computer. The software does not get installed until users select the shortcut for the first time.

Software that has been published or assigned is also installed if users double-click a file with the extension supported by the published or assigned application.

Repairing Applications

Windows Installer Service maintains configuration information on each application installed via the Windows Installer. The MSIEXEC.exe program can repair an application in the event that one or more of an application's files become damaged or deleted. MSIEXEC.exe offers several command-line switches. The default options if no switches are specified on the command line are **/fpecms**. For more details on using MSIEXEC.exe, go to the Windows XP Professional Help and Support Center (the Windows XP help system) and search on MSIEXEC.

The syntax for the repair options for MSIEXEC.exe is

MSIEXEC /f [p] [o] [e] [d] [c] [a] [u] [m] [s] [v] *filename.msi* *[ProductCode]*

The commands in brackets are optional.

The syntax for advertising an MSI application is **MSIEXEC /j**, **MSIEXEC /ju** to advertise to the current user, or **MSIEXEC /jm** to advertise to all users of the computer. To apply a transform file (MST) to the installation, specify the **/t** switch on the command line. To write all installation errors to a log file, add the **/L*v** *logfile.txt* option to the command line.

Multiple-Language Support and Regional Options

Windows XP offers excellent support for multiple languages. It enables you to support people and companies that need to communicate in different languages by adding installed services for each input language that you need supported. Installed services include the input language and the keyboard layout for that input language. In addition, the Multilingual User Interface (MUI) Pack for Windows XP lets administrators or users specify the language for the user interface for any of the 33 supported languages. If your organization operates in a single language other than English, you can deploy one of 24 different localized versions of Windows XP Professional. For example, if you are responsible for maintaining PC desktops in a company that operates only in French, you could obtain the French-localized version of Windows XP Professional. Your users would still have support to view, edit, and print in hundreds of languages, but the interface would only be available in French.

Windows XP Multilingual User Interface Pack

The *MUI Pack* is an add-on to the English version of Windows XP Professional and is available only via volume licensing programs to corporate users. The Windows XP MUI Pack eases the deployment and maintenance of multilingual computing environments by helping administrators to define a single corporate standard for desktops worldwide, enabling administrators to apply service packs or updates one time for all supported language environments, and allowing workstations to be shared by users who speak different languages. The MUI Pack also supports users logging on anywhere and getting the user interface in their own language.

Language Options

All versions of Windows XP Professional offer support for editing documents in multiple languages. Users or administrators can install Complex Script and Right-to-Left or East Asian language options as needed. All editions of Windows XP provide support for editing documents in several different languages, and the world's languages have been categorized by Microsoft into three major Language Collections: Basic Collection, Complex Script Collection, and East Asian Collection. The Basic Collection includes support for languages spoken in Western and Central Europe and the United States, along with support for Baltic, Greek, Cyrillic, and Turkic languages. The Complex Script Collection is optionally installed depending on the localized language version of Windows XP and includes complex script support and right-to-left languages such as Thai, Hebrew, Arabic, Vietnamese, and Armenian. The East Asian Collection is always installed on the Asian versions of Windows XP Professional and can be optionally installed on all other versions. This collection includes Japanese, Korean, Simplified Chinese, as well as Traditional Chinese. The following are the three key areas of language configuration settings within the Regional and Language Options applet from the Windows XP Control Panel:

➤ Regional Options

➤ Languages

➤ Advanced

Regional Options: Locales

A *locale* is a collection of Windows XP Professional settings that reflects a specific country or region's language and cultural conventions. For example, the English (United Kingdom) and English (United States) locales reflect different countries or regions that may share a common language but use different dialects, currencies, and even date and time formats. Applications use the locale information to input the correct symbols and characters.

A locale contains information about standards and formats such as the following:

➤ Number

➤ Currency

➤ Time and date formats

➤ Localized calendar settings

➤ Character code page conversion tables

➤ Country abbreviation

The Regional Options tab on the Regional and Language Options dialog box gives you the ability to select a country from the Standards and Formats dropdown list box. When you select a country, the corresponding formats and standards for that locale are listed under Samples. To change the default settings for a locale, click the Customize button.

Configuring Regional Options

You configure all regional (locales) and language settings through the Regional and Language Options applet in the Control Panel folder (see Figure 5.14). Perform the following steps to select a regional setting for standards and formats:

1. Open the Regional and Language Options applet in the Control Panel.

2. Select the Regional Options tab.

3. Select your preferred locale from the Standards and Formats drop-down list.

4. Click OK.

No reboot is required. The change of locale takes effect immediately. In addition, applications that depend on these settings reflect the new locale immediately. As an alternative to selecting a specific locale, you can click the Customize button to individually adjust the regional settings for Numbers, Currency, Time, and Date from the Customize Regional Options dialog box. To configure Windows XP for multiple locations, click the Location drop-down arrow at the bottom of the

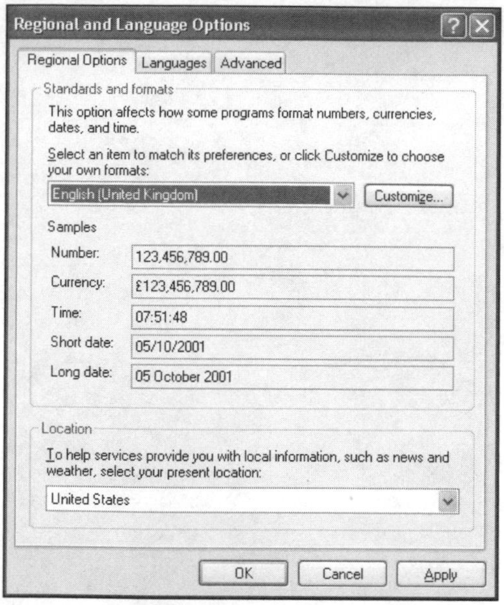

Figure 5.14 The Regional Options tab for the Regional and Language Options Control Panel applet.

Regional Options tab and choose a different country than the one listed under Standards and Formats.

Configuring Text Services and Input Languages

You can add, remove, and configure support for input languages and associated keyboard layouts from the Languages tab on the Regional and Language Options dialog box. From this tab, you can add supplemental language support for East Asian languages and/or add support for complex script and right-to-left languages. Click the Details button to change the default input language, to add or remove Installed Services for input languages, or to set preferences for the Language Bar and Key Settings, as shown in Figure 5.15.

As soon as you add an additional input language (besides the default language), an icon appears on the taskbar next to the system tray; it indicates the input language that is currently being used. A quick way to select input languages (besides assigning hot keys) is to click the Language icon on the taskbar and then select the specific input language that you need, as shown in Figure 5.16. By clicking the Key Settings button on the Text Services and Input Languages dialog box, you can assign keystroke combinations for easy switching between different installed input languages.

Note: Additional input locales are available for each new language that is installed. For example, if a user needs an input locale for Estonian, install the Baltic language setting.

Figure 5.15 The Text Services and Input Languages dialog box for the Regional and Language Options Control Panel applet.

Figure 5.16 Input language selections from clicking the Language icon on the taskbar.

Configuring Advanced Language Settings

Use the Advanced tab of the Regional and Language Options dialog box to specify the language to use for displaying menus and dialog boxes for non-Unicode applications. Use the Code Page Conversion Tables section to add or remove Code Page Conversion Tables on your Windows XP Professional computer. Click the Apply All Settings To The Current User Account And To The Default User Profile checkbox to allow all new user accounts on the computer to take advantage of all the Regional and Language Options dialog box settings that you have configured.

File Settings and Transfer Wizard

The new *File Settings and Transfer (FAST) Wizard* is a special GUI version of the User State Migration Tool that has been available in the Windows 2000 Resource Kit. The FAST Wizard makes it easier to move user configuration settings, folders, and files from one computer to another. This wizard enables users to migrate Internet Explorer, Outlook Express, and Outlook settings; store dial-up connections, phone and modem options, accessibility settings, classic desktop screen saver settings, fonts, folder options, taskbar settings, mouse and keyboard settings, sound settings, regional options, Office settings, Network Drives and Printers folders, My Documents folder, My Pictures folder, Favorites folder, Cookies folder, common Office file types; and transfer user-specified files. The FAST Wizard supports three types of transfer techniques:

➤ Via direct cable connection using an RS-232 serial port or using a parallel (LPT) port

➤ Via floppy disk or other removable media such as Zip disks

➤ Via other media or connections such as network drives or removable hard drives

The "old" computer that you want to transfer settings *from* must be running one of the following Microsoft operating systems:

➤ Windows 95

➤ Windows 98/Windows 98 Second Edition (SE)

➤ Windows Millennium Edition (ME)

➤ Windows NT 4

➤ Windows 2000

➤ Windows XP

Transferring Settings from One Computer to Another

The FAST Wizard offers several options for copying user and application settings to a new computer. The Direct Cable Connection and the Network Connection options are the fastest and easiest methods. To transfer settings and files from one computer to another using a network connection, follow these steps:

On the old computer:

1. Run the FASTWIZ.exe program from the \SUPPORT\TOOLS folder on the Windows XP Professional CD-ROM.

2. At the Welcome window, click Next to continue (see Figure 5.17).

3. Select a transfer method—to use a network connection, click either Home Or Small Office Network or Other and specify a local or network folder in which to store the captured settings. Click Next.

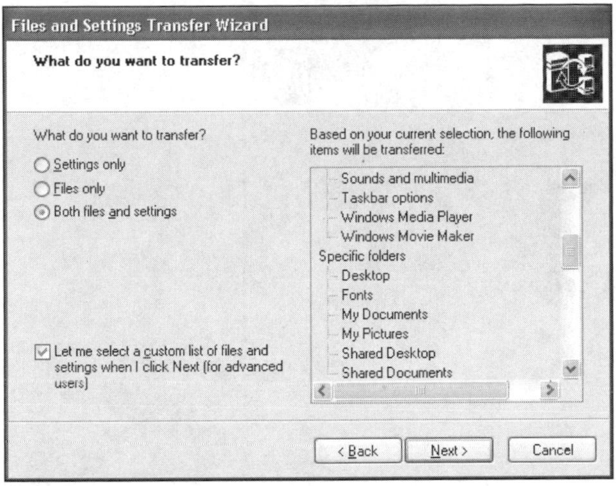

Figure 5.17 Selecting files and settings to copy using the File Settings and Transfer Wizard.

4. If the wizard displays a message about certain applications that need to be installed on the new computer before you transfer settings, take note of them and click Next again.

5. Click Finish after the wizard notifies you that it has successfully copied all the files and settings that you specified.

On the new (Windows XP) computer:

1. Click Start|All Programs|Accessories|System Tools|File And Settings Transfer Wizard.

2. At the Welcome window, click Next to continue.

3. Click New Computer and click Next.

4. Click I Don't Need The Wizard Disk, I Have Already Collected My Files And Settings From My Old Computer, and click Next again.

5. Click Other (For Example, A Removable Drive Or Network Drive) and specify the exact location of the FAST Wizard's transfer files (see Figure 5.18). Click Next. The transfer process will begin and you must wait for it to complete.

6. Click Finish to complete the wizard after it notifies you that your files and settings were transferred successfully.

7. Click Yes to log off. Log back on to have the new settings take effect.

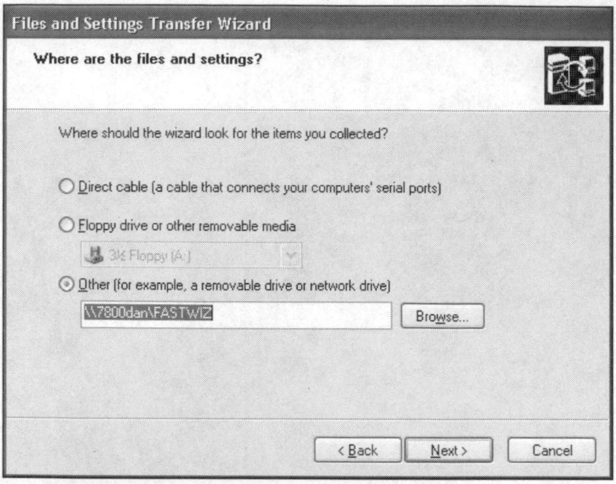

Figure 5.18 Choosing a method and location for copying settings to the new computer using the File Settings and Transfer Wizard.

Accessibility Options

Windows XP provides several options to make navigating and using the operating system easier. You can enhance the interface and keyboard settings for users who have limited vision, hearing, or manual dexterity.

Accessibility Options Applet

The *Accessibility Options applet* in the Control Panel contains several useful tabs: Keyboard, Sound, Display, General, and Mouse.

Keyboard Tab

Several options are available on the Keyboard tab to control repeat rate and key combinations:

➤ *StickyKeys*—Enables a user to press multiple keystrokes, such as Ctrl+Alt+Delete, by using one key at a time. To enable this feature, select the StickyKeys option in the Accessibility Options applet. You can also enable it by pressing the Shift key five times. At that point, a dialog box appears; it asks the user if this feature should be turned on. Click OK to enable and close the dialog box. In addition, a StickyKeys icon appears in the system tray. Double-clicking this icon opens the Accessibility Options applet.

➤ *FilterKeys*—Enables you to control the keyboard repeat rate, ignore repeated keystrokes, and control the rate at which a key repeats the keystroke if a user holds it down. You can apply granular settings to configure the repeat delay in number of seconds. If, for example, a user presses the L key and holds the key down, the letter L will repeat every x seconds (x represents the number of seconds for the repeat key delay). When you have enabled FilterKeys, an icon in the shape of a stopwatch appears in the system tray. You can also enable FilterKeys by holding down the right Shift key for eight seconds.

 If a user has enabled FilterKeys but finds that the keystrokes repeat with no delay, either someone has selected the No Keyboard Repeat setting or the repeat time delay has been configured to its lowest setting.

➤ *ToggleKeys*—When enabled, this option causes a high-pitched sound to be played when the Num Lock, Caps Lock, or Scroll Lock key is pressed. This feature is enabled via the Accessibility Options applet or by holding down the Num Lock key for five seconds.

Sound Tab

On the Sound tab, you can enable the following two sound features to help notify users of warnings and other events:

➤ *SoundSentry*—When enabled, this option displays visual warnings when Windows XP generates audible alerts. This feature is helpful for users with a hearing impairment. A user can specify which part of the screen actually flashes when a sound is generated. The options are Flash Active Window, Flash Active Caption Bar, or Flash Desktop. To enable this feature, simply select the SoundSentry checkbox. No shortcut is available for this feature.

➤ *ShowSounds*—When applications use sounds to convey messages and information, this feature displays text captions that represent those sounds. Selecting the ShowSounds checkbox enables this feature. No shortcut is available for ShowSounds.

Display Tab

The Display tab enables you to specify high-contrast colors and fonts and to set cursor options:

➤ *High Contrast*—When enabled, this feature informs applications to change the color scheme to a High Contrast scheme to allow for easier reading. For example, you can enable a white-on-black scheme, a black-on-white scheme, or one of the many other high-contrast schemes, or you can choose from any of the installed appearance schemes on your Windows XP system. Doing so enables users to adjust colors and font sizes for Windows XP and all applications. To enable this feature, select the Use High Contrast checkbox, or press the left Alt+left Shift+Print Screen keys as a shortcut. When you press these three keys at the same time, a dialog box appears that asks if the feature should be turned on.

➤ *Cursor Options*—You can adjust the Blink Rate slider bar to achieve a faster or slower blink rate for your Windows XP cursor. You can adjust the Width slider bar to set the cursor width to be narrower or wider.

Mouse Tab

The Mouse tab enables you to use the keyboard as a mouse using the following feature:

➤ *MouseKeys*—When enabled, this feature allows a user to use the numeric keypad to move the mouse pointer. The keypad can also perform single-click, double-click, and drag-mouse actions. In addition, you can assign settings that control the pointer speed. To enable this feature, select the MouseKeys checkbox or press left Alt+left Shift+Num Lock. A dialog box will appear asking whether the MouseKeys feature should be enabled. If you click the OK button, an icon will appear in the system tray to graphically indicate that the feature has been enabled.

General Tab

The General tab enables you to specify settings for all accessibility features:

➤ *Automatic Reset*—You can turn off StickyKeys, FilterKeys, ToggleKeys, SoundSentry, High Contrast, and MouseKeys after a specified idle period has passed. For example, you could assign a five-minute idle period. These six features would then all be turned off if the computer were idle for five or more minutes. To assign an idle period, click the Turn Off Accessibility Features After Idle For checkbox and select a timeout period from the drop-down list box.

➤ *Notification*—You can have the system alert you whenever an accessibility feature is turned on or off by having a warning message pop up and/or by having the system make a sound.

➤ *SerialKey Devices*—Enable this option for users who cannot use a standard keyboard and must install an alternative input device into a serial port.

➤ *Administrative Options*—You can choose Apply All Settings To Logon Desktop to allow the current user to use the Accessibility Options when logging on to the system. In addition, you can mark the checkbox Apply All Settings To Defaults For New Users to have the current settings applied to all new user accounts created by this Windows XP computer.

Accessibility Wizard

You can configure most of the accessibility options quite easily through the Accessibility Wizard. The wizard asks a series of questions to determine whether you need to configure keyboard, sound, display, and mouse accessibility features. For example, the wizard displays a sentence in varying font sizes. The user then selects a sentence with the font size that is easy to read. After the user has answered all the questions, the interface immediately changes to reflect larger fonts and any other options that were configured.

Additional Accessibility Features

Windows XP provides three additional accessibility tools that are not available in the Accessibility Options applet. These tools, which you can locate by navigating to Start|All Programs|Accessories|Accessibility, are the following:

➤ *Narrator*—This tool is for people who have low vision or who are completely vision-impaired. When enabled, the Narrator uses a synthesized voice to read what is displayed (such as menu options, text, dialog boxes, and alerts).

➤ *Magnifier*—This tool splits the screen into two portions, magnified and nonmagnified. The magnified portion of the screen magnifies the size of anything that the mouse pointer is hovering over. The nonmagnified area selects what needs to be magnified. You can increase or decrease the magnification level and the size of the magnification.

➤ *On-Screen Keyboard*—This tool displays a virtual keyboard on the Windows XP desktop. Users use the mouse pointer to press the virtual keys. They can also use a joystick with the on-screen keyboard to select keys.

Utility Manager

Utility Manager enables users to access these three accessibility tools from one central location. You can also use Utility Manager to check the status, and start or stop the tools. An administrator can configure these tools to start when Windows XP starts. Users who have administrator privileges can configure one, two, or all three of these accessibility tools to start whenever Utility Manager launches. Users can also start these accessibility utilities before logging on to the computer by pressing the Windows key+U at the Welcome screen. Narrator, the built-in text-to-speech program, starts when Utility Manager opens so that users who have impaired vision can obtain immediate access to Utility Manager. Using Utility Manager, you can tell Windows to automatically start accessibility programs each time you log on to your computer, when you lock your computer desktop, or when Utility Manager starts. For example, you can specify that Magnifier launches automatically every time that you log on to your system.

Advanced Video Display Options

Windows XP Professional offers support for enhanced video-display features not found under previous operating systems, such as Windows 2000. One of the advanced video display options is ClearType, a font-smoothing technology for mobile computers and flat-screen monitors that use LCD technology. Another advanced display feature is called Dualview, which extends the Windows XP desktop over two computer displays using a mobile PC's built-in LCD screen plus an external monitor. Each of these advanced features enhances your computing experience when working with Windows XP.

ClearType Display Support

ClearType makes reading LCD screens easier by smoothing the display of fonts for mobile computer displays and flat-screen monitors. On ordinary (non-LCD) desktop monitors, ClearType may make the display appear blurry. ClearType is not compatible with the Magnifier utility. When you select either Standard or ClearType from the Use The Following Method To Smooth Edges Of Screen Fonts drop-down list, the computer's video adapter and monitor must support at least 256 colors. High Color (24-bit) or Highest Color (32-bit) are recommended settings to use with ClearType. To enable ClearType technology:

1. Open the Display applet in the Control Panel.

2. Go to the Appearance tab and click the Effects button.

3. Mark the checkbox labeled Use The Following Method To Smooth Edges Of Screen Fonts and select ClearType from the drop-down list box.

4. Click OK to close the Effects dialog box and then click OK to close the Display Properties window and enable ClearType.

Dualview Multiple Display Support

Dualview is related to the Multi-Monitor feature that was first introduced in Windows 98. The Multi-Monitor feature is also available under Windows XP, but Dualview extends the concept both to mobile computers that have only one video card installed and to desktop computers that have one video card installed with two video output ports. With Dualview, you cannot specify which monitor is the primary display. On mobile PCs, the primary display is always the built-in LCD screen. On desktop PCs, the primary display is always the monitor connected to the first video output port. To configure Dualview support, launch the Display applet in the Control Panel *after* you have connected and powered on the second (external) monitor. From the Display Properties window, click the Settings tab and then select the Extend My Windows Desktop Onto The Monitor option.

Not all display adapters are supported under Dualview. At the time of the initial release for Windows XP, Microsoft specified only three mobile display adapters that support this feature: the S3 Savage MX, the Trident 3D, and Trident XP video adapters. Be sure to check the Microsoft Hardware Compatibility List and Microsoft Knowledge Base article Q307397 for a list of supported adapters.

Fax Features

Windows XP provides support for sending and receiving faxes via an internal or external modem or through a remote fax device connected over a network. The Windows XP Fax service is not installed by default when you first install Windows XP. To install the Fax service, open the Printers and Faxes folder from the Start menu and select Set Up Faxing from the Printer Tasks section, or select File|Set Up Faxing from the Printers and Faxes menu bar. As an alternative method, you can open the Add or Remove Programs applet from the Control Panel and select Add/Remove Windows Components. Mark the Fax Services checkbox, click Next, wait for the components to be installed, and then click Finish to complete the Windows Components Wizard.

After you have installed the Fax service, you need to configure the service using the Fax Console. The first time that you click Start|All Programs|Accessories| Communications|Fax|Fax Console after installing the Fax service, you'll be greeted by the Fax Configuration Wizard, which assists you in setting up your computer to send and receive faxes. Enter your Sender Information, specify which fax device to use, and configure fax send and receive options. By default, the Fax service is configured to allow users to only send faxes, not receive them. Mark the Enable Receive checkbox to turn on the fax-receiving feature. Enter your Transmitting Subscriber Identification (TSID) number and your Called Subscriber Identification (CSID) number through the Fax Configuration Wizard.

The wizard also asks you for routing options—whether to print a received fax on a certain print device and/or whether to store an *additional* copy of each fax within a specific folder. After you complete the wizard, the Fax Console window opens. You can access the Fax Console window by selecting Start|All Programs|Accessories| Communications|Fax|Fax Console, by right-clicking the Fax icon in the Printers and Faxes folder and selecting Open from the pop-up menu, or simply by double-clicking the Fax icon in the Printers and Faxes folder.

To fax a document, follow these steps:

1. Click File|Send A Fax from the Fax Console, click File|Print from an application program, or click File|Send To|Fax Recipient.

2. If you select File|Print from an application, select the fax printer and then click OK to submit the fax. For any of the three options you choose, the Send Fax Wizard launches. The wizard enables you to enter the recipient's name and fax number, cover page information, and other configurations. Figure 5.19 shows the Send Fax Wizard.

The Fax Console: Managing Faxes, Settings, and Options

The *Send Fax Wizard* gathers some information, such as the sender's name and fax number. This information is gathered from settings contained in the properties of the Fax Console. To work with fax settings, right-click the Fax icon in the Printers and Faxes folder and select Properties. You can access the Printers and Faxes window from the Start menu or by clicking the Printers and Faxes icon in the Control Panel. The Fax Properties windows displays five tabs:

➤ *General*—Enables you to assign a location, comment, and configure specific fax features.

➤ *Sharing*—Fax sharing is not supported under Windows XP Professional.

➤ *Devices*—Enables you to specify fax device settings and send and receive options for each device.

➤ *Tracking*—Enables you to specify a fax device to monitor and to set send and receive notification options.

➤ *Archives*—Enables you to specify whether to archive incoming and/or outgoing faxes and where to store those archives.

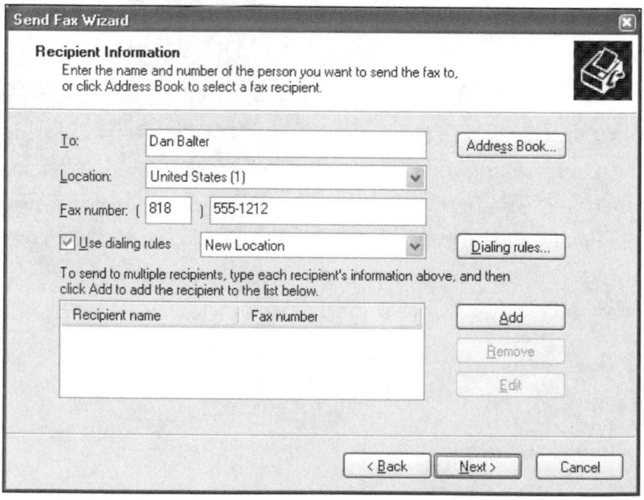

Figure 5.19 The Send Fax Wizard.

To work with Fax Security permissions, right-click the Fax icon in the Printers and Faxes folder, press and hold down the Ctrl key, and then select Properties. The Fax Properties window will appear with an additional tab—*Fax Security*. By default, three groups have Fax Security permissions: Administrators, Everyone, and Interactive. Under default permissions, Interactive users can send documents as low-, normal-, or high-priority faxes. They can view fax jobs, manage fax jobs, view the Fax service configuration, and view incoming fax and outgoing fax archives. Administrators, by default, can additionally manage the Fax service configuration plus manage incoming and outgoing fax archives.

You use the Fax Console itself to troubleshoot and monitor fax transmissions. You can perform the following functions with the Fax Console:

➤ Send a fax

➤ Receive a fax

➤ Change sender information

➤ Manage personal cover pages

➤ Check fax printer status

➤ Run the Fax Configuration Wizard to reconfigure the Fax service

➤ Open the Fax Properties window

➤ Launch the Fax Monitor

The Fax Console window displays four folders for organizing faxes:

➤ Incoming

➤ Inbox

➤ Outbox

➤ Sent Items

If faxes aren't being sent or received, verify that a user has permission to use the fax device and make sure the fax device is configured to send and receive faxes. If those settings are correct and faxes are still not being sent or received, stop and restart the Fax service.

Scheduled Tasks

With the advent of Internet Explorer (IE) 5 (and later versions), Microsoft introduced the Scheduled Tasks folder, which replaced the older AT scheduler service. Under Windows XP, Microsoft has further refined this GUI utility that is designed to automatically run tasks at specified times. This utility is quite similar to the Windows 98 Task Scheduler.

You can open the Scheduled Tasks folder from the Control Panel by double-clicking the Scheduled Tasks icon or by clicking Start|All Programs|Accessories| System Tools|Scheduled Tasks. Unlike Windows 2000 Professional, the Scheduled Tasks folder is *not* shared by default. You still can, however, create a task on a Windows XP computer and then copy it to another Windows XP computer. This is helpful if a similar task needs to run on many computers. By copying the task from one computer to another, you don't have to re-create it multiple times.

Creating a Task

To create a new task, open the Scheduled Tasks folder and double-click the Add Scheduled Task icon to launch the Scheduled Task Wizard. This wizard steps users through the process of selecting a program, batch file, or script to run automatically at a scheduled time. The Scheduled Tasks service runs under the security context of the Windows XP local system account. However, for each scheduled task, you must specify a user account and password that determines the security context under which each scheduled task will execute. You still have the option of using the legacy **AT** command via the command line to set up scheduled events. Events scheduled using the **AT** command may be run under a different security context by selecting Advanced|AT Service Account from the Scheduled Tasks folder's menu. You can then specify a particular user account whose security context will be used for *all* events that are scheduled using the **AT** command. Perform the following steps to create an automated task using the Scheduled Tasks folder:

1. Double-click the Add Scheduled Task icon and then click Next at the Scheduled Task Wizard window.

2. Select the application program that you want to schedule from the list, or click Browse to locate the appropriate program and click Next.

3. Choose how often the task should run and then click Next. The options are as follows:

   ➤ Daily

   ➤ Weekly

   ➤ Monthly

   ➤ One Time Only

   ➤ When My Computer Starts

   ➤ When I Log On

4. Depending on what you chose in Step 3, users may have to set up what time of the day, what days of the week, or what months of the year the task should run. Choose the appropriate options and then click Next.

5. The next step requires you to enter a username and password. The username must have the right to run the selected application. Click Next.

6. The last dialog box of the wizard asks users whether or not to open the Advanced Properties dialog box after the task has been created. The Properties dialog box enables the user to edit the schedule, delete the task if it is not scheduled to run again, stop the task, start the task during idle periods, and not start the task if the computer is running on batteries. Also, you can assign security permissions to the task to control which users can modify the task options. Click Finish.

After you have closed the Scheduled Task Wizard and the Advanced Properties sheet, an icon that represents the task is created. Users can double-click a task to view and configure its advanced properties after they have created the task, as shown in Figure 5.20.

Troubleshooting Tasks

The Scheduled Task Wizard makes it very easy to create tasks. However, sometimes, tasks do fail to run. The most common reason for this is that the wrong

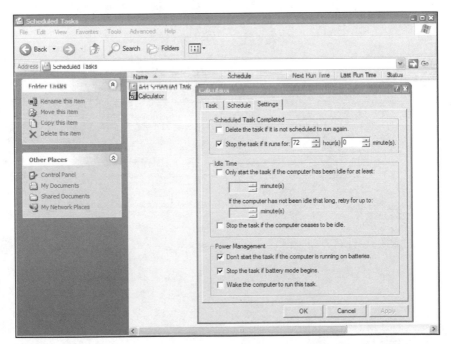

Figure 5.20   The Scheduled Tasks window displaying the advanced settings for a task.

username or password was entered for the task. If a task failed, verify that you entered the correct username and password on the task.

Another area where an incorrect account can cause problems is if a task has been created for old 16-bit applications. It may fail to run if the system account is used on the Task Service. If an error relating to the Task Service is generated, change the account used to run the service. Use the **AT** command to create a scheduled event and select Advanced|AT Service Account from the Scheduled Tasks folder's menu. You can then specify a particular user account whose security context will be used for *all* events that are scheduled using the **AT** command. If the task still won't run, stop and restart the Task Service. You can configure it to restart automatically if it fails. To do so, go to Start|Control Panel|Administrative Tools and open the Services console. Right-click the Task Scheduler service and choose Properties. Click the Recovery tab and specify actions for service failures.

Practice Questions

Question 1

> As a network administrator for your company, you log on to a Windows XP Professional workstation computer. You suspect that several different users are logging on to this workstation, so you want to view all the user profiles that are stored locally. You look in the c:\Documents and Settings folder, but no user profiles exist. The c:\ drive is the only volume on the computer. What has happened to all the user profiles for this system?
>
> ○ a. The system is configured to use only roaming profiles.
>
> ○ b. The system is configured to use only mandatory roaming profiles.
>
> ○ c. Fast User Switching is turned on, so user profiles exist only on a domain controller.
>
> ○ d. The user profiles are located in %systemroot%\Profiles.

Answer d is correct. The computer must have been upgraded from Windows NT Workstation 4. Upgraded systems continue to store user profiles in the same folder as the Windows NT 4 default location—%systemroot%\Profiles. All profiles get stored on the local computer, including roaming and mandatory roaming profiles, so answers a and b are incorrect. Fast User Switching has nothing to do with user profile locations.

Question 2

> WRKSTN3 is a Windows XP Professional computer that is connected to a workgroup named SALESDEPT. All computers in the workgroup are configured with default settings. A user named Alexis makes sure that she shares her GROUPDOCS folder with the network and leaves the default settings for caching. A user named Brendan, working on WRKSTN7, connects to Alexis' GROUPDOCS share. He right-clicks one of the files in the shared folder to make it available offline; however, that option does not exist on the pop-up menu. How can Brendan solve this problem?
>
> ○ a. Make sure that his computer's DNS settings are correct.
>
> ○ b. Turn off Fast User Switching.
>
> ○ c. Run the Network Settings Wizard to enable Offline Files.
>
> ○ d. Make the computer a member of a Windows 2000 Server or a Windows .NET Server Active Directory domain.

Answer b is correct. The Offline Files feature, also known as Client-side Caching, is disabled whenever Fast User Switching is turned on. DNS settings are used to insure proper TCP/IP name resolution, so answer a is incorrect. Answer c is incorrect because the Network Settings Wizard does not configure Offline File support. A Windows XP Professional computer does not need to be a member of a domain for Offline Files to function; therefore, answer d is also incorrect.

Question 3

Alison always works on several Excel files and Word documents at the same time. She's tired of having so many buttons cluttering her taskbar. What can Alison do to improve the organization of all the buttons representing all of her open application programs on the taskbar?

- ○ a. Enable Dualview display.
- ○ b. Enable the Taskbar Switching option.
- ○ c. Turn on the Group Similar Taskbar Buttons option in Control Panel|Display Properties.
- ○ d. Add the Quick Launch toolbar to the taskbar.

Answer c is correct. By enabling the Group Similar Taskbar Buttons feature, all running application buttons will be grouped together on the taskbar. Answer a is incorrect because Dualview is related to the Multiple Monitor option that supports two displays from one video output port. Answer b is incorrect because no Taskbar Switching option exists. The Quick Launch toolbar adds icons to the taskbar for starting application programs, not for grouping program buttons that are already running. Therefore, answer d is incorrect.

Question 4

As a system administrator, you need to modify the Windows XP Professional boot settings so that the computer will generate a boot log file each time that it restarts. You can't remember the exact boot option switch and you'd prefer not to edit the Boot.ini file directly. How can you accomplish this task?

- ○ a. Run the SYSEDIT utility.
- ○ b. Run the MSCONFIG utility.
- ○ c. Boot into Safe Mode and use the BOOTVRFY utility.
- ○ d. Use RegEdit to modify the Registry data for the value WindowsBoot under HKEY_LOCAL_MACHINE\SOFTWARE\Microsoft\Windows NT\CurrentVersion\Winlogon.

Answer b is correct. The MSCONFIG utility allows you to set a variety of system startup options, including adding command-line switches to the Boot.ini file. The SYSEDIT tool does not allow you to modify any part of the Boot.ini file, so answer a is incorrect. The **BOOTVRFY.exe** command does not support editing the Boot.ini file, so answer c is incorrect. Values for the Boot.ini file are not stored in the Windows XP Registry, so answer d is also incorrect.

Question 5

You want to use two different legacy applications under Windows XP Professional. One application requires a Windows NT 3.51 environment. The other program requires a Windows NT 4 Service Pack 6a environment. Which application program can Windows XP provide legacy support for?

- ○ a. The Windows NT 4 Service Pack 6a application.
- ○ b. The Windows NT 3.51 application.
- ○ c. Both applications can be properly supported.
- ○ d. Neither application can be properly supported.

Answer d is correct. Windows NT 3.51 applications are not supported by Windows XP Compatibility Support. Although Windows NT 4 Service Pack 5 applications are supported, Windows NT 4 Service Pack 6a–specific programs are not explicitly supported. Other supported environments are Windows 95/98/ME/2000.

Question 6

Jon is a network administrator who has created a ZAP file for a legacy 16-bit application. He wants to assign the application to the users in the Marketing OU within his company's Active Directory domain. How can Jon accomplish this using a software Group Policy?

- ○ a. Create a Computer Configuration policy to assign the application using the ZAP file.
- ○ b. Create a User Configuration policy to assign the application using the ZAP file.
- ○ c. Create an MSI Windows Installer Package file for the legacy application using third-party repackaging software.
- ○ d. Create an administrative template to add to the User Configuration settings for the Group Policy of the OU.

Answer c is correct. You can only publish, not assign, legacy applications using ZAP files. Answer a is incorrect because applications installed using ZAP files can only be published; therefore, you cannot use ZAP files for software Group Policies under Computer Configuration. Answer d is incorrect because you create software Group Policies from the Software Settings folder of the Group Policy MMC snap-in, not by using additional Administrative Templates.

Question 7

Zachary, a network administrator, wants to use the Windows Installer Program executable to advertise a new application to all users on a standalone Windows XP Professional workstation. The name of the program's installer package is App1.msi. He'd like to modify the installation with a transform file he's created by the name of App1.mst. He also wants to log any and all error messages to a file named Logfile.txt on the root of the c:\ drive. How can he accomplish this?

○ a. Use the following command line syntax: **MSIEXEC.exe /jm c:\setup\app1.msi /t c:\setup\app1.mst /L*v c:\logfile.txt**.

○ b. Run setup.exe to install the application and specify **/transform=c:\setup.app1.msi /log=c:\logfile.txt** as command line arguments for the setup program.

○ c. Create an MST Windows Installer Package Transform file for the legacy application using third-party repackaging software. Specify **MSIEXEC /t c:\setup\app1.mst** on the command line.

○ d. Use the following command line syntax: **MSIEXEC.exe /fm c:\setup\app1.msi /t c:\setup\app1.mst /L*v c:\logfile.txt**.

Answer a is correct. The syntax for **MSIEXEC.exe** is: **MSIEXEC [options] msi_filename.msi [/t transform_filename.mst] [/L*v driveletter:\logfile_name.txt]** where parameters in square brackets are optional. Answer b is incorrect because you need to run **MSIEXEC** to advertise applications using the command line option **/ju** to advertise to the current user or **/jm** to advertise to all users of the computer. Answer c is incorrect because you must specify both the Windows Installer Package (.msi) file as well as the Transform file, and no logging is specified. Answer d is incorrect because the **/fm** option means to perform a repair of an existing application by re-writing all computer specific registry entries.

Question 8

Which computer configuration transfer techniques are supported by the File And Settings Transfer (FAST) Wizard? [Check all correct answers]

- ❑ a.   Serial port connections (one RS-232 cable connected between two computers)
- ❑ b.   Parallel port connections (one LPT cable connected between two computers)
- ❑ c.   USB connections (one USB cable connected between two computers)
- ❑ d.   Zip or Jaz drive cartridges
- ❑ e.   IEEE 1394 (FireWire) connections (one FireWire cable connected between two computers)
- ❑ f.   Infrared connections
- ❑ g.   Wireless 802.11 connections

Answers a, b, d, f, and g are all correct. The FAST Wizard supports a direct cable connection using either serial ports or parallel ports and appropriate cables. Removable media are supported, which includes Zip and Jaz drives. Infrared connections are supported indirectly because you can copy the FAST Wizard's files via an infrared connection. Wireless networking support is also included, because *any* network connection will work. Answer c is incorrect because a direct USB connection between two computers is not supported. Answer e is incorrect because a direct FireWire connection between two computers is also not supported.

Need to Know More?

 Microsoft Corporation. *Administering Microsoft Windows XP Professional Resource Kit Documentation.* Redmond, WA: Microsoft Press, 2001. ISBN 0-73561-485-7. This all-in-one reference is a compilation of technical documentation and valuable insider information that computer-support professionals and administrators can reference to install, customize, and support Windows XP.

 Bott, Ed and Carl Siechert. *Microsoft Windows XP Inside Out.* Redmond, WA: Microsoft Press, 2001. ISBN 0-73561-382-6. This book offers timesaving tips, troubleshooting techniques, and workarounds. It focuses on techniques such as taking advantage of the rich integration of devices, applications, and Web services in Windows XP.

 Minasi, Mark. *Mastering Windows XP Professional.* Alameda, CA: Sybex, Inc., 2001. ISBN 0-78212-981-1. This book provides in-depth coverage of installing, configuring, and administering Windows XP Professional.

Search the Microsoft TechNet CD (or its online version through **www.microsoft.com**) using keywords such as "Offline Files", "MSCONFIG", "Fax", "Scheduled Tasks", and "Windows Installer Service".

Installing, Configuring, and Troubleshooting Hardware Devices and Drivers

6

Terms you'll need to understand:

✓ Universal Serial Bus (USB)

✓ Universal Plug and Play (UPnP)

✓ Advanced Power Management (APM)

✓ Advanced Configuration and Power Interface (ACPI)

✓ Add Hardware Wizard

✓ Device Manager

✓ Driver signing

✓ FireWire, or IFEE (Institute of Electrical and Electronics Engineers) 1394

✓ Driver Rollback

✓ Smart cards and smart card readers

✓ Multilink support

✓ Digital Versatile Disc (DVD)

✓ Infrared Data Association (IrDA) devices

✓ Network adapter, or network interface card (NIC)

✓ Multiple monitor support

✓ Video adapter

✓ Power mode options

✓ Hardware profiles

✓ Multiprocessor support

Techniques you'll need to master:

✓ Installing, configuring, and troubleshooting hardware devices and drivers

✓ Updating drivers and system files

✓ Rolling back drivers to a previous version

✓ Managing and troubleshooting driver signing

✓ Managing and troubleshooting various types of input/output (I/O) devices

✓ Configuring and troubleshooting Multilink support for a dial-up connection

✓ Configuring and troubleshooting multiple monitor support, hardware profiles, and multiprocessor support

Implementing, Managing, and Troubleshooting Hardware

Hardware includes any physical device that is connected to your computer and that your computer's processor controls. This includes equipment that was connected to your computer when it was manufactured, as well as equipment that you added later. Modems, disk drives, CD-ROM drives, printers, network cards, keyboards, display adapter cards, and USB cameras are all examples of devices. Windows XP offers full support for Plug and Play (PnP) devices and partial support for non-Plug and Play devices. "Partial" support means only one thing: Some work, others do not. Sometimes, testing a device may be the only sure way to determine if it will work with Windows XP. Always consult the latest Windows XP Hardware Compatibility List (HCL) before installing a new device.

For a device to work properly with Windows XP, software (a device driver) must be installed on the computer. Each hardware device has its own unique device driver(s), which the device manufacturer typically supplies. However, many device drivers are included with Windows XP and work even *better* with Windows XP than the manufacturer's own driver. Look for Microsoft to recommend using its own drivers for a given device rather than those of the manufacturer, because Microsoft understands the inner workings of the operating system better than anyone else.

Because Windows XP controls your computer's resources and configuration, you can install PnP hardware devices and many other devices *without* restarting your computer. Windows XP automatically identifies the new hardware and installs the drivers it needs. If you are using an older computer that does not support Advanced Power Management (APM), or the current standard, Advanced Configuration and Power Interface (ACPI), you must set up the device manually and restart your computer when installing new hardware devices. For now, you need ACPI-compliant hardware to make your Windows XP hardware setup experience smoother. We will discuss APM and ACPI in greater detail later in this chapter.

Universal Plug and Play—The Enhanced PnP Standard

Starting with Windows 95, Microsoft has built hardware device PnP capabilities directly into the operating system, which makes installing and configuring peripherals on a personal computer a great deal easier. The Universal Plug and Play (UPnP) standard extends this simplicity to include the entire networked environment, enabling discovery and control of networked devices and services, such as network-attached printers, Internet gateways, and even consumer electronics equipment. UPnP is more than just a simple extension of the PnP peripheral model. It is designed to support zero-configuration, "invisible" networking, as well as automatic device discovery for a vast array of different types of devices developed by a wide range of manufacturers.

With UPnP, a device can dynamically join a network, obtain an IP address, communicate its capabilities, and discover the presence and capabilities of other devices—completely automatically. Devices can subsequently communicate with each other directly, further enabling transparent peer-to-peer networking (with no user intervention).

The scope of UPnP is large enough to encompass many exciting implementations, such as home automation, printing and imaging, audio and video entertainment, kitchen appliances, and automobile networks.

UPnP takes advantage of open, standard protocols such as TCP/IP, HTTP, and XML, enabling it to seamlessly fit into existing networks. Because UPnP is based on a distributed, open network architecture, it is not dependent on any specific operating system or programming language. UPnP does not require the use of specific APIs (application programming interfaces—calls to operating system functions) that applications must use. Operating system developers are free to create their own APIs that will meet their customers' needs. Devices on a UPnP network can be connected using any type of connection, including radio frequency (RF, wireless), phone lines, power lines, IrDA (Infrared), Ethernet (LAN), and IEEE 1394 (FireWire). In other words, any medium that can be used to connect network-enabled devices together can enable UPnP. An important issue to consider is whether the network connection being utilized supports the bandwidth required for the intended use.

Installing, Configuring, and Managing Hardware

You configure devices on Windows XP machines using the Add Hardware icon in the Control Panel or by clicking the Add Hardware Wizard button from the Hardware tab on the System Properties window. Keep in mind that in most cases, you need to be logged on to the local machine as a member of the Administrators group to add, configure, and remove devices.

Installing PnP or UPnP Devices

Connect the device to the appropriate port or slot on your computer according to the device manufacturer's instructions. You may need to start or restart your computer, but this happens *much less often* than it did with previous versions of Windows. If you are prompted to restart your computer, do so. Windows XP should detect the device and then immediately start the Found New Hardware Wizard.

Installing Non-PnP Devices

To install a device that is not Plug and Play, follow these steps:

1. Click the Add Hardware icon in the Control Panel.

2. Click Next and then click Yes, I Have Already Connected The Hardware. Click Next again.

3. Scroll down the Installed Hardware list to the very bottom, select Add A New Hardware Device, and click Next.

4. Select one of the following options:

   ➤ *Search For And Install The Hardware Automatically (Recommended)*—Do this if you want Windows XP to try to detect the new non–Plug and Play device you want to install.

   ➤ *Install The Hardware That I Manually Select From A List (Advanced)*—Do this if you know the type and model of the device you are installing and you want to select it from a list of devices.

5. Click Next, and then follow the instructions on your screen.

6. You may be prompted to restart your computer, depending on the type of non–Plug and Play device you just installed.

Tips on Installing Devices

Using a PnP driver to install a *non*–PnP device may provide *some* PnP support. (Don't get your hopes up.) Although the system cannot recognize the hardware and load the appropriate drivers on its own, PnP can oversee the installation by allocating resources, interacting with Power Options in the Control Panel, and recording any issues in the Event Log.

If your computer is connected to a network, network policy (Group Policy) settings may prevent you from installing any devices on your computer. To add and set up a *non*–PnP device connected directly to your computer, you *must* be logged on as an administrator or a member of the Administrators group.

If an administrator has already loaded the drivers for the device, you can install the device *without* having administrator privileges.

Troubleshooting Installed Hardware Devices

To troubleshoot an installed device, perform the following steps:

1. Click the Add Hardware icon in the Control Panel.

2. Click Next and then click Yes, I Have Already Connected The Hardware. Click Next again.

3. Select the installed hardware device that you are having trouble with and click Next.

4. Follow the subsequent instructions on your screen. To launch a troubleshooter from the Windows XP Help and Support Center, click Finish and go through the troubleshooter's steps to try to resolve the problem.

Device Driver Updates

Keeping drivers and system files updated ensures that your operating system performs at its peak level. Microsoft recommends using *Microsoft* digitally signed drivers whenever possible. The Driver.cab cabinet file on the Windows XP CD-ROM contains all the drivers that Windows XP ships with. This cabinet file is copied to the %systemroot%\Driver Cache\i386 folder when Windows XP is installed. Whenever a driver is updated, Windows XP looks in the Driver.cab file first. The location of Driver.cab is stored in a Registry key and can be changed via HKLM\Software\Microsoft\Windows\CurrentVersion\Setup\DriverCachePath.

Automatic Device Drivers Updates

Windows XP supports automatic updating of device drivers and other critical operating system files. In Windows XP Professional, you must be logged on as either the local administrator or as a member of the Administrators group to install updated components or to change Automatic Updates settings. If your computer is a member of a Windows Active Directory domain, Group Policy settings may further restrict your ability to modify these settings and install updated components.

To turn on, turn off, or modify Windows XP Automatic Updates notification settings, follow these steps:

1. Log on the computer as the administrator or as a member of the Administrators group.

2. Right-click the My Computer icon from the Start menu and select Properties.

3. Click the Automatic Updates tab.

4. Select from one of three available Notification Settings buttons, as shown in Figure 6.1:

➤ Download The Updates Automatically And Notify Me When They Are Ready To Be Installed (default).

➤ Notify Me Before Downloading Any Updates And Notify Me Again Before Installing Them On My Computer.

➤ Turn Off Automatic Updating. I Want To Update My Computer Manually.

5. Click OK to accept the new settings.

After the successful installation of certain updated components, Windows XP may prompt you to restart the computer. As a best practice, you should always restart the machine immediately as instructed. Failure to follow these instructions may result in an unstable or unusable computer.

If you choose not to install one or more updates that have been downloaded to your PC, Windows XP deletes those update files from your computer. If you later decide that you want to install any of the updates that you have previously declined, click the Restore Declined Updates button on the Automatic Updates tab. If any of the previously declined updates still apply to your system, Windows XP will display them the next time that the system notifies you of newly available updates.

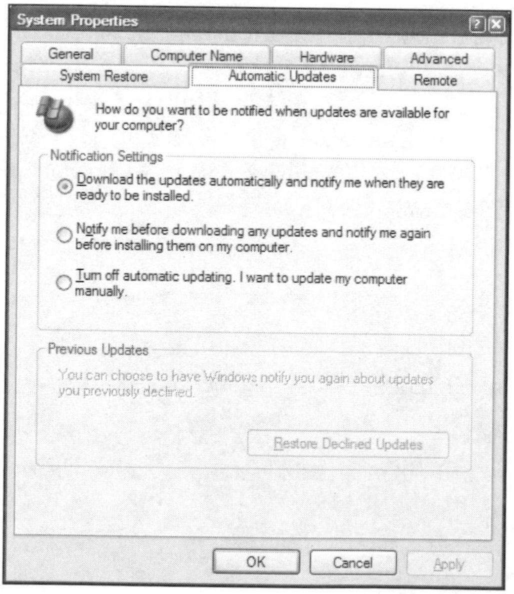

Figure 6.1 The Automatic Updates tab of the System Properties dialog box.

Manually Updating Drivers

To update individual drivers, perform the following steps:

1. Right-click My Computer from the Start menu, or open the System icon from the Control Panel.

2. From the System Properties window, click the Hardware tab and click the Device Manager button.

3. Perform one of these steps:

   ➤ Right-click the device that you want to update, select Update Driver from the pop-up list, and follow the on-screen instructions.

   ➤ Right-click the device that you want to update and select Properties from the pop-up list. Click the Update Driver button and follow the on-screen instructions.

You can use the Driver Verifier utility to troubleshoot and isolate driver problems. It is *not* enabled by default. To use it, you must enable it by running the Driver Verifier Manager part of Verifier.exe by executing it from the GUI first, or by changing a Registry setting and then restarting the computer. When you run the Driver Verifier tool (Verifier.exe) from the command line, it offers several options for troubleshooting drivers. For example, if you run the command **verifier /all**, it verifies all the drivers installed on the system. See the Microsoft Knowledge Base article Q244617 for more information.

Updating Your System Files Manually from the Windows Update Web Site

Windows Update is a Microsoft database of items such as drivers, patches, help files, and Internet components that you can download to keep your Windows XP installation up to date. Using the Product Updates section of Windows Update, you can scan your computer for outdated system files, drivers, and help files, and automatically replace them with the most recent versions.

To update your system files using Windows Update, follow these steps:

1. Go to Windows Update at **http://windowsupdate.microsoft.com/**. (This Web site address may change at any time, because Microsoft is prone to shuffling Web page locations frequently.) You can also open Windows Update by clicking Start|All Programs|Windows Update.

2. Click Yes if you are prompted about whether to allow ActiveX or other components from Microsoft Corporation to be downloaded to your system.

3. Click Scan For Updates.

4. Follow the on-screen instructions to review and install all or some of the applicable updates to your system.

 You may be required to be logged on as an administrator or a member of the Administrators group to complete the installation of certain Windows Update components or procedures. If your computer is connected to a network, network (Group Policy) settings may prevent you from updating any system files or drivers.

The Driver Rollback Feature

Driver Rollback is a new feature of Windows XP. If you encounter problems with a hardware device after you have installed an updated driver for it, you can now easily revert back to the previously installed software driver for that device by using the Driver Rollback option. To restore a device driver back to its previously installed version, open Device Manager, right-click the device you are having trouble with, and select Properties. Click the Driver tab and then click the Roll Back Driver button, as shown in Figure 6.2.

Managing and Troubleshooting Device Conflicts

You configure devices using the Add Hardware Wizard in the Control Panel or from the Hardware tab on the System Properties window, which can also be accessed from the Control Panel. Each resource—for example, a memory address

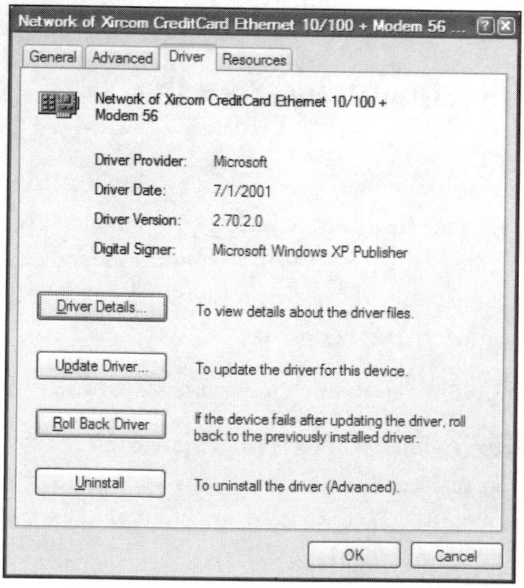

Network of Xircom CreditCard Ethernet 10/100 + Modem 56 ... ? ⊠

| General | Advanced | Driver | Resources |

Network of Xircom CreditCard Ethernet 10/100 + Modem 56

Driver Provider: Microsoft
Driver Date: 7/1/2001
Driver Version: 2.70.2.0
Digital Signer: Microsoft Windows XP Publisher

[Driver Details...]   To view details about the driver files.

[Update Driver...]   To update the driver for this device.

[Roll Back Driver]   If the device fails after updating the driver, roll back to the previously installed driver.

[Uninstall]   To uninstall the driver (Advanced).

[OK]   [Cancel]

Figure 6.2   The Driver tab on a hardware device's Properties dialog box provides the Roll Back Driver button option.

range, inters pt request (IRQ), input/output (I/O) port, Direct Memory Access (DMA) channel, and so on—that is assigned to your device must be unique or the device won't function properly. For PnP devices, Windows XP attempts to ensure automatically that these resources are configured properly. If a device has a resource conflict or is not working properly, you see next to the device name a yellow circle with an exclamation point inside it.

Occasionally, two devices require the same resources, but keep in mind that this does not always result in a device conflict—especially if the devices are PnP- or UPnP-compliant. If a conflict arises, you can manually change the resource settings to be sure that each setting is unique. Sometimes, two or more devices can share resources, such as interrupts on Peripheral Connection Interface (PCI) devices, depending on the drivers and the computer. For example, you may see Windows XP share IRQ 9 among multiple devices on many mobile computers.

When you install a non-PnP device, the resource settings for the device are not automatically configured. Depending on the type of device you are installing, you may have to manually configure these settings. The appropriate range of settings should be supplied in the user's manual that ships with your device.

 Generally, you should *not* change resource settings manually, because when you do so, the settings become fixed, and Windows XP then has less flexibility when allocating resources to other devices. If too many resources become fixed, Windows XP may not be able to install new PnP devices.

Managing and Troubleshooting Driver Signing

Microsoft is promoting driver signing for devices as a method to advance the quality of drivers and to reduce support costs for vendors and total cost of ownership (TCO) for customers. Windows XP uses a driver-signing process to make sure drivers have been certified to work correctly with the Windows Driver Model (WDM) in Windows XP. If you are having problems, it may be because you are using a driver not correctly written for Windows XP. To identify such drivers, use the Signature Verification tool. This utility, Sigverif.exe, helps you to quickly identify unsigned drivers if a device is not working or if you want to ensure that all drivers in use are properly signed.

Using the Signature Verification Tool

To use the Signature Verification tool, perform the following steps:

1. Start Sigverif.exe (Start|Run|Sigverif.exe).

2. Click the Advanced button.

3. Select the option Look For Other Files That Are Not Digitally Signed.

4. Mark the checkbox to include subfolders.

5. Click the Logging tab to make any changes for the log file, and then click OK. Note the log file name: Sigverif.txt.

6. Click Start to run the utility.

Configuring Driver-Signing Options from the GUI

Windows XP offers a good degree of control over whether users can install signed or unsigned drivers, or both, for a chosen device. Signed drivers are software device drivers that have been tested by Microsoft for compatibility with Windows XP (or other versions of Windows). Microsoft embeds a digital signature into each device driver that successfully passes its compatibility test. Therefore, unsigned drivers are drivers that either have not been tested or that are actually not compatible with specific versions of Windows. To change the system's driver-signing options, right-click My Computer, select Properties, click the Hardware tab, and click the Driver Signing button. Select one of the following actions for Windows XP to take when you attempt to install an unsigned device driver (as shown in Figure 6.3):

➤ *Ignore*—Selecting this setting ignores whether a driver is signed or not, allowing the user to proceed with the driver installation.

➤ *Warn*—Selecting this setting issues a dialog box warning if an unsigned driver is encountered during a device installation. It gives the user the option of continuing with the installation or terminating the device's setup.

➤ *Block*—This option is the most restrictive of the three settings. To prevent the installation of any unsigned device drivers, this is the option you should select.

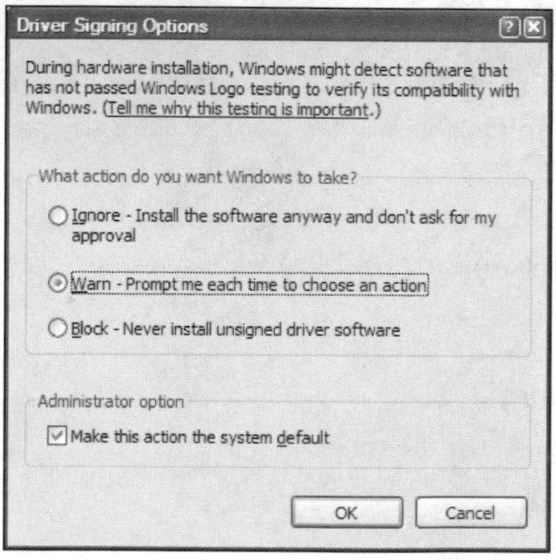

Figure 6.3 The Driver Signing Options dialog box.

Controlling the Use of Signed and Unsigned Drivers Using Group Policy

Instead of modifying the driver-signing options from the GUI, you can manipulate Windows XP driver-signing options using a Group Policy Object (GPO) setting under the Local Computer Policy. This GPO setting is located in Computer Configuration|Windows Settings|Security Settings|Local Policies|Security Options. The policy is named Devices: Unsigned Driver Installation Behavior. The three choices for this unsigned driver behavior policy (as shown in Figure 6.4) are the following:

➤ *Silently Succeed*—Selecting this setting ignores whether a driver is signed or not, allowing the user to proceed with the driver installation.

➤ *Warn But Allow Installation*—Selecting this setting issues a dialog box warning if an unsigned driver is encountered during a device installation. It gives the user the option of continuing with the installation or terminating the device's setup.

➤ *Do Not Allow Installation*—This option is the most restrictive of the three settings. To prevent the installation of any unsigned device drivers, this is the option you should select.

Using Cameras and Scanning Devices

The *Scanners And Cameras applet,* part of the Control Panel, enables you to configure properties for scanners and digital cameras. If you have a PnP camera or scanner, Windows XP detects it and installs it automatically. You can use the Scanners And Cameras applet to install other scanners, digital still cameras, digital video cameras, and image-capturing devices.

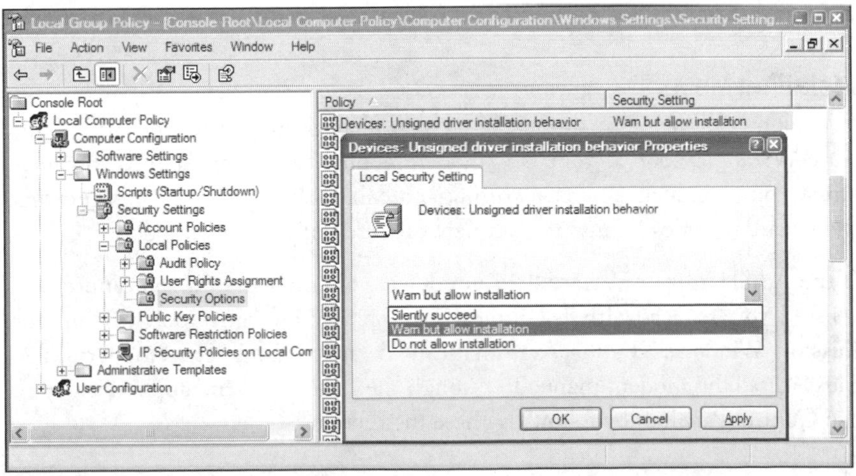

Figure 6.4 The Group Policy settings for unsigned driver installation behavior.

After a device is installed, Scanners And Cameras can link it to a program on your computer. For example, when you push Scan on your scanner, you can have the scanned picture automatically open in the program you want.

Installing Scanners or Digital Cameras

To install a scanner or digital camera, perform the following steps:

1. Open Scanners And Cameras in the Control Panel.

2. Click Add An Imaging Device, and then follow the instructions on the screen.

Remember that you must be logged on as an administrator or a member of the Administrators group to complete this procedure. If your computer is connected to a network, network policy settings may prevent you from installing devices.

Testing Scanners or Digital Cameras

To test a scanner or digital camera, perform the following steps:

1. Open Scanners And Cameras in the Control Panel.

2. Right-click the scanner or camera you want to test, and then click Properties.

3. On the General tab, click Test Scanner Or Camera.

An on-screen message tells you if the camera or scanner completed the test successfully. You can also check your Event Log to see if the test was successful.

Using Modems

At one time or another, if you've used a computer, you have probably used a modem to connect to your office or to an Internet service provider (ISP) using a dial-up connection. This section details what you need to know about modem support and troubleshooting in Windows XP Professional.

Installing Modems

If Windows XP launches the Install New Modem dialog box for the Add Hardware Wizard as soon as your new modem is physically connected to your machine, you are in luck! You have nothing more to do than follow the prompts that the wizard provides (if any) to complete the setup of your new modem.

If the Add Hardware Wizard does not detect your modem or if you cannot find it listed, you are faced with installing an unsupported modem. Good luck on your mission. Windows XP *cannot* automatically detect certain internal modems. You must install the modem manually through the Add Hardware applet located in the Control Panel, or by following these instructions:

1. Open Phone And Modem Options in the Control Panel.

2. (Optional) If you are prompted for location information, enter dialing information for your location and click OK.

3. Click the Modems tab and then click the Add button.

4. Follow the instructions for the Add Hardware Wizard.

Using Multilink Support

Multilinking, or multiple-device dialing, allows you to combine two or more modems or integrated services digital network (ISDN) adapters into one logical link with increased bandwidth. The Network And Dial-up Connections feature performs PPP Multilink dialing over multiple ISDN, X.25, or modem lines. The feature combines multiple physical links into a logical bundle, and the resulting aggregate link increases your connection bandwidth. For example, you could use Multilink to combine the power of two 33.6Kbps modems to achieve approximately a 67.2Kbps dial-up connection. Detailed information on Multilink support under Windows XP can be found in the Microsoft Knowledge Base article Q307849.

Configuring Multilink

To configure Multilink, perform the following steps:

1. Open the Control Panel and double-click the Network Connections icon.

2. Right-click the connection on which you want to enable Multilink, and then select Properties.

3. On the General tab, mark the checkbox next to each device that you want to use with this connection, and click OK.

Multilink Tips

If you use multiple devices to dial a server that requires callback, only one of your Multilinked devices is called back, because only one phone number is stored in a user account. Therefore, only one device connects, all other devices fail to complete the connection, and your connection loses Multilink functionality. You can avoid this problem if the Multilinked phonebook entry is to an ISDN line or modem with two channels that have the same phone number.

To dial multiple devices, both your connection and your remote access server must have Multilink enabled.

Troubleshooting Modems

You can verify that your modem is working properly by clicking the Query Modem button found on the Diagnostics tab of the Properties dialog box for the modem (the Query Modem button is also accessible from the modem's Properties dialog box in Device Manager). Another option for troubleshooting a modem problem is to use the Troubleshoot button, which is also available from the modem's Properties dialog box, but you should use this only as a last resort, because it just invokes the Windows XP Help and Support Center and runs you through a basic troubleshooting checklist.

Configuring and Managing Compact Disc (CD) and Digital Versatile Disc (DVD) Devices

Windows XP supports a variety of CD read-only memory (CD-ROM), CD recordable (CD-R), CD rewritable (CD-RW), DVD read-only memory (DVD-ROM), DVD recordable (DVD-R), DVD rewritable (DVD-RW), and DVD random access memory (DVD-RAM) drives and disc formats. Check with the most recent Hardware Compatibility List (HCL) or your hardware vendor to see if your CD or DVD device will work with Windows XP.

If the CD or DVD device is PnP-compliant, you can rely on Windows XP to detect the device and install the appropriate drivers, as well as allocate system resources for the device. If you are using a CD or DVD drive that is not PnP-compliant, use the Add Hardware applet in the Control Panel to install the drivers and assign resources for the device.

The Windows XP Compact Disc File System (CDFS) reads CDs that are formatted according to the ISO 9660 standard. Windows XP also supports the Joliet standard, which is an extension to the ISO 9660 standard. Joliet supports Unicode characters and supports a folder hierarchy extending deeper than eight levels of subfolders. Windows XP also offers integrated support for writing data directly onto CD-R and CD-RW media without requiring any third-party CD-burning software such as Roxio's CD Creator by Adaptec.

A DVD drive needs either a hardware or software decoder to play movies on your Windows XP computer, even if you want to use the built-in Windows Media Player as the preferred playback device. Of course, the computer also requires a Windows XP–compatible sound card and video display card with their respective drivers to play multimedia DVD titles. Your decoder must be Windows XP–compliant to play movies after you install Windows XP if you upgrade from a previous Windows version. You do not need a decoder for reading data DVDs.

The Universal Disk Format (UDF)

UDF is based on the ISO 13346 standard, and Windows XP uses this standard for reading removable media such as DVDs; CD-ROMs; CD-Rs; CD-RWs; write once, read many (WORM) discs; and magneto-optical (MO) discs. Windows XP supports UDF versions 1.02, 1.50, 2.0, and 2.01 through the Udfs.sys driver. You can format DVD-RAM discs with the FAT32 file system under Windows XP; however, you cannot natively format DVD-RAM discs using NTFS, nor can you write directly to UDF volumes (including DVD-RAM discs) without using a third-party application.

Installing, Configuring, and Troubleshooting USB Devices

Windows XP offers built-in support for many Universal Serial Bus (USB) devices. Because all USB devices fully support Plug and Play, USB peripherals can be easily connected to (and disconnected from) Windows XP computers that have USB ports by using standard USB cables and connectors. In theory, USB devices can be safely connected and disconnected while the computer is running. Windows XP detects USB devices when they are plugged into the PC and attempts to install the proper device driver for each detected USB device. If Windows XP cannot locate an appropriate device driver, it will prompt you to insert a driver diskette or CD-ROM from the manufacturer of the device.

Overview: USB Controllers, USB Hubs, and Daisy-Chaining USB Devices

To support USB, a computer needs either a USB host controller to be built into the motherboard or a USB controller add-in adapter card to be installed. The USB host controller directs all USB traffic and also serves as a hub that USB devices connect to. Additional (external) USB hubs may be connected to enable multiple USB devices to be connected to the host controller, also known as the root hub. Hubs are either self-powered or bus-powered. Some devices, like mice and keyboards, can function fine when plugged into bus-powered USB hubs. Other devices, such as external hard drives, printers, and scanners, may require more power than bus-powered hubs can provide. Connect these kinds of USB devices to self-powered hubs. USB supports up to a maximum of 127 devices connected to one USB host controller (root hub) with no more than seven tiers (seven layers of USB hubs daisy-chained together). No more than five external hubs may be used in one physical chain of hubs. Each device can be no more than five meters away from the port of the hub that it is connected to.

USB devices that install and function properly under Windows 98, Windows Me, or Windows 2000 are not guaranteed to work flawlessly under Windows XP. Be sure to check for upgraded drivers before you upgrade a computer to Windows XP. Verify that USB peripherals are on the Windows XP HCL or check with the USB device vendor regarding compatibility with Windows XP.

Viewing Power Allocations for USB Hubs

To view power allocations for USB hubs, perform the following steps:

1. Open Device Manager.

2. Expand the entry for Universal Serial Bus Controller.

3. Right-click USB Root Hub, and then click Properties.

4. On the Power tab, view the power consumed by each device in the Attached Devices list.

 As mentioned previously, hubs for USB devices are either self-powered or bus-powered. Self-powered hubs (hubs plugged into an electrical outlet) provide maximum power to the device, whereas bus-powered hubs (hubs plugged only into another USB port) provide minimum power. Devices that require a lot of power, such as cameras, should be plugged into self-powered hubs. Universal Serial Bus Controller appears only if you have a USB port on your computer. The Power tab appears only for USB hubs.

Troubleshooting USB Devices

Sometimes, when you install a USB device on a computer, the computer might start functioning poorly or the system might even freeze entirely. The first step to take in such a scenario is to power off the computer, wait about 60 seconds, and then power it back on. If that doesn't help, try one or more of the following steps:

➤ Follow the manufacturer's installation instructions, which may require that you run a setup program before connecting the USB device to the computer.

➤ Connect the device to a different computer to verify that it is not defective.

➤ Plug the device directly into a USB hub on the back of the computer instead of plugging it into a USB hub.

➤ Look at the Windows XP Event Log for USB-related error messages.

➤ Check Device Manager to verify that all USB devices on the Universal Serial Bus Controller's tree are operating correctly.

➤ Check whether one or more USB devices are drawing more power (more than 500 milliamps) than the bus or hub can provide. Use a separate power adapter for high-power-consumption devices (if available) or use a self-powered USB hub for such devices.

➤ Try replacing the USB cables.

➤ Make sure that no more than five hubs are connected in one continuous chain.

Using Network Adapters

You can install network adapters using the Add Hardware applet in the Control Panel. You can make changes to the binding order of protocols and the network provider order by selecting the Advanced Settings option under the Advanced menu of the Network Connections window (accessed from the Network Connections icon in the Control Panel). Each network adapter has its own separate icon in the Network Connections folder. Right-click a network adapter icon to set its properties, install protocols, change addresses, or perform any other configuration changes for the connection.

Using Infrared Data Association (IrDA) Devices

Windows XP supports IrDA protocols that enable data transfer over infrared connections. This provides an infrastructure that allows other devices and programs to communicate with Windows XP through the IrDA interface. Windows XP installs with the Wireless Link tool, which transfers files to or from another computer that runs Windows XP, Windows 2000, or Windows 98.

Windows XP's PnP architecture automatically detects and installs the infrared component for computers with built-in IrDA hardware. For computers without built-in IrDA hardware, a user can attach a serial port IrDA transceiver to a serial COM port and use the Add Hardware Wizard to install the device under Windows XP.

After an infrared device is installed, the Wireless Link icon appears in the Control Panel. When another IrDA transceiver comes in range, the Wireless Link icon appears on the desktop and on the taskbar. You can then send a file over the infrared connection with any of the following actions:

➤ Specify a location and one or more files using the Wireless Link dialog box.

➤ Use drag-and-drop operations to move files onto the Wireless Link icon on the desktop.

➤ Right-click any selection of files on the desktop, in Windows Explorer, or in My Computer, and then click Send To Infrared Recipient.

➤ Print to a printer configured to use an infrared port.

In addition to sending or printing files, you can create a network connection that connects two computers using the infrared port. You can use this capability to map shared drives on a host computer and work with files and folders in Windows Explorer or My Computer. You can also use an infrared network connection to connect directly to another computer without modems, cables, or network hardware.

Enabling or Disabling Receiving Files via IrDA Connections

To enable or disable receiving files using an infrared link, perform the following steps:

1. Open the Wireless Link applet in the Control Panel.

2. On the Infrared tab, mark or clear the checkbox labeled Allow Others To Send Files To Your Computer Using Infrared Communications and click OK.

Wireless Local Area Networking (WLAN) Support

Windows XP Professional includes support for the IEEE standard 802.11 for WLANs. WLAN support under Windows XP includes a new roaming feature that enables the operating system to detect a move to a new wireless access point and forces reauthentication to verify appropriate network access at a new location. By default, WLAN support under Windows XP uses the zero client configuration feature to automatically configure and use IEEE 802.11 authentication on the wireless network. You can configure WLAN networking settings by opening the Network Connections window from the Control Panel, right-clicking the wireless connection you want to modify, and selecting Properties. From the wireless connection's Properties dialog box, you can enable or disable the automatic wireless configuration, set up or disable IEEE 802.11 authentication, and specify a connection to a wireless network with or without a Wired Equivalent Privacy (WEP) Network Key.

Installing, Configuring, and Supporting Video Display Adapters

When Windows XP is being installed, your system's BIOS selects the primary video display adapter based on PCI slot order. You can install and configure any additional video adapters you want to use with your system by using the Display applet or the Add Hardware applet in the Control Panel. Video problems often occur for one of three reasons:

➤ An incorrect video device driver has been installed.

➤ The display settings for the video adapter have been configured incorrectly.

➤ The graphics hardware acceleration setting has been set too high.

If you select an incorrect video driver or if you configure a video driver's settings incorrectly, your Windows XP system may become unusable or even display the dreaded blue screen of death (BSOD). Fortunately, Windows XP offers several ways to restore the previous (functional) video display settings. When you restart the computer, press the F8 key as Windows XP is restarting, which enables you to select one of the following options from the Windows Advanced Options menu:

➤ *Safe Mode*—Enables you to manually update, remove, or even roll back the problem video driver.

➤ *Enable VGA Mode*—Enables you to boot the system using standard VGA 640×480 resolution with just 16 colors. You can then correct any incorrect video settings.

➤ *Last Known Good Configuration (your most recent settings that worked)*—Enables you to revert the system's Registry and device driver configurations back to how they were the last time that a user started the computer and logged on successfully.

Configuring Multiple-Monitor Support

Windows XP continues to support multiple-monitor functionality that increases your work productivity by expanding the size of your desktop. Multiple displays still must use PCI or Accelerated Graphics Port (AGP) port devices to work properly with Windows XP. PCI or AGP video adapters that are built into the motherboard are also supported under the multiple-monitor feature.

 You can connect up to 10 individual monitors to create a desktop large enough to hold numerous programs or windows.

You can easily work on more than one task at a time by moving items from one monitor to another or by stretching them across numerous monitors. Edit images or text on one monitor while viewing Web activity on another. Or you can open multiple pages of a single, long document and drag them across several monitors to easily view the layout of text and graphics. You could also stretch a spreadsheet across two monitors so you can view numerous columns without scrolling.

One monitor serves as the primary display. This is the monitor on which you see the Logon dialog box when you start your computer. In addition, most programs display their windows on the primary monitor when you initially open them. You can set different resolutions and different color depths for each monitor. You can also connect multiple monitors to individual graphics adapters or to a single adapter that supports multiple outputs.

Arranging Multiple Monitors

To arrange multiple monitors, perform the following steps:

1. Open the Display applet in the Control Panel.

2. Click the monitor icons and drag them to positions that represent how you want to move items from one monitor to another, and then click OK or Apply to view the changes (see Figure 6.5). You can also click the Identify button to briefly flash the monitor number on each monitor's screen as assigned by Windows XP.

The icon positions determine how you move items from one monitor to another. For example, if you are using two monitors and you want to move items from one monitor to the other by dragging left and right, place the icons side by side. To move items between monitors by dragging up and down, place the icons one above the other. The icon positions do not have to correspond to the physical positions of the monitors. You can place the icons one above the other even though your monitors are side by side.

Changing the Primary Monitor

To change the primary monitor, perform the following steps:

1. Open the Display applet in the Control Panel.

2. On the Settings tab, click the monitor icon that represents the monitor you want to designate as the primary one.

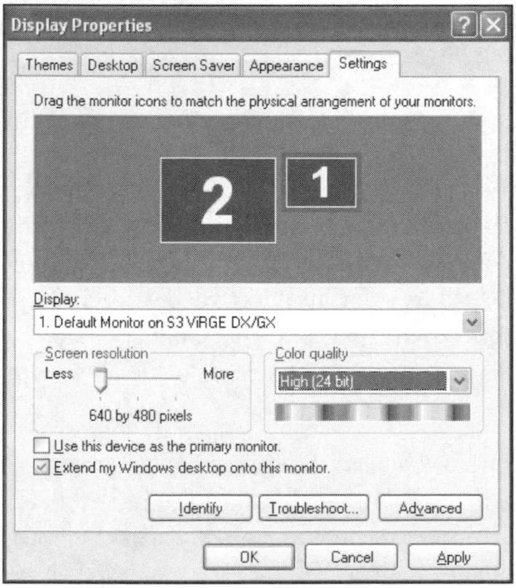

Figure 6.5 The Display Properties dialog box enables you to configure multiple monitors when multiple video adapters are installed.

3. Select the Use This Device As The Primary Monitor checkbox (see Figure 6.5). This checkbox is unavailable when you select the monitor icon that is currently set as your primary monitor.

The monitor that is designated as the primary monitor displays the Logon dialog box when you start your computer. Most programs display their window on the primary monitor when you first open them.

Moving Items between Monitors or Viewing the Same Desktop on Multiple Monitors

To move items between monitors, or to view the same desktop on multiple monitors, perform the following steps:

1. Open the Display applet in the Control Panel.

2. On the Settings tab, click the monitor icon that represents the monitor you want to use in addition to your primary monitor.

3. Select the Extend My Windows Desktop Onto This Monitor checkbox (refer to Figure 6.5). Selecting this checkbox enables you to drag items across your screen onto alternate monitors. You can also resize a window to stretch it across more than one monitor.

Troubleshooting Multiple Displays

The default refresh frequency setting is typically 60Hz, although your monitors may support a higher setting. A higher refresh frequency might reduce flicker on your screens, but choosing a setting that is too high for your monitor may make your display unusable, and may even damage your hardware.

If your refresh frequency is set to anything higher than 60Hz and your monitor display(s) goes black when you start Windows XP, restart the system in Safe Mode. Change your refresh frequency for all monitors to 60Hz. You may need to double-check this setting in your Unattended Installation script file, commonly called Unattend.txt. Again, set it to 60Hz.

Multiple-display support in Windows XP presents some challenges when you are dealing with some older applications and DOS applications. If you start a DOS application on your multiple-monitor Windows XP machine, and then both of your screens flicker and completely go dark, you can fix the problem without much difficulty. Multiple-display support allows you to adjust the display settings so that your application runs and is viewable on both monitors. First, you may need to restart your system. Then, you select Safe Mode at the F8 startup menu. Finally, after you can see the contents of your desktop, you can configure the DOS application to run in a window and change your Display settings from Default to Optimal.

Removable Storage Support

Windows XP Professional provides removable storage services for applications and network administrators that enhance the sharing and management of removable media hardware like backup tape drives, optical discs, and automated (robotic) media pool libraries. Removable storage and media support in Windows XP precludes the need for third-party software developers to write custom application programs to support each different type of removable media device. In addition, removable storage services allow organizations to leverage their investment in expensive removable storage equipment by having multiple removable storage applications share these devices.

Windows XP Removable storage implements a set of APIs that enable third-party software solutions to catalog all removable media, such as DVDs, tapes, and optical discs. Both offline (shelved) as well as online (housed in a library) media can be cataloged. Removable storage organizes media using media pools. These media pools control access to the removable media, categorize the media according to each type of use, and permit the media to be shared by applications. Removable storage tracks the application programs that share the removable media. Removable storage is logically structured into five basic components: media units, media libraries, media pools, work queue items, and operator requests. You manage Removable storage from the MMC snap-in named, strangely enough, Removable storage.

Managing Tape Devices

Windows XP provides comprehensive control of tape devices. You can back up or restore from tape devices, enable or disable specific tapes in your library, insert and eject media, and mount and dismount media. Tape devices are not the only media that the Windows Backup program supports. You can back up to network shares, to local hard drives, or to removable media such as Zip disks or Jaz disks. Backing up to tape is still very popular, however, despite some of its drawbacks.

 The Windows XP Backup utility does not support backing up directly to CD-R or CD-RW media. You can copy files directly to a CD-R or a CD-RW disc, or you can copy a backup file that was created by the Backup utility to a CD-R or CD-RW disc. During a restore, the Windows XP Backup program can read directly from CD-R or CD-RW media to perform the restore procedure.

If the tape device is PnP-compliant, you can rely on Windows XP to detect the device and install the appropriate drivers, as well as allocate system resources for the device. If you are using a tape device that is not PnP-compliant, use the Add

Hardware applet in the Control Panel to install the drivers and assign resources for the device. Use Device Manager to enable, disable, or edit settings for any tape device.

Upgrading a System from One to Two Processors (CPUs)

Windows XP Professional supports a maximum of two processors; Windows XP Home supports only one processor. When more than one processor is present in the computer when the operating system is installed, Windows XP Professional uses symmetric multiprocessing (SMP). However, if Windows XP is installed with just one CPU present and you want to add a second processor later, you must use the Update Hardware Wizard to enable support for multiple processors.

To install support for multiple CPUs, perform the following steps:

1. Right-click My Computer and then select Properties.

2. Click the Hardware tab, and then click the Device Manager button.

3. Expand the Processors node and note the type of support you currently have.

4. Right-click the icon for the currently installed processor and select Update Driver to launch the Update Hardware Wizard. Alternatively, you can right-click the icon for the currently installed processor, select Properties, and then click the Driver tab, as shown in Figure 6.6. Next, click the Update Driver

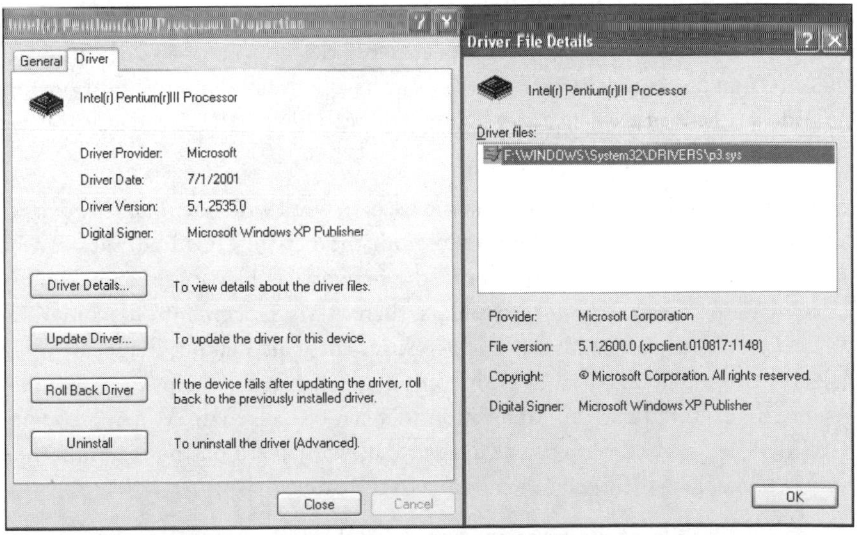

Figure 6.6 The Processor Properties dialog box enables you to add support for a second processor by clicking the Update Driver button.

button from this dialog box, and you will also launch the Update Hardware Wizard. Follow the on-screen instructions to load the proper Hardware Abstraction Layer (HAL) for the CPU that you have added.

5. You must restart the computer for the change to take effect.

 You can use this procedure only to upgrade from a single-processor HAL (Hardware Abstraction Layer) to a multiple-processor HAL. If you use this procedure to change from a standard HAL to an ACPI HAL (for example, after a BIOS upgrade) or vice versa, unexpected results may occur, including an inability to boot the computer. If you upgrade the BIOS from supporting APM to ACPI, you need to reinstall Windows XP so that the operating system will properly support that type of upgrade.

Mobile Computing

PCMCIA (PC Card) adapters, USB ports, IEEE 1394 (FireWire), and infrared devices are fully supported in Windows XP. You manage these through Device Manager. Support is provided in Windows XP Professional for both the APM and the ACPI power management standards, which are covered near the end of this chapter.

Hot (computer is fully powered) and cold (computer is in Suspend mode) docking and undocking are fully supported for computers with a Plug and Play BIOS. Hibernate (complete power down while maintaining the state of open programs and connected hardware) and Suspend (deep sleep with some power) modes are also supported for extending battery life.

When you install a PC Card, USB, or infrared device, Windows XP automatically recognizes and configures it (if it meets Plug and Play specifications). If Windows does not have an entry in its Driver.cab file for the new hardware, you are prompted to supply one.

Support for Offline Files enables mobile users to work with documents and other files even when they are disconnected from the network. Offline Files can be synchronized when users reconnect to the network. Folder Redirection enables administrators to redirect system folders, such as My Documents, to store users' files at an alternate location on a network server while making it appear to the users that the folder is local to their computer. This feature helps to ensure that users' data is stored in a central location that can be backed up. When used with Offline Files, mobile users can take their data with them on the road and then synchronize their files when they return to the office.

Equipping mobile computers with Smart Cards and implementing the NTFS file system in conjunction with the Encrypting File System decreases the likelihood of confidential data being compromised if the computer is stolen, lost, or simply placed into the wrong hands.

Managing Hardware Profiles

A *hardware profile* stores configuration settings for a collection of devices and services. Windows XP can store different hardware profiles so that users' needs can be met even though their computer may frequently require different device and service settings depending on the circumstances. A good example is a portable computer that is used in an office with a docking station. The computer is then undocked so the user can travel with the notebook PC. These two situations require different power management settings, possibly different network settings, and various other hardware configuration changes.

You can enable and disable devices in particular profiles through their Properties dialog box in Device Manager, as shown in Figure 6.7. You manage services using the Services snap-in for the MMC, as shown in Figure 6.8. You create and manage hardware profiles using the System applet in the Control Panel, or by right-clicking My Computer and choosing Properties. Once inside the System applet, go to the Hardware tab and click the Hardware Profiles button to open the Hardware Profiles dialog box, shown in Figure 6.9. At installation, Windows XP creates a single hardware profile called Profile 1 (Current), which you can rename. You are prompted to select a hardware profile at system startup only when two or more hardware profiles are stored on your machine. You can create

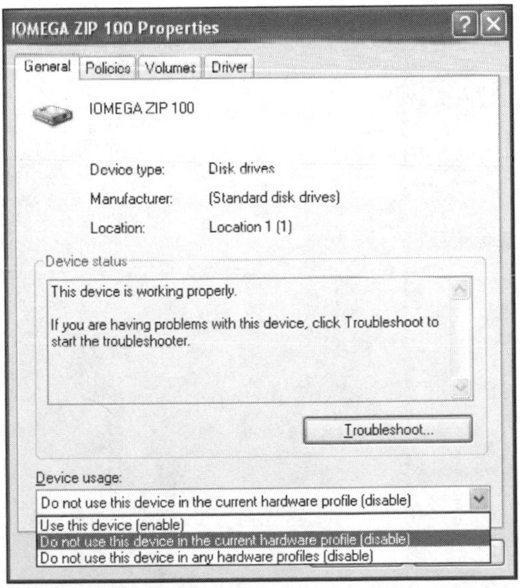

Figure 6.7   The Properties dialog box for a device allows you to enable or disable it for the current hardware profile using the Device Usage dropdown list box.

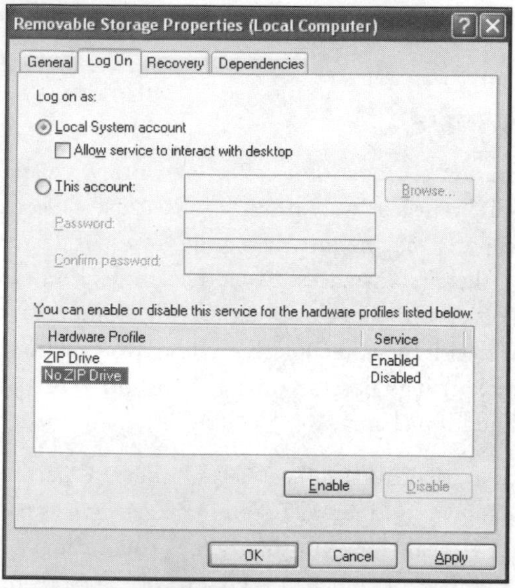

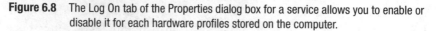

Figure 6.8 The Log On tab of the Properties dialog box for a service allows you to enable or disable it for each hardware profiles stored on the computer.

and store as many hardware profiles on your machine as you like. You select the desired hardware profile at Windows XP startup to specify which device and service configuration settings you need for the current session.

To configure a hardware profile, copy the default profile and rename it appropriately. Restart the computer and select the profile you want to configure, if you are

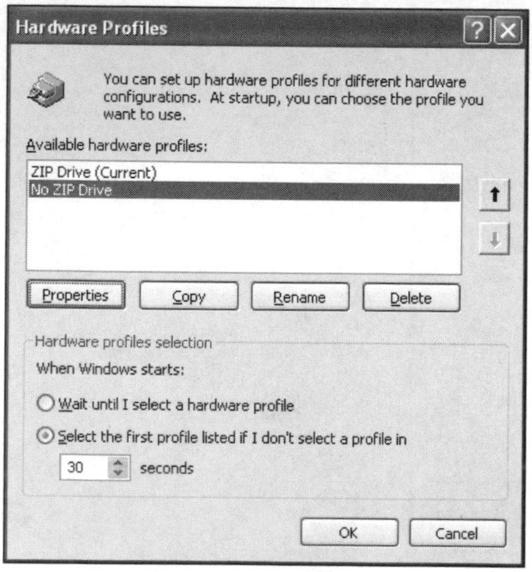

Figure 6.9 The Hardware Profiles dialog box enables you to copy, remove, and configure hardware profiles.

configuring hardware devices. In the Properties dialog box for any device, you can specify whether that device is enabled or disabled for the current profile. To configure services, you can specify which hardware profile a particular service is enabled or disabled for—the computer does not need to be restarted with a specific hardware profile when you configure services.

If Windows XP detects that your computer is a portable (laptop or notebook), it tries to determine whether your system is docked or undocked; it then selects the appropriate hardware profile for the current conditions. Do not confuse hardware profiles with *user profiles*—the two are not related! Hardware profiles deal with devices and services settings for the entire computer; user profiles deal with user configuration settings for individual users.

Advanced Power Management

Windows XP supports the APM version 1.2 specification. APM helps to greatly reduce your computer's power consumption, which is particularly helpful for mobile users. You use the Power Options applet in the Control Panel to configure power management settings on your computer. If your computer does not have an APM-compliant BIOS, Windows XP cannot install APM—this means no APM support for your machine, plus no APM tab in the Power Options applet in the Control Panel. Keep in mind, though, that your machine can still function as an ACPI computer if your BIOS is ACPI-compliant. The ACPI-based BIOS will take over your system configuration and power management from the Plug and Play BIOS.

Advanced Configuration and Power Interface

The ACPI standard has replaced the older APM specification. ACPI is an open-industry specification that defines a flexible and extensible hardware interface for your system board. Windows XP is a fully ACPI-compliant operating system. Software developers and designers use the ACPI specification to integrate power management features throughout a computer system, including hardware, the operating system, and application software. This integration enables Windows XP to determine which applications are active and to handle all the power management resources for computer subsystems and peripherals.

ACPI enables the operating system to control power management on a wide range of mobile, desktop, and server computers and peripherals. ACPI is the foundation for the OnNow industry initiative, which allows manufacturers to deliver computers that will start at the touch of a key on a keyboard.

ACPI design is *essential* when you want to take full advantage of power management and UPnP features in Windows XP. If you are not sure if your computer is

ACPI-compliant, check your manufacturer's documentation. To change power settings that take advantage of ACPI, use the Power Options applet in the Control Panel.

If you upgrade a computer's BIOS so that the computer will support the ACPI standard, you must reinstall Windows XP if you want the system to take advantage of ACPI features.

Power Options Overview

By using Power Options in the Control Panel, you can reduce the power consumption of several computer hardware components or you can have it impact your entire system. You do this by choosing a *power scheme*, which is a collection of settings that manages your computer's power usage. You can create your own power schemes or use the ones provided with Windows XP.

You can also adjust the individual settings in a power scheme. For example, depending on your hardware, you can do the following:

➤ Turn off your monitor and hard disks automatically to save power.

➤ Put your computer in Standby mode, which puts your entire system in a low-power state, if you plan to be away from your computer for a while. While in Standby mode, your entire computer switches to a low-power state, where devices such as the monitor and hard disks turn off and your computer uses less power. When you want to use the computer again, it comes out of Standby quickly, and your desktop is restored exactly as you left it. Standby is useful for conserving battery power in portable computers.

Standby mode does not save your desktop state to disk, so if a power failure occurs while the computer is in Standby mode, you can lose unsaved information. If an interruption in power occurs, information in memory is lost. If this concerns you, using Hibernate mode or completely powering off might be better choices to consider.

➤ Put your computer in Hibernate mode. When you restart your computer, your desktop is restored exactly as you left it. It takes longer to bring your computer out of Hibernate mode than out of Standby. Put your computer in Hibernate mode when you will be away from the computer for an extended period of time.

The Hibernate feature saves everything in memory to disk, turns off your monitor and hard disk, and then turns off your computer.

Managing Battery Power on a Portable Computer

Using the Power Options applet in the Control Panel, you can reduce consumption of battery power on your portable computer and still keep the computer available for immediate use. You can view multiple batteries separately or as a whole, and set alarms to warn you of low-battery conditions.

Managing Power When Installing a Plug and Play Device

Plug and Play works with Power Options in the Control Panel to be sure that your system runs efficiently while you are installing or removing hardware devices. Power Options controls the power supply to the devices attached to your computer, supplying power to those that you are using and conserving power for those you are not. Windows XP automatically manages the power for devices. However, some devices may have options you can set in Device Manager.

To take full advantage of Plug and Play, you need to use Windows XP on an ACPI-compliant computer that is running in ACPI mode, and the hardware devices must be PnP- and/or ACPI-compliant. In an ACPI-compliant computer, the operating system, not the hardware, configures and monitors the computer's devices. Windows XP Professional supports ACPI wake events for ACPI-compliant devices. These events include wake-on-ring for modems, wake-on-LAN for network cards, and wake-on-critical-battery.

Managing Card Services

Card services play an important role in Windows XP Professional. Support for card services includes PC Cards as peripheral devices and Smart Card technology for logon authentication. The operating system supports both the PC Card (formerly known as PCMCIA) standard as well as the CardBus (PC Card 32) standard. The many benefits of these devices include their compact size, low power requirements, and support for the Plug and Play standard. The CardBus specification is a combination of the PC Card 16 standard and the Peripheral Component Interconnect (PCI) standard. This combination provides 32-bit performance and the PCI bus in a compact, portable size. You can find several types of PC Cards that are usually used in mobile computers: network adapter cards, hard drive cards, modem cards, wireless network cards, and so on.

Smart Cards

Support for Smart Card technology is fully integrated into Windows XP. Smart Cards play an important role in Windows XP's Public Key Infrastructure (PKI) security architecture for logon authentication and other security-related services.

Smart Cards are credit card–sized devices that have integrated circuits built into them. These electronic cards securely store both public and private encryption keys and also perform cryptographic functions such as digital-signature and key-exchange operations.

Microsoft supports only PnP-compliant Smart Card reader devices. Smart Card readers connect to standard PC interfaces such as serial (RS-232) ports, PS/2 ports, USB ports, and PC Card slots. To install a Smart Card reader, use the Add Hardware applet in the Control Panel. Smart Card configurations typically use the Extensible Authentication Protocol-Transport Level Security (EAP-TLS) authentication protocol. When you use a Smart Card to log on to a Windows XP Professional computer, at least one Cryptographic Service Provider (CSP) service must be installed and running on the system. CSPs enable other application programs to have access to the cryptographic services of a Smart Card, such as digital signature, key generation, and key exchange.

Before a user can log on to a system with a Smart Card, the user must be enrolled for a Smart Card certificate by an administrator who has the proper security privileges to enroll other users. This enrollment process creates a certificate and a public encryption key for the user. The user also needs to create or to be assigned a personal identification number (PIN) code, which must be used in conjunction with the Smart Card when logging on to a Smart Card–enabled computer.

Practice Questions

Question 1

Brendan has just installed a brand new updated version of the software driver for his Zip drive removable media device. After the driver installs successfully, he is prompted to restart his Windows XP computer. Unfortunately, whenever he attempts to copy files to a Zip disk now, he receives an error message and the files do not get copied to the disk. He doesn't have the original Zip disk driver diskette, but he wants to replace the new driver with the previous version. What is the fastest and easiest way that he can accomplish this?

- ○ a. Restart the computer, press the F8 key during startup, and select the Last Known Good Configuration option.

- ○ b. Restart the computer, press the F8 key during startup, and select the Safe Mode option. Uninstall the printer and then reinstall it and let Windows locate the correct driver.

- ○ c. Open Device Manager, right-click the Zip device, select Properties, click the Driver tab, and click the Roll Back Driver button.

- ○ d. Click Start|All Programs|Windows Update and download a driver from the Windows Update Web site.

Answer c is correct. The Driver Rollback feature is the quickest and easiest way to return a device driver to its previous version. Answer a is incorrect because the Last Known Good Configuration option can't help you once you have successfully logged on to the computer after a configuration change. Answer b is incorrect because Safe Mode is no better for installing drivers than booting normally, and this action would not return the driver to its previous version. Answer d is incorrect because the Windows Update Web site would also not return the driver to its previous state.

Question 2

Brandy is a network administrator who wants to control the type of device drivers that can be installed in the Windows XP Professional workstations in her office. Which Group Policy Object (GPO) can she use along with which setting so that unsigned device drivers cannot be installed?

○ a. Brandy can go to User Configuration|Windows Settings|Security Settings|Local Policies|Security Options and set the Devices: Unsigned Driver Installation Behavior policy to Silently Succeed.

○ b. Brandy can go to Computer Configuration|Administrative Templates|System and set the Devices: Unsigned Driver Installation Behavior policy to Silently Succeed.

○ c. Brandy can go to User Configuration|Administrative Templates|System and set the Devices: Unsigned Driver Installation Behavior policy to Do Not Allow Installation.

○ d. Brandy can go to Computer Configuration|Windows Settings|Security Settings|Local Policies|Security Options and set the Devices: Unsigned Driver Installation Behavior policy to Do Not Allow Installation.

Answer d is correct. The policy setting for Devices: Unsigned Driver Installation Behavior is a global, computer-related GPO, and the setting Do Not Allow Installation blocks unsigned drivers from being installed on the system. Answer a is incorrect because the policy setting for Devices: Unsigned Driver Installation Behavior is a global, computer-related GPO, it is not user-specific, and the setting Silently Succeed allows both signed and unsigned drivers to be installed. Answer b is incorrect because the setting Silently Succeed allows both signed and unsigned drivers to be installed. Answer c is incorrect because the GPO is not located in the User Configuration container and the policy is not under Administrative Templates.

Question 3

Alexis has several USB devices plugged into several different USB hubs that are all connected to a USB port on her Windows XP computer. She buys a new USB mouse and plugs it into one of the daisy-chained USB hubs using a USB cable that is 12 feet in length. The computer does not detect the new mouse. Even when she tries to install it using the Add Hardware Wizard, the system cannot find the new USB device. What is the most likely cause of this problem?

○ a. The mouse is not compatible with Plug and Play or Universal Plug and Play.

○ b. The USB hub that the mouse is plugged into is connected as the sixth hub in a row of hubs.

○ c. The 12-foot USB cable used for the mouse is longer than the supported USB cable length.

○ d. The USB mouse requires a self-powered hub instead of a bus-powered hub.

Answer b is correct. No more than five external hubs may be used in one physical chain of hubs. Answer a is incorrect because all USB devices are PnP–compatible. Answer c is incorrect because the maximum supported cable length between a USB device and a USB hub or port is 5 meters (12 feet is less than 5 meters). Answer d is incorrect because high power consumption devices like hard drives, cameras, and scanners often require self-powered hubs—generally, devices like keyboards and mice do not

Question 4

Which of the following five methods can you employ to fix a severe video driver problem where the display is no longer visible? [Check all correct answers]

❑ a. Restart the computer in Safe Mode and then update or change the driver.

❑ b. Don't restart the computer and use the Driver Rollback feature.

❑ c. Restart the computer in VGA Mode.

❑ d. Restart the computer under the Last Known Good Configuration option.

❑ e. Restart the computer and select a different hardware profile.

Answers a, c, and d are correct. You can restart the computer in Safe Mode to fix the driver problem, you can restart the computer and select VGA Mode and then fix the problem, or you can simply restart the computer under the Last Known Good Configuration option and the video settings will revert back to how they were previously. Answer b is incorrect because you can't use the Driver Rollback feature if you can't see the display. Answer e is incorrect because the computer may have only one hardware profile present, and any other hardware profiles may not necessarily apply to the video display settings.

Question 5

How many monitors will Windows XP support if you install one PCI video adapter, one AGP video adapter, and one ISA video adapter, and the computer already has an integrated AGP video adapter on the motherboard?

○ a. The computer will support three monitors.

○ b. The computer will support four monitors.

○ c. The computer will support two monitors.

○ d. The computer will support one monitor.

Answer a is correct. Windows XP supports the multiple-monitor feature using only PCI or AGP video display adapters—it's okay if one adapter is built into the motherboard. Answer b is incorrect because the multiple-monitor feature is not supported for ISA video adapters. Answer c is incorrect because the multiple-monitor feature is supported on both PCI and AGP adapters—built-in adapters are also acceptable.

Question 6

What is the most efficient way that can you update Windows XP Professional to support a second processor if only a single processor was present when you first installed the operating system?

○ a. Use the Uptomp.exe utility from the Windows XP Professional Resource Kit.

○ b. Reinstall Windows XP Professional on the system.

○ c. Launch the Hardware Update Wizard by right-clicking the existing processor in Device Manager and selecting Update Driver.

○ d. Copy the Halmps.dll file from the Windows XP Professional Setup CD-ROM to the %systemroot%\system32 folder and then restart the computer.

Answer c is correct. Windows XP Professional supports a maximum of two processors. To upgrade the operating system to support a second installed processor, you use the Hardware Update Wizard. Answer a is incorrect because the Uptomp.exe utility was used for Windows NT 4, but is not used for Windows XP. Answer b is incorrect because although performing a reinstallation should update the system to support multiple processors, it would take much more time than to simply run the Hardware Update Wizard. Answer d is incorrect because copying DLL files from the Windows XP CD-ROM is not supported for upgrading support for two processors.

Question 7

How can you update Windows XP to support ACPI after you have upgraded the computer's BIOS from supporting APM to supporting ACPI?

- ○ a. Go to the Power Options applet in the Control Panel, click the Advanced tab, click the Enable ACPI option button, and then restart the computer for the change to take effect.

- ○ b. Reinstall Windows XP Professional on the system.

- ○ c. Launch the Hardware Update Wizard by right-clicking the existing processor in Device Manager and selecting Update Driver.

- ○ d. Copy the Halacpi.dll file from the Windows XP Professional Setup CD-ROM to the %systemroot%\system32 folder and then restart the computer.

Answers b is correct. The only way that you can enable ACPI support after you have upgraded your system's BIOS to support ACPI is to reinstall Windows XP. Answer a is incorrect because there is no option button for Enable ACPI under the Power Options applet in the Control Panel. Answer c is incorrect because the Hardware Update Wizard does not support enabling ACPI on systems that were not installed with ACPI support. Answer d is incorrect because copying DLL files from the Windows XP CD-ROM is not supported for upgrading the operating system to support ACPI.

Question 8

Which of the following statements about support for DVD and CD media are not true under Windows XP Professional? [Check all correct answers]

❑ a. You can write to CD-R and CD-RW media under Windows XP without using any third-party applications.

❑ b. You can write to DVD-R and DVD-RW media under Windows XP without using any third-party applications.

❑ c. You can play back DVD movies without third-party decoder software or hardware by using the new Windows Media Player that ships with Windows XP.

❑ d. You cannot read DVD data discs without using a third-party application.

Answers b, c, and d are correct. You cannot write to DVD-R or DVD-RW media without a third-party utility. You cannot play back DVD movies without third-party decoder hardware or software. You can read DVD data discs natively under Windows XP without requiring a third-party utility. Answer a is incorrect because Windows XP does support writing to both CD-Rs and CD-RWs natively.

Need to Know More?

Bott, Ed, and Carl Siechert. *Microsoft Windows XP Inside Out.* Redmond, WA: Microsoft Press, 2001. ISBN 0-73561-382-6. This book offers timesaving tips, troubleshooting techniques, and workarounds. It focuses on techniques such as taking advantage of the rich integration of devices, applications, and Web services in Windows XP.

Microsoft Corporation. *Microsoft Windows XP Professional Resource Kit Documentation.* Redmond, WA: Microsoft Press, 2001. ISBN 0-73561-485-7. This all-in-one reference is a compilation of technical documentation and valuable insider information that computer-support professionals and administrators can reference to install, customize, and support Windows XP.

Minasi, Mark *Mastering Windows XP Professional.* Alameda, CA: Sybex, Inc., 2001. ISBN 0-78212-981-1. This book provides in-depth coverage of installing, configuring, and administering Windows XP Professional.

Search the Microsoft TechNet CD (or its online version through **www.microsoft.com**) using keywords such as "ACPI", "Driver Signing", "Universal Plug and Play", "Hardware Profiles", and "Multiple Monitors".

Implementing, Managing, and Troubleshooting Disk Drives and Volumes

Terms you'll need to understand:

- ✓ Basic vs. dynamic disks
- ✓ Partitions, volumes, and logical drives
- ✓ Simple, spanned, and striped volumes
- ✓ Diskperf.exe utility
- ✓ Diskpart.exe utility
- ✓ File allocation table (FAT or FAT16) file system volumes
- ✓ 32-bit file allocation table (FAT32) file system volumes
- ✓ NTFS volumes
- ✓ Convert.exe utility
- ✓ Mounted drives and mount points
- ✓ Disk quotas
- ✓ NTFS compression
- ✓ NTFS data encryption

Techniques you'll need to master:

- ✓ Using the Disk Management console
- ✓ Monitoring and troubleshooting disks using the Performance console
- ✓ Using the Disk Cleanup Wizard and Disk Defragmenter
- ✓ Selecting a file system for Windows XP Professional
- ✓ Using Convert.exe to convert a FAT volume to NTFS
- ✓ Using Diskpart.exe to manage disk drives and volumes from the command line
- ✓ Creating mounted volumes
- ✓ Managing NTFS compressed files and folders
- ✓ Managing NTFS encrypted files and folders

If you are familiar with managing hard disks and volumes under Windows 2000, you should feel quite at home working with disk storage administration in Windows XP. Hard disk management under Windows XP Professional is strikingly similar to the Disk Management console under both the Server and Professional editions of Windows 2000. For administrators who are more accustomed to working with Windows NT 4, Windows XP Professional introduces some new concepts, such as basic and dynamic disk storage. Even so, the Disk Management MMC (Microsoft Management Console) snap-in has a resemblance to the old Disk Administrator utility used under Windows NT 4.

Disk Storage Management

This chapter discusses how to manage and troubleshoot hard disks in Windows XP Professional. It looks at available options under Windows XP for creating partitions on a hard disk, creating and formatting drive volumes, and disk administration. In addition, this chapter uncovers the features of the new disk storage types that were first introduced with Windows 2000. Windows XP Professional supports two disk configuration types—basic storage and dynamic storage. This chapter compares the differences between basic and dynamic storage, and explains how to configure and manage disks that have been initialized with either type of configuration.

Basic Disks

A Windows XP *basic disk*, which is similar to the disk configuration used under earlier versions of Windows, is a physical disk with primary and extended partitions. As long as you use the file allocation table (FAT) file system (discussed in detail later in this chapter), Windows XP Professional and Home editions, Windows 2000, Windows NT, Windows 9x, and MS-DOS operating systems can access basic disks. You can create up to three primary partitions and one extended partition on a basic disk, or just four primary partitions. You can create a single extended partition with logical drives on a basic disk; however, you *cannot* extend a basic disk. Extending a disk enables you to use a second hard disk volume for storage while the operating system makes the extra volume appear to be part of the same volume on the first disk. You gain more disk storage while maintaining the same drive volume letter.

Basic disks store their configuration information in the master boot record (MBR), which is stored on the first sector of the hard drive. The configuration of a basic disk consists of the partition information on the disk. Basic fault-tolerant sets inherited from Windows NT Server 4 are based on these simple partitions, but they extend the configuration with some extra partition relationship information, which is stored on the first track of the disk.

Basic disks may contain spanned volumes (volume sets), mirrored volumes (mirror sets), striped volumes (stripe sets), and Redundant Array of Independent (or Inexpensive) Disks (RAID) level 5 volumes (stripe sets with parity) that were created using Windows NT 4 or earlier. These kinds of volumes are covered later in this chapter.

Mirrored and RAID-5 volumes are *fault-tolerant* volumes that are only available under the Windows 2000 Server or Windows .NET Server family of server operating systems. These types of volumes cannot be created on basic *or* dynamic disks using Windows XP Professional. Fault-tolerant volumes are designed to withstand a single disk failure within a set of disks and to continue functioning until the failed disk is replaced. A mirror set duplicates data to a second physical disk; a RAID-5 set writes data across several disks (between 3 and 32 physical disks) and stores parity information across all the drives to be able to retrieve data in the event of a single failed disk.

Dynamic Disks

A Windows XP *dynamic disk* is a physical disk that does not use partitions or logical drives. Instead, a single partition is created that includes the entire disk, which can then be divided into separate volumes. Also, dynamic disks do not have the same constraints of basic disks. For example, a dynamic disk can be resized on-the-fly without requiring a reboot. Dynamic disks are associated with *disk groups*, which are disks managed as a collection, which helps to organize dynamic disks. All dynamic disks in a computer are members of the same disk group. Each disk in a disk group stores replicas of the same configuration data. This configuration data is stored in a 1MB region at the end of each dynamic disk.

Dynamic disks can contain any of the types of volumes discussed later in this chapter. You can extend a volume on a dynamic disk. Dynamic disks can contain an unlimited number of volumes, so you are not restricted to four volumes per disk, as you are with basic disks. Regardless of the type of file system employed, only computers running Windows XP, Windows 2000, or Windows .NET Server can *directly* access dynamic volumes on hard drives that are physically connected to the computer. However, computers that are not running Windows XP, Windows 2000, or Windows .NET Server can access the dynamic volumes *remotely* when they are connected to shared folders over the network.

Dynamic disks are not available under Windows XP Home edition.

Comparing Basic Disks to Dynamic Disks

When you install Windows XP, the system automatically configures the existing hard disks as basic disks. Windows XP does *not* support dynamic disks on mobile PCs (laptops or notebooks), and, if you're using an older desktop machine that is not Advanced Configuration and Power Interface (ACPI)-compliant, the Upgrade To Dynamic Disk option (discussed later in this chapter) is not available. Dynamic disks have some additional limitations. You can install Windows XP on a dynamic volume that you *converted* from a basic disk, but you can't extend either the system or the boot partition. The process of upgrading volumes is covered later in this chapter. Any troubleshooting tools that cannot read the dynamic Disk Management database work only on a basic disk.

> Dynamic disks are only supported on desktop or server systems using Small Computer System Interface (SCSI), Fibre Channel, Serial Storage Architecture (SSA), Integrated Drive Electronics (IDE), Enhanced Integrated Drive Electronics (EIDE), Ultra Direct Memory Access (DMA), or Advanced Technology Attachment (ATA) interfaces. Portable computers, removable disks, and disks connected via Universal Serial Bus (USB) or Firewire (IEEE 1394) interfaces are *not* supported for dynamic storage. Dynamic disks are also not supported on hard drives with a sector size of less than 512 bytes. Cluster disks—groups of several disks that serve to function as a single disk—are not supported either.

Basic and dynamic disks are Windows XP's way of looking at hard disk configuration. If you're migrating to Windows XP from Windows NT 4, the dynamic disk concept might seem odd in the beginning; but once you understand the differences, working with dynamic disks is not complicated. You can format partitions with FAT16, FAT32, or NT File System (NTFS) on a basic or a dynamic disk. FAT and NTFS are discussed later in this chapter. However, you can only format a dynamic volume as NTFS from the Disk Management console. You must use Windows XP Explorer to format a dynamic volume as FAT or FAT32. Table 7.1 compares the terms used with basic and dynamic disks.

Upgrading Disks

When you perform a new installation of Windows XP Professional or when you perform an upgrade installation from Windows 98, Windows ME, or Windows NT Workstation 4, the computer system defaults to basic disk storage. Only if you upgrade from Windows 2000 Professional (or if you import a "foreign disk" from Windows 2000 Server or a later version) could one or more of the disk drives be configured as dynamic. Dynamic disks are proprietary to Windows 2000 and Windows XP Professional and they provide support for advanced disk configurations such as disk striping and disk spanning. On Windows 2000 Server and later server versions, dynamic disks provide support for fault tolerant

Table 7.1 A cross-reference of terms used with basic and dynamic disks.	
Basic Disks	**Dynamic Disks**
Active partition	Active volume
Extended partition	Volume and unallocated space
Logical drive	Simple volume
Mirror set	Mirrored volume (server only)
Primary partition	Simple volume
Stripe set	Striped volume
Stripe set with parity	RAID-5 volume (server only)
System and boot partitions	System and boot volumes
Volume set	Spanned volumes

configurations such as disk mirroring and disk striping with parity (also known as Redundant Array of Inexpensive Disks—RAID level 5).

Upgrading Basic Disks to Dynamic Disks

You use Windows XP's Disk Management console (an MMC snap-in) to upgrade a basic disk to a dynamic disk. To access Disk Management, click Start|All Programs|Administrative Tools|Computer Management. Or, simply right-click the My Computer icon from the Start menu and select Manage. You'll find Disk Management by expanding the Storage folder. You must be a member of the local Administrators group to make any changes to the computer's disk management configuration.

For the upgrade to succeed, any disks to be upgraded must contain at least 1MB of unallocated space. Disk Management automatically reserves this space when creating partitions or volumes on a disk, but disks with partitions or volumes created by other operating systems may not have this space available. (This space can exist even if it is not visible in Disk Management.) Before you upgrade disks, close any programs that are running on those disks. Windows XP requires this minimal amount of disk space to store the dynamic database, which is maintained by the operating system that created it. This is why it is not a good idea to dual-boot between Windows XP and Windows 2000 (or .NET Server) if you are using dynamic disks.

To change or convert a basic disk to a dynamic disk from the Disk Management console, perform the following steps:

1. Open the Disk Management tool.

2. Right-click the basic disk you want to change to a dynamic disk and then click Convert To Dynamic Disk.

When you upgrade a basic disk to a dynamic disk, you do not need to reboot. However, if you do upgrade your startup disk or upgrade a volume or partition, you must restart your computer for the change to take effect. The good news is that you do not need to select a special command like Commit Changes Now before restarting your computer or closing the Disk Management tool.

To change or convert a basic disk to a dynamic disk from the Windows XP command line, perform these steps:

1. Open a command prompt window, type "diskpart", and press Enter.

2. Type "commands" or "help" to view a list of available commands.

3. Type "select disk 0" to select the first hard disk ("select disk 1" to select the second hard disk, and so on) and press Enter.

4. Type "convert dynamic" and press Enter.

5. Type "exit" to quit the Diskpart.exe tool and then restart the computer to have the new configuration take effect (see Figure 7.1).

Note: In addition to Diskpart.exe, Windows XP administrators can take advantage of another command-line tool for managing FAT, FAT32, and NTFS file systems—Fsutil.exe. With Fsutil.exe, Windows XP administrative users can perform tasks such as managing disk quotas, reparsing (mount) points, and several other advanced disk-related tasks. Type "Fsutil /?" at a command prompt to view a list of supported commands.

When you upgrade a basic disk to a dynamic disk, any existing partitions on the basic disk become simple volumes on the dynamic disk. Any existing mirrored volumes, striped volumes, RAID-5 volumes, or spanned volumes become dynamic mirrored volumes, dynamic striped volumes, dynamic RAID-5 volumes, or dynamic spanned volumes, respectively.

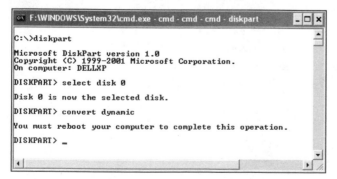

Figure 7.1   Using the Diskpart.exe command-line utility to convert from a basic disk to a dynamic disk.

You *cannot* dual-boot to another operating system if you upgrade a basic disk to a dynamic disk, which typically isn't an issue for servers. However, it's something to consider for Windows XP Professional machines. After you upgrade a basic disk to a dynamic disk, you cannot change the dynamic volumes back to partitions. Instead, you must *delete* all dynamic volumes on the disk and then use the **Convert To Basic Disk** command.

Note: Upgrading to a dynamic disk is a one-way process. Yes, you can convert a dynamic disk with volumes back to a basic disk, but you'll lose all of your data. Obviously, this is a major downside! If you find yourself needing to do this, though, first save your data, convert the disk to basic, and then restore your data.

Because the upgrade from basic to dynamic is per physical disk, all volumes on a physical disk must be either basic or dynamic. Again, you do not need to restart your computer when you upgrade from a basic to a dynamic disk from the Disk Management Console. You must restart your computer only if you use the Diskpart.exe command-line tool, upgrade your startup disk, or upgrade a volume or partition.

When you upgrade or convert a basic disk to a dynamic disk, at least 1MB of free space must be available for the dynamic disk database. Under normal circumstances, this should not be a problem.

Converting Dynamic Disks to Basic Disks

You must remove all volumes from the dynamic disk before you can change it back to a basic disk. After you change a dynamic disk back to a basic disk, you can create only partitions and logical drives on that disk. After being upgraded, a dynamic disk cannot contain partitions or logical drives, nor can any operating systems other than Windows XP, Windows 2000, or Windows .NET Server access it.

To convert a dynamic disk to a basic disk, perform the following steps:

1. Open Disk Management.

2. Right-click the dynamic disk you want to change back to a basic disk and then click Convert To Basic Disk.

Moving Disks to Another Computer

To move disks to another computer, perform the following steps:

1. Before you disconnect the disks, look in Disk Management and make sure the status of the volumes on the disks is healthy. If the status is not healthy, repair the volumes *before* you move the disks.

2. Turn the computer off, remove the physical disks, and then install the physical disks on the other computer. Restart the computer that contains the disks you moved.

3. Open Disk Management.

4. Click Action and then click Rescan Disks.

5. Right-click any disk marked Foreign, click Import Foreign Disks, and then follow the instructions on your screen.

Guidelines for Relocating Disks

Every time you remove disks from or import disks to a computer, you must click Action|Rescan Disks from the Disk Management console menu and then verify that the disk information is correct. Aside from following the preceding Steps 1 through 5, you can choose which disks from the group you want to add by choosing the Select Disk option when you right-click a Foreign disk—you do not have to import all the new disks at the same time.

Disk Management describes the condition of the volumes on the disks before you import them. Review this information carefully. If any problems exist, you will know what will happen to each volume on these disks after you have imported them. After you import a dynamic disk from another computer, you can see and use any existing volumes on that disk. Be sure to move together all disks that are part of a volume set or a stripe set. If you move only some of the disks that are members of a volume set or stripe set, you render the set unusable. You may even damage the set and lose the data stored on the set if you do not move all the disks that make up the set. You can also use the Diskpart.exe command-line tool to import disks.

Reactivating a Missing or Offline Disk

A dynamic disk may become missing when it is corrupted, powered down, or disconnected. Only dynamic disks can be reactivated—not basic disks. Sorry!

To reactivate a missing or offline disk, perform the following steps:

1. Open Disk Management.

2. Right-click the disk marked Missing or Offline, and then click Reactivate Disk.

3. The disk should be marked Online after the disk is reactivated.

Basic Volumes

Basic volumes include partitions and logical drives, as well as volumes created using Windows NT 4 or earlier operating systems. Before Windows 2000, basic *disks* contained all volume types: basic volumes, volume sets, stripe sets, mirror sets, and stripe sets with parity (also known as RAID level 5 sets). For Windows 2000 and Windows XP, these volumes have been *renamed* to spanned volumes, striped volumes, mirrored volumes, and RAID-5 volumes. Under Windows XP, you can create basic volumes on basic disks only. In addition, *fault-tolerant* volumes (mirrored volumes and RAID-5 volumes) can only be created on dynamic disks under a Windows 2000 or a Windows .NET *Server* operating system. See the upcoming section "Dynamic Volumes" to find out how to migrate data from stripe sets or volume sets that are stored on a basic disk under Windows NT 4 Workstation or Windows 2000 Professional.

Because Windows XP Professional is a desktop (client-side) network operating system, it does not support any type of fault-tolerant volumes, even on dynamic disks. Only Microsoft server operating systems support fault-tolerant features such as mirrored volumes and RAID 6 volumes (stripe sets with parity). Windows 2000 Server and later server operating systems require fault-tolerant volumes to be stored on dynamic disks.

Partitions and Logical Drives on Basic Disks

You can create primary partitions, extended partitions, and logical drives only on basic disks. You should create partitions instead of dynamic volumes if your computer also runs a down-level Microsoft operating system. You must be an administrator or a member of the Administrators group to create, modify, or delete basic volumes.

Partitions and logical drives can reside only on basic disks. You can create up to four primary partitions on a basic disk, or up to three primary partitions and one extended partition. You can use the free space in an extended partition to create multiple logical drives.

Note: You can extend a basic volume, but it must be formatted as NTFS, it must be adjacent to contiguous unallocated space on the same physical disk, and it can be extended only onto unallocated space that resides on the same physical disk.

You should create basic volumes, such as partitions or logical drives, on basic disks if you want computers running earlier versions of Microsoft operating systems to be able to access those volumes.

Creating or Deleting a Partition or Logical Drive

To create or delete a partition or logical drive, you may use the Diskpart.exe command-line tool, or use the GUI and perform the following steps:

1. Open the Disk Management console.

2. Right-click an unallocated region of a basic disk and then click New Partition. Alternatively, you can right-click an area of free space in an extended partition and then click New Logical Drive. To remove the partition, select Delete Partition from the right-click menu.

3. Using the Create Partition Wizard, click Next. Click Primary Partition, Extended Partition, or Logical Drive and follow the instructions presented by the wizard.

If you choose to delete a partition, all data on the deleted partition or logical drive is lost. You cannot recover deleted partitions or logical drives. You cannot delete the system partition, boot partition, or any partition that contains an active paging file. The operating system uses one or more paging files on disk as virtual memory that can be swapped into and out of real system memory as the system's load and volume of data dictate.

 Windows XP requires that all logical drives or other volumes in an extended partition be deleted before you can delete the extended partition.

Dynamic Volumes

What were called *sets* (such as mirror sets and stripe sets) under earlier operating systems are called *volumes* (such as mirrored volumes and striped volumes) in Windows 2000 and Windows XP. Dynamic volumes are the only type of volume you can create on dynamic disks. With dynamic disks, you are no longer limited to four volumes per disk (as you are with basic disks). You can install Windows XP Professional onto a dynamic volume; however, these volumes must contain the partition table (which means that these volumes must have been *converted* from basic to dynamic under Windows XP or Windows 2000). Windows XP cannot be installed onto dynamic volumes that have been created under Windows XP directly from unallocated space. Only computers running Windows XP Professional, the Windows 2000 family of operating systems, or the Windows .NET Server family of products can access dynamic volumes. The five types of dynamic volumes are simple, spanned, mirrored, striped, and RAID-5. Windows XP Professional only supports simple, spanned, and striped dynamic volumes. You must be an administrator or a member of the Administrators group to create, modify, or delete dynamic volumes.

Simple Volumes

A *simple volume* is made up of disk space on a single physical disk. It can consist of a single area on a disk or multiple areas on the same disk that are linked together.

To create a simple volume, perform the following steps:

1. Open Disk Management.

2. Right-click the unallocated space on the dynamic disk where you want to create the simple volume and then click New Volume.

3. Using the New Volume Wizard, click Next, click Simple, and then follow the instructions on your screen.

Here are some guidelines about simple volumes:

➤ You can create simple volumes on dynamic disks only.

➤ Simple volumes are not fault tolerant.

➤ Simple volumes cannot contain partitions or logical drives.

➤ Neither MS-DOS nor Windows operating systems other than Windows XP (and Windows 2000) can access simple volumes.

Spanned Volumes

A *spanned volume* is made up of disk space from more than one physical disk. You can add more space to a spanned volume by extending it at any time.

To create a spanned volume, perform the following steps:

1. Open Disk Management.

2. Right-click the unallocated space on one of the dynamic disks where you want to create the spanned volume and then click New Volume.

3. Using the New Volume Wizard, click Next, click Spanned, and then follow the instructions on your screen.

Here are some guidelines about spanned volumes:

➤ You can create spanned volumes on dynamic disks only.

➤ You need at least two dynamic disks to create a spanned volume.

➤ You can extend a spanned volume onto a maximum of 32 dynamic disks.

➤ Spanned volumes cannot be mirrored or striped.

➤ Spanned volumes are not fault tolerant.

Extending a Simple or Spanned Volume

To extend a simple or spanned volume, perform the following steps:

1. Open Disk Management.

2. Right-click the simple or spanned volume you want to extend, click Extend Volume, and then follow the instructions on your screen.

Here are some guidelines about extending a simple or a spanned volume:

➤ You can extend a volume only if it contains no file system or if it is formatted using NTFS. You cannot extend volumes formatted using FAT or FAT32.

➤ You can extend a simple volume within its original disk or onto additional disks, provided that the volume was converted to a dynamic volume under Windows XP (not Windows 2000). If you extend a simple volume across multiple disks, it becomes a spanned volume.

➤ After a volume is extended onto multiple disks (spanned), you cannot mirror or stripe it.

➤ After a spanned volume is extended, no portion of it can be deleted without the entire spanned volume being deleted.

➤ You can extend a simple or extended volume only if the volume was created as a dynamic volume. You cannot extend a simple or extended volume that was upgraded from basic to dynamic under Windows 2000.

➤ You can extend simple and spanned volumes on dynamic disks onto a maximum of 32 dynamic disks.

➤ Spanned volumes only write data to subsequent disks as each disk volume fills up. Therefore, a spanned volume writes data to physical disk 0 until it fills up, then writes to physical disk 1 until its available space is full, then writes to physical disk 2, and so on. If just *one* disk fails in the spanned volume—*only the data contained on that failed disk is lost for that spanned volume.*

Note: You cannot extend a system volume or boot volume. You cannot extend striped, mirrored, and RAID-5 volumes.

Striped Volumes

A *striped volume* stores data in stripes on two or more physical disks. Data in a striped volume is allocated alternately and evenly (in stripes) to the disks of the striped volume. Striped volumes can substantially improve the speed of access to your data on disk.

To create a striped volume, perform the following steps:

1. Open Disk Management.

2. Right-click unallocated space on one of the dynamic disks where you want to create the striped volume and then click New Volume.

3. Using the New Volume Wizard, click Next, click Striped, and then follow the instructions on your screen.

Here are some guidelines about striped volumes:

➤ You need at least two physical, dynamic disks to create a striped volume.

➤ You can create a striped volume onto a maximum of 32 disks.

➤ Striped volumes are not fault tolerant and cannot be extended or mirrored.

Mirrored Volumes and RAID-5 Volumes

You can create mirrored volumes and RAID-5 volumes *only* on dynamic disks running on Windows 2000 Server or Windows .NET Server computers.

Note: Mirrored and RAID-5 volumes are available only on computers that are running Windows 2000 Server or Windows .NET Server. Windows XP Professional computers can use basic and dynamic disks, but they cannot host software-based fault-tolerant disk configurations such as mirrored volumes and stripe sets with parity (RAID-5) volumes. You can, however, use a computer running Windows XP Professional to create mirrored and RAID-5 volumes on a remote computer running a Windows 2000 Server or Windows .NET Server network operating system. The Disk Management MMC snap-in can administer both local and remote disk storage

Limitations of Dynamic Disks and Dynamic Volumes

You can use dynamic disks and dynamic volumes in specific circumstances; you need to understand when you can and cannot use them.

When You Are Installing Windows XP

If you create a dynamic volume *from unallocated space* on a dynamic disk, you cannot install Windows XP on that volume. The setup limitation occurs because Windows XP Setup recognizes only dynamic volumes that contain partition tables. Partition tables appear in basic volumes and in dynamic volumes only when they have been upgraded from basic to dynamic. If you create a new dynamic volume on a dynamic disk, that new dynamic volume does not contain a partition table.

When You Are Extending a Volume

If you upgrade a basic volume to dynamic (by upgrading the basic disk to a dynamic disk), you can install Windows XP on that volume, but you *cannot* extend the volume. The limitation on extending volumes occurs because the boot volume, which contains the Windows XP files, cannot be part of a spanned volume. If you extend a simple volume that contains a partition table (that is, a volume that was upgraded from basic to dynamic), Windows XP Setup recognizes the spanned volume but cannot install to it, because the boot volume cannot be part of a spanned volume.

You can extend volumes that you created only after you convert the disk to a dynamic disk. You can extend volumes and make changes to disk configuration in most cases without rebooting your computer. If you want to take advantage of these features in Windows XP, you must change or upgrade a disk from basic to dynamic status, as covered earlier in this chapter. Use dynamic disks if your computer runs only Windows XP and you want to create more than four volumes per disk or want to extend, stripe, or span volumes onto one or more dynamic disks.

When You Are Upgrading from Windows NT 4 with Volume Sets on a Basic Disk

If you need to upgrade a computer running Windows NT 4 that has hard drives configured as volume sets or stripe sets, you must first back up all the data stored on each volume set or stripe set, because Windows XP Professional does not support volume sets or stripe sets on a basic disk. Striped and spanned volumes are only supported by dynamic disks under Windows XP Professional.

To migrate data on volume sets or stripe sets from Windows NT 4 to Windows XP Professional, perform the following steps:

1. Under Windows NT 4, back up the data.

2. Delete the volume(s).

3. Upgrade the operating system to Windows XP Professional.

4. Convert the appropriate hard disks from basic to dynamic disks.

5. Create the appropriate volume(s).

6. Restore the backed up data.

When You Are Upgrading from Windows 2000 Professional with Volume Sets on a Basic Disk

If you need to upgrade a computer running Windows 2000 Professional that has hard drives configured as volume sets or stripe sets, you must still back up all the data stored on each volume set or stripe set because Windows XP Professional does not support volume sets or stripe sets on a basic disk. Under Windows 2000 Professional, volume sets and stripe sets are supported on basic disks for backward compatibility, although you cannot create such sets on basic disks. Under Windows XP Professional, volume sets and stripe sets are strictly not supported. Windows XP Professional Setup will not allow an installation to complete if stripe sets or volume sets are present on basic disks.

To migrate data on volume sets or stripe sets stored on basic disks from Windows 2000 Professional to Windows XP Professional, perform the following steps:

1. Under Windows 2000, back up the data.

2. Under Windows 2000, use the Disk Management console to convert the basic disks to dynamic disks.

3. Upgrade the operating system to Windows XP Professional.

Troubleshooting Disks and Volumes

If a disk or volume fails, naturally you want to repair it as soon as possible to avoid losing data. The Disk Management snap-in makes it easy to locate problems quickly. In the Status column of the list view, you can view the status of a disk or volume. The status also appears in the graphical view of each disk or volume.

Diagnosing Problems

To diagnose disk and/or volume problems, perform the following steps:

1. Open Add Hardware in the Control Panel. Click Next. Windows XP tries to detect new Plug and Play devices.

2. Click Yes, I Have Already Connected The Hardware, and then click Next.

3. Choose the device you want to diagnose and fix, and then click Next.

4. The wizard will inform you of the device's current status. Click Finish to invoke the Hardware Troubleshooter as part of the Help and Support Center, or click Cancel to exit the Add Hardware Wizard.

Another way to troubleshoot hardware problems is with Device Manager. Right-click the My Computer icon from the Start menu and select Properties. Click the Hardware tab and then click the Device Manager button. Expand the hardware category that you need to troubleshoot and right-click the device that you want to inquire about. Select Properties from the context menu to display the properties window for that device, as shown in Figure 7.2. All the pertinent information about the device is available from this window, including its device status as determined by the operating system.

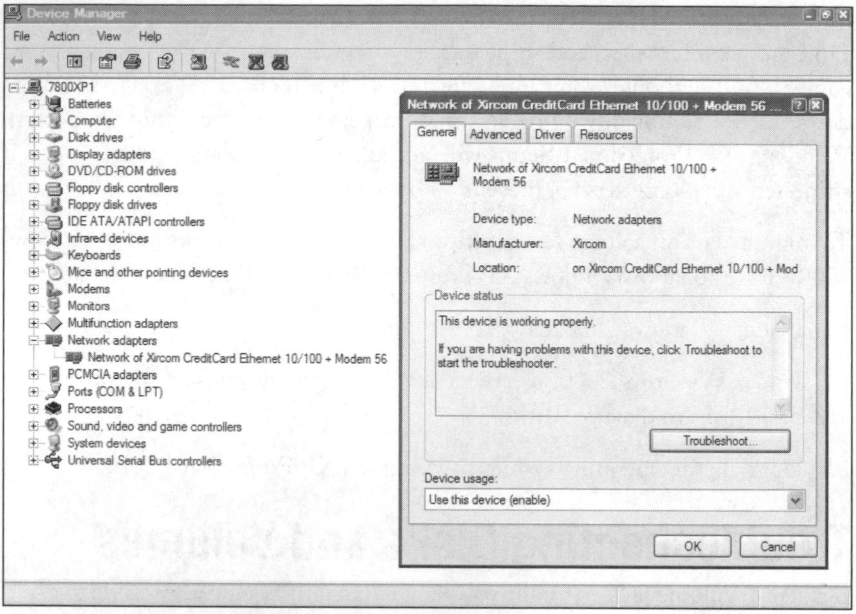

Figure 7.2   Using Device Manager to troubleshoot hardware issues.

Monitoring Disk Performance

The *Windows XP performance monitoring tool* is composed of two parts: System Monitor, and Performance Logs and Alerts. The MMC snap-in is simply named Performance. With *System Monitor*, you can collect and view real-time data about disk performance and activity in graph, histogram, or report form. *Performance Logs and Alerts* enables you to configure logs to record performance data and to set system alerts to notify you when a specified counter's value is above or below a defined threshold.

To open Performance, perform the following steps:

1. Click Start|Control Panel.

2. In the Control Panel, double-click Administrative Tools, and then double-click Performance. You will use System Monitor within Performance to monitor disk activity.

The Diskperf.exe command-line tool was used to control the types of physical and logical disk counters that you could enable for monitoring system performance under earlier versions of Windows. Under Windows XP, disk performance counters are *permanently enabled* and the LogicalDisk object counters have been removed. Instead of using the LogicalDisk object counters for measuring disk performance, Windows XP maps physical drives to logical drives by applying the same instance name. For example, if a computer contains a dynamic volume that is comprised of two physical hard disks, the logical drives might appear as Disk 0 C: and Disk 1 C:, which denotes that drive C spans physical disks 0 and 1. For a PC that has three logical volumes on one physical disk, the instance would appear as 0 C: D: E:.

Detecting and Repairing Disk Errors

In previous Windows operating systems, ScanDisk detected and fixed disk errors. In Windows XP, you can use the Error-Checking tool to check for file system errors and bad sectors on your hard disk.

To run the Error-Checking tool, perform the following steps:

1. Open My Computer and right-click the local disk you want to check.

2. Select Properties.

3. Click the Tools tab.

4. Under Error Checking, click Check Now.

5. Under Check Disk Options, select the Scan For And Attempt Recovery Of Bad Sectors checkbox and click Start.

All files must be closed for the Error-Checking process to run. Your volume is not available to run any other tasks while this process is running. If the volume is currently in use, a message asks if you want to reschedule the disk checking for the next time you restart your system. Then, the next time you restart your system, disk-checking runs. If your volume is formatted as NTFS, Windows XP automatically logs all file transactions, replaces bad clusters automatically, and stores copies of key information for all files on the NTFS volume.

The Disk Defragmenter Tool

Disk Defragmenter rearranges files, programs, and unused space on your computer's hard disk(s), allowing programs to run faster and files to open more quickly. Putting the pieces of files and programs in a more contiguous arrangement on disk reduces the time the operating system needs to access requested items.

To run Disk Defragmenter, perform the following steps:

1. Click Start|All Programs|Accessories|System Tools and then click Disk Defragmenter. Alternatively, you can right-click a drive letter in My Computer, select Properties, click the Tools tab, and click Defragment Now.

2. Select which disk(s) you would like to defragment and any additional options you would like to set.

3. Click the Defragment button to start the defragmentation process.

Note: Windows XP Professional ships with a command-line version of the disk defragmenter—Defrag.exe. You can run this program within a batch file or inside of a Windows script, which in turn can be scheduled to run automatically using the Scheduled Tasks folder.

Understanding Why Files Are Not Moved to the Beginning of NTFS Volumes

On NTFS volumes, Windows XP reserves a portion of the free space for a system file called the *master file table (MFT)*. The MFT is where Windows stores all the information it needs to retrieve files from the volume. Windows stores part of the MFT at the beginning of the volume. Windows reserves the MFT for exclusive use, so Disk Defragmenter cannot and does not move files to the beginning of volumes.

Using the Disk Cleanup Wizard

Disk Cleanup helps free up space on your hard drive by searching your drive(s) and then showing you a list of temporary files, Internet cache files, and potentially unnecessary program files that you can safely delete. You can instruct Disk Cleanup to delete none, some, or all of those files.

To use the Disk Cleanup Wizard, perform the following steps:

1. Click Start|All Programs|Accessories|System Tools.

2. Click the Disk Cleanup icon and follow the on-screen instructions.

File Systems Supported in Windows XP

The Compact Disc File System (CDFS) has full support for CD-based media in Windows XP. Although Windows XP does not support the High Performance File System (HPFS) as used under IBM's OS/2 operating system, it fully supports the FAT, FAT32, and NTFS file systems.

FAT and FAT32

Windows XP has full FAT (also known as FAT16) and FAT32 file system support with the following conditions or specifications:

➤ Preexisting FAT32 partitions up to 2TB are supported in Windows XP.

➤ By design, Windows XP allows you to create new FAT32 volumes of only 32GB or less.

➤ FAT volumes are limited to a maximum size of 4GB and can support a maximum file size of 2GB.

➤ FAT32 volumes can support a maximum file size of 4GB.

➤ You can install Windows XP onto a FAT, FAT32, or NTFS partition. Keep in mind that you have no local security for Windows XP unless you place the operating system on an NTFS partition.

➤ If you initially install Windows XP onto a FAT or FAT32 partition and then later use the Convert.exe utility to convert the partition to NTFS, default security settings are not applied to the %systemroot% folder or its subfolders. The %systemroot% environment variable maps to the Windows XP system folder, which, by default, is installed as the \Windows folder located on the root of the designated boot drive. Under Windows 2000 and previous versions of Windows NT, the %systemroot% folder was named the \Winnt folder by default.

The Windows XP NTFS File System

Windows XP Professional inherits the Windows 2000 NTFS version 5 file system. NTFS is Windows XP's native file system. This version of NTFS includes capabilities such as support for very granular file and folder permissions, support for disk quotas, the Encrypting File System (EFS), and a number of other useful features. The disk quotas feature is covered later in this chapter.

When you install Windows XP, existing legacy NTFS volumes are automatically upgraded to NTFS 5. No options are presented to choose NTFS 5 during the installation. The existing volumes are simply converted to NTFS 5 whether you want it or not.

When you install Windows XP to an NTFS partition, part of the Setup process is to apply default security settings to the system files and folders located on the boot partition (essentially the \Windows and \Program Files folders).

All local NTFS volumes, including removable media, are upgraded to the new version 5 of NTFS. This occurs after you restart your computer the first time after the graphical portion of Setup. Any NTFS volumes that are removed or powered off during the installation or upgrade process are upgraded automatically when those drives are mounted. If, during the installation, the system detects a version of Windows NT earlier than Windows NT 4 with Service Pack 4 (SP4), you will see a warning message indicating that an earlier version of Windows NT was found and that Windows NT will not be accessible if you continue. Windows NT Workstation 4 *can* be upgraded to Windows XP Professional without applying service packs. However, if you want to create a new installation of Windows XP and dual-boot with Windows NT 4, then you will see the warning.

If you want to configure your computer to run Windows NT 4 and Windows XP, you need to upgrade your version of Windows NT 4 to SP4 or later. An updated NTFS.SYS driver is included in NT 4 SP4 and later SPs that enables NT 4 to read from and write to NTFS 5 volumes created with Windows 2000 or Windows XP. If you expect to dual-boot Windows 98 (or Windows Me) with Windows XP, remember that Windows 98/Me can read only FAT and FAT32 file systems.

Converting from One File System to Another

Windows XP supports converting from one file system to another, with some special caveats and limitations that you need to be well aware of.

Converting a FAT or FAT32 Partition to an NTFS Partition

Let's say that you want to convert drive D: to NTFS, from either FAT or FAT32. No problem! From the command line (click Start|Run, type "CMD.EXE", and click OK), enter the command "convert d: /fs:ntfs". If the FAT or FAT32 partition is the boot partition, the conversion takes place when the machine next reboots, because many of the operating system files are locked. This command is a one-way ticket only and is *not reversible*. However, if you convert the *boot* volume, you do have one option *before* the computer restarts. The boot volume should not be confused with what Microsoft calls the system volume (the first logical operating system partition, usually denoted as the C: drive). Figure 7.3 shows an example of the Disk Management console where both the system and boot volumes are identified in parentheses for the C: drive and the F: drive, respectively. Of course, the system volume and the boot volume may be one and the same.

If you decide to undo the conversion to NTFS for the boot volume (the volume that contains the \Windows folder, also known as the %systemroot% folder), *before*

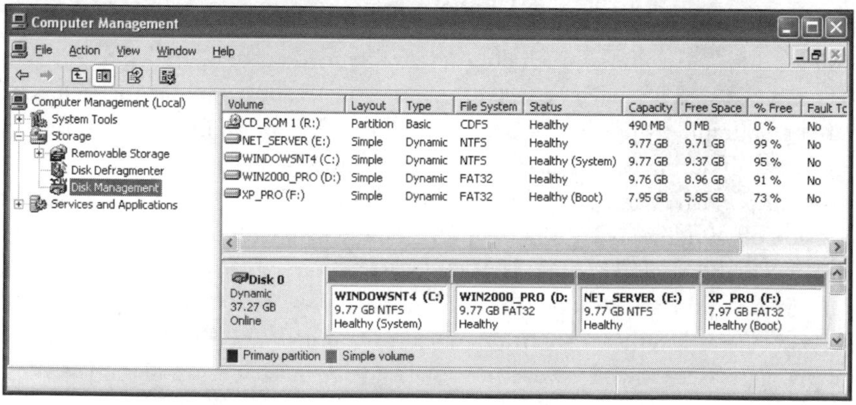

Figure 7.3   The Disk Management console shows which drive volume is the system volume and which is the boot volume.

you restart the computer, you may edit the Windows XP Registry to remove the NTFS file system conversion flag that gets placed by the Convert.exe utility. As a warning: Editing the Windows XP Registry is a risky procedure that can render a computer unstable or unbootable—be sure to have a good, recent backup before editing the Registry. You can use the Regedit.exe tool to modify the following Registry entry: HKEY_LOCAL_MACHINE\CurrentControlSet\Control\ Session Manager. Change the BootExecute value data from "autoconv \DosDevices\ x: /FS:NTFS" to "autocheck autochk*", where x: denotes the volume drive letter to be converted.

After the conversion, NTFS file permissions are set to Full Control for the Everyone group. However, if the %systemroot% folder resides on a newly converted NTFS volume, the permissions for the \Winnt folder and \Program Files folder and associated files should be properly secured using NTFS permissions.

Myth: Converting an NTFS Partition to a FAT Partition

You *cannot* convert an NTFS partition to a FAT partition. A simple conversion using the Convert.exe command-line utility is not possible. Your only course of action, if you want to keep the data, is to back up all the data on the drive. Then, use the Disk Management tool to reformat the disk to the flavor of FAT you prefer and restore your backed up data to your newly formatted disk.

Reapplying Default NTFS Permissions

You may need or want to reapply the default NTFS permissions to the system boot partition if you changed them or never applied them to begin with (because you converted the boot partition to NTFS after installation). To reapply the default NTFS permissions, use the Secedit.exe utility, which comes with Windows XP, from the command prompt. The computer must still be bootable under Windows XP for this approach to work.

Assigning, Changing, or Removing Drive Letters

To assign, change, or remove a drive letter, perform the following steps:

1. Open Disk Management.

2. Right-click a partition, logical drive, or volume, and then click Change Drive Letter And Paths.

3. Do one of the following:

   ➤ *To assign a drive letter*—Click Add, select the drive letter you want to use, and then click OK.

➤ *To change a drive letter*—Click Change, select the drive letter you want to use, and then click OK.

➤ *To remove a drive letter*—Click Remove, either click Yes to confirm the removal or click No to cancel the removal, and then click OK.

An old "gotcha" still applies. Be careful when assigning drive letters, because many MS-DOS and Windows applications refer to a specific drive letter, especially during installation. For example, the PATH environment variable shows specific drive letters in conjunction with program names.

You can use up to 24 drive letters, from C: through Z:. Drive letters A: and B: are reserved for floppy disk drives. However, if you do not have a floppy disk drive B:, you can use the letter B: for a network drive. You cannot change the drive letter of the system volume or boot volume.

An error message may appear when you attempt to assign a letter to a volume, CD-ROM drive, or other removable media device, possibly because a program in the system is using it. If this happens, close the program that is accessing the volume or drive, and then click the Change Drive Letter And Paths option again.

Windows XP allows you to statically assign drive letters on volumes, partitions, and CD-ROM drives. This means that you permanently assign a drive letter to a specific partition, volume, or CD-ROM drive. When you add a new hard disk to an existing computer system, it does not affect statically assigned drive letters. You can also mount a local drive through an empty folder on an NTFS volume by using a drive path instead of a drive letter. This feature is known as using mounted drives.

Mounted Drives

Mounted drives, also known as *mount points* or *mounted volumes*, are useful for increasing a drive's "size" without disturbing it. For example, you could create a mount point to drive E: as C:\CompanyData, thus seeming to increase the size available on the C: partition, which would specifically allow you to store more data in C:\CompanyData than you could otherwise. Drive paths are available only on empty folders on NTFS volumes. The NTFS volumes can be basic or dynamic.

Creating a Mounted Drive

To create a mounted drive, perform the following steps:

1. Open Disk Management.

2. Right-click the partition or volume you want to mount and then click Change Drive Letter And Paths.

3. Do one of the following:

➤ *To mount a volume*—Select Add. Click Mount In The Following Empty NTFS Folder and type the path to an empty folder on an NTFS volume, or click Browse to locate it.

➤ *To unmount a volume*—Select the drive letter path and then click Remove. Confirm your selection by clicking Yes to remove the mount point, or click No to retain it.

When you mount a local drive in an empty folder on an NTFS volume, Windows XP assigns a drive path to the drive rather than a drive letter.

To modify a drive path, remove it and then create a new drive path using the new location. You cannot modify the drive path directly. If you are administering a local computer, you can browse NTFS folders on that computer. If you are administering a remote computer, browsing is disabled and you must type the path to an existing NTFS folder.

Support for FAT32 on DVD-RAM Disks

Under Windows XP Professional, DVD-RAM disks can be used as CD-ROM devices, as DVD-ROM devices, or as recordable and rewritable media. Windows XP employs the FAT32 file system for both read and write operations on DVD-RAM disks. The Universal Disk Format (UDF) file system is utilized for read-only operations. Windows XP support for DVD-RAM disks includes multiple session recording and logical block addressing. See the Windows XP Hardware Compatibility List (HCL) on the Microsoft Web site (**www.microsoft.com/ hcl/default.asp**) for a current listing of supported DVD-RAM drives.

Disk Quotas

Windows XP disk quotas track and control disk usage on a per-user, per-volume basis. You can apply disk quotas only to Windows XP NTFS volumes. Quotas are tracked for each volume, even if the volumes reside on the same physical disk. The per-user feature of quotas enables you to track every user's disk space usage regardless of which folder the user stores files in. Disk quotas do not use compression to measure disk space usage, so users cannot obtain or use more space simply by compressing their own data. To enable disk quotas, open the Properties dialog box for a disk, select the Quota tab, and configure the options as shown in Figure 7.4.

When a user no longer stores data on a volume, you need to delete disk quota entries. The catch to this is that you can delete the user's quota entries only after you have removed from the volume all files that the user owns, or after another

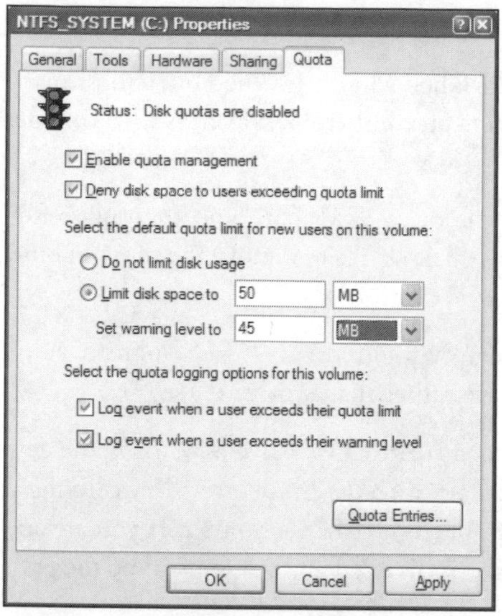

Figure 7.4 The Quota tab of the Properties dialog box for an NTFS volume enables you to configure Windows XP disk quota options.

user has taken ownership of the files. By default, only members of the Administrators group can view and change quota entries and settings. In addition, all members of the Administrators group inherit *unlimited* disk quotas by default. To work with disk quota entries, click the Quota Entries button on the Quota tab of an NTFS drive volume's Properties dialog box. The Quota Entries window is shown in Figure 7.5.

Set identical or individual disk quota limits for all user accounts that access a specific volume. Then, use per-user disk quota entries to allow more (a fairly common scenario) or less (for those disk space hogs!) disk space to individual users when necessary.

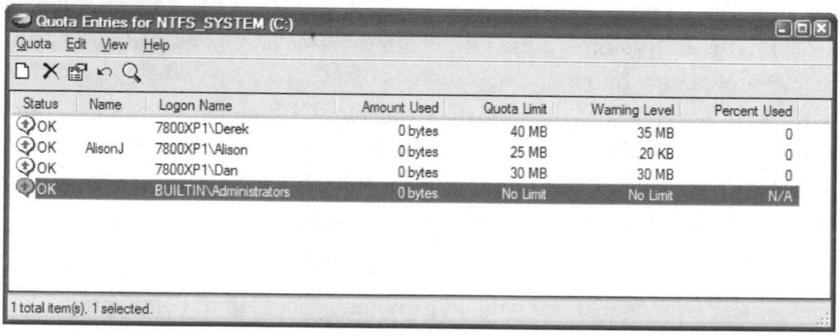

Status	Name	Logon Name	Amount Used	Quota Limit	Warning Level	Percent Used
OK		7800XP1\Derek	0 bytes	40 MB	35 MB	0
OK	AlisonJ	7800XP1\Alison	0 bytes	25 MB	20 KB	0
OK		7800XP1\Dan	0 bytes	30 MB	30 MB	0
OK		BUILTIN\Administrators	0 bytes	No Limit	No Limit	N/A

1 total item(s), 1 selected.

Figure 7.5 The Quota Entries window enables you to set and remove disk quota limits and warning levels for individual users.

Data Compression

Windows XP Professional supports two types of data compression: NTFS compression and a new Compressed (Zipped) Folders feature. Files and folders compressed using the Compressed (Zipped) Folders feature remain compressed under all three supported file systems—NTFS, FAT, and FAT32. Compressing any system folders, such as the \Windows folder or the \Program Files folder, is not recommended. Compressed (Zipped) Folders are identified by a zipper icon that is part of the folder's icon. To create a Compressed (Zipped) Folder, right-click a folder, point to Send To, and click Compressed (Zipped) Folder. This action actually creates a Zip file that Windows XP recognizes as a Compressed (Zipped) Folder that contains the folder you selected to be compressed along with all of that folder's contents. You can also use any popular third-party utility, such as WinZip or PKZip, to read, write, add, or remove files to any Compressed (Zipped) Folder.

The NTFS file system under Windows XP enables you to compress individual files and folders so that they occupy less space on the NTFS volume. Any Windows- or DOS-based program can read and write to NTFS compressed files without having to decompress them first. The compressed files decompress when opened and recompress when closed. The Windows XP NTFS file system handles this entire process transparently to the user. You can use Windows Explorer to have compressed items displayed in a different color than uncompressed items.

Setting the compression state (compressed or uncompressed) on a file or folder is as simple as setting a file or folder attribute. Simply right-click the file or folder that you'd like to compress or uncompress and select Properties. On the General tab, click the Advanced button. Check or clear the Compress Contents To Save Disk Space checkbox. Click OK twice to exit both dialog boxes.

Instead of compressing individual files or even individual folders, you can choose to compress an entire NTFS drive volume. To compress an entire NTFS volume, right-click an NTFS drive volume in My Computer or in Windows Explorer, select Properties, and mark the checkbox labeled Compress Drive To Save Disk Space, as shown in Figure 7.6. Click OK to close the drive volume's Properties dialog box.

Moving and Copying Compressed Files and Folders

A simple method exists for remembering whether the original compression attribute of an object is retained or inherited when you are moving and/or copying files and folders. For Zipped Compressed folders, they retain their compression no matter where they are copied to. For NTFS-compressed files and folders: When you *move* a compressed or uncompressed file or folder from one location

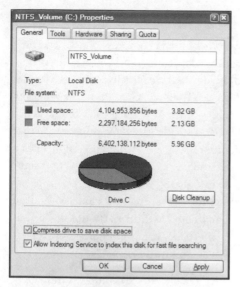

Figure 7.6 The Properties dialog box for an NTFS drive volume where you can mark the checkbox to Compress Drive To Save Disk Space.

to another within the same NTFS volume, the original compression attribute is *retained*. That is all you need to remember about NTFS compression, because in *all* other scenarios, the compression attribute is *inherited* from the *new*, or target, location.

NTFS Compression Guidelines

NTFS allocates disk space based on the *uncompressed* size of a file. If you try to copy a compressed file to an NTFS volume with enough space for the compressed file, but not the uncompressed file, you get an error message telling you there is inadequate disk space to copy the file to the target. Plan ahead.

 If you attempt to copy or move an NTFS-compressed file to a floppy, be prepared for the Insufficient Disk Space error. If the uncompressed size of the file is larger than the capacity of the floppy, you cannot copy or move the file. Use a third-party compression tool, such as WinZip, for this operation.

Make it a practice to use NTFS compression only on static data, and not on data that frequently changes, because applying or removing the compression attribute does incur system overhead. NTFS encryption and compression are mutually exclusive. You can encrypt or compress a file or folder, but not both. Windows XP does not support NTFS compression for volumes with cluster sizes larger than 4KB because of the performance degradation it would cause.

Data Encryption

The NTFS file system for Windows XP Professional also supports data encryption. Just as with NTFS data compression, data encryption is set as an advanced attribute for a file or a folder. With NTFS data encryption, Microsoft has given you a secure method for keeping confidential documents private.

Keeping Data Private with the Encrypting File System (EFS)

Microsoft designed EFS for Windows XP to ensure the confidentiality of sensitive data. EFS employs public key/private key–based cryptography. EFS works only with the NTFS 5 file system under Windows XP and Windows 2000. Its use is transparent to users. You can either compress or encrypt files and folders, but you can't do both. Files that are encrypted using EFS remain encrypted even if you move or rename them. Encrypted files that are backed up or copied also retain their encryption attributes as long as they reside on NTFS-formatted drive volumes. EFS leaves no file remnants behind because it modifies an encrypted file, nor does it leave any traces of decrypted data from encrypted files in tempo rary files or in the Windows XP paging file. You can encrypt and decrypt files and folders from the graphical user interface (GUI) by using Windows Explorer, as well as from the command line by using the Cipher.exe tool.

Encrypting Folders and Files

The best practice for using encryption is to first encrypt a folder and then move files into the encrypted folder. Folders do not actually become encrypted; folders get marked with the encryption attribute. The files contained within an encrypted folder are the objects that actually become encrypted. You can also individually encrypt files without their having to reside within a folder that is marked for encryption. To encrypt and decrypt files physically located on a Windows 2000 server or on a Windows .NET server over the network, that server must be trusted for delegation. By definition, domain controllers are already trusted for delegation. Member servers require this Trust For Delegation setting. To encrypt a file or folder from Windows Explorer, follow these steps:

1. Right-click the file or folder and select Properties.

2. From the General tab, click the Advanced button.

3. Click the Encrypt Contents To Secure Data checkbox in the Advanced Attributes dialog box.

4. Click OK.

5. Click OK in the Properties dialog box. The folder then becomes encrypted, and any files and folders that are placed within it are encrypted. If subfolders or files exist within the folder, the Confirm Attribute Changes dialog box, shown in Figure 7.7, appears.

6. Click either Apply Changes To This Folder Only or Apply Changes To This Folder, Subfolders And Files to specify the object(s) that you want encryption to affect.

7. Click OK; the encryption attribute is applied to the appropriate objects.

If you want to unencrypt a file or folder, perform the same steps as outlined previously and simply clear the Encrypt Contents To Secure Data checkbox in the Advanced Attributes dialog box.

Issues to Remember about Using EFS

Only files and folders located on NTFS volumes may be encrypted. If you encrypt a file or folder that is already compressed using NTFS compression, that file or folder will become uncompressed. You cannot (and should not) encrypt any files that are marked with the System attribute, nor can you encrypt files that are stored within the %systemroot% folder structure, which, by default, is the \Windows folder. Windows XP offers you the option of displaying both compressed and encrypted folders and files in a different color. This feature enables you to readily identify objects that have one of these advanced attributes. You configure this feature as a part of the View tab of the Folder Options dialog box available from the Control Panel, as shown in Figure 7.8.

Accessing Encrypted Files and Data Recovery Agents (DRAs)

Encryption is just an extended (or advanced) attribute of a file or folder. If you set NTFS permissions to deny the Write Attributes permission on a file or folder, the users to whom you have assigned this Deny permission cannot use encryption. To work with NTFS permissions on a Windows XP computer that is not a member of an Active Directory domain, you must clear the Use Simple File

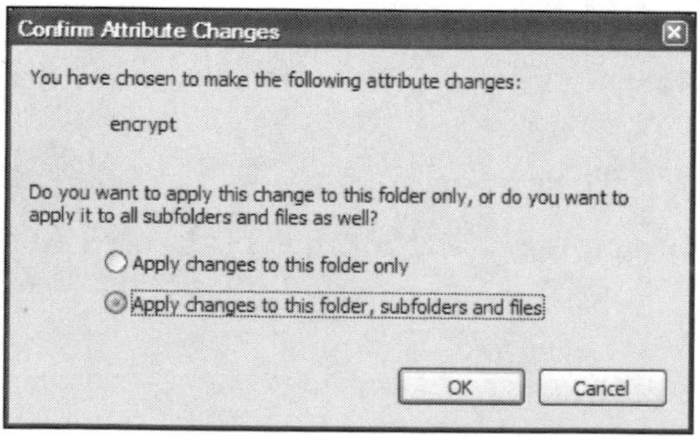

Figure 7.7 The Confirm Attribute Changes dialog box.

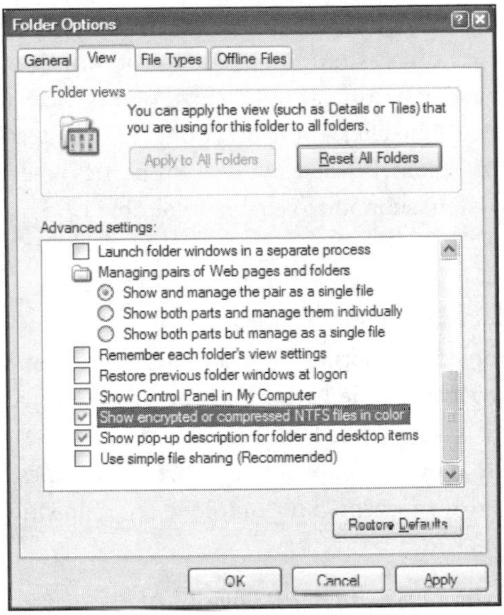

Figure 7.8 The Show Encrypted Or Compressed NTFS Files In Color option on the View tab of the Folder Options dialog box.

Sharing (Recommended) checkbox from the Folder Options dialog box. After a file has the encryption attribute, only the user who encrypted it or the DRA can access it. DRAs are users who are designated as recovery agents for encrypted files. Only these users have the ability to decrypt *any* encrypted file, no matter who has encrypted it. Other users who attempt to access an encrypted file receive an Access Is Denied message. The default DRAs are as follows:

➤ Users who are members of the local Administrators group for Windows XP Professional nondomain member computers

➤ Users who are members of the local Administrators group for Windows 2000 Server and Windows .NET Server nondomain member servers

➤ Users who are members of the Domain Administrators group for Windows 2000 Server or Windows .NET Server domain controllers, Windows domain member servers, and Windows XP Professional domain member computers

DRAs can log on to a system and decrypt files and folders so that they are once again accessible to other users. Nondomain member Windows XP Professional computers issue a default self-signed certificate that designates the default Administrator user as the DRA. If you remove any and all DRAs from a standalone Windows XP computer or from a Windows Active Directory domain, no Data Recovery policy is in place and, therefore, EFS will *prohibit* users from encrypting files and folders. You can manage the EFS recovery policy for the local Windows

XP computer via the Group Policy snap-in for the Microsoft Management Console (MMC). Expand the Group Policy snap-in node for Computer Configuration|Windows Settings|Security Settings|Public Key Policies. Select the Encrypting File System subnode. Right-click the Encrypting File System subnode and select Add Data Recovery Agent, or you can select Properties when you right-click the Encrypting File System subnode to enable or disable EFS on the computer, as shown in Figure 7.9.

Moving and Copying Encrypted Files

Encrypted files that are moved or copied to another NTFS folder remain encrypted. Encrypted files that are moved or copied to a FAT or FAT32 drive volume become decrypted because EFS is supported only on NTFS 5 volumes. Files also become decrypted if they are moved or copied to a floppy disk. Unless users have been granted shared access to an encrypted file or folder, the following rules apply:

➤ Users who did not originally encrypt a file or folder receive an Access Is Denied message if they try to copy an encrypted file or folder.

➤ If users other than the one who encrypted the file attempt to move it to a different NTFS volume, or to a FAT or FAT32 drive volume, they receive an Access Is Denied error message.

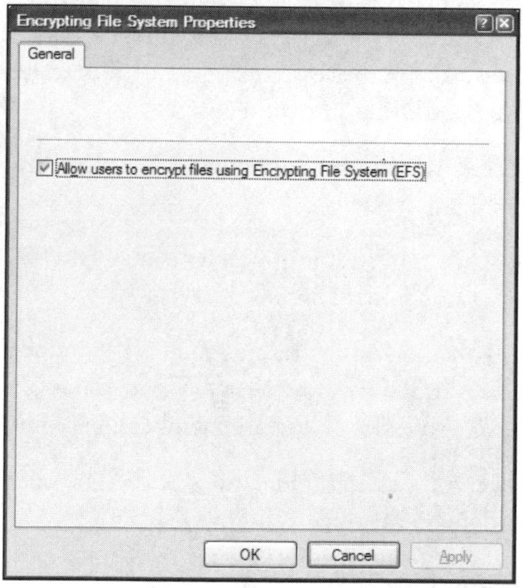

Figure 7.9 The Properties dialog box for the local Recovery Policy for the Encrypting File System.

➤ If users other than the one who encrypted the file attempt to move the encrypted file to a different folder located on the *same* NTFS volume, the file is moved.

Sharing Access to Encrypted Files with Other Users

You can now share confidential access to encrypted files under Windows XP Professional. This shared access applies only on a file-by-file basis; it does not apply to folders. To grant other users access to an encrypted file, each user must have already encrypted at least one file or folder previously so that either the local Windows XP system or the Active Directory domain has issued the user an EFS-compatible certificate. To add or remove users for shared access to encrypted files, you must be the original user who encrypted the file or you must be one of the users already listed as having shared access to the file. Perform the following steps to share access to an encrypted file with one or more other users:

1. Right-click a file that you have already encrypted under EFS and select Properties.

2. Click the Advanced button from the General tab.

3. Click the Details button to display the Encryption Details dialog box for the encrypted file.

4. Click the Add button to display the Select User dialog box, as shown in Figure 7.10. The Find User button is only available when the computer is a member of an Active Directory domain.

5. Click the user with whom you want to share access to this file and then click OK. Repeat this step for each user with whom you want to share access to this file.

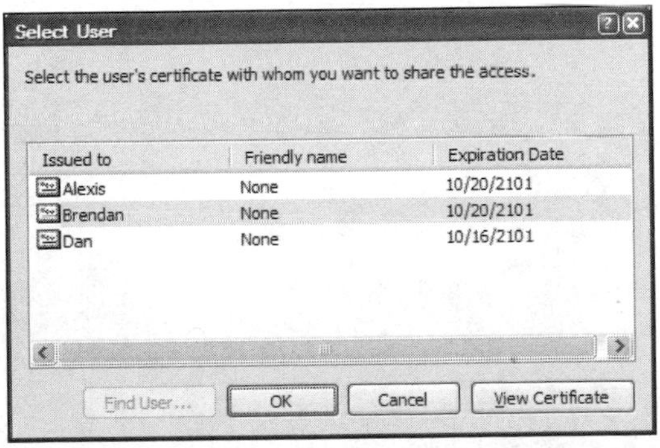

Figure 7.10   The Select User dialog box enables you to pick other users with whom to share access to an encrypted file.

6. Click OK to close the Encryption Details dialog box. This dialog box should display all the users who can transparently access the encrypted file, similar to Figure 7.11.

7. Click OK to close the Advanced Attributes dialog box, and then click OK again to close the encrypted file's Properties dialog box.

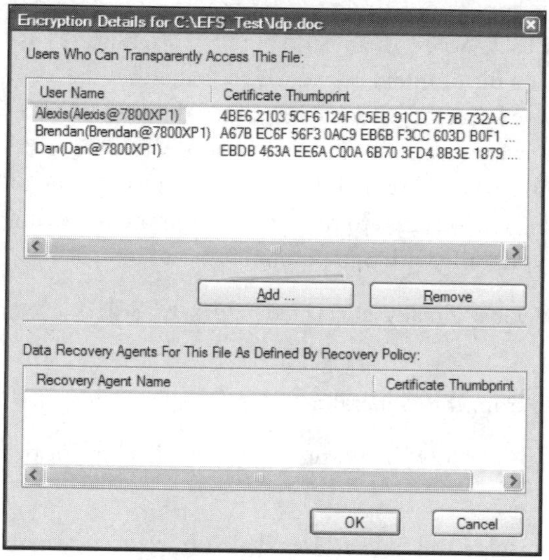

Figure 7.11   The Encryption Details dialog box enables you to view, add, and remove users who can access the encrypted file.

Practice Questions

Question 1

Brendan wants to convert one of the hard drives connected to his Windows XP Professional desktop computer from a basic disk to a dynamic disk. In the Disk Management console, he right-clicks the physical disk designated as Disk 1, but the option to Convert To Dynamic Disk is unavailable. Why would the option to convert the drive to a dynamic disk be disabled?

○ a. There are already drive volumes with data stored on that physical disk.

○ b. The drive is an external drive connected via USB or IEEE 1394 bus connections.

○ c. The drive is an external Fibre Channel device.

○ d. The drive has a sector size of greater than 512 bytes.

Answer b is correct. Hard disks connected via USB or Firewire (IEEE 1394) buses are not supported for dynamic disks. Answer a is incorrect because you are allowed to convert disks with existing drive volumes and data to dynamic disks—you cannot convert back to a basic disk without deleting all existing volumes (and therefore the data on those volumes), however. Answer c is incorrect because dynamic disks do support Fibre Channel drives. Answer d is incorrect because only disks that have a sector size of less than 512 bytes are not supported by dynamic disks.

Question 2

Alexis wants to convert physical hard disk number 2 on her Windows XP Professional desktop computer from a basic disk to a dynamic disk using only the command line. Is a command-line tool available to accomplish this task? If so, what is the name of this utility and does it differ from the Disk Management console?

- ○ a. The command-line tool is called Diskperf.exe. Only administrative users may use it.

- ○ b. No command-line tool equivalent to the Disk Management MMC exists.

- ○ c. The command-line tool is called Diskpart.exe. You must restart the computer for the conversion process to take effect.

- ○ d. The command-line tool is called Convert.exe. You do not need to restart the computer for the conversion to take place unless you are converting the boot disk.

Answer c is correct. Diskpart.exe is the command-line equivalent to Disk Management. You must restart the computer for the conversion to take effect. Answer a is incorrect because Diskperf.exe enables and disables hard disk performance counters on earlier versions of Windows; it does nothing for converting basic disks to dynamic disks. Answer b is incorrect because a command-line utility functionally equivalent to Disk Management exists—Diskpart.exe. Answer d is incorrect because the Convert.exe command-line tool is used to convert a FAT or FAT32 volume to NTFS.

Question 3

What are the three types of dynamic volumes that are supported by dynamic disks under Windows XP Professional? [Check all correct answers]

- ❑ a. Spanned volumes

- ❑ b. Extended volumes

- ❑ c. RAID-5 volumes

- ❑ d. Simple volumes

- ❑ e. Volume sets

- ❑ f. Striped volumes

- ❑ g. Mirrored volumes

Answers a, d, and f are correct. Spanned volumes enable you to store data sequentially over two or more physical disks, but Windows XP displays the disks as one logical drive volume. Simple volumes are the most fundamental dynamic volumes, with each simple volume residing on only one physical disk. Striped volumes are also supported under Windows XP, enabling you to store data in stripes across two or more physical disks, but Windows XP displays the disks as one logical drive volume. Answer b is incorrect because there is no such volume as an extended volume on a dynamic disk. Answer c is incorrect because Windows XP Professional does not support the fault-tolerant RAID-5 volume configuration. Answer e is incorrect because volume sets were supported for basic disks under Windows NT—these are known as spanned volumes under Windows XP. Answer g is incorrect because Windows XP Professional does not support the fault-tolerant mirrored volume configuration.

Question 4

Sue has a Windows XP Professional computer that has two physical hard drives installed—both disks have been converted to dynamic disks. The first disk (disk 0) has a capacity of 20GB with 1GB of unallocated free space, a drive C: (system and boot) volume of 2GB, and a drive D: volume of 7GB. The second disk (disk 1) has a capacity of 30GB with 20GB of unallocated free space. Sue needs to extend drive D: (a simple volume) on her computer so that the volume will have an increased amount of total disk space—from 7GB to 14GB. How can she accomplish this without deleting any existing data? [Check all correct answers]

- ❑ a. Repartition and reformat drive C:.
- ❑ b. Extend drive D: to an area of free space on disk 1.
- ❑ c. Extend drive D: to an area of free space on disk 0.
- ❑ d. Convert disk 1 to basic and extend the volume.

Answers b and c are correct. A simple volume on a dynamic disk may be extended onto unallocated free space of additional dynamic disks up to a maximum of 32 dynamic disks—this automatically turns the volume into a spanned volume. A simple volume on a dynamic disk may also be extended onto an area of unallocated free space on the same dynamic disk. Answer a is incorrect because repartitioning and reformatting a disk deletes any data stored on the disk. Answer d is incorrect because converting a disk from dynamic to basic deletes any data stored on the disk.

Question 5

To make accessing several different hard drive volumes and removable drives easier on a local Windows XP computer, you want your users to be able to access each drive volume through different folder names located on the same drive letter. How can you accomplish this?

○ a. Use the Subst.exe command-line utility to specify each folder as a unique drive letter.

○ b. Use the Disk Management console to create mount points for each hard drive volume letter through empty folders on the same FAT or FAT32 volume.

○ c. Use Diskpart.exe to create mount points for each hard drive volume letter through empty folders on the same NTFS volume.

○ d. Use Diskperf.exe to create mount points for each hard drive volume letter through empty folders on the same NTFS volume.

Answer c is correct. You may use either Diskpart.exe or the Disk Management MMC snap-in to create mount points for a drive letter through empty NTFS folders. Answer a is incorrect because the Subst.exe command associates a specific drive letter path with a different drive letter root folder. Answer b is incorrect because you can only create mount points on empty NTFS folders. Answer d is incorrect because Diskperf.exe enables and disables hard disk performance counters on earlier versions of Windows.

Question 6

What is the easiest way to convert an NTFS drive volume configured as drive D: to the FAT32 file system without losing any existing data? Assume that the volume is not the system or boot volume.

○ a. Use the command "convert d: /fs:fat32".

○ b. Use the command "convert d: /fs:-ntfs".

○ c. Use the Disk Management console to revert the volume back to FAT or FAT32.

○ d. Back up all the data stored on the NTFS drive volume, use Diskpart.exe or the Disk Management console to delete the volume, create a new volume, format the volume as FAT32, and then restore the backed up data.

Answer d is correct. Windows XP does not offer a conversion tool for converting an existing NTFS volume to FAT, FAT32, or any other file system. You must back up all the data on the volume, create a new volume, format it, and restore the data. Answer a is incorrect because the Convert.exe command does not support the conversion to the FAT or FAT32 file system. Answer b is incorrect because the Convert.exe command-line tool only supports a conversion to NTFS— prepending a minus sign (-) to the NTFS parameter is not supported. Answer c is incorrect because the Disk Management console only supports reformatting an existing NTFS drive volume to convert it to the FAT or FAT32 file system.

Question 7

How can you set disk quotas on NTFS drive volumes for the Power Users group and for the Administrators group?

O a. Right-click the drive lettor In My Computer, select Properties, click the Quota tab, and mark the checkboxes for Enable Quota Management and Deny Disk Space To Users Exceeding Quota Limit. Click Apply and click the Quota Entries button. Configure quota entries for the Power Users group and for the Administrators group.

O b. Right-click the drive letter in My Computer, select Properties, click the Quota tab, and mark the checkboxes for Enable Quota Management and Deny Disk Space To Users Exceeding Quota Limit. Click Apply and click the Quota Entries button. Configure quota entries for the Power Users group.

O c. Right-click the drive letter in My Computer, select Properties, click the Quota tab, and mark the checkboxes for Enable Quota Management and Deny Disk Space To Users Exceeding Quota Limit. Click Apply and click the Quota Entries button. Configure quota entries for each member of the Power Users group.

O d. Create a new local group named Super Users and make all the members of the Power Users group and the Administrators group members of this new group. Right-click the drive letter in My Computer, select Properties, click the Quota tab, and mark the checkboxes for Enable Quota Management and Deny Disk Space To Users Exceeding Quota Limit. Click Apply and click the Quota Entries button. Configure quota entries for the Super Users group.

Answer c is correct. Windows XP Professional supports disk quotas on NTFS drive volumes only for individual users, not for groups. Therefore, you would have to create a quota entry for each member of the Power Users group—you cannot assign a quota limit to a group. All members of the Administrators group inherit a no-limit disk quota by default, so you cannot set quotas on members of this group. Answer a is incorrect for the reasons just cited. Answer b is incorrect because you cannot set quotas on groups. Answer d is incorrect for the same reason.

Question 8

Brandy wants to move an NTFS-compressed file from NTFS drive D: to an uncompressed folder on NTFS drive F:. What will happen to the file when she performs this operation?

○ a. The compressed file will become uncompressed when it is moved to drive F:.

○ b. The compressed file will remain compressed when it is moved to drive F:.

○ c. Windows XP will prompt the user as to whether the file should remain compressed or should be uncompressed after it is moved.

○ d. Brandy will receive an error message when she attempts to move the file to an uncompressed folder.

Answer a is correct. When you move a compressed file from one NTFS volume to a different NTFS volume, the file inherits the compression attribute from the target location. Answer b is incorrect because an NTFS compressed folder or file only retains its compression attribute when it is moved to another folder on the same NTFS volume. Answer c is incorrect because Windows XP never prompts the user as to whether a folder or file should remain compressed or uncompressed. Answer d is incorrect because Windows XP does not generate error messages for moving compressed files to an uncompressed folder.

Question 9

Terry encrypts an NTFS folder named SECRET DOCS on the hard drive of a Windows XP Professional computer. Terry is the only user with access to all the encrypted files in the SECRET DOCS folder (except for the DRA). Terry shares the computer with her associate, Kim. Kim is not the DRA. Later, Kim logs on to the same computer and attempts to copy one of the files stored inside of the SECRET DOCS folder, named Salaries.xls, to a floppy disk in drive A. After that, Kim tries to move the same file to an unencrypted folder on the same NTFS drive volume named PUBLIC DOCS. What are the results of Kim's file operations?

○ a. Kim will receive an error message for trying to copy the encrypted file to a floppy disk, but he will successfully be able to move the encrypted file to the PUBLIC DOCS unencrypted NTFS folder, where the file will remain encrypted.

○ b. Kim will receive an error message for trying to copy the encrypted file to a floppy disk and he will also receive an error message for attempting to move the encrypted file to the PUBLIC DOCS unencrypted NTFS folder.

○ c. Kim will receive an error message for trying to copy the encrypted file to a floppy disk, but he will be able to successfully move the encrypted file to the PUBLIC DOCS unencrypted NTFS folder, where it will lose its encryption attribute.

○ d. Kim will successfully copy the encrypted file to a floppy disk, where it will remain encrypted, and he will successfully be able to move the encrypted file to the PUBLIC DOCS unencrypted NTFS folder.

Answer a is correct. Only the user who originally encrypted the file (or any users given shared access to the encrypted file) may copy the file to a non-NTFS drive volume or to any type of removable media. In addition, only the user who originally encrypted the file (or any users given shared access to the encrypted file) may copy the file or move it to a folder located on a different NTFS volume. A user without shared access to an encrypted file is only permitted to move the file to another folder located on the same NTFS volume, where the file remains encrypted. Answer b is incorrect because, although Kim will receive an error message when he attempts to copy the file to a floppy disk, he will not receive an error message when he attempts to move the encrypted file to an unencrypted NTFS folder located on the same NTFS volume. Answer c is incorrect because, although Kim will receive an error message when he attempts to copy the file to a floppy disk, he will be allowed to move the encrypted file to an unencrypted NTFS folder located on the same NTFS volume, but the file will not lose its encryption attribute. Answer d is incorrect because Kim will receive an error message when he attempts to copy the encrypted file to a floppy disk.

Need to Know More?

 Bott, Ed and Carl Siechert. *Microsoft Windows XP Inside Out*. Redmond, WA: Microsoft Press, 2001. ISBN 0-73561-382-6. This book offers timesaving tips, troubleshooting techniques, and workarounds. It focuses on techniques such as taking advantage of the rich integration of devices, applications, and Web services in Windows XP.

 Microsoft Corporation. *Microsoft Windows XP Professional Resource Kit Documentation*. Redmond, WA: Microsoft Press, 2001. ISBN 0-73561-485-7. This all-in-one reference is a compilation of technical documentation and valuable insider information that computer-support professionals and administrators can reference to install, customize, and support Windows XP.

 Minasi, Mark. *Mastering Windows XP Professional*. Alameda, CA: Sybex, Inc., 2001. ISBN 0-78212-981-1. This book provides in-depth coverage of installing, configuring, and administering Windows XP Professional.

Search the Microsoft TechNet CD (or its online version through **www.microsoft.com**) using keywords such as "Fsutil", "Diskpart", "Disk Quotas", "NTFS Encryption", and "Dynamic Disks".

Implementing, Managing, and Troubleshooting Network Protocols and Services

Terms you'll need to understand:

- ✓ Transmission Control Protocol/Internet Protocol (TCP/IP)
- ✓ Dynamic Host Configuration Protocol (DHCP)
- ✓ Domain Name System (DNS)
- ✓ Windows Internet Naming Service (WINS)
- ✓ Automatic Private IP Addressing (APIPA)
- ✓ File Transfer Protocol (FTP)
- ✓ Simple Mail Transfer Protocol (SMTP)

- ✓ Address Resolution Protocol (ARP)
- ✓ **ipconfig**
- ✓ **ping**
- ✓ **route**
- ✓ **tracert**
- ✓ TCP/IP profiles
- ✓ Bridged connection
- ✓ Windows Messenger
- ✓ Remote Desktop
- ✓ Remote Assistance

Techniques you'll need to master:

- ✓ Configuring and troubleshooting TCP/IP
- ✓ Configuring protocols to inter-operate with Unix and Novell
- ✓ Configuring a network bridge

- ✓ Using Windows Messenger
- ✓ Configuring and troubleshooting Remote Desktop
- ✓ Configuring and troubleshooting Remote Assistance

The idea of a protocol in the networking world is rather simple. When one computer needs to communicate with another computer, they must talk the same language and be on the same connection. The protocol is the language that the computers talk, and the network itself (typically an Ethernet network) is the connection over which the protocols travel. Many different protocols exist to choose from, including NetBEUI, IPX/SPX, and TCP/IP. Microsoft supports all three of these protocols and more. Windows XP Professional must be configured with TCP/IP if it is going to be communicating on a network that runs Microsoft's Active Directory. The configuration of the TCP/IP protocol can be confusing, and troubleshooting communication problems related to TCP/IP can be more difficult. However, after an overview of the technology, configurations, and tools, the confusing aspects of protocols and network services will be crystal clear.

Configuring and Troubleshooting TCP/IP

TCP/IP encompasses a vast array of utilities and network services. This suite of services has evolved to become the industry standard for both the Internet and for local area networks (LANs) using personal computer network operating systems like Novell NetWare 5, Unix, and Windows XP.

TCP/IP is the default protocol when you install Windows XP Professional. It provides a means for connecting dissimilar computer systems. TCP/IP scales well and is typically the best choice for any size of organization. TCP/IP and its name resolution partner, Domain Name System (DNS), are both required components for implementing Active Directory in the Windows 2000/.NET Server family of products.

Deciphering the TCP/IP Protocol Suite for Windows XP

TCP/IP is more than just a standardized specification for data transport over a network wire. It is a sophisticated toolbox of data transport services, name resolution services, and troubleshooting utilities. Microsoft's implementation of TCP/IP for Windows XP includes the following network services and components:

➤ *Dynamic Host Configuration Protocol (DHCP)*—This service is based on an industry-standard specification for automatically assigning (or leasing) IP addresses to computers connected to the network. The addresses are assigned from a predefined pool (or *scope*) of IP addresses that an administrator must configure. DHCP makes the chore of assigning and maintaining TCP/IP addresses on hundreds or thousands of computers much easier than having to maintain an exhaustive list of IP addresses and computer names by hand. However, administrators should manually assign static IP addresses for domain controllers, file and print server computers, and printers. You can install the DHCP service only in the Windows 2000 Server product line, but DHCP can assign addresses to both servers and workstations. Any operating system that can make DHCP-enabled requests for IP addresses can use a DHCP server that is running Windows 2000. DHCP-enabled operating systems include Windows 3.x, 9x, ME, NT, 2000, and XP.

➤ *DNS server*—Computers understand and work well with numbers, but humans remember names much more easily than numbers. TCP/IP requires that each network device be assigned a numeric IP address. DNS, in conjunction with DNS servers, maps numeric IP addresses to computer (host) names and vice versa. DNS employs a hierarchical system of domains and subdomains that helps to make this name resolution service very scalable. DNS servers mitigate the need for a manually maintained HOSTS file to be stored on each computer. Windows 2000 DNS servers offer added functionality such as Active Directory Integrated Zones, Incremental Zone Transfers, and Secure Dynamic Updates. DNS is a requirement for implementing Active Directory.

➤ *Windows Internet Naming Service (WINS)*—This service is Microsoft's implementation of a name resolution mechanism to match IP addresses to NetBIOS computer names and vice versa. WINS servers can greatly reduce NetBIOS traffic on networks by decreasing the amount of broadcast traffic that occurs when computers attempt to resolve unknown NetBIOS computer names to IP addresses. For an Active Directory–based network in Windows 2000 native mode with no applications that require NetBIOS, nor any legacy Windows clients, WINS becomes unnecessary.

➤ *Automatic Private IP Addressing (APIPA)*—Microsoft first introduced this feature in Windows 98. For computers that are configured to obtain an IP address automatically, APIPA kicks in if no DHCP server is available on the network to lease out an IP address. APIPA automatically queries the other computers on the network to ensure it does not duplicate an IP address, and then assigns a unique IP address to the local computer using the IP address scheme of 169.254.x.y with the subnet mask of 255.255.0.0. The Internet Assigned Numbers Authority (IANA) has reserved the IP address range of 169.254.0.0 through 169.254.255.255 for APIPA. This ensures that any IP address that APIPA generates does not conflict with any public, routable addresses. This feature is turned on by default in Windows XP Professional.

➤ *Serial Line Internet Protocol (SLIP)*—This specification is an older Unix standard for serial communications. Windows XP supports SLIP for backward-compatibility purposes. You can use SLIP only for outbound connections on Windows XP Professional.

➤ *Point-to-Point Protocol (PPP)*—PPP has effectively replaced SLIP. PPP is a remote access/dial-up protocol that supports industry-standard network protocols such as TCP/IP, NWLink, NetBEUI, and AppleTalk. PPP is optimized for low-bandwidth connections, so it is the preferred remote access protocol for dial-up/modem connections.

➤ *Point-to-Point Tunneling Protocol (PPTP)*—The only Virtual Private Network (VPN) protocol that shipped with Windows NT 4, PPTP encapsulates TCP/IP, Internet Protocol Exchange (IPX), or NetBEUI data packets and encrypts the data being transmitted as it is tunneled through the Internet. PPTP clients can connect to any Microsoft-compatible PPTP servers via the Internet with proper security credentials. This service, shipped with Windows XP Professional, allows users to connect to the Internet using local (non-long-distance) connections and offers them a way to connect to PPTP computers in remote locations without incurring toll charges or requiring dedicated data lines.

➤ *Layer 2 Tunneling Protocol (L2TP)*—An alternative to PPTP, L2TP was new to Windows 2000 and offers similar functionality to PPTP. However, L2TP is an industry-standard VPN protocol and is shipped with Windows XP Professional. L2TP also encapsulates TCP/IP, IPX, or NetBEUI data packets and encrypts the data being transmitted as it is tunneled through the Internet. You can also use L2TP in conjunction with Microsoft IP Security (IPSec) for enhanced security. L2TP is covered in more detail later in this chapter.

➤ *IPSec*—This is a relatively new Internet security protocol, also referred to as Secure IP. It provides computer-level authentication in addition to data encryption for VPN connections that use the L2TP protocol. IPSec negotiates between the client computer and the remote tunnel server before an L2TP connection is established, which secures both authentication passwords and data. L2TP uses standard PPP-based authentication protocols, such as Extensible Authentication Protocol (EAP), Microsoft Challenge Handshake Authentication Protocol (MSCHAP), CHAP, Shiva Password Authentication Protocol (SPAP), and Password Authentication Protocol (PAP) with IPSec.

➤ *World Wide Web (WWW) publishing service*—This is a major component of Internet Information Services (IIS), which ships with Windows XP Professional. Although not installed by default in Windows XP Professional, IIS and the WWW publishing service provide Web page hosting for HTML-based and Active Server Pages (ASP)-based documents.

➤ *File Transfer Protocol (FTP) service*—This is another major component of IIS. FTP is an industry-standard protocol for transferring files between computers over TCP/IP-based networks, such as the Internet.

➤ *Simple Mail Transfer Protocol (SMTP)*—The Microsoft SMTP service implements the industry-standard SMTP to transport and deliver email messages. The SMTP service for Windows XP is also a component of IIS.

Understanding TCP/IP Computer Addresses

TCP/IP assigns a unique set of numbers to each computer that is connected to a TCP/IP-based network or internetwork. This set of numbers consists of four separate numbers, each delimited by a period or a dot (.). For example, an IP address of 192.168.1.20 illustrates this concept, known as *dotted-decimal notation*. Each device on a TCP/IP-based network must be assigned a *unique* IP address so that it can send and receive data with the other devices on the network. A network device can be a computer, a printer, a router, a firewall, and so on.

We write IP addresses in a dotted-decimal format for ease and convenience. However, TCP/IP addresses are actually 32-bit *binary* numbers! By converting these binary numbers into decimal, most of us can work with these addresses much more easily than if we had to work with them in their native binary format. The real binary address of 192.168.1.20, previously mentioned, translates into 11000000.10101000.00000001.00010100.

 If you're not sure how to convert decimal numbers into binary or vice versa, just use the Windows Calculator by selecting Start|Run, typing "calc", and clicking OK. Select View|Scientific and you can easily perform those conversions.

Certain IP addresses are reserved for specific functions:

➤ The address 255.255.255.255 (11111111.11111111.11111111.11111111 in binary) is reserved for network broadcasts.

➤ The IP address 127.0.0.1 (1111111.00000000.00000000.00000001 in binary) is reserved as a loopback address for testing proper configuration of the IP address(es) for the local host computer.

➤ The address schemes 192.168.x.y, 172.16.0.0 to 172.31.255.255, and 10.0.x.y have been reserved as nonroutable by the bodies that govern the Internet.

Therefore, IP addresses such as 192.168.1.20 and 10.0.0.7 are restricted to being used only for the internal addressing of LANs. By definition, you cannot route these addressing schemes onto the Internet. Routers (devices that route network data packets) do not forward any data packets that originate with a nonroutable addressing scheme.

Understanding Classful IP Addressing

A look at Classful IP addressing takes us back to the beginning of TCP/IP itself. Classful addressing was adopted as RFC 791, and was the first major addressing scheme. Three address classes were used for typical network communication.

These three ranges include A, B, and C class ranges. The difference between each class was the number of bits that made up the class prefix. For example, an IP address of 10.1.1.1 would be in the Class A range, because the first octet, 10, starts with a prefix that is within the Class A range. Table 8.1 shows the different classes and the corresponding prefix ranges.

> **TIP**
>
> You can quickly determine the class ranges by starting off with an octet of all zeros and turning on bits from the leftmost part of the octet range. For a Class A range, the starting number would be an octet of all zeros up to an octet with the first bit turned on, 10000000. This would be a range of 0 to 127. The actual value of the octet with the first bit turned on is 128, which is the start of the next range. Then, the end of the next range would be up to the second bit turned on, 11000000. So, the Class B would be a range of 128 to 191. If you follow this pattern for the remaining ranges, you will never be at a loss as to which range an IP address falls into.

When you see a reference to a Classful IP address scheme, it is referring to an address scheme that does not break up these classes. It is no surprise that these address ranges are already purchased, due to the influx of the Internet. If you want to get a range of IP addresses, you will need to contact an Internet service provider (ISP).

Understanding Variable-Length Subnet Masks

When you contact that ISP, you might be surprised that you can't obtain your own Class B range. What you will find instead is that you might get a portion of a Class B range. When a Classful IP address range is broken down into smaller pieces, you need to use a variable-length subnet mask (VLSM). The standard subnet masks that come with the Classful IP ranges are as follows:

➤ Class A—255.0.0.0

➤ Class B—255.255.0.0

➤ Class C—255.255.255.0

Table 8.1 Classful network addresses and their prefix range.	
Prefix Range	**Address Class**
0–127	A
128–191	B
192–223	C
224–239	D
240–255	E

When you want to use only a portion of the address class range, you need to alter the standard subnet mask. A typical example of using VLSM is when you need to break up a Class C range into smaller ranges. A typical Class C range contains 254 IP addresses for hosts. Many smaller companies don't need this many addresses, so they will use a Class C address range that uses a VLSM to break up the range. This is done to create smaller pools of IP addresses. If you had a company that needed only 50 IP addresses, you could use a subnet mask of 255.255.255.192 with a Class C range of IP addresses. This subnet mask would break up the original Class C range and create four IP address ranges containing 62 IP addresses each.

Understanding Classless Interdomain Routing

The technology that we just looked at, VLSM, takes a Classful IP address range and makes more IP networks with fewer IP addresses. This is great for smaller companies or companies that want to break up the network into segments to reduce broadcasts. However, what if you are a larger company and you require additional IP addresses for one network segment? For this solution, you will need to combine IP address ranges together. This is called Classless Interdomain Routing (CIDR). With CIDR, multiple subnets are seen as a single logical network of IP addresses. CIDR does have limitations such as routing protocols and hardware devices. However, if your network can support CIDR, it just might be the solution that you are looking for.

When you are determining whether or not two IP address ranges can be combined with CIDR, you need to first determine if they share the higher order bits. Here, examples will help explain how this works:

Example 1	Bits
10.1.2.0/24	00001010.00000001.00000010.00000000
10.1.3.0/24	00001010.00000001.00000011.00000000
Example 2	Bits
10.3.2.0/24	00001010.00000011.00000010.00000000
10.1.3.0/24	00001010.00000001.00000011.00000000

The first example can use CIDR, because the first 23 bits are the same, and therefore can be combined into a single network by the use of a classless network. This would be accomplished by using a new subnet mask of 255.255.254.0. This would result in a new subnet that would have a total of 510 host addresses. The second example will not work with a shortened CIDR subnet, because only the first 14 bits are the same.

Note: To get further information on CIDR, refer to the Microsoft Windows 2000 Resource Kit, Chapter 1, Introduction to TCP/IP.

Configuring TCP/IP

TCP/IP is installed by default when you install Windows XP Professional. However, you can override this default setting if your network does not require it or if you will not be on a network with Active Directory. In addition, the protocol's default configuration is to *obtain an IP address automatically.* This means that the computer automatically requests a unique TCP/IP address for your network from a DHCP server. If no DHCP server is available, the operating system invokes APIPA to query the other computers that are currently powered on and connected to the network so that it can assign itself a unique IP address.

To work with TCP/IP, you need to become familiar with the following terms:

➤ *Subnet mask*—This is essentially an IP address filter that gets applied to each unique IP address. The subnet mask determines which part of the IP address for a computer specifies the network segment where the computer is located, versus which part of the IP address specifies the unique host address for that individual computer. As an example, an IP address of 192.168.1.20 with a subnet mask of 255.255.255.0 is determined to have the network ID of 192.168.1. The host address for the computer, therefore, is 20. This is analogous to the street name of a postal address versus the actual house number of the address. The street may have many houses, but only one house has a house number of 20.

➤ *Default gateway*—This IP address specifies the router for the local network segment (or subnet). If this address is absent, the computer cannot communicate with other computers that are located outside of the local network segment. Default gateway information is often obtained through DHCP if the computer is configured to obtain an IP address automatically.

➤ *Preferred and alternate DNS servers*—Having more than one DNS server on a network helps provide load balancing and fault tolerance for client computers that need to perform hostname-to-IP address lookups as well as IP address-to-hostname lookups. DNS is also used to find domain-based services such as domain controllers, DFS roots, and Global Catalog servers. Name resolution is a critical issue in TCP/IP. DNS server information is often obtained through DHCP if the computer is configured to obtain an IP address automatically.

➤ *WINS addresses*—WINS provides name resolution between NetBIOS computer names and IP addresses. WINS server addresses are often obtained through DHCP if the computer is configured to obtain an IP address automatically.

To manually set up a Windows XP Professional computer with a static IP address for the TCP/IP network protocol, select Start|Control Panel|Network Connections, and then select the Local Area Connection that you want to configure. After the window appears, click the Properties button. If TCP/IP is not currently installed, follow these steps:

1. Click Install from the Local Area Connection's Properties dialog box.

2. Click Protocol and then click Add.

3. Click Internet Protocol (TCP/IP) and then click OK.

4. Restart the computer.

To configure the necessary settings so that TCP/IP can communicate with other computers and devices over the network, follow these steps:

1. Click Internet Protocol (TCP/IP) and then click Properties.

2. Click Use The Following IP Address

3. Type the IP Address, Subnet Mask, and Default Gateway.

4. Type the proper IP address for a Preferred DNS Server and an Alternate DNS Server (if any).

5. Click the Advanced button to add additional IP addresses and default gateways. You can also add, edit, or remove DNS server address information, and you can change other DNS settings. You can specify IP addresses for any WINS servers on the network, enable NetBIOS name resolution using an LMHOSTS file, and enable or disable NetBIOS over TCP/IP. You can also set up IPSec and TCP/IP filtering as optional settings from the Advanced TCP/IP Settings Properties sheet.

6. Click OK to close the Advanced TCP/IP Settings Properties dialog box.

7. Click OK to close the Internet Protocol (TCP/IP) Properties dialog box.

8. Click OK to close the Local Area Connection Properties dialog box.

Troubleshooting TCP/IP

Windows XP Professional comes with several software tools and utilities to help you isolate and resolve TCP/IP-related issues. You must run all of these utilities from the command line. Connectivity tools include the following:

➤ *Finger*—Displays information about a user for a particular computer. The target computer must be running the Finger service.

➤ *FTP*—Transfers files to and from FTP servers over a TCP/IP connection.

➤ *LPR*—Sends one or more files to be printed via a line printer daemon (LPD) printer.

➤ *RCP*—Copies files between a Windows XP Professional computer and a computer system running the remote shell daemon (RSHD). Windows 2000 and XP clients cannot run the RSHD daemon, but Unix systems can.

➤ *REXEC*—Executes commands on remote computer systems that are running the REXEC service. Windows 2000 and XP clients do.

➤ *RSH*—Executes commands on remote computer systems that are running the RSH service. Windows 2000 and XP clients do not run the RSH service.

 A utility included with the Windows 2000 Server Resource Kit enables the RSH service to run on a Windows 2000 system. The utility is called RSHSVC.EXE.

➤ *Telnet*—Establishes a terminal emulation session for working on remote systems, including environments such as Unix, Mainframe, and minicomputers.

➤ *Trivial File Transfer Protocol (TFTP)*—Copies files to and from remote computers that are running the TFTP service.

Diagnostic tools include the following:

➤ *Address Resolution Protocol (ARP)*—Lists and edits the IP-to-Ethernet (or Token Ring) physical translation tables that ARP uses.

➤ *HOSTNAME*—Lists the name of the local host (computer).

➤ *IPCONFIG*—Shows all of the current TCP/IP configuration settings for the local computer, such as its IP address, subnet mask, and any WINS servers and DNS servers assigned to the computer.

 There are special switches that deal with the DNS portion of the IP session. These would be the **/registerdns**, **/displaydns**, and **/flushdns** switches. These switches will register the client with DNS, show the DNS cache, and flush out the DNS cache, respectively.

➤ *LPQ*—Shows the current status of the print queue on a computer that is running the LPD service.

➤ *NBTSTAT*—Delineates network protocol statistics and lists the current connections that are using NetBIOS over TCP/IP.

Don't forget about the **–R** and **–RR** switches that can help refresh the cache, as well as send release packets to WINS, and then refresh the client connection.

➤ *NETSTAT*—Delineates network protocol statistics and lists the current TCP/IP connections.

➤ *PING*—Is used to test TCP/IP-related connectivity to remote computers. This command also verifies the proper TCP/IP configuration of the local host computer by attempting to ping the loopback address for the local host (computer). For example: **ping 127.0.0.1.**

➤ *ROUTE*—Edits the local computer's routing tables.

➤ *TRACERT*—Displays the route (path) that data packets follow as they travel from the local computer to a remote destination computer.

Troubleshooting TCP/IP Configuration and Connectivity

Whenever you initially set up TCP/IP, you should always test and verify that the protocol is working properly. Here are the steps you can take to check the computer's TCP/IP configuration and to test its connectivity:

1. Open a command prompt window; **ipconfig** and **ping** are strictly command-line utilities.

2. Run **ipconfig** to display the computer's current IP configuration. Use **ipconfig /all** to display more detailed information, as shown in Figure 8.1.

3. Use the **ping** command to ping the computer's loopback address: **ping 127.0.0.1.** This tests whether TCP/IP is correctly installed and bound to the network adapter card. Figure 8.2 shows the response from pinging the loopback IP address.

4. Ping the IP address of the local computer to verify the uniqueness of the IP address on the network.

5. Ping the IP address of the default gateway for the local subnet to check that the default gateway is up and running. This step also demonstrates whether the computer can successfully communicate over the local network segment.

6. Ping the IP address of a computer that is located on a different network segment. This step indicates whether the computer can send and receive network data packets through a router.

```
Command Prompt                                                    _ □ x
C:\>ipconfig /all

Windows IP Configuration

        Host Name . . . . . . . . . . . . : xpprorc2
        Primary Dns Suffix . . . . . . . :
        Node Type . . . . . . . . . . . . : Hybrid
        IP Routing Enabled. . . . . . . . : No
        WINS Proxy Enabled. . . . . . . . : No

Ethernet adapter Local Area Connection:

        Connection-specific DNS Suffix  . :
        Description . . . . . . . . . . . : Xircom CardBus Ethernet II 10/100
        Physical Address. . . . . . . . . : 00-10-A4-16-27-F7
        Dhcp Enabled. . . . . . . . . . . : Yes
        Autoconfiguration Enabled . . . . : Yes
        IP Address. . . . . . . . . . . . : 10.10.10.55
        Subnet Mask . . . . . . . . . . . : 255.255.255.0
        Default Gateway . . . . . . . . . : 10.10.10.10
        DHCP Server . . . . . . . . . . . : 10.10.10.10
        DNS Servers . . . . . . . . . . . : 24.1.240.33
                                            24.1.240.34
                                            10.10.10.1
        Lease Obtained. . . . . . . . . . : Saturday, September 15, 2001 2:14:06
  PM
        Lease Expires . . . . . . . . . . : Friday, September 21, 2001 2:14:06 P
M

C:\>
```

Figure 8.1 An example of running the **ipconfig** command with the **/all** switch.

```
Command Prompt                                                    _ □ x

C:\>ping loopback

Pinging xpprorc2 [127.0.0.1] with 32 bytes of data:

Reply from 127.0.0.1: bytes=32 time<1ms TTL=128
Reply from 127.0.0.1: bytes=32 time<1ms TTL=128
Reply from 127.0.0.1: bytes=32 time<1ms TTL=128
Reply from 127.0.0.1: bytes=32 time<1ms TTL=128

Ping statistics for 127.0.0.1:
    Packets: Sent = 4, Received = 4, Lost = 0 (0% loss),
Approximate round trip times in milli-seconds:
    Minimum = 0ms, Maximum = 0ms, Average = 0ms

C:\>ping 127.0.0.1

Pinging 127.0.0.1 with 32 bytes of data:

Reply from 127.0.0.1: bytes=32 time<1ms TTL=128
Reply from 127.0.0.1: bytes=32 time<1ms TTL=128
Reply from 127.0.0.1: bytes=32 time<1ms TTL=128
Reply from 127.0.0.1: bytes=32 time<1ms TTL=128

Ping statistics for 127.0.0.1:
    Packets: Sent = 4, Received = 4, Lost = 0 (0% loss),
Approximate round trip times in milli-seconds:
    Minimum = 0ms, Maximum = 0ms, Average = 0ms

C:\>
```

Figure 8.2 An example of pinging a computer's loopback IP address.

Using APIPA

If a computer is set up to obtain an IP address automatically from a DHCP server but no DHCP servers are available, APIPA temporarily assigns an IP address to the local computer while it searches the network to make sure that no other network devices have been assigned the same IP address. By running **ipconfig**, you can view the current TCP/IP information for the local computer. An address such as 169.254.x.y generally indicates that APIPA is currently in effect.

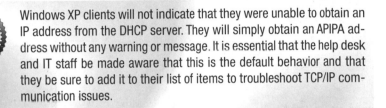

Windows XP clients will not indicate that they were unable to obtain an IP address from the DHCP server. They will simply obtain an APIPA address without any warning or message. It is essential that the help desk and IT staff be made aware that this is the default behavior and that they be sure to add it to their list of items to troubleshoot TCP/IP communication issues.

Working with TCP/IP Profiles

You now know that when a DHCP-enabled client can't find a DHCP server, it will be allocated an IP address from the APIPA range. A new feature that Windows XP offers is the alternate TCP/IP configuration option, sometimes referred to as a TCP/IP profile. This feature is excellent for laptop users who need to connect to multiple networks. A good example of this might be an executive who receives a DHCP-allocated IP address at work, but needs a static IP address for the home office network.

The new IP allocation process follows these steps:

1. The DHCP-enabled client attempts to locate a DHCP server.

2. The client will attempt to contact a DHCP server for approximately 60 seconds, and then will try to configure its own IP address.

3. The computer will use the information configured on the Alternate Configuration tab to determine whether to use APIPA or to use the alternate configuration information. Figure 8.3 illustrates the options available for the Alternate Configuration tab.

The Alternate Configuration tab is only available if the initial TCP/IP configuration is set to Obtain An IP Address Automatically.

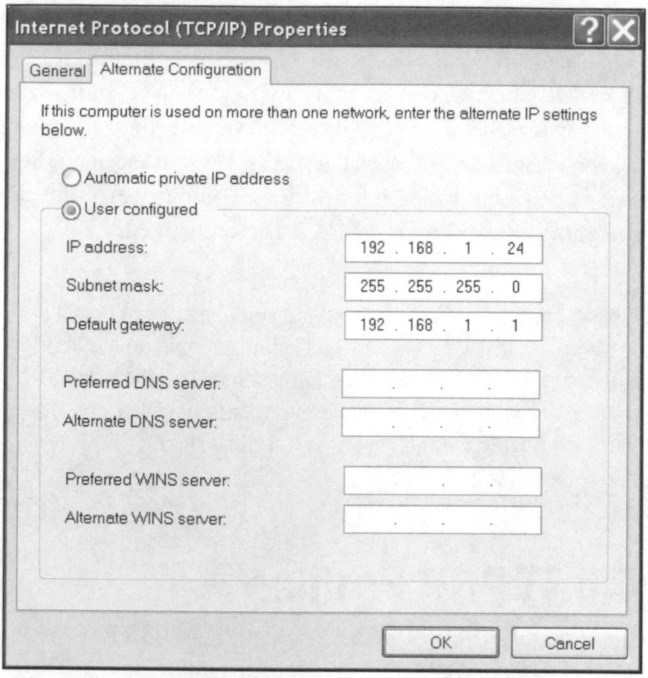

Figure 8.3   The Alternate Configuration tab for TCP/IP profiles.

Connecting to Novell NetWare Networks and Unix-Based Computer Systems

Microsoft has always made an effort to allow its client operating systems the connectivity that they need to communicate with other network operating systems. Windows XP does not stray from these efforts. Microsoft's OSs have always had the capability to connect with Novell networks, and Microsoft continues to add capabilities to connect to other companies' network OSs as they become more common in the business marketplace.

Novell NetWare Connectivity

When connecting to a Novell network, the version of NetWare and connectivity requirements will determine the Windows XP configuration. Of course, we are all familiar with the protocol that is used to communicate with most of the Novell networks in existence: IPX/SPX. Microsoft has renamed its version of this protocol to incorporate NetBIOS, which it calls NWLink. If you are running Novell NetWare 3.x or 4.x, you will need to install NWLink on some, if not all, of your Microsoft clients for communication. If you are running Novell NetWare 5.x, then you can run TCP/IP natively, allowing for a limited number of protocols to be installed on the Microsoft clients.

Beyond the protocol, you also need to consider the client redirector. Since the NT days, the Microsoft client redirector for a Novell network has been Client Service for NetWare (CSNW). This client allows Microsoft clients access to file and print sharing with NetWare servers. When this client is installed, the client also installs the NWLink protocol to function properly.

Another service designed to help the communication gap with NetWare is Gateway Service for NetWare (GSNW). This service is only available on Microsoft servers and functions as a proxy between the Microsoft network and the NetWare network. If this service is implemented, the clients running Windows XP only need TCP/IP installed. The server running the service will need both TCP/IP and NWLink installed to communicate with both the Microsoft network and the NetWare network.

CSNW and GSNW do not function with TCP/IP, even with NetWare 5.x servers. These services are designed to function only with the IPX/SPX protocol suite.

Another important aspect of communicating with a NetWare network is the frame type that is associated with the IPX/SPX protocol. To ensure communication is upheld, be sure to check with the following list of frame types when configuring your Windows XP Professional clients:

➤ Netware 2.x through 3.11—802.3

➤ Netware 3.12 and later, including 4.x and 5.x—802.2

An option is available to set the frame type to autodetect, but it will only detect one type at a time. The order in which the frame types are detected is 802.2, 802.3, ETHERNET_II, and 802.5. The frame type 802.5 is used with Token Ring and is not usually used.

Unless you are running some form of metadirectory or software to synchronize the account information between Microsoft and NetWare, you will need to change your password for the NetWare environment separately from the Microsoft environment. One option is to use the **SETPASS.EXE** command from the Windows XP Professional client. The other option is to change the NetWare password from the Change Password option available when you press Ctrl+Alt+Delete. This enables the Windows XP Professional user to change their password on a NetWare 4.x and higher server that is running Novell Directory Services (NDS).

Unix Connectivity

Microsoft has made a valiant effort to incorporate better connectivity with Unix servers, and has produced many new services and applications that allow better communication. However, the tools still have not made their way into the base operating system. The standard tools are available with Windows XP:

➤ *Print Services for Unix*—This service enables Line Printer Remote (LPR) ports to be installed on your Windows XP client. An LPR port can send a document to a print spooler service on another computer or Unix printer. The Line Printer Daemon (LPD) service is also installed with Print Services for Unix. This allows the receipt of a print job.

➤ *Services for Unix (SFU)*—This service can be installed on a Windows system to allow the Windows system to communicate with Unix file and print servers. The different services that are installed include: Telnet client, Telnet server, Unix shell and utilities, and Client for NFS. SFU is not a free product, but can be purchased online or from a Microsoft vendor.

Other Protocols

A Microsoft OS comes with more than just the standard TCP/IP and NWLink protocols. Microsoft has continued to integrate additional protocols to communicate with a variety of different OSs and network resources. The following is a list of the different protocols that are available:

➤ *Data Link Control (DLC)*—Used in a Microsoft world for two main purposes: to communicate with AS/400 devices or IBM emulators, and to communicate with network printers, such as HP Directjet devices

➤ *AppleTalk*—Allows Windows XP Professional computers to communicate with Apple printers

➤ *NetBEUI*—Is an older protocol that is used for a network that is not running Active Directory nor connected to the Internet

Network Bridging

The *Windows XP network bridge option* is not unlike a typical bridge. It connects different network segments into a single network, appearing as a single network subnet. This will be ideal for the small office and home office (SOHO) networks. The technology will allow different network media to be bridged as well. Some of these different network media might include Ethernet, FireWire, and wireless Ethernet.

To get the network bridge established, you will highlight both of the network adapters that will be part of the bridge. After highlighting the adapters, you will right-click one of them and select the Bridge Connections menu option. After the bridge is established between the two network cards, the bridge will function as a single, logical network card. The two original network cards will not be configurable, because they are now part of the bridge. The bridge will obtain an IP address and will function as a single network card between the two different networks.

> You can confirm that the bridge is working properly by running the **ipconfig** command. The results of the command should indicate that the network bridge is the only connection and that it now has the IP address and TCP/IP configurations needed to communicate with both networks.

It is possible to add more than two network cards to a network bridge. Actually, it is possible to add as many network cards as your computer will support. After the network card is added to the network bridge, it is located under the Network Bridge section in the Network Connections properties interface, as shown in Figure 8.4.

Windows Messenger

It is no surprise that Microsoft put a messenger service inside of Windows XP. The popularity of Microsoft Instant Messenger is nothing new to computer users. The tool that Microsoft placed into the Windows XP default configuration replaces MSN Messenger. Of course MSN Messenger is the tool that you will continue to use on your pre-Windows XP clients. If you are a NetMeeting user,

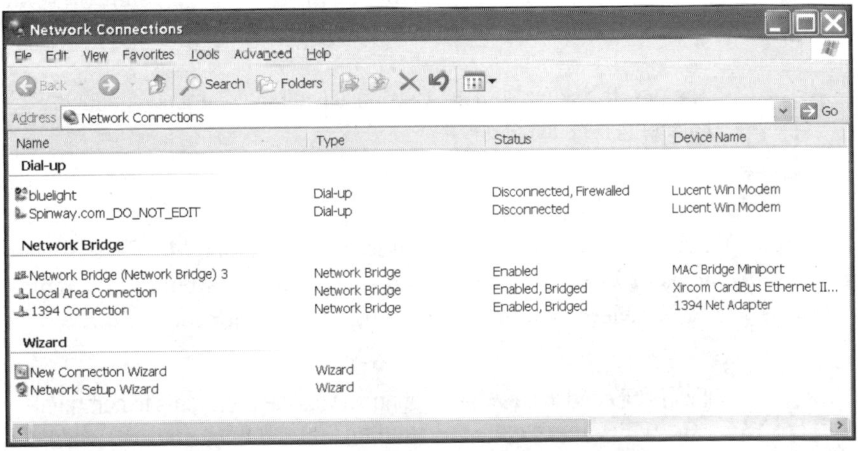

Figure 8.4 Network bridge interface showing the different network connections that are part of the bridge.

you will also be able to switch over to Windows Messenger for your collaboration and communication needs.

If you have not used MSN Messenger before, you will most likely become very familiar with the application as soon as you get your XP client running. Windows Messenger allows you to communicate with other users on the Internet, as well as share files. The following is a list of functions that you can perform with Windows Messenger:

➤ Chat with employees, clients, or friends who are also online.

➤ Use the contact list and notification capabilities to determine whether other employees, clients, or friends are online. This reduces the time spent attempting to contact someone who is not available.

➤ Communicate with employees, clients, or friends using audio and video conferencing.

➤ Make voice calls using the built-in capabilities of the messenger application.

➤ Communicate to cell phones and pagers by sending text messages.

➤ Transfer files and documents quickly and easily.

➤ Share a whiteboard or program online to collaborate with employees, clients, or friends.

To get Windows Messenger up and running, you need to get a .NET Passport account established. You can either establish a Passport with a free MSN (or Hotmail) account or link it to an existing email account that you own. The Passport information can be saved with your user account, either as a domain or local account. After you have the information stored with your user account, you will have pass-through authentication with a single username and password.

One way to ask for Remote Assistance is directly through Windows Messenger menu options.

This new Windows Messenger is compatible with the older MSN Messenger for the capabilities of MSN Messenger. However, if you are attempting to communicate with a NetMeeting user, you will find that it is not compatible.

If you still need to have NetMeeting on your XP Pro clients to communicate with others who are running NetMeeting, you can access NetMeeting from the XP Pro CD.

Remote Desktop

Remote Desktop is brand new for Windows XP. Microsoft wanted to allow you to access a session that is running on your computer while you are sitting at another computer. This is a great solution for those employees who want to connect to their computer at work while working from home. You will have access to applications, files, and other network resources from the comfort of your home. You will even be able to see the existing applications that were left open on your desktop.

Configuring Remote Desktop

To get Remote Desktop up and running, you will need to configure the computer that will be connected to, which is called the *work computer* in this discussion. The computer that will be connecting to the work computer is called the *home computer*. We will look at the requirements for the home computer in just a little bit.

For the work computer, you must be running Windows XP Professional. You must enable the work computer to allow Remote Desktop. To access this option, you need to follow this path: Control Panel|Performance and Maintenance| System|Remote tab. After you get to the interface for this path, you can just enable Remote Desktop, as shown in Figure 8.5.

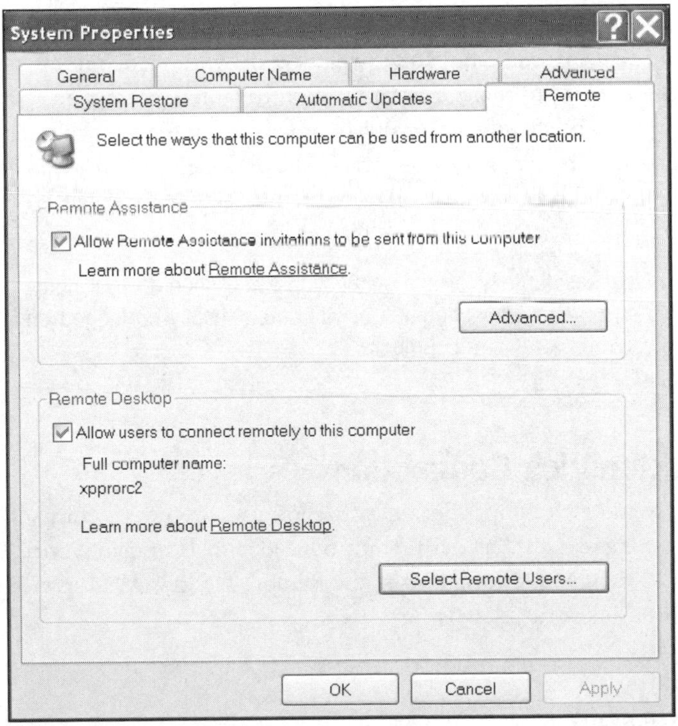

Figure 8.5 Remote Desktop options under System Properties.

After you get Remote Desktop enabled, you will then need to configure which users will have the ability to connect. This is accomplished by adding the correct users to the Remote Desktop Users group. This is the group that users must belong to in order to gain access to the work computer from the home computer. You can add users to this group by using the interface shown in Figure 8.5 or by using the Local Users and Groups option in the Computer Management snap-in.

Administrators automatically have Remote Desktop access without being placed into the group.

Connecting with Remote Desktop

When a user wants to connect to a computer that has Remote Desktop enabled, they will only need to run a simple application. The application is installed by default on all Windows XP Professional computers. To access the application, go to Start|All Programs|Accessories|Communications|Remote Desktop Connection. You will be prompted to input the computer name (or IP address) of the work computer. After clicking the Connect button, you will be prompted for a username and password for the Remote Desktop connection.

Microsoft put in a security feature for the work computer. The feature locks the desktop and puts up a screen so no one can see what you are working on remotely. As long as you are connected to the computer through Remote Desktop, no one will be able to connect to the computer locally. In order for you to gain access to your computer after you get back to work, you press Ctrl+Alt+Delete to be prompted you for your username and password, enabling you to unlock the system.

If you have accidentally left the connection established on your home computer to your work computer, it will automatically be logged off when you unlock the work computer.

Remote Desktop Web Connection

Another feature of Remote Desktop is the ability to allow users to connect through a Web browser. This is a feature that was first introduced with Terminal Services and is ported over to Remote Desktop. To get the Remote Desktop Web service installed, you need to follow these steps:

1. Open Add Or Remove Programs in Control Panel.

2. Select Add/Remove Windows Components.

3. Select Internet Information Services (IIS), as well as the Details button for this option.

4. After selecting World Wide Web Service in the IIS Details screen, click the Details button for this option.

5. Select the Remote Desktop Web Connection option and click OK for all of the Windows that you have opened, and then click Next when you get to the Windows Components Wizard screen.

This will install the Remote Desktop capabilities, which are really a portion of IIS. If you go into the IIS management tool, you will see a virtual directory named tsweb that supports the Remote Desktop functionality.

The connecting computer only needs to have Microsoft Internet Explorer 4 or higher. To make the connection, just open the browser and type in the following URL: "http://<computername>/tsweb". This will prompt the user for the computer that you want to connect to, and then the proper credentials for authentication. Figure 8.6 shows the IE interface for connecting through the Remote Desktop Web Connection.

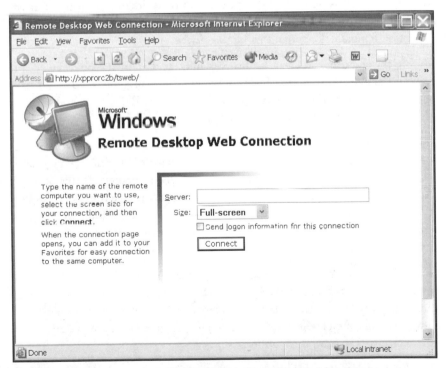

Figure 8.6   Interface for the Remote Desktop Web Connection with Internet Explorer.

Regardless of whether you are connecting through the Remote Desktop Web Connection interface or the Web-based Remote Desktop interface, the user whom you are connecting with must have a password. A blank password is not acceptable for the use of Remote Desktop.

Understanding Remote Assistance

The underlying technologies of Remote Desktop and Remote Assistance are the same, but the application is much different. As you just saw with Remote Desktop, the goal is to allow a user access to their work computer from their home computer. With *Remote Assistance*, the goal is to have another user, typically a help desk or IT employee, remotely help the end user with an issue that they are experiencing on their Windows XP Professional computer.

Remote Assistance will be similar to the existing remote control software that you currently use, such as PCAnywhere, Funk Proxy, or VNC. However, this software is built into the OS and allows for better control and security. With this technology, the end user is able to invite someone to help them troubleshoot or walk through an issue that they are having on their desktop. The end user will simply fill out a small questionnaire and ship it to the desired support personnel. This questionnaire is referred to as an *invitation*.

Before the end user can create and successfully send an invitation, they need to enable Remote Assistance on their computer. This is accomplished by going to Control Panel|Performance and Maintenance|System|Remote tab and selecting the option to enable Remote Assistance, as shown in Figure 8.7.

This interface shown in Figure 8.7 also allows for advanced options to be configured for the Remote Assistance session. The first advanced option configuration is the ability to allow the computer to be controlled remotely. If this option is selected, it indicates that the support person not only is able to see the desktop, but also can take control of it with their mouse and keyboard. The second option controls the amount of time that the invitation is valid. It would not be wise to have an invitation sitting untouched for too long, due to security concerns.

To create an invitation, the user selects Get Help From A Friend By Using Remote Assistance from the Start|Help And Support menu option. The invitation has many steps that need to be well understood. The first step is to determine how you will contact your support person, or *assistant*, as they are referred to in the interface. You have three options:

➤ *Windows Messenger*—This requires that you have an existing MSN Messenger account or have configured a .NET Passport.

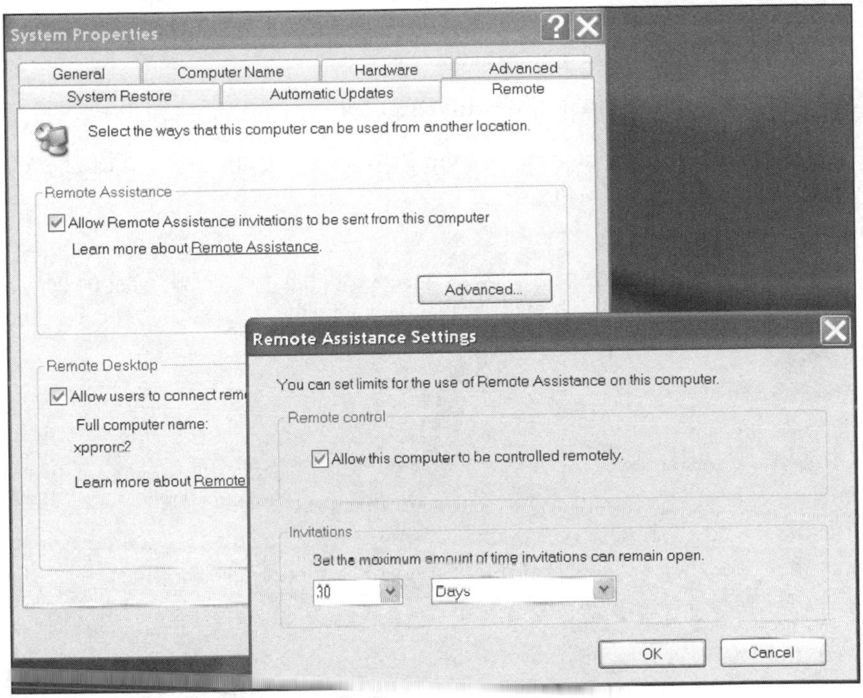

Figure 8.7 Remote Assistance options under System Properties.

➤ *Email*—This requires that you have Microsoft Outlook or Outlook Express configured.

Both you and the assistant must have Windows Messenger or a MAPI-compliant email tool such as Outlook or Outlook Express.

➤ *File*—This is the advanced option, but allows the most freedom in getting the invitation out to the assistant.

During the creation of the invitation, you first are prompted to give the name that will appear on the invitation and the duration the invitation will be valid. Next, you are given an opportunity to give the invitation a password. This is a critical step in configuration for the overall security of the process. It is highly recommended that you configure the password, but keep the password complex. Here are some tips to ensure the password is complex:

➤ The password should contain multiple characters, at least six or seven.

➤ The password should contain more than one type of character, such as a combination of alpha and numeric characters.

➤ The password should not contain the computer name or username.

➤ The password should not be a common word, especially one that can be referenced from a dictionary.

Because the password is not sent with the invitation, it must be communicated with the assistant before the invitation is sent. This can be via an email or phone conversation.

After this information is input, the invitation needs to be saved. The name of the ticket can be anything and should be descriptive for the event. The extension for the file should not be altered, which is .msrcincident. The file is actually an XML file that gives the pertinent information for the invitation and connection to the remote computer.

After you have sent the invitation or created the invitation file, you can access the log of invitations through the XP interface. Just go to Start|Help And Support and select the View Invitation Status option. This will display the different invitations that you have sent or created.

When the assistant receives the invitation, they will just click to accept the invitation and connect to your computer. After they connect, they will be able to view your desktop and chat with you in realtime. Both the assistant and the computer being controlled must be running Windows XP Professional. If the computer being controlled has been configured to allow remote control, then the assistant will be able to use their mouse and keyboard to control the remote desktop. The remote control requires permission, so it is not an automatic feature. Another feature that is possible after the connection is made is audio help. If both parties have full-duplex sound cards or sound through the USB port, speakers, and a microphone, they will be able to communicate verbally to help resolve any issues.

To stop Remote Assistance, you can click the Stop option on the chat window. Another option is to press the Esc key, which will also put an end to the current session. If you want to just disconnect the current session but keep the Remote Assistant window open, you can select the Disconnect option in the chat window.

Some final comments about Remote Assistant start with security. Not all firewalls will allow this form of communication. If it is necessary to allow this assistance to your Windows XP clients, you will want to start by opening port 3398 on the firewall. All of the sessions are encrypted, so the security of the information being transferred back and forth should be extremely high. As far as creating a new invitation, you can do this with a command line if you feel so brave. The HELPCTR.EXE tool can create almost any view of the Help and Support Center, including starting a Remote Assistance session.

Practice Questions

Question 1

You are the administrator of a small company that has 20 nodes on the network. The network is currently split into two distinct network segments. You are looking for an inexpensive solution to allow the computers on one network segment to communicate with the users on the other network segment. What will you implement to allow this communication?

○ a. Set up a DHCP relay agent.

○ b. Configure ICS on one of the client computers.

○ c. Configure a TCP/IP profile for each node.

○ d. Set up a network bridge.

Answer d is correct. A network bridge connects different network segments into a single network, allowing them to appear as a single network subnet. Answer a is incorrect because the DHCP relay agent is only for DHCP clients, not for allowing normal network traffic communication. Answer b is incorrect because it does not allow a network of computers access to the Internet, through a single computer. Answer c is incorrect because a TCP/IP profile is designed to allow a single computer multiple IP configuration options at boot time.

Question 2

You have just been promoted to the sales manager for the Braincore.net corporation. As part of your job responsibilities, you are required to access a database to monitor the sales trends. You discover that the database is not updated until well after you get home in the evenings, but your report is due early in the morning. You do not want to make the drive into work to generate the report from the database information. What do you do instead?

○ a. Configure your system at work to allow Remote Assistance.

○ b. Configure your system at work to receive dial-up access.

○ c. Configure your system at work to allow Remote Desktop access.

○ d. Configure your system at work to allow a Virtual Private Network connection.

Answer c is correct. Remote Desktop allows someone to access a session that is running on one computer while sitting at another computer. This is an excellent solution for someone who works at home and needs to gain access to their computer at work. Answer a is incorrect because Remote Assistance allows for another person to access your computer to help you with an issue. Answers b and d are incorrect because the Remote Desktop option is preferred due to security and access permissions. If you were to configure you computer at work to accept dial-up or VPN access, then there would need to be a local account for authentication, which is frowned upon in most enterprises.

Question 3

You are the network administrator for a growing Web development company. You have needed to purchase multiple Class C address ranges to keep up with the growth of the company and the number of computers. You need to combine two of the Class C licenses that you have to increase the number of clients on a single network segment. How will you accomplish this?

- a. Use DHCP instead of statically configuring your IP addresses.
- b. Use Classless Interdomain Routing to combine the two IP address ranges into one.
- c. Use Classful IP address ranges to combine the two IP address ranges into one.
- d. Use variable-length subnet masking to combine the two IP address ranges into one.

Answer b is correct. Classless Interdomain Routing (CIDR) is the technology that allows two or more IP address ranges to appear as if they are on the same network segment. Answer a is incorrect because CIDR will still be needed, even if DHCP is used. Answer c is incorrect because a Classful IP address range will not solve the problem of combining the two Class C licenses together. Answer d is incorrect because VLSM would make more network segments, not reduce them.

Question 4

You have just installed Windows XP Professional and want to use the new built-in Windows Messenger service. You have been using MSN Messenger but want to take advantage of the new features that the Windows Messenger offers. To keep security tight, you want to keep the information for Windows Messenger stored with your domain account. What will you do to perform this task?

○ a. Create a certificate and store it with your account.

○ b. Use IP Security.

○ c. Establish an Internet firewall, which stores domain account information as well as Internet access passwords, such as Windows Messenger.

○ d. Create a .NET Passport and store it with your account.

Answer d is correct. Windows Messenger uses a .NET Passport to authenticate and gain access to the service. It is possible to store this information with the user account for pass-through authentication. Answer a is incorrect because a certificate will not allow this type of double or multiple authentication using the Windows Messenger service. Answer b is incorrect because IP Security will not allow the storage of the Windows Messenger account with the domain account. Answer c is incorrect because the use of an Internet firewall will not store the domain account information, nor the Internet access passwords. This would be a severe security hole if this was the case.

Question 5

You have just acquired an application that runs on a NetWare 3.11 server. There are numerous Windows XP clients that need to gain access to this application, the files that are generated from the application which are placed on the NetWare server, as well as the other domain-based Microsoft resources on the network. These clients cannot have static IP addresses, due to the limited number of IP addresses that are available. What protocols or services will these Windows XP clients need to run? [Check all correct answers]

❑ a. TCP/IP that is dynamically configured

❑ b. IPX/SPX that uses frame type 802.2

❑ c. TCP/IP that is manually configured

❑ d. GSNW

❑ e. IPX/SPX that uses frame type 802.3

❑ f. CSNW

Answers a, e, and f are correct. To have the client automatically receive an IP address, it must be configured to dynamically receive an IP address. Another term for this is to be DHCP-enabled. Because the version of NetWare that is being used is 3.x, the frame type must be 802.3. The use of IPX/SPX is also a requirement, because the NetWare server cannot communicate with the XP Pro client without it. The Windows XP client must also have CSNW installed to allow communication to the file and print services running on the NetWare server. Answer b is incorrect because the 802.2 frame type would not be correct for the NetWare 3.11 server that is being used. Answer c is incorrect because the question clearly states that static or manual IP addresses are not allowed. Answer d is incorrect because the GSNW service is for servers, not for Professional computers.

Question 6

You are attempting to connect to your Windows XP Professional computer at work named XPPROWORK. This computer has an IP address of 24.15.199.1. You are attempting to connect from your Windows 98 computer at home, named HOME. This computer has been assigned an IP address of 20.1.20.1 from your ISP. You do not have the correct client installed on your Windows 98 computer, but have installed the Remote Desktop Web Connection on the work computer. How will you connect to the work computer from the Windows 98 computer?

- ○ a. You cannot connect to a Windows XP Professional computer from a Windows 98 computer using Remote Desktop.
- ○ b. Connect using Internet Explorer and a URL of http://HOME/tsweb.
- ○ c. Connect using Internet Explorer and a URL of http://XPPROWORK/ tsweb.
- ○ d. Connect using Internet Explorer and a URL of http://20.1.20.1/ tsweb.

Answer c is correct. As long as the Windows 98 client has IE4 or higher, it can connect to the Windows XP computer using the virtual directory that was configured on that system for Remote Desktop. The virtual directory is named tsweb by default, and can be referenced with either the computer name or the IP address. Answer a is incorrect because it is possible to connect to a Windows XP Professional computer from a Windows 98 computer using Remote Desktop. Answer b is incorrect because HOME is the name of the Windows 98 computer, not the Windows XP computer. Answer d is incorrect because this is the IP address of the Windows 98 computer, not the Windows XP computer.

Question 7

You are having trouble getting an application to work properly on your Windows XP Professional computer. You know of another person in the IT department who can help you with the issue, but they are working at home today. What Windows XP component will allow them to help you with your issue?

- ○ a. Remote Desktop Web Access
- ○ b. Remote Desktop
- ○ c. Remote Assistance
- ○ d. Application Compatibility

Answer c is correct. Remote Assistance will allow someone to gain access to your computer and assist you with a problem or issue. This tool will allow remote control, chat, and voice communications. Answers a and b are incorrect because they are related to Remote Desktop, not Assistance. With Remote Desktop, someone can take control of your computer, but they can't assist you with the problem. Answer d is incorrect because Application Compatibility will attempt to run applications in another OS environment, not help someone connect to your computer.

Question 8

> You have been given the task of documenting the IP network and the Classful subnets that make up your network. To make the correct classification for the subnets, you need to have the correct ranges for each different class of IP address. You also need to specify which IP address ranges are functional on the internal network, but not routable on the Internet. Which is the correct set of IP address ranges for the A, B, and C classes, and which is the set of IP addresses that are within those ranges, but are not routable on the Internet? [Check all correct answers]
>
> ☐ a. 0 to 128 for Class A, 129 to 192 for Class B, and 193 to 224 for Class C
>
> ☐ b. 0 to 126 for Class A, 128 to 191 for Class B, and 192 to 223 for Class C
>
> ☐ c. Nonroutable ranges of 10.x.y.z and 192.168.x.y
>
> ☐ d. Nonroutable ranges of 127.x.y.z and 192.168.x.y

Answers b and c are correct. The Classful ranges for IP addresses go up to the binary range of the number, but don't include the next value. For example, the Class A range includes 0 to 126, but does not include 128, which is the beginning of the next range of addresses. The nonroutable ranges include the 10.x.y.z range from Class A and 192.168.x.y from the Class C range. There is another range that is not routable, which is 172.16.0.0 to 172.31.255.255 from the Class B range. Answer a is incorrect because the IP address ranges are too large, not leaving room between the Class ranges. Answer d is incorrect because 127.x.y.z is not a functional address range, because it is used for local computer configurations.

Question 9

You are trying to find the last Remote Assistance file that you created, but are unable to track down the location where you stored the file. When you saved the file, you did not use the default location, to increase the security of the invitation. Now you need to try to search for the file. What file extension will you look for?

○ a. .msrcincident

○ b. .assistant

○ c. .help

○ d. .info

Answer a is correct. When an invitation for Remote Assistance is saved to a file, the default file extension is .msrcincident. Another extension is valid, but you will manually have to connect the file to the correct application when accessing it. Answers b, c, and d are incorrect because these are not the correct extensions for the Remote Assistance files.

Need to Know More?

 Microsoft Corporation. *Microsoft Windows 2000 Professional Resource Kit.* Redmond, WA: Microsoft Press, 2000. ISBN 1-57231-808-2. This book reviews the core aspects of TCP/IP and the related protocol tools.

 Minasi, Mark. *Mastering Windows XP Professional.* Alameda, CA: Sybex, Inc., 2001. ISBN 0-78212-981-1. This book reviews all of the standard TCP/IP overviews, configurations, and troubleshooting tips and tools.

 Search the TechNet CD (or its online version through **www.microsoft. com**) and the *Windows 2000 Professional Resource Kit* CD using the keywords "TCP/IP", "APIPA", "DNS", "Network Bridge", "Remote Assistance", and "Remote Desktop".

System Monitoring, Performance Optimization, and Recovery Features

- -

Terms you'll need to understand:

✓ Windows XP Backup

✓ Normal Backup

✓ Differential Backup

✓ Incremental Backup

✓ System State

✓ Volume Shadow Copy Technology

✓ Advanced startup options

✓ Safe Mode

✓ Last Known Good Configuration

✓ Recovery Console

✓ System Restore

✓ Automated System Recovery (ASR)

✓ Counters

✓ Objects

✓ Sample (or Update) interval

✓ Baselining

✓ Paging file

Techniques you'll need to master:

✓ Backing up and restoring data

✓ Starting a Windows XP system in the appropriate Safe Mode

✓ Using the Last Known Good Configuration

✓ Installing and using the Recovery Console

✓ Using and configuring System Restore

✓ Using the Automated System Recovery (ASR) tool

✓ Creating restore points

✓ Using System Monitor

✓ Creating a log with Performance Logs and Alerts

✓ Setting performance alerts

✓ Viewing performance with Task Manager

After a Windows XP system has been successfully installed, configured, and secured, one of the major goals of a system administrator is to ensure stable, reliable, and optimal performance. Windows XP Professional offers more system troubleshooting and recovery features than any previous Microsoft operating system. This chapter explores the skills required to properly prepare for and recover from computer system failures. This chapter also examines how to maintain systems to run under peak conditions by providing a foundation for performance monitoring and system optimizing.

Backing Up and Restoring Data

In Windows XP, *Windows Backup* helps you plan for and recover from data loss by enabling you to back up and restore files, folders, and System State data (which includes the Registry) manually, or on a schedule. The new-and-improved backup tool supports all kinds of storage devices and media, including tape drives, logical drives, removable disks, and recordable CD-ROMs by integrating the Removable Storage feature. The term media refers to any fixed or removable objects that store computer data such as hard disks, floppy disk, tape cartridges, compact discs (CDs), and Digital Versatile Discs (DVDs). The Windows Backup tool also has wizards to help administrators new to Windows XP to implement backup and recovery processes.

Using Windows Backup

To run the Windows Backup utility, perform one of the following actions:

➤ Click Start|Run, type "ntbackup", and click OK.

➤ Select Start|All Programs|Accessories|System Tools and click Backup.

➤ Use the NTBackup.exe tool from the command line. Run "ntbackup /?" from a command prompt window to view all of its command-line options.

By default, Windows Backup runs the Backup Or Restore Wizard, which steps you through the choices and configurations related to backing up and restoring data. To change this default behavior, clear the Always Start In Wizard Mode checkbox. You can bypass the wizard by clicking the Advanced Mode link on the Welcome To The Backup Or Restore Wizard window.

Required Permissions for Backing Up Files

To successfully back up or restore data on a Windows XP system, users must have appropriate *permissions*. Users who are members of either the Local Administrators group or the Local Backup Operators group may back up any and all files on a local Windows XP computer. Users who are members of either the Administrators group or the Backup Operators group for a Windows domain may back up any and all files on any Windows XP Professional computer that is a member of that domain. If a user is not a member of one of these groups, he or she must be an owner of all the files and folders that he wants to back up. If a user is neither an owner of the files and folders nor a member of Backup Operators or Administrators, he or she must be granted at least one of the following permissions on those files and folders: Read, Read and Execute, Modify, or Full Control. Only members of Administrators are permitted to back up System State data, which contains very important internal configuration information for Windows XP systems, including the Registry. Moreover, System State data can only be backed up on a local computer. You cannot back up the System State remotely over the network to another Windows XP computer.

Backup Types

Several different types of backup jobs enable you to create a backup procedure that maximizes efficiency, minimizes media used, and minimizes performance impact. Each file has an archive attribute, also called a *backup marker*. When a file is changed, the archive attribute or marker is set, indicating that the file has been modified since the last backup. This marker is the focus of the different backup types because some types look for the marker; others do not. Some types clear the marker; others do not. Table 9.1 clarifies the different backup types.

Note: The Windows XP Backup program skips backing up and restoring certain files by default. These files include temporary files such as Pagefile.sys, Hiberfil.sys, Win386.swp, 386spart.par, Backup.log, and Restore.log. Files that are open or locked during the backup procedure are also skipped unless they reside on a local NTFS volumes, and enough disk space is available on a local NTFS drive volume for a volume shadow copy to be created. Volume shadow copies are covered later in this chapter.

NTFS File System Offers The Change Journal Attribute

The Change Journal is a new and faster method for keeping track of changes under the NTFS 5 file system used in Windows XP and Windows 2000. The Change Journal keeps track of changes similar to the archive attribute, but in addition, it goes beyond the archive attribute in that it can also keep track of changes to permissions and changes to a document's name. These are features that the archive attribute simply doesn't offer.

Table 9.1	Windows XP backup types.		
Backup Type	**Looks for Marker**	**Clears Marker**	**Backup Set Created**
Normal	No	Yes	Backup of all selected files and folders. The most complete backup and the most straightforward to recover, but also the lengthiest to create.
Copy	No	No	Copies all selected files and folders.
Differential	Yes	No	Backup of selected files that have changed since the last normal backup. If you create a normal backup, then one week later create a differential backup, and then another week later create another differential backup, you could restore all data using the normal backup and the second differential backup, which contains all files that have changed since the normal backup. You could, in this example, discard the first differential backup.
Incremental	Yes	Yes	Backup of all data that has changed since the most recent (normal or incremental) backup. If you create a normal backup, then one week later create an incremental backup, and then another week later create a second incremental backup, you would need all three backups to recover data.
Daily	Yes	No	Backup of all files and folders that have changed during the day.

Backup Strategies

Backup strategies generally combine different backup types. Some backup types require more time to create the backup. A normal backup takes the most time to create because it backs up all selected files; however, it creates a "baseline," or complete backup. The second backup could be incremental or differential—the result would be the same. The third and subsequent backups are where the difference starts to be significant. If the second and third backups are differential, the third backup includes all files changed since the normal backup. If the second and third backups are incremental, the third backup includes only files changed since the second (incremental) backup.

So, why wouldn't you just do a normal backup and then do incremental backups until the end of time? Because incremental backups take longer than a differential backup to *recover*. Imagine recovering a machine that had a normal backup one year ago, and an incremental backup every week since. To recover that system after a catastrophe, you would have to restore the normal backup and then restore 51 incremental backups. If you had used differential backups, you would have to restore only the normal backup and the most recent differential backup.

Therefore, you should balance the "cost" of backup time against the "cost" of recovery time. Also, factor in the media required to support your backup plan. You must save incremental backups until the next normal backup. You need keep only the most recent differential backup, along with the most recent normal backup.

Configuring File and Folder Backup

When you create a backup job using the Backup Wizard or the Backup tab of the Windows Backup utility, you can specify the following:

➤ Drives, files, or folders to back up. Place a checkmark next to the drive, file, or folder that you want to back up. The selected items are backed up according to the backup type. Items whose checkboxes are cleared are not backed up. A grayed-out but marked checkbox indicates a container (disk or folder) in which only some, but not all, of its contents are selected.

➤ A backup destination. You can back up to a file or to any other storage device configured on your system. However, you cannot back up directly to CD-R or CD-RW media.

➤ A path and file name for the backup file, or a tape to use.

➤ Backup options such as backup type and log file type.

➤ A description of the job, to help you identify the job.

➤ Whether the backup medium already contains existing backup jobs.

➤ Advanced backup options, including compression and data verification.

The Windows XP Backup utility does not support backing up directly to CD-R or CD-RW media. You can back up to a local or network drive and then copy the backup file onto CD-R or CD-RW media. Fortunately, you can restore directly from one or more CD-R or CD-RW discs with the Windows XP Backup program.

Backing Up the System State

The Backup tool can back up what is called *System State* data, which includes critical files that you can use to rebuild the system. You can reinstall a failed system with the Windows XP CD-ROM. Then, you can restore the System State data, bringing the system back to its original condition as of the date of the System State backup.

Be familiar with backing up the System State. You should understand that the backup program can provide you with a backup of the system's Registry as a whole, but it cannot back up individual components of System State data.

System State data includes the following:

➤ The Registry

➤ The component services class registration database—Component Object Model + (COM+) objects

➤ System startup files

➤ Certificate Services database; applies only to Windows 2000 Server and Windows .NET Server domain controllers (DCs) and member servers running Certificate Services, not Windows XP

➤ Active Directory—Applies only to DCs, not Windows XP

➤ Sysvol folder—Applies only to DCs, not Windows XP

Configuring the System State Backup

To configure the System State backup using the Backup Wizard, perform the following steps:

1. In the Backup Wizard, on the What Do You Want To Back Up? page, select Let Me Choose What To Back Up and then click Next.

2. On the Items To Back Up page, expand My Computer and mark the checkbox for System State, click Next, and follow the remaining instructions from the wizard.

To configure the System State backup using Advanced Mode, perform the following steps:

1. Click the Backup tab.

2. Expand My Computer and mark the checkbox for System State, click Next, and follow the remaining onscreen instructions.

Scheduling Backup Jobs

You can use the Backup utility in conjunction with Task Scheduler to schedule backups to occur at regular intervals or during periods of relative inactivity on the network.

Scheduling a Backup with the Backup Wizard

To schedule a backup when using the Backup Wizard, perform the following steps:

1. In the Backup Wizard, on the Completing The Backup Or Restore Wizard page, click the Advanced button.

2. Select the backup type, if you need to change it, and click Next.

3. Select any options that you want and click Next again.

4. Select either to append this backup to any existing backups on the backup media or to replace any existing backups on the backup media, and then click Next.

5. On the When To Back Up page, click Later, type in a Job Name, and click the Set Schedule button.

6. Specify the schedule for the backup job as shown in Figure 9.1 and click OK.

7. Click Next to display the Set Account Information dialog box. Type in the user account under which this scheduled backup job will run, type in the password for the user account, and then confirm the password. Click OK.

8. Click Finish to complete the wizard.

Configuring a Job Using the Scheduled Jobs Tab

To configure a job using the Scheduled Jobs tab, perform the following steps:

1. In the Windows Backup utility, click Advanced mode, and click the Scheduled Jobs tab.

2. Double-click the day you wish to start scheduled backups, or click the Add Job button at the bottom of the Scheduled Jobs window.

3. Complete the information for the Backup Wizard.

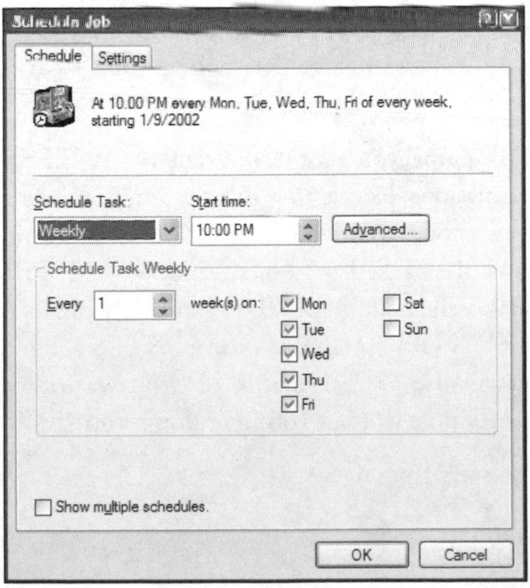

Figure 9.1 The Schedule Job dialog box for the Windows Backup program.

Volume Shadow Copy Technology

Microsoft introduces Volume Shadow Copy Technology (VSCT) to enable back-ups to be made of data files and application files even when they are currently locked and in use. Whenever a backup procedure begins, an instant shadow copy is created of the original volume(s) that is (are) being backed up. VSCT is enabled by default.

Volume shadow copies are created only for NTFS-formatted volumes running under Windows XP Professional. Enough available free disk space must exist on *any* available local NTFS volume for the shadow copy to be made. If none of the local NTFS volumes contain enough free disk space to hold the shadow copy, no shadow copy is created.

By creating an exact duplicate copy of the original volume being backed up, the Backup program can back up all of the files from the shadow copy rather than from the original volume. After the copy is made, it does not change, even if data on the original volume changes during the backup procedure. After the backup procedure is completed, the shadow copy is deleted. VSCT enables applications and services to be backed up even when they are still running. Open files appear closed on the shadow copy for backup purposes and the data within those open files is frozen as of the time that the shadow copy is created. Open files on the original volume remain open and their data may continue to change.

Restoring Files and Folders

You can restore files and folders by using the Backup utility, through the Restore Wizard, or by manually restoring them (without using the wizard). When you restore files and folders, you must specify which ones to restore, the restore location (original location, alternate location, or a single folder), and options (such as to replace existing files with backup files).

If you backed up data from an NTFS volume, you must restore data to an NTFS 5 disk volume to preserve security permissions, Encrypting File System (EFS) settings (encryption), disk quota settings, mounted drive configuration settings, and remote storage information. Restoring files backed up from a Windows XP NTFS volume onto a FAT or FAT32 volume will result in *all* NTFS settings being lost. If you attempt to restore Windows XP NTFS-stored files onto an NTFS volume running under Windows NT 4, you will lose all EFS settings, disk quota settings, advanced NTFS 5 permissions, and Remote Storage configuration information.

Troubleshooting and Repairing Windows XP Professional Systems

Windows XP Professional offers several advanced startup options for troubleshooting and repairing the operating system. In addition to supporting various options when you restart the computer, Windows XP also offers more effective ways to recover from reconfiguration errors, or from intentional or accidental system damage than any other previous Microsoft operating system. With Windows XP, disaster recovery no longer needs to be an overly arduous process.

Safe Mode and Other Advanced Startup Options

Safe Mode enables you to start your system with a minimal set of device drivers and services. For example, if newly installed device drivers or software are preventing your computer from starting, you may be able to start your computer in Safe Mode and then remove the software or device drivers from your system. Safe Mode does not work in all situations, especially if your system files are corrupted or missing, or if your hard disk is damaged or has failed. All Safe Modes start using standard VGA and create a boot log, which is useful when you are determining the exact cause of system startup problems. As a precautionary measure, when you boot into Safe Mode, Windows XP does not update the Last Known Good Configuration information. So, you always have the option of booting the computer using the Last Known Good Configuration even after you have restarted the computer under Safe Mode and perhaps changed some settings. You can go back to the original settings under the Last Known Good Configuration and discard any changes you may have made under Safe Mode.

In Safe Mode, Windows XP uses default settings, including the VGA monitor, Microsoft mouse driver, no network connections, and the minimum device drivers required to start Windows. Support for audio devices, as well as for most USB and FireWire (IEEE 1394) devices, is disabled by Safe Mode. Users' applications that normally run at startup do not run at startup under Safe Mode. If your computer does not start successfully using Safe Mode, you may need to use the Recovery Console feature or the Automated System Recovery (ASR) feature, covered later in this chapter, to repair your system.

Windows XP also provides several startup modes to help you troubleshoot and repair Windows XP systems, as well as recover from various types of disaster. Understanding each mode enables you to make informed decisions about the best startup method to use in a particular crisis situation. To select an advanced startup option, press the F8 key during the Windows XP startup process. The startup options definitely provide extra troubleshooting capabilities for your Windows XP machines. The following sections describe the Windows Advanced Options

Menu items that are available when you press the F8 key during startup for Windows XP Professional.

Safe Mode

As previously mentioned, this option loads only a minimal set of drivers and system services so that Windows XP can run in a very basic state. User startup programs do not load automatically.

Safe Mode with Networking

This option starts Windows XP using only Safe Mode drivers, services, and drivers required to enable network connections. Logon scripts run, security settings get applied, and Group Policy settings get applied. If you are confident that network issues are not the cause of your problem, it can be useful to boot to this mode, which enables you to connect to a remote system, access installation files, install service packs, or back up data.

Safe Mode with Command Prompt

This option uses the Safe Mode configuration, but displays the command prompt instead of the Windows graphical user interface (GUI) after you log on successfully. This is useful if you believe that a process spawned by the Explorer shell may be causing your problem.

Enable Boot Logging

This option starts Windows XP and creates a log file that details all drivers and services that the operating system loads (or fails to load). The log file is called Ntbtlog.txt and is located in the %systemroot% folder (by default, this is the \Windows folder). Safe Mode, Safe Mode with Networking, and Safe Mode with Command Prompt also create a boot log file. This option creates the log file without booting into Safe Mode. The boot log is useful when you are determining the exact cause of system startup problems.

Enable VGA Mode

This option employs the extremely stable and well-debugged standard VGA driver for Windows XP. This mode is useful when you have installed a new video card, if you have configured incorrect settings for the video display, or if you have installed a corrupted or poorly written video device driver. Video is a common troubleshooting issue in the Windows environment. This stable video driver is used when booting into each of the Safe Modes.

Last Known Good Configuration

Windows XP starts using the Registry configuration (ControlSet) that was saved at the last successful logon to Windows XP. Last Known Good Configuration helps you recover from incorrect configuration of hardware device drivers and services. However, it does not solve problems caused by corrupted or missing drivers or files. Any changes made to the ControlSet key of the Registry because the last successful startup and logon are lost when you select to start up with the Last Known Good Configuration. You should try this option before resorting to the Automated System Recovery feature, discussed later in this chapter.

Directory Services Restore Mode

This option applies only to Windows 2000 Server and Windows .NET Server domain controllers, and is used to restore Active Directory and the sysvol folder. This option is not applicable to Windows XP, even though it is one of the menu choices.

Debugging Mode

In this mode, Windows XP can send debugging information through a serial cable to another computer for troubleshooting the operating system kernel and system analysis.

Start Windows Normally

This option simply starts Windows XP normally without selecting any advanced startup option.

Reboot

This option restarts Windows XP Professional.

Return to the OS Choices Menu

This option takes you back to the operating system selection menu, if your computer has more than one operating system installed.

System Recovery Settings

To specify Windows XP's behavior if the system stops unexpectedly, follow these steps:

1. Right-click the My Computer icon (not a shortcut) and then select Properties.

2. On the Advanced tab, click the Settings button under the Startup And Recovery section. From the System Failure section and from the Write Debugging Information section, select the actions that Windows XP should perform if a stop error occurs, which shuts down the operating system and usually results in the infamous BSOD (Blue Screen Of Death).

Available Recovery Actions

The following are the available recovery actions that only members of the Administrators group may configure from the Startup And Recovery dialog box, as shown in Figure 9.2:

➤ Write An Event To The System Log

➤ Send An Administrative Alert

➤ Automatically Restart

➤ Small Dump Directory—Specify the small memory dump location and folder name

➤ Dump File—Specify the dump file location and file name

The Write Debugging Information drop-down list enables you to select from four different options: None, Small Memory Dump (64KB), Kernel Memory Dump, and Complete Memory Dump. The Complete Memory Dump option requires a paging file on the boot volume at least as large as the computer's installed physical RAM, plus 1MB. If you select the Kernel Memory Dump option, Windows XP writes only kernel information to the listed file instead of the entire contents of system memory. The Small Memory Dump option requires at least a 2MB paging file on the boot volume.

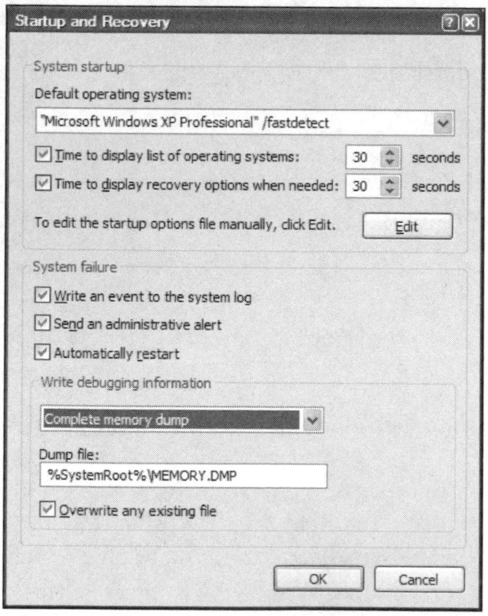

Figure 9.2   System Failure and Write Debugging Information option settings.

If you contact Microsoft Product Support Services about a stop error, the support engineer may ask for the system memory dump file generated by the Write Debugging Information options. Except for small memory dumps, Windows always writes to the same file name for each dump file generated. To save successive dump files, change the file name after each stop error, or change the location path or file name setting in the Dump File text box. For small memory dumps, a new file name is created each time the system stops unexpectedly.

Setting Up Recovery Actions to Occur When a Service Fails

To set up recovery actions to take place when a service fails, perform the following steps:

1. Open the Services MMC snap-in.

2. Right-click the service for which you want to set recovery actions and then click Properties.

3. On the Recovery tab, select the actions you want the system to take for the First Failure, Second Failure, and Subsequent Failures, as shown in Figure 9.3.

If you select Run A Program, do not specify programs or scripts that require user input. If you select Restart The Computer, you can specify how long to wait before restarting the computer by clicking the Restart Computer Options button. You can also create a message to send to remote users before the computer restarts.

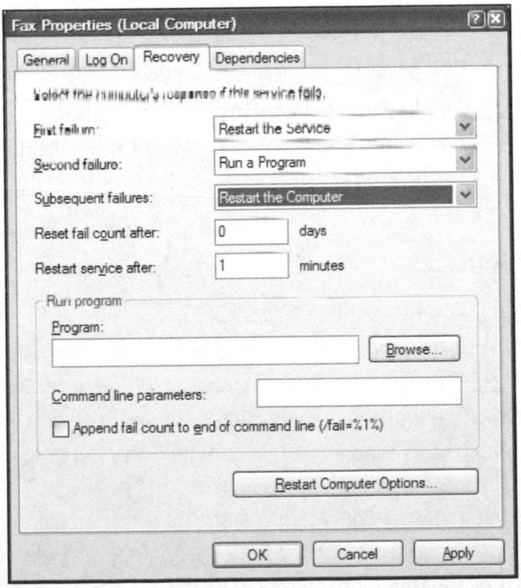

Figure 9.3   The Recovery tab of a service's Properties dialog box enables you to select actions that the system will take if the service fails.

The Recovery Console

The *Recovery Console* is a startup option that provides you with a command-line interface that enables you to repair system problems using a limited set of command-line commands. Using the Recovery Console, you can start and stop services, read and write data on a local drive (including drives formatted as NTFS), format drives, repair a corrupted master boot record, and perform many other administrative tasks. This feature gives you maximum control over the repair process; only advanced users and administrators should use it.

The Recovery Console is particularly useful if you need to repair your system by copying a file from a floppy or CD-ROM to your hard drive. It can also help you when you need to reconfigure a service that is preventing your computer from starting properly. You should try this option if the Last Known Good Configuration option is unsuccessful and you cannot start the system in Safe Mode.

Running the Recovery Console on a System that Will Not Start

To run the Recovery Console on a system that will not start, perform the following steps:

1. Be sure that your computer is configured to boot from the CD-ROM drive by selecting the proper options in the BIOS settings; insert the Windows XP Professional Setup CD-ROM into your CD-ROM or DVD-ROM drive.

2. Restart your computer.

3. Follow the directions on the screen; you may need to press a key to boot from the CD. It may take several minutes to load the files. Choose the option to repair your Windows XP installation ("press R") to start the Recovery Console. If you have other installations of Windows XP or Windows 2000 on your computer, the Recovery Console will prompt you to select which installation you want to work with.

4. Type the Administrator password and press the Enter key when prompted.

Before you encounter a system failure, open a command prompt window in Windows XP, and from the i386 folder on the Windows XP CD-ROM or from a shared network installation folder, enter the command "winnt32.exe /cmdcons". Doing so installs the Recovery Console on the local hard drive (this requires 7MB of disk space) and configures it as a valid startup option. Then, if you wish to start the system using the Recovery Console, you do not need the Windows XP CD-ROM installation files. Simply boot the machine and press the F8 key to display the startup options.

Launching the Recovery Console

The Recovery Console is quite powerful, so only advanced users who have a thorough understanding of personal computers and Windows XP should use it. Also, it is recommended that you install the Recovery Console on each Windows XP machine so that it is always an available startup option.

If you install the Recovery Console as a startup option on a FAT or FAT32 volume and then convert that volume to NTFS, the Recovery Console will no longer function. You must reinstall the Recovery Console if you convert the system's boot drive to NTFS.

After you start the Recovery Console, you must choose which installation of Windows XP or Windows 2000 that you want to log on to (if you have a dual-boot or multiboot system), and you must log on with a local administrator account and password. You are allowed three attempts to enter the correct password. *If you enter three incorrect passwords, the system automatically restarts the computer.* The design of the Recovery Console grants the administrator access to the root of the hard drives, the \Cmdcons directory if it exists, and the \Windows directory and all directories below it. You have read-only access to CD-ROM drives, to floppy drives, and to other removable media. These limitations are in place for security concerns, and access to other devices or systems is functionally beyond the scope and purpose of the Recovery Console. The main purpose of the Recovery Console is to allow you to repair the existing installation and to successfully boot Windows XP.

Recovery Console Commands

The easiest way to work in the Recovery Console—as in any unfamiliar environment—is to type "help" at the command prompt and then press the Enter key. The commands available in the Recovery Console are listed in Table 9.2.

You can use Group Policy in conjunction with a **Set** command to enable write access for removable media while using the Recovery Console. Run GPEdit.msc from the Start|Run box to launch the Local Group Policy snap-in and expand Computer Configuration|Windows Settings|Security Settings|Local Policies. Click Security Options. Double-click the policy named Recovery Console: Allow Floppy Copy And Access To All Drives And All Folders, and click the Enabled button. Click OK to save the new setting and exit from the Group Policy snap-in. The next time that you boot into the Recovery Console, type the following command: "Set AllowRemovableMedia = TRUE". Be sure to insert a space before and after the equal sign. When you enable this environment variable setting after turning on the Group Policy setting, you have access to all local hard drive volumes and folders, in addition to being able to copy files to floppy disks and other removable media.

Table 9.2	Recovery Console commands.
Command	**Description**
attrib	Changes file attributes
batch	Runs a list of commands stored in a text file
bootcfg	Scans the hard drives to modify or rebuild the Boot.ini file so that the system will boot properly
chdir (cd)	Displays the name of the current folder or changes the current folder
chkdsk	Checks a disk and displays a status report
cls	Clears the screen
copy	Copies a single file to another location
delete (del)	Deletes one or more files
dir	Displays a list of files and subfolders in a folder
disable	Disables a system service or a device driver
diskpart	Adds and deletes hard drive partitions
enable	Starts or enables a system service or a device driver
exit	Exits the Recovery Console and restarts your computer
expand	Expands compressed files such as Windows XP setup files and CAB files
fixboot	Writes a new partition boot sector onto the system partition
fixmbr	Repairs the master boot record of the partition boot sector
format	Formats a disk
help	Displays a list of the commands that you use in the Recovery Console
listsvc	Displays all available services and drivers installed on the system along with their startup status
logon	Logs on to a Windows 2000 or Windows XP installation
map	Displays the drive letter mappings
mkdir (md)	Creates a folder
more	Displays a text file
net	Maps a network share to a drive letter
rename (ren)	Renames a single file
rmdir (rd)	Deletes a folder
set	Specifies environment variables for the Recovery Console session
systemroot	Sets the current folder to the %systemroot% folder for the system that you are currently logged on to
type	Displays a text file

System Restore

The *System Restore feature* enables you to restore a Windows XP Professional system back to a prior operational state and configuration. This feature can be quite helpful if you ever want to go back to a previous configuration, because the system is encountering a problem with a new setting or a new driver, or even if the system is having compatibility problems with a new application program that you installed. You must be a member of the Administrators group to work with System Restore.

System Restore monitors several critical operating system files and application program files that are listed in a file named FileList.xml located in the %systemroot%\ system32\restore folder. The main function of System Restore is the ability to get a Windows XP computer back up and running properly again; its job is not to act as a backup and restore agent for user data files. Several data folders and files are *not* tracked by the System Restore feature, such as: the paging file; data files stored in My Documents; Favorites; temporary folders; BMP, JPG, and EPS image files, and any data files not listed in FileList.xml, including file names ending in .doc, .xls, .mdb, and .pot.

Restore Points

System Restore automatically creates restore points based on several types of events. You can also manually create your own restore points. The initial restore point is created when you start your Windows XP system for the very first time, either after performing an upgrade installation or a brand new installation. After that, Windows XP automatically creates its own restore points every 24 hours, or every 24 hours that the computer remains powered on. If the machine is powered off for more than 24 hours, a restore point is created the next time that the computer is turned on. Restore points are automatically created whenever you update the system, perform a recovery from the Windows XP Backup utility, install a new application, restore the system from a restore point, or install an unsigned device driver.

To change the amount of disk storage allocated to System Restore, right-click the My Computer icon (not a shortcut), click Properties, and click the System Restore tab. System Restore is enabled by default. To turn off this feature, click the Turn Off System Restore On All Drives checkbox. To increase or decrease the amount of disk space used for restore points, select a drive letter from the Available Drives list and click the Settings button. Drag the slider bar (as shown in Figure 9.4) to the right to increase the amount of disk space used for restore points, or drag it to the left to decrease the amount of disk space used.

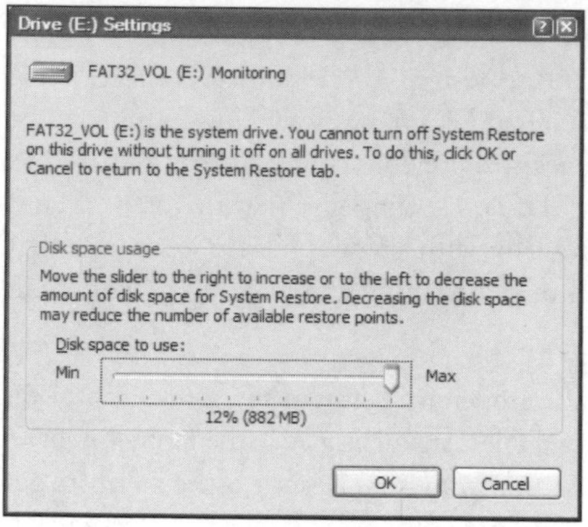

Figure 9.4 The Settings dialog box for configuring disk space usage for restore points.

The System Restore Wizard

Use the *System Restore Wizard* to manually create restore points and to restore the system to an earlier configuration by selecting a previously created restore point. You find the System Restore Wizard by clicking Start|All Programs| Accessories|System Tools|System Restore. To manually create a restore point, launch the System Restore Wizard and click the Create A Restore Point button. Click Next. Type in a restore point description and click Create.

To restore the system to a previous state, launch the System Restore Wizard and click the Restore My Computer To An Earlier Time button. Click Next and then click a boldfaced date on the calendar (boldfaced dates contain restore points). More than one restore point may exist for a given date—select the restore point that you want, and then click Next. Click Next again to confirm the restore point selected after you close all open applications. Your Windows XP system will shut down and then restart using the configuration settings specified by the restore point that you chose.

Automated System Recovery

The new *Automated System Recovery (ASR) process* replaces the Emergency Repair Disk (ERD) used with Windows 2000 and Windows NT. ASR is an advanced feature of the Windows XP Professional Backup tool (NTBackup.exe). The aim of ASR is to get a Windows XP Professional system back up and running when other recovery tools like Safe Mode, the Recovery Console, or the Last Known Good Configuration won't work due to issues such as physical problems with a hard drive, for example. ASR is *not* for backing up or restoring data! ASR actually formats the system drive volume (the volume denoted by the %systemdrive% environment variable)—any data files present on this volume will be lost if an ASR restore is performed.

You should always attempt to restore the system using the System Restore feature before you decide to use ASR.

Creating an ASR Backup

You use the Windows XP Backup program to create ASR backups. One floppy disk is required in addition to using backup media to store the operating system files, settings, and the System State data. To create an ASR backup, perform the following steps:

1. Launch the Windows XP Backup program and use Advanced Mode.

2. Click the Automated System Recovery Wizard button and click Next at the welcome screen.

3. Select a backup media type and name and click Next.

4. Click Finish to complete the wizard and begin the backup process, and then follow the instructions on the screen.

Performing an ASR Restore

The ASR restore process requires three critical components: the bootable Windows XP Professional CD-ROM, your most recent ASR backup floppy disk, and your system's most recent ASR backup media set (usually stored on tape or other removable media). To perform an ASR restore, perform the following steps:

1. Insert the Windows XP Professional CD-ROM and restart the computer.

2. Press a key when prompted to Press Any Key To Boot From CD as the computer starts.

3. When prompted to invoke Automated System Recovery, press the F2 key as the Windows Setup program loads.

4. Insert your ASR floppy disk when prompted by Windows Setup.

5. Insert your ASR backup media when prompted by Windows Setup.

6. Specify a location for the %systemroot% folder (for example, C:\Windows).

7. Follow the instructions on the screen to complete the process.

You should specify the same folder name for the %systemroot% target folder as on the backup media. You cannot perform an ASR restore from an ASR backup residing on a network share. The ASR backup must be stored on a locally attached device such as a tape drive, a Zip or Jaz drive, a CD drive, other removable media, or other hard disks.

Performance Optimizing and Troubleshooting

Although Windows XP Professional performs extremely well as a general work-station platform, with the right tools, techniques, and knowledge, you can further optimize the operating system for particular roles and you can more easily troubleshoot performance challenges. This section looks at System Monitor, Performance Logs and Alerts, Task Manager, and other tools that you can use to improve Windows XP's performance.

System Monitor

The *System Monitor MMC snap-in* is a node of the Performance Console (accessed by selecting Start|All Programs|Administrative Tools|Performance) and is available for inclusion in custom MMC consoles. This tool enables you to visually inspect the activity of system components, such as the memory, processor, disk subsystem, network cards, paging file, and applications. The plethora of performance metrics, or *counters*, available for monitoring can make the task a daunting one, indeed. We will examine the most useful counters after a tour of the Performance Console's major components.

Configuring System Monitor

System Monitor, like all MMC snap-ins, is best controlled by right-clicking. If you right-click the main portion of the Details pane, you can select Add Counters, which opens the Add Counters dialog box, shown in Figure 9.5. Counters are the basic elements that track specific aspects of system performance. The thousands of available counters are organized hierarchically as follows:

➤ *Computer*—You can monitor performance of the local system (default) or of a remote system.

➤ *Performance Object*—Any system component, such as processor, memory, disk, network protocol, or service.

➤ *Counter*—You use these objects as performance metrics related to the specific performance object on the specific computer selected. Literally thousands of counters may be available for monitoring, so take advantage of the Explain button in the Add Counters dialog box—clicking Explain produces a description of the selected counter.

➤ *Instance*—When an object occurs more than once on a computer, you see instances. For example, a multiprocessor machine has instances for each processor when you select the processor object. When you select the logical disk

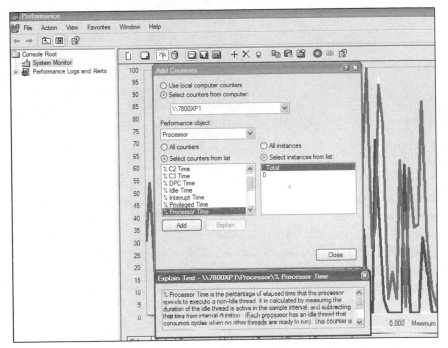

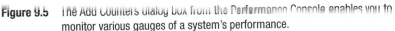

Figure 9.5   The Add Counters dialog box from the Performance Console enables you to monitor various gauges of a system's performance.

object, you see instances for each drive volume on a system. Often, instances are numbered, with the first instance being 0, the second instance 1, and so on. Usually, an additional instance provides the total for all the instances. For example, a dual processor system has a "_Total", which reflects the combination of processors 0 and 1.

After you select a computer, object, counter, and (if necessary) instance, click Add to add the counter to your System Monitor view. By right clicking the view (the right-hand pane of the Performance Console) and choosing Properties, you can alter all properties of the System Monitor view, including the display color of counters, the scale and sample rate, and the format of the monitor's display—which can be in a graph (default), a histogram (bar chart), or a report (numeric display) format.

Performance Logs and Alerts

The *Performance Logs and Alerts snap-in*, also part of the Performance Console, enables you to collect and save performance data, as well as proactively configure a system to send notifications based on various performance thresholds.

Configuring Alerts

Alerts enable you to generate actions based on a counter reaching a particular threshold. For example, you might want to be notified when a disk's capacity reaches 90 percent so that you might work to increase the disk's capacity before it fills up. By specifying a counter (such as %Free Space for a logical disk) and a threshold (under 10 percent), you can cause an event to be logged, a program to be run, a log to be started, or a network message to be sent.

To configure alerts, select the Alerts node in the Performance Logs and Alerts snap-in. Then, right-click in the Details pane and choose New Alert Settings. Enter a name for your alert settings—the name is for your use only. Then, in the Properties dialog box, add the counter(s) appropriate for the alert you are configuring. For each counter, you must specify a threshold (over or under a particular amount). You select either Under or Over from the Alert When The Value Is drop-down list, and then specify the threshold amount in the Limit text box on the General tab. You can then configure, on the Action tab, what will happen when those alerts are generated. The General and Action tabs are shown in Figure 9.6. On the Schedule tab, you can specify when the selected counters should be scanned. If you specify no schedule, scanning will begin as soon as you click OK. The alert settings you have specified will appear in the Alerts node of the Performance Logs and Alerts snap-in. Right-click an alert setting to change its configuration, to delete it, or to stop or start scanning.

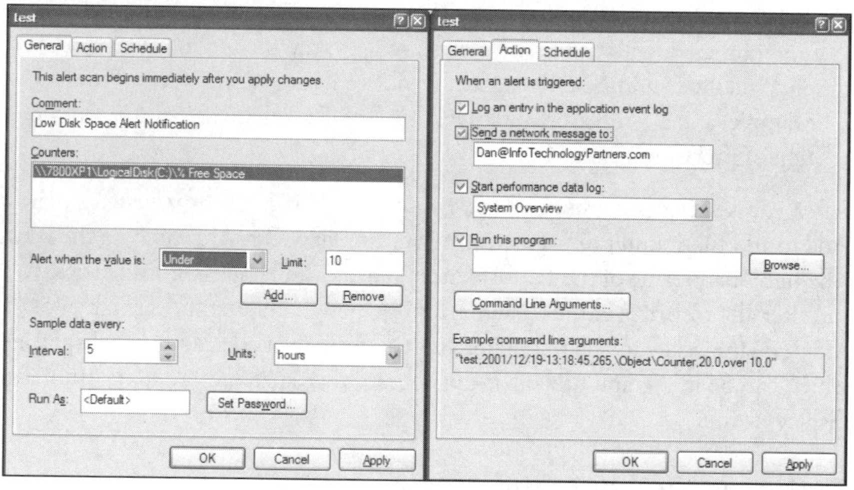

Figure 9.6 The General tab of an alert's Properties dialog box enables you to set counters and thresholds, while the Action tab enables you to specify what actions should be taken when the alert conditions are met.

Configuring Logs

Logs collect and store performance counters' data. You can view logs by using System Monitor, retrieve them in a spreadsheet such as Excel, or import them into a database. The following are the two types of logs:

➤ *Counter logs*—Record data captured over a span of time and are useful for detecting trends, setting baselines of performance, and spotting performance bottlenecks. Baselines are discussed later in this chapter.

➤ *Trace logs*—Collect performance data when an event such as a process creation, disk input/output (I/O), or page fault occurs. Trace logs are useful for troubleshooting and debugging.

To create a counter log, select the Counter Logs node of the Performance Logs and Alerts snap-in and then right-click the Details (right-hand) pane and choose New Log Settings. Give the log a name that will help you identify it in the future, and then click OK. On the General tab of the new log's Properties dialog box, add one or more counters to be recorded and then specify the sample rate—the interval at which counter data will be collected. Obviously, a shorter sample rate provides more data but also fills up the log more quickly.

 You can also configure and manage counter logs and trace logs directly from the command line by using the new Logman.exe tool. Type "Logman.exe /?" at a command prompt to view all of this command's syntax, parameters, and options.

Logs are stored, by default, in the \Perflogs folder off the root of the same drive volume where the %systemroot% folder is located. The default format is binary (.blg extension). You can stop and start logs as desired and view them in System Monitor. To view a log using the System Monitor: Click System Monitor, right-click the right-hand (view) pane of the Performance Console, and choose Properties. Then, on the Source tab, click Log Files and click Add to browse for the log file name. To analyze a log with Excel, Access, or other database and reporting tools, save the log as a comma- or tab-delimited file (.csv or .tsv extension, respectively).

Managing Performance

Monitoring, troubleshooting, and optimizing performance are some of the most important tasks you will perform as an administrator of Windows XP Professional systems. Managing performance involves several steps:

1. Create a baseline.

2. Proactively monitor.

3. Evaluate performance.

4. Identify potential bottlenecks.

5. Take corrective action.

6. Monitor the effectiveness and stability of the change.

7. Return to Step 2.

Creating a Baseline

One of the most important, and most often overlooked, steps of managing performance is creating a baseline. A *baseline* is a range of acceptable performance of a system component under normal working conditions. Baselining, or establishing a baseline, requires that you capture key counters while a system performs with normal loads and all services running. Then, you can compare future performance against the baseline to identify potential bottlenecks, troubleshoot sudden changes in performance, and justify system improvements.

 A baseline should cover a relatively large timeframe so that it captures a range of data reflecting acceptable performance. The sample interval for the log should be somewhat large as well, so the baseline log does not become enormous. You should generate baselines regularly, perhaps even once a month, so that you can identify performance trends and evaluate bottlenecks pertaining to system and network performance. If you follow these guidelines, you will produce a baseline that gives an accurate overview of system performance.

The most useful objects to understand and monitor are the following:

➤ *Cache*—Physical memory used to store recently accessed disk data.

➤ *Memory*—RAM used to store code and data.

➤ *Paging file*—The file used to extend physical RAM and create virtual memory.

➤ *Physical disk*—The disk drive or redundant array of independent disks (RAID) device. A physical disk may contain multiple logical disks.

➤ *Logical disk*—The disk volume, including simple, logical, spanned, striped, mirrored, or RAID-5 volumes. A logical disk may span multiple physical disks.

➤ *Process*—Executable programming code that represents a running application.

➤ *Processor*—The Central Processing Unit (CPU).

➤ *Server*—The server service, which offers data and print services, even on a Windows XP Professional system.

➤ *System*—Counters that apply to all system hardware and software.

➤ *Thread*—Executable programming code that the processor is processing.

Baselines should include these critical objects as well as the other counters discussed in this chapter.

Managing Memory Performance

The counters in the Memory object represent the memory available via the system's physical RAM and via the system's virtual memory (paging file). The most important counters in the memory object are the Pages/sec counters and the Available Bytes counter:

➤ *Memory:Pages/sec, threshold over 20 pages/sec* This counter, and all related counters (including Page Reads/sec, Page Writes/sec, Page Faults/sec, Page Inputs/sec, and Page Outputs/sec) reflect the transfer of data and code from physical RAM to the virtual paging file, and paging-related events. When any one of these counters is high, it indicates a potential memory shortage, because when a system does not have enough RAM to satisfy its needs, inactive data and code are moved from physical RAM to the virtual paging file to make room for active data and code.

➤ *Memory:Available Bytes, threshold under 4MB*—Available Bytes reflects the amount of physical RAM available after the working sets of applications and the cache have been served. Windows XP Professional trims working sets and page memory to the disk to maintain at least 4MB of available RAM. If this counter is consistently lower than 4MB, it generally indicates a memory shortage.

> Memory is often the first performance bottleneck in the "real world." The counters related to processor and hard drive utilization might be well beyond their thresholds simply because inadequate memory is causing paging, which impacts those two components. So always check the memory counters to make sure that they are not the "root cause" of the performance bottleneck.

To correct a memory shortage, your first reaction might be to add more RAM, which is certainly one solution. However, it is often equally valid to optimize memory usage by stopping unnecessary services, drivers, and background applications, or by moving services or applications to systems with excess capacity.

Managing the Paging File

Just as every Windows 2000 computer requires a paging file to avoid dismally slow performance, each Windows XP Professional system needs a paging file as well. When physical RAM is not sufficient to support active processes, the *Virtual Memory Manager (VMM)* moves less active data or code from physical RAM to virtual memory stored in the paging file. When a process later attempts to address data or code currently in the paging file, the VMM transfers that memory space back into physical RAM. The paging file thus provides for efficient utilization of a system's physical RAM and allows a system to support more activity than its physical RAM alone would allow. Transfer of pages, 4KB blocks of memory, to and from the paging file is normal on any system, but excessive paging, or *thrashing*, indicates a memory shortage. In addition, the paging file itself can impede performance if it is not properly optimized.

You configure the paging file using the System applet in Control Panel. Click the Advanced tab, click the Performance Options button, and then, in the Virtual Memory section, click Change. The paging file, called Pagefile.sys, is created on the %systemroot% volume by default. Microsoft recommends that the paging file size should be 1.5 times the amount of physical RAM installed in the computer. You can configure the paging file to be placed on other volumes or to be split across multiple volumes, in which case there will be a Pagefile.sys file on each selected volume. The total size of the paging file is considered to be the sum total of all the paging files that the system uses. You can also configure the paging file's Initial Size (the space created initially by the VMM and reserved for paging activity) and its Maximum Size (a setting that can permit the VMM to expand the paging file to a size greater than the Initial Size).

You can optimize paging by performing the following:

➤ Remove the paging file from the system and boot partitions. The system partition is technically the partition that is used to start the system—it contains the NTLDR file and the boot sector. To make things confusing, the boot partition contains the operating system and is indicated by the variable %systemroot%. Luckily, most computers are configured with Windows XP on the C drive (the first partition), making the boot partition, the system partition, and %systemroot% all equal to C:. To remove the paging file from a partition, set its Initial Size and Maximum Size to zero (0) and click the Set button.

➤ Configure the paging file to reside on multiple physical disks, and configure the Initial Size and Maximum Size identically on all drives. The paging subsystem then spreads written pages evenly across all available Pagefile.sys files.

➤ Configure the paging file to reside on fast, less active drives. If you have drives of various speeds, put the paging file on the fastest one. If you have drives that are less active, put the paging file on those so that the paging system doesn't have to compete as often with other read or write operations.

➤ Before moving the paging file, defragment the volumes on which you will put the paging file. This practice helps to prevent a fragmented paging file.

➤ Set the Initial Size to be sufficient for the system's paging requirements, and then set the Maximum Size to the same size. When the Maximum Size is greater than the Initial Size, and the system must expand the paging file, the expansion puts an additional burden on both the processor and disk subsystems. In addition, the paging file is likely to become fragmented, further hitting the performance of paging.

The ideal paging file configuration is to split it evenly over multiple *physical* disks, except for the disk(s) containing the system and boot partitions.

Managing Disk Performance

The **PhysicalDisk** and **LogicalDisk** performance objects collect metrics related to individual disk drives and logical disk volumes, respectively. **PhysicalDisk** counters focus on a storage device, so you should use them to analyze hardware performance. Use **LogicalDisk** counters, which focus on a specific volume, to analyze disk read and write performance.

For Windows XP systems, you no longer need to enable **LogicalDisk** counters with the **Diskperf.exe** command so that you can monitor their performance with the System Monitor snap-in—**LogicalDisk** counters are automatically enabled on demand. **Diskperf.exe** is needed only for remote administration of computers running Windows NT and Windows 2000.

The following disk counters will help you to monitor and manage disk performance:

➤ *PhysicalDisk/LogicalDisk: %DiskTime, threshold close to 100%*—This reports the amount of time that a disk is busy servicing read or write requests.

➤ *PhysicalDisk/LogicalDisk: Disk Queue Length, threshold 2*—The Average and Current disk queue length counters reflect the read/write requests that are pending and being serviced. If the queue is long, processes are being delayed.

When disk performance is a bottleneck, you can add capacity; replace disks with faster hardware; move applications, services, or data to underused disks; or implement spanned, striped, or RAID-5 volumes.

Managing Network Performance

Although Windows .NET Server and Windows 2000 Server can support Network Monitor for relatively sophisticated network traffic analysis, Windows XP Professional has limited network performance tools. Counters are available for the number of bytes and packets received and sent over a particular network interface. However, you cannot analyze the contents or properties of packets using only Windows XP Professional tools from the GUI.

To conduct detailed network analysis for a Windows XP Professional system, perform the following steps:

1. Install the Network Monitor Driver.

2. From the Network Connections folder, right-click a connection, choose Properties, and then click Install.

3. Select the Protocol component and click the Add button. Select Network Monitor Driver and click OK.

4. Click Close to exit from the connection's Properties dialog box.

The Network Monitor Driver can collect packets that the Windows XP system's network interfaces send or receive. You can then analyze those packets using a version of Network Monitor that ships with Systems Management Server (SMS), Windows 2000 Server, or Windows .NET Server. You can also use a new tool that ships with Windows XP Professional, the Netcap.exe command-line utility, to analyze your system's network packets.

Managing Processor Performance

A system's processor is one of the more difficult components to optimize because every other component impacts it. Low memory leads to paging, which increases processor usage; fragmented disk drives increase processor usage; hardware interrupts keep the processor busy; and, of course, applications and services place many demands on the processor. Therefore, to optimize a processor, you need to look at Processor counters, as well as counters for other objects. Some of the most useful Processor counters are the following:

➤ *Processor:%ProcessorTime, threshold near 100%*—A processor being fully utilized (100 percent) is not necessarily a sign of a performance bottleneck—in fact, one would hope that you would be using this expensive system component at its full capacity. Therefore, although %ProcessorTime is a flag that indicates a potential bottleneck, it is not in itself enough to prescribe a solution. Check Memory:Pages/sec to examine paging and determine whether low memory is causing excessive paging.

➤ *Processor:Interrupts/sec, threshold varies*—A malfunctioning hardware device may send excessive interrupts to the processor. Compare this counter to a baseline; a significant increase in this counter without a corresponding increase in system activity may indicate a bad device. Network cards are particularly notorious for generating bogus interrupts.

➤ *System:Processor Queue Length, threshold 2*—A queue length that is regularly above 2 indicates that threads are backing up as they wait for processor attention.

➤ *Process:%ProcessorTime (Instance—each service or application)*—This counter enumerates the activity of individual applications and services, allowing you to identify processes that are placing demands on the processor.

If Processor Queue Length is low and %ProcessorTime is averaging above 85 percent for extended periods of time, these settings indicate that a single threaded application or service is keeping the processor busy. A faster processor may improve performance of such a system. However, if Processor Queue Length is high, a second processor would be a better solution, or you might consider moving processes to underutilized systems.

Task Manager

Task Manager enables you to view applications and processes, and a number of other common performance counters. To open Task Manager, right-click the taskbar and choose Task Manager, or press Ctrl+Shift+Esc. The Applications tab enumerates active applications. The Processes tab can display a number of process-related counters. With the Processes tab displayed, click View|Select Columns from the menu bar to specify which counters you wish to view. The Performance tab displays useful performance metrics such as CPU usage and paging file usage—these statistics start running whenever Task Manager is opened. The Networking tab is new to Windows XP—it displays the network utilization percentage for the system.

Managing Application Performance

Windows XP preemptively multitasks active processes, ensuring that all threads gain access to the processor. Processes do run at different priorities, however. Priority levels of 0 to 31 are assigned to a process, and higher-level processes are executed before lower-level processes. As a user, you can specify process priority using Task Manager. Right-clicking a process on the Processes tab enables you to set a process's priority. Processes are assigned a priority of Normal by default.

Choosing Above Normal or High will increase the priority of a process and thereby increase the frequency with which its threads are serviced. Choosing Below Normal or Low will diminish the servicing of a process.

 Do not use the Realtime priority. This priority should be reserved for real-time data gathering applications and operating system functions. Setting an application to Realtime priority can cause instability and can be difficult to reverse without restarting the system.

Process priority can also be controlled when an application is launched, using the **start** command with the **/low, /belownormal, /normal, /abovenormal, /high,** and **/realtime** switches.

On dual-processor Windows XP Professional computers, you can also assign one or more specific processes to a specific processor of your choosing. When you right-click a process in Task Manager from the Processes tab, the Set Affinity option is available in addition to the Set Priority option. The Set Affinity option is not displayed at all on single CPU systems.

Monitoring Event Logs

The new Eventtriggers.exe command-line tool displays and configures actions to be taken based on events (system messages, warnings, and failures) that occur, which are tracked by the Windows XP Event Viewer. The Eventtriggers.exe utility works on both local and remote computers and monitors the Application log, System log, Security log, DNS Server log, and Directory log. You must be a member of the Administrators group to use Eventriggers.exe. To view a current list of event triggers, type "eventtriggers" (without any parameters) at a command prompt. For more details on this tool, search on the keyword "eventtriggers" in the Windows XP Professional Help and Support Center, or type "eventtriggers / ?" at a command prompt.

Practice Questions

Question 1

If your Windows XP system gets a stop error (blue screen) after you have installed an updated video driver, what is the best and most efficient course of action to take to get your system back up and running so that you can fix the problem?

○ a. Restart the system using the Last Known Good Configuration advanced startup option.

○ b. Restart the system using the Recovery Console.

○ c. Perform a restore operation using the Automated System Recovery feature.

○ d. Restart the system using the Enable VGA Mode advanced startup option.

Answer d is correct. Restarting the system under VGA mode would be the fastest and most efficient way to get back into the system, and either roll back or uninstall the poorly behaving video driver. Answer a is incorrect because the Last Known Good Configuration would also erase any other configuration changes that you might have made just prior to updating the video driver. Answer b is incorrect because you do not need to boot into the Recovery Console just to change the video driver. Answer c is incorrect because an Automated System Recovery restore formats the system drive and reinstalls Windows XP, which would be time-consuming and completely unnecessary in this case.

Question 2

Jan's Windows XP Professional computer does not have a tape drive installed on it. Fortunately, the important data that she needs to back up requires only about 575MB of storage space. Jan remembers that Windows XP supports writing directly to CD-R and CD-RW media, so she runs the Windows XP Backup program to create a backup of her data onto a CD-R disc. How can Jan get her data backed up onto a CD-R?

○ a. Specify a CD-R as the target media for the Windows Backup program.

○ b. Specify a CD-RW as the target media for the Windows Backup program.

○ c. Use the Windows XP Backup program to back up the data to a different hard drive or to a network drive, and then copy the backup file onto CD-R or CD-RW media.

○ d. Specify a DVD-R as the target media for the Windows Backup program.

Answer c is correct. The Windows XP Backup program does *not* support backing up directly to CD-R or CD-RW media, but you can copy a previously created backup file to a CD-R or CD-RW disc. Answer a is incorrect because the Windows XP Backup program does not support backing up directly to CD-Rs. Answer b is incorrect because the Windows XP Backup program does not support backing up directly to CD-RWs. Answer d is incorrect because the Windows XP Backup program does not support backing up directly to DVD-Rs, nor can you natively write to DVD-RAM media.

Question 3

Bob has a Windows XP Professional computer that has applications processing data 24 hours a day, 7 days a week. He upgraded the computer to Windows XP from Windows 98 and he has left the file systems intact. He knows he needs to have frequent, regular backups, but he's concerned about not being able to back up several important data files that are always open and critical application files that are always locked. What can Bob do to back up his important data and application files?

○ a. Turn off 50 percent of the important applications and close their data files during nonpeak intervals and perform a backup of those files; turn off the other 50 percent at different nonpeak intervals and perform a second backup of those files.

○ b. Rely on Windows XP's Volume Shadow Copy Technology to enable the Windows XP Backup program to back up those open data files and locked application files.

○ c. Let the Windows XP Backup program skip the open and locked files for now; those files may be closed and unlocked during the next scheduled backup.

○ d. Use the Inuse.exe utility from the Windows 2000 Professional Resource Kit to unlock any locked files and then perform a backup.

Answer a is correct. Volume Shadow Copy Technology (VSCT) is not available for data or application files stored on FAT or FAT32 drive volumes; Bob must create a backup window interval during which the Backup program can back up his important files. Answer b is incorrect because VSCT is not available for data or application files stored on FAT or FAT32 drive volumes. Answer c is incorrect because open and locked files do not get backed up, and you should not leave good backups to chance. Answer d is incorrect because the Inuse.exe tool is meant for replacing locked operating system files, not for helping to back up locked or open files.

Question 4

> How can you boot your Windows XP system into the Recovery Console after
> you have just installed Windows XP Professional on the computer? [Check
> all correct answers]
>
> ❑ a. Restart the system, press the F8 key as Windows XP starts up, and
> select Recovery Console from the default list of advanced startup
> options.
>
> ❑ b. Restart the system by booting from the Windows XP Professional
> CD-ROM and select the repair option when prompted.
>
> ❑ c. Click Start|Run, and run the command "winnt32.exe /cmdcons"
> from the i386 folder on the Windows XP Professional CD-ROM.
> Restart the system, press the F8 key as Windows XP starts up, and
> select Recovery Console from the list of advanced startup options.
>
> ❑ d. Restart the system, press the F8 key as Windows XP starts up, and
> select Safe Mode Using Recovery Console from the default list of
> advanced startup options.

Answers b and c are correct. You can boot into the Windows XP Recovery Console by booting from the Windows XP Professional CD-ROM and selecting the repair option, or by first installing the Recovery Console onto your system using the **winnt32.exe /cmdcons** command and then you can restart the system'select Recovery Console as an advanced startup option. Answer a is incorrect because the Recovery Console is not a default startup option; you must manually install it first. Answer d is incorrect because there is no Safe Mode Using Recovery Console advanced startup option.

Question 5

After making several configuration settings changes, Edie wants to restore her Windows XP Professional system to the configuration that it had yesterday, before she made any changes. Unfortunately, she forgot to set any restore points. Her computer has been left powered on in her office for the last week. Can she restore her system to its previous state, and if so, using which technology?

○ a. Yes, she can use the System Restore Wizard to restore her system.

○ b. No, she can't restore her system to its previous state from yesterday, but she can restore it to its original state when it was first installed using the System Restore Wizard.

○ c. Yes, she can easily restore her system to its previous state using the Last Known Good Configuration.

○ d. Yes, she can restore her system's configuration using the Windows XP Professional CD-ROM, an ASR floppy disk, and the ASR tape backup that she created from the night before.

Answer a is correct. By default, System Restore automatically creates a restore point every 24 hours or every 24 hours that the computer is powered on. She can use the System Restore Wizard to restore her system from the restore point that was created approximately 24 hours earlier. Answer b is incorrect because she can restore her system to its previous state from approximately 24 hours earlier. Answer c is incorrect because the Last Known Good Configuration holds the **CurrentControlSet** information after you successfully log on to the system—it cannot revert to a previous configuration after successfully logging on to the system. Answer d is incorrect because when you perform an ASR restore, it reformats the system drive and returns all settings to their installation defaults.

Question 6

Which of the following system tools is best suited to help you create a historical baseline of overall system performance for a Windows XP Professional computer?

○ a. Performance Logs and Alerts

○ b. System Monitor

○ c. Task Manager

○ d. Network Monitor Driver and the Netcap.exe utility

Answer a is correct. The Performance Logs and Alerts snap-in captures performance activity for all of the objects and their associated counters that you add to a performance counter log. By tracking such activity over time for key components, such as memory, processor, network interfaces, physical and logical disks, you can create a baseline against which to compare future activity. Answer b is incorrect because the System Monitor snap-in displays only current activity or past activity—it does not store such data. Answer c is incorrect because the Task Manager displays only current activity for applications, processes, performance, and networking—it does not store such data. Answer d is incorrect because the Network Monitor Driver and the Netcap.exe utility capture and analyze network data packets—they do not store any other performance-related data.

Question 7

Which of the following actions represents a best practice approach to configuring virtual memory on a Windows XP Professional computer that has three physical hard disks (assigned as drives C, D, and E), the %systemroot% folder located on the C drive, and 256MB of memory installed?

- ○ a. Place the paging file on the C drive with an initial size of 192MB and a maximum size of 256MB.

- ○ b. Place a paging file on the D drive with an initial size of 192MB and a maximum size of 192MB, and place a second paging file on the E drive, also with an initial size of 192MB and a maximum size of 192MB.

- ○ c. Place a paging file on the E drive with an initial size of 128MB and a maximum size of 256MB.

- ○ d. Place a paging file on the E drive with an initial size of 192MB and a maximum size of 192MB, and place a second paging file on the C drive, also with an initial size of 192MB and a maximum size of 192MB.

Answer b is correct. The optimal paging file configuration is to split it evenly over multiple physical disks without placing it on the system or boot volumes. The recommended paging file size is 1.5 times the installed memory. For a system with 256MB RAM installed, that would be 384MB split over two drives (192MB each). Answer a is incorrect because it is not a best practice to place the paging file on the system or boot volumes. Answer c is incorrect because it is not optimal to make the initial size lower than the maximum size, because this will cause the paging file to be expanded, which takes system resources. Answer d is incorrect because it is not a best practice to place the paging file on the system or boot volumes, even if you place other paging files on different volumes.

Question 8

Which of the following Windows XP system components can you configure
or monitor from the Task Manager window for a dual-processor computer?
[Check all correct answers]

- ❑ a. Network utilization and current condition
- ❑ b. Processor usage and page file usage
- ❑ c. Processor affinity for specific processes
- ❑ d. Processor priority for specific processes
- ❑ e. Available system memory
- ❑ f. List of processes running from all users

Answers a, b, c, d, e, and f are all correct. Network utilization percentage is displayed on the Networking tab, processor and page file usage is displayed on the
Performance tab, and processor affinity settings and processor priority settings
for specific processes are managed on the Processes tab. Available system memory
is shown on the Performance tab, and you can expand the list of processes to
include all users on the machine by marking the Show Processes From All Users
checkbox at the bottom of the Processes tab.

Need to Know More?

Bott, Ed and Carl Siechert. *Microsoft Windows XP Inside Out*. Redmond, WA: Microsoft Press, 2001. ISBN 0-73561-382-6. This book offers timesaving tips, troubleshooting techniques, and workarounds. It focuses on techniques such as taking advantage of the rich integration of devices, applications, and Web services in Windows XP.

Microsoft Corporation. *Microsoft Windows XP Professional Resource Kit Documentation*. Redmond, WA: Microsoft Press, 2001. ISBN 0-73561-485-7. This all-in-one reference is a compilation of technical documentation and valuable insider information that computer-support professionals and administrators can reference to install, customize, and support Windows XP.

Minasi, Mark. *Mastering Windows XP Professional*. Alameda, CA: Sybex, Inc., 2001. ISBN 0-78212-981-1. This book provides in-depth coverage of installing, configuring, and administering Windows XP Professional.

Search the Microsoft TechNet CD (or its online version through **www.microsoft.com**) using keywords such as "Backup", "System Restore", "Automated System Recovery", "Safe Mode", and "Performance".

Installing, Administering, and Troubleshooting Remote Access Services

Terms you'll need to understand:

- ✓ Authentication protocol
- ✓ Internet Protocol Security (IPSec)
- ✓ Point-to-Point Tunneling Protocol (PPTP)
- ✓ Layer 2 Tunneling Protocol (L2TP)
- ✓ Extensible Authentication Protocol (EAP)
- ✓ Smart Card
- ✓ Encryption
- ✓ Dial-up connection
- ✓ Virtual Private Network (VPN)
- ✓ Internet Connection Firewall (ICF)
- ✓ Internet Connection Sharing (ICS)

Techniques you'll need to master:

- ✓ Configuring the proper authentication for a remote access client
- ✓ Determining when it is best to use PPTP or L2TP for your VPN connections
- ✓ Establishing the requirements and configurations to use a Smart Card
- ✓ Knowing what the default encryption levels are for your remote access connections
- ✓ Configuring ICF to secure your computer on the Internet
- ✓ Knowing when to configure ICS to allow multiple computers on your network access to the Internet

Dial-up connectivity still maintains an important role for connecting remote computers. In Microsoft terms, *dial-up connections* generally refer to client computers dialing out to server computers. Remote Access Services (RAS) generally refers to server computers that accept inbound remote connections from dial-up clients. Dial-up connections usually involve regular phones using analog modems and/or dial-up integrated services digital network (ISDN) lines.

Authentication Protocols

Windows XP Professional provides advanced support for remote access authentication protocols over older versions of Windows operating systems. These new authentication protocols offer enhanced security and dynamic bandwidth allocation for remote access. These authentication protocols, authenticate the logon credentials for all users who attempt to connect to a Windows-based network. Windows XP Professional supports all the authentication protocols that Windows 2000 offered, including PAP, CHAP, MSCHAP (v1 and v2), EAP, SPAP, PPTP, and L2TP. Figure 10.1 shows the new interface for configuring an XP Professional's authentication protocols.

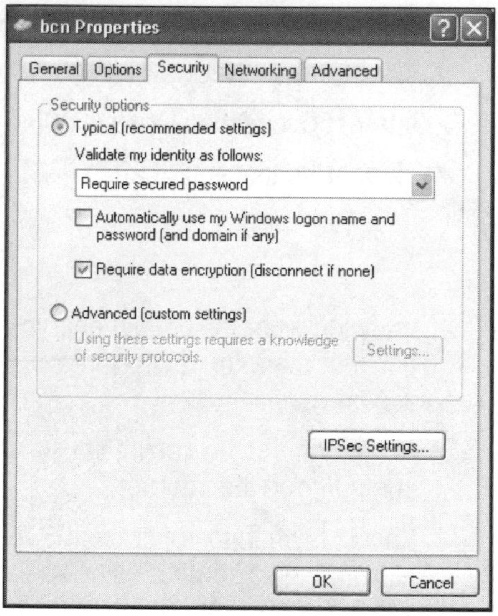

Figure 10.1 Security configurations for a dial-up or VPN connection.

Note: The Security tab has two different configuration options: Typical and Advanced. Choosing the Typical option enables you to make a fast configuration setting. If you want to see what the Typical settings are and perhaps make changes to them, just select the Advanced option and then click the Settings button. Clicking the Settings button will give all the detailed settings that are configured for the current settings.

The default authentication protocols for a dial-up connection are PAP, SPAP, MS-CHAP, and MS-CHAPv2. The default protocols for a VPN connection are MS-CHAP and MS-CHAPv2.

EAP

Extensible Authentication Protocol (EAP) is an extension of PPP for dial-up networking (DUN), L2TP, and PPTP clients. EAP supports a negotiated authentication model where the actual authentication mechanism is determined between the dial-up connection client and the remote access server. EAP provides support for a few authentication protocols, including the following:

➤ *Message Digest 5 Challenge Handshake Authentication Protocol (MD5-CHAP)*— Encrypts usernames and passwords using its own MD5 algorithm.

➤ *Transport Level Security (TLS)*—Works with Smart Cards and other types of security certificates. A Smart Card stores a user's security certificate and private key electronically on the card. Smart Card technology requires physical cards and card readers.

Note: By using EAP application programming interfaces (APIs), software developers can design and implement new authentication methods for Smart Cards, generic token cards, and even biometric devices such as fingerprint identification scanners. In this way, EAP can support authentication technologies that will be developed in the future. To add EAP authentication methods, go to the Security tab of the remote access server's Properties dialog box.

IPSec

IP Security (IPSec) is a suite of security-related protocols and cryptographic functions for establishing and maintaining private and secure IP connections. IPSec is easy to implement and offers superb security for potential network traffic sniffing. IPSec-enabled clients establish a Security Association (SA) with the server that serves as a private key for encrypting data. IPSec uses simple on/off configurations, or you can configure policies for configuring its security services. IPSec policies support different gradations of security levels for different types of network traffic. Administrators can set IPSec policies at the Local, Organizational

Unit, Domain, or Site level. You configure IPSec policies with the IP Security Policy Management snap-in of the Microsoft Management Console (MMC).

L2TP

You can compare the *Layer 2 Tunneling Protocol (L2TP)* to the Point-to-Point Tunneling Protocol (PPTP) in that it provides an encrypted "tunnel" for data to pass through an untrusted (public) network such as the Internet. Both L2TP and PPTP use PPP to establish initial communications. Some of the major differences between L2TP and PPTP include the following:

➤ L2TP exploits IPSec for encryption services; PPTP uses the encryption functions of PPP.

➤ L2TP offers support for tunnel authentication; PPTP does not support tunnel authentication. If you implement IPSec tunneling in conjunction with L2TP or PPTP, L2TP tunnel authentication isn't needed, because this will be handled by the IPSec tunnel.

RADIUS

Remote Authentication Dial-in User Service (RADIUS) offers accounting services and centralized authentication functions for distributed dial-up connections. Windows XP Professional can take on the role of a RADIUS server or a RADIUS client, or it can assume the roles of both. A RADIUS client is often used as a remote access server for an Internet service provider (ISP). The RADIUS client forwards authentication requests to a RADIUS server. You configure RADIUS client settings from the Security tab of the remote access server's Properties dialog box.

RADIUS servers validate requests from RADIUS clients. For authentication, Windows 2000 provides Internet Authentication Services (IAS) as an optional Windows component that you can add during installation or through the Add/Remove Programs icon in the Control Panel. RADIUS servers maintain RADIUS accounting data from RADIUS clients in associated log files.

BAP

Bandwidth Allocation Protocol (BAP) works in conjunction with the Bandwidth Allocation Control Protocol (BACP) as an enhancement to the Multilink feature found in Windows NT 4. Multilink enables you to bind together two or more modems or ISDN lines, allowing you to achieve higher throughput (more bandwidth) than you would if you used the lines individually. BAP and BACP work together to dynamically add or drop lines for multilinked devices on an on-demand basis. Both protocols serve as PPP control protocols. These protocols provide a means for optimizing bandwidth while holding down connection costs by responding to network bandwidth needs on demand. For organizations that incur line-usage charges based on bandwidth use (such as ISDN lines), BAP and BACP can significantly cut costs.

Administrators can turn on the Multilink feature as well as BAP and BACP from the PPP tab of each remote access server's Properties dialog box. You configure BAP settings using remote access policies. By implementing a remote access policy using BAP, you can specify that an extra line should be dropped if the connection for that line falls below a specified percentage. If two different users need to have different BAP settings, multiple remote access policies can be configured, where each of them uses a different percentage. The easiest way to configure the different remote access policies is to associate the settings to a Windows group, which will easily apply the policy settings to the correct type of user.

Encryption

Encryption is the technology of locking down data or network traffic with digital keys. These keys are only available to those who are transferring the information. Multiple levels of encryption exist, and with each increase in a level of encryption, you will have a hit to performance. It simply takes longer to create and decode higher encryption.

By default, dial-up connections have the encryption level set to optional, and VPN connections have the encryption level set to required. In these instances, a dial-up session does not have to use encryption, whereas VPN sessions do. Of course, the main reason for this is the lack of security that VPNs endure, because they are traveling across the Internet. You can alter this default behavior, but in the case of the VPN, it is always best to keep the security at this level or higher.

The following are the four different encryption levels that you can set on any remote network connection, as shown in Figure 10.2:

➤ *No Encryption Allowed*—This does not allow the dial-up or VPN client to connect with any form of encryption. Not allowing any encryption will be rare, but in the case of a very slow connection, this can be useful.

➤ *Optional Encryption*—This will use encryption if the remote access server is suggesting that it be used or requiring that encryption be used.

➤ *Require Encryption*—This will require that the remote access client use encryption with the remote access server. The encryption level used will be the standard level for either the MPPE or IPSec.

➤ *Maximum Strength Encryption*—This will require that both the remote access client and server negotiate the communication with strong encryption.

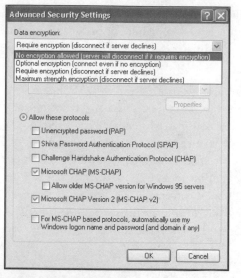

Figure 10.2   Security configurations for a dial-up or VPN connection.

Two different levels of encryption can be required for a remote access connection. Table 10.1 gives you the information about how the different levels are seen in the interface and what each means.

Connecting to Remote Access Servers

You create new connections to remote access servers from the Network Connections window. You can make new connections as well as modify or delete existing network connections from this window. To create a new network connection, you would simply start the New Connection Wizard from the Network Connections window. During this wizard, you can create connections for your LAN, dial-up, VPN, or direct connection. Figure 10.3 shows the wizard in action, including some of the options that are available.

As soon as you complete the New Connection Wizard for a remote access connection, a Connect dialog box appears. It prompts you for a User Name and a Password. Click the Connect button to initiate the connection. Click the Properties button to modify the remote connection's properties.

Table 10.1   Required encryption levels.

Interface Text	Encryption Level	MPPE	IPSec
Require Encryption	Standard	40-bit	56-bit (DES)
Maximum Strength Encryption	Strong	128-bit	168-bit (3DES)

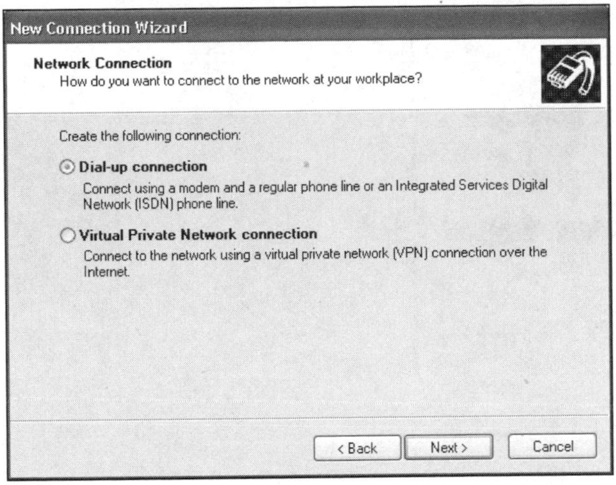

Figure 10.3 New Connection Wizard options for connecting to a workplace.

You can modify the properties of any network connection listed in the Network Connections window by right-clicking the connection's icon and selecting Properties. From the connection's Properties dialog box, you can configure connection devices (modems and so on), list alternate phone numbers, and configure dialing options and redialing options. You can specify security options, configure dial-up server settings, and modify network connection components. You can also set up Internet Connection Sharing (ICS) from the Sharing tab, if this connection will be used to connect other users on the network to the Internet. ICS is covered in more detail later in this chapter.

The Networking tab of a dial-up connection's Properties dialog box enables you to configure several essential components for successful connections (see Figure 10.4). Be sure to specify the proper dial-up server type to which you will be connecting (either PPP or SLIP). You can change PPP settings by clicking the Settings button (as shown in Figure 10.5). Be sure that your connection has at least one dial-up network protocol in common with the remote access server to which it will be attempting to connect. You can install and uninstall networking components, such as protocols, from the Networking tab. You can also enable or disable any listed component by marking or clearing its checkbox.

Setting Up and Configuring VPN Connections

Setting up and configuring VPN connections is similar to establishing dial-up connections. VPN connections enable you to connect to remote computers anywhere in the world by tunneling through the Internet using a VPN protocol such as PPTP or L2TP. VPN protocols encapsulate TCP/IP, NetBEUI, or NWLink

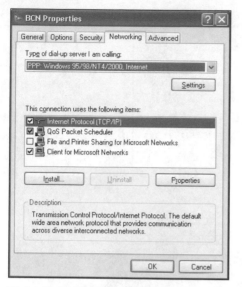

Figure 10.4   The Networking tab of a dial-up connection's Properties dialog box.

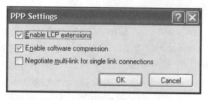

Figure 10.5   The PPP Settings dialog box.

data packets for transport over TCP/IP via the Internet. PPTP and L2TP use encryption to secure all the data that they encapsulate as it travels to the destination VPN server.

When you double-click the Virtual Private Connection icon to access a VPN server, you are prompted to connect to the Internet using the dial-up connection you specified. After you have established a connection to the Internet, Windows XP Professional attempts to connect to the remote VPN server.

Configuring Internet Connection Firewall

Internet Connection Firewall (ICF) is an excellent addition to Windows XP Professional. The product is considered to be a stateful firewall, in that it monitors all aspects of the traffic that crosses the interface, which includes inspecting the source and destination addresses, for further control. ICF needs to track traffic that has originated from the computer running ICF, as well as from computers on the Internet. To do this in an efficient manner, the computer keeps track of all traffic that originates from the computer. This might be traffic that it is sending on behalf of another computer through the ICS service. If this is the case, the ICF service will check with the ICS translation table to see if there is an internal computer that should be receiving the traffic. If so, the ICF service will allow the traffic to pass and reach the final internal computer destination.

In the case where the traffic originated from the Internet, the ICF computer will handle this traffic in a much different manner. In this case, the traffic will be dropped by default, unless the traffic is associated with a service that is listed on the Services tab, as shown in Figure 10.6.

When configuring one of these services, you will need to provide the name or IP address of the computer on the network that is running the selected service. If you don't find a service that you need to translate for Internet users or you need to customize a service, you can do so by clicking the Add button within the Services tab. After you click the Add button, you will be prompted to input critical information for the service, as shown in Figure 10.7.

ICF Logging

When there is traffic that is dropped by the ICF service, no message appears to the user of the system. The reason for this is obvious: If there is an abundance of dropped packets, there could be an overwhelming number of messages hindering

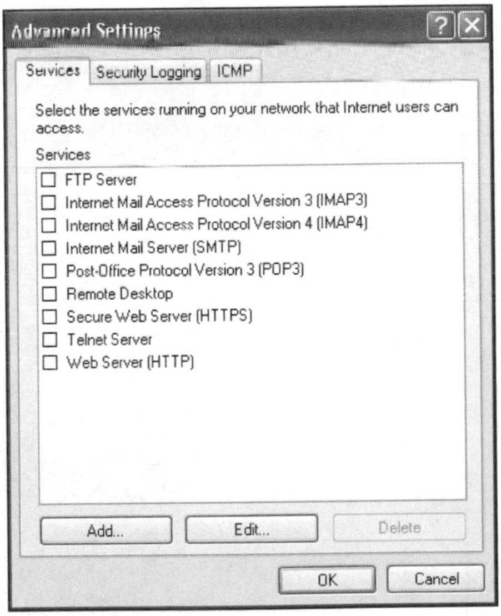

Figure 10.6   Services tab for an ICF connection.

Figure 10.7 Custom service window for use with the ICF service.

the user. In many instances, the information about dropped packets will be important, whether for troubleshooting or for tracking down security issues. For these cases where it is important to get information about the traffic that is being dropped, a log file is available that can store information about the dropped packets, successful connections, or both. Figure 10.8 illustrates the configurations that are possible for the ICF log configurations.

 Remember that HTTP traffic will be logged as port 80 and FTP traffic will be logged as ports 20 and 21.

Figure 10.8 Log file configuration for the ICF service.

Configuring and Troubleshooting ICS

Windows XP Professional enables you to have one IP address from an ISP and share that connection (through the Windows XP Professional computer) with other computers on the network. This feature is known as Internet Connection Sharing (ICS). ICS translates (or maps) a set of nonroutable IP addresses (by default, from the 192.168.x.y network range) to an external (public) IP address that exists on the Internet. Computers on the LAN can then access external resources on the Internet, such as Web sites and FTP sites, but the LAN computers are somewhat sheltered from outside intrusions because the LAN computers are using nonroutable IP addresses.

Configuring ICS

To set up ICS, perform the following steps:

1. Click Start|Control Panel|Network Connections.

2. Right-click a connection icon for an Internet connection and select Properties.

3. Click the Advanced tab.

4. Click the Allow Other Network Users To Connect Through This Computer's Internet Connection checkbox. After you have marked this checkbox, the other settings for ICS become available.

5. Select the Establish A Dial-Up Connection Whenever A Computer On My Network Attempts To Access The Internet checkbox if you want this Internet connection to automatically dial and establish a connection to the Internet when another computer on the LAN attempts to access Internet resources through this computer.

6. Click the Settings button. On the Services tab, you can mark the checkboxes for each Internet-related service you want to enable for this shared connection. You can also add services that are not currently listed by clicking the Add button.

7. Click OK to close the Internet Connection Sharing Settings dialog box.

After you have set up ICS, you should verify that the computer's IP address is now set to 192.168.0.1 with a subnet mask of 255.255.255.0. Test the local Internet connection to verify that the computer can connect to the Internet successfully. For each Windows XP Professional computer on the LAN that wants to take advantage of the shared Internet connection, perform the following steps:

1. Click Start|Control Panel|Network Connections.

2. Right-click the LAN connection and select Properties.

3. Click Internet Protocol and then click Properties.

4. Configure TCP/IP to obtain an IP address automatically. This is the preferred method to use with ICS (as opposed to obtaining the address manually, covered shortly). When you enable ICS, the Windows XP Professional DHCP Allocator uses the default IP addressing range of 192.168.0.2 through 192.168.0.254, and the DNS Proxy service becomes enabled so that clients on the network can connect to the shared Internet resource.

As an alternative, you can manually set up workstations to work with ICS; however, this is not the recommended method according to Microsoft. To do this, perform these steps:

1. Click Start|Control Panel|Network Connections.

2. Right-click the LAN connection and select Properties.

3. Click Internet Protocol and click Properties.

4. Click Use The Following IP Address and type a unique IP address in the range from 192.168.0.2 through 192.168.0.254.

5. Type "255.255.255.0" for the Subnet Mask.

6. Type "192.168.0.1" for the Default Gateway (the IP address for the Windows XP Professional computer that is hosting the shared Internet connection).

7. Type the Preferred DNS Server according to your ISP's documentation (if your ISP does not provide this information automatically).

8. Type the Alternate DNS Server according to your ISP's documentation (if your ISP does not provide this information automatically).

9. Click OK in the Internet Protocol (TCP/IP) Properties dialog box.

10. Click OK in the LAN connection Properties dialog box.

Troubleshooting ICS

Here are some tips for troubleshooting ICS:

➤ If you encounter problems with computers on the network not being able to connect to Web sites through the shared Internet connection, verify the DNS server IP addresses with your ISP.

➤ To verify that the new IP settings have taken effect, type "ipconfig" at a command prompt; sometimes you may need to restart the computer for all the settings to become active.

➤ Check the subnet mask; it must read 255.255.255.0 or else the computer that is attempting to connect to the ICS computer cannot connect.

➤ Make sure that each IP address that you assign to the other computers on the network falls within the range of 192.168.0.2 through 192.168.0.254, with no duplicate addresses on any computer.

If you have network devices that need to have static IP addresses while using ICS, you will need to modify the Registry. The update will modify the STOP value, which needs to be set to the maximum IP address within the 192.168.0.0/24 network that will be given out to clients. For example, if you set the STOP value to 192.168.0.220, the DHCP service within the ICS service will only give out IP addresses between 192.168.0.1 and 192.168.0.220. You would set your network devices to an IP address above 192.168.0.221.

➤ If computers on the network can connect to the Internet only after you manually initiate the Internet connection from the ICS host computer, check that Establish A Dial-Up Connection Whenever A Computer On My Network Attempts To Access The Internet is checked on the Advanced tab of the Internet connection's Properties dialog box.

Practice Questions

Question 1

Bob is a consultant for an IT outsourcing company. He has a number of clients that have network infrastructures that enable him to access their internal networks via a Virtual Private Network (VPN). One of his new clients, ACME Corp., needs Bob to check the status of its Exchange Server. Bob configures a VPN connection for ACME on his Windows XP Professional workstation to use a Smart Card. Bob tries to check Automatically Use My Windows Logon Name And Password but the option is grayed out. What should Bob do to enable this option?

○ a. Change the Security option setting from Use Smart Card to Require Secured Password.

○ b. Change the Security option setting from Typical to Advanced.

○ c. Change the Security option setting from Require Secured Password to Allow Unsecured Password.

○ d. Disable his Smart Card.

Answer a is correct. The option Automatically Use My Windows Logon Name And Password is only available when the Security option setting Require Secured Password is selected. When using a Smart Card for authorization, the logon name and password entry will be secured and there is no need to have the system require a secured password. Answer b is incorrect because selecting Advanced on the Security option setting will gray out the option, not make it available. Answer c is incorrect because the Allow Unsecured Password option is only available with dial-up clients. Answer d is incorrect because you cannot disable the Smart Card and allow Bob to log on.

Question 2

Your manager informs you that you need to set up dial-up networking for all the clients in your network. She is concerned about ensuring that the clients will use the appropriate authentication protocols as the remote users dial in to the network. You want to calm her fears. Which authentication protocols does Windows XP Professional install, by default, when dial-up networking is installed on the computer? [Check all correct answers]

❑ a. PAP

❑ b. SPAP

❑ c. MS-CHAP

❑ d. MS-CHAPv2

❑ e. CHAP

All the answers are correct. An authentication protocol is a set of standards for exchanging logon name and password information between the two network devices. Microsoft Windows XP supports the most common authentication protocols and includes their own version of CHAP. For a dial-up connection, all of these protocols are selected and are supported for the remote access client.

Question 3

You are the network administrator of an international tar factory. You have 200 Windows 2000 servers and 4,500 Windows XP Professional workstations. Two hundred fifty of the Windows XP Professional workstations are for the remote sales force. This remote sales force will access the corporate LAN via Virtual Private Networking and connect to a Windows 2000 Advanced Server running RRAS. You instruct the remote users on how to configure their workstations to use the corporate network via VPN. A few days later, one of the remote users calls you, explaining that he cannot access the Internet when he is connected to the corporate LAN. How should you resolve the issue?

- ○ a. Clear the checkbox Use Default Gateway On Remote Network on the General tab of the TCP/IP dialog box.

- ○ b. Ensure that the checkbox Use Default Gateway On Remote Network on the General tab of the TCP/IP dialog box is checked.

- ○ c. Ensure that the checkbox Allow Other Network Users To Connect Through This Computer's Internet Connection on the Internet Connection Sharing section on the Advanced Dial-Up properties sheet is checked.

- ○ d. Clear the checkbox Require Data Encryption (Disconnect If None) on the Security tab of the VPN Properties dialog box.

Answer a is correct. The checkbox applies when you are connected to a local network and a dial-up network simultaneously. When checked, data that cannot be sent on the local network is forwarded to the dial-up network. Answer b is incorrect because the browser is using the remote server as its gateway (which is incorrect) and will not be able to connect to the Internet. Answer c is incorrect because the issue is about connecting to remote computers, not computers connecting to the user's computer. You would check the box if you wanted others to access the Internet through your computer. Answer d is incorrect because it wouldn't affect whether the user could access the Internet.

Question 4

You have several clients that have installed Windows XP Professional on their corporate workstations. One of your clients calls, requesting that you connect to his machine using Remote Desktop. You have a direct Internet connection and Internet Connection Firewall (ICF) enabled. You attempt to connect to your client's network via VPN. You have problems connecting to the client's machine. What is the first thing you should do?

- O a. Disable Internet Connection Firewall on the VPN connection.
- O b. Ensure that Internet Connection Firewall on the VPN connection is enabled.
- O c. Check the Dial Another Connection First box on the General tab of the VPN Properties dialog box.
- O d. Disable your direct Internet connection and dial in to your client's network.

Answer a is correct. You should not enable ICF on VPN connections because it will interfere with the operation of file sharing and other VPN functions. Answer b is incorrect because, by default, the option is already enabled. Answer c is incorrect because you would have the same problems with ICF. Although it seems that answer d would work, nothing in the scenario suggests that it is possible to dial in to the network.

Question 5

You have 250 Windows XP Professional computers in various OUs in your domain. You have 100 remote Windows XP Professional computers that use VPN connections to connect to the corporate LAN. You want the connections to be encrypted, so you use L2TP with IPSec on the VPN connection. What type of authentication is being used by default during the negotiation of security settings?

- O a. Preshared key authentication
- O b. Certificate-based authentication
- O c. Pass-through authentication
- O d. Internet Authentication Service

Answer b is correct. When you make an L2TP with IPSec connection, an IPSec policy is automatically created to specify that the Internet Key Exchange (IKE) will use certificate-based authentication during the negotiation of security settings for L2TP. This means that both the L2TP client and L2TP server must have a computer certificate (also known as a machine certificate) installed before a successful L2TP-over-IPSec connection can be established. Answer a is incorrect because Microsoft does not recommend frequent use of preshared key authentication, because the authentication key is stored, unprotected, in the IPSec policy. Preshared key methodology is provided *only* for interoperability purposes and to adhere to the IPSec standards set forth by the Internet Engineering Task Force (IETF). Answer c is incorrect because pass-through authentication is for access to resources, not the negotiation of security settings. Answer d is incorrect because IAS performs centralized authentication, authorization, auditing, and accounting of connections for dial-up and VPN remote access and demand-dial connections; it does not negotiate security settings.

Question 6

John is the network administrator for SofaKing, Inc., which has 15 print devices distributed throughout the enterprise. SofaKing uses Internet Connection Sharing in its company to provide Internet access to its users. The users' computers receive an address from the server that is sharing the Internet connection. The print devices must have static TCP/IP addresses. You want to ensure that the Dynamic Host Control Protocol (DHCP) service does not assign a conflicting IP address. How should you accomplish this?

- ○ a. Edit the Registry and change the STOP value to 192.168.0.200.
- ○ b. Edit the Registry value, STOP, to 192.168.0.1.
- ○ c. Exclude the print devices' IP address from the DHCP scope.
- ○ d. Exclude the servers' IP address from the DHCP scope.

Answer a is correct. To ensure that the Dynamic Host Control Protocol (DHCP) service does not assign a conflicting IP address, you must edit the Registry and change the STOP value to 192.168.0.200. You would then assign to the printers static IP addresses from the range above 192.168.0.200, including 192.168.0.201 through 254. Answer b is incorrect because the value expressed in the answer would not allow enough addresses for the clients on the network. Answer c is incorrect because the DHCP scope is hard-coded and cannot be modified. Answer d is incorrect because the server IP addresses would not be in the DHCP scope.

Question 7

You are the administrator for a national bank and your current protocol requires that you use Smart Cards for both local and remote user logons. You want the remote users to be able to use the Internet while connected to the corporate LAN. You do the following:

- Enable a Smart Card logon process for the domain.

- Enable the Extensible Authentication Protocol (EAP) and configure the Smart Card or other certificate (TLS) EAP type on the remote access router computer.

- Enable Smart Card authentication on the VPN connection on the remote access client computer.

What else must you do to ensure the successful connection of your VPN clients? [Check all correct answers]

- ❑ a. Install a computer certificate on the remote access router.

- ❑ b. Configure remote access on the remote access router.

- ❑ c. Ensure that the checkbox Use Default Gateway On Remote Network on the General tab of the TCP/IP Properties sheet is checked.

- ❑ d. Ensure that Internet Connection Firewall on the VPN connection is enabled.

Answers a and b are correct. You must install a computer certificate on the remote access router because you are using Smart Cards. You must also configure remote access on the remote access router that remote clients can connect to. Answer c is incorrect because it would cause the remote clients to not be able to connect to the Internet. Answer d is incorrect because it would cause the remote clients to have connectivity problems if ICF is installed.

Question 8

You want to host a family Web site from your home on your Windows XP Professional workstation. You want to enable your family to access the Web site and add content via FTP. You create the site, register its name, and enable Internet Connection Firewall. Later, you receive reports that your family can access the Web page without problem, but no one can upload their files. What can you do to resolve the issue?

○ a. Ensure that the FTP box on the Services tab of the Advanced Settings page of the ICF VPN Properties dialog box is checked.

○ b. Ensure that the FTP box on the Services tab of the Advanced Settings page of the ICF VPN Properties dialog box is cleared.

○ c. Ensure that the HTTP box on the Services tab of the Advanced Settings page of the ICF VPN Properties dialog box is checked.

○ d. Ensure that the HTTP box on the Services tab of the Advanced Settings page of the ICF VPN Properties dialog box is cleared.

Answer a is correct. Any service that you want to provide for remote clients must be enabled on the Services tab of the Advanced Settings page on the ICF VPN Properties dialog box. Answer b is incorrect because the FTP service option must be selected, not cleared. Answer c is incorrect because the scenario clearly indicates that users are able to connect to the Web site, so the option had to have been checked. Answer d is incorrect because that would cause the users to not be able to connect to the Web site, which is *not* what you want.

Need to Know More?

 Microsoft Corporation. *Microsoft Windows XP Professional Resource Kit Documentation.* Redmond, WA: Microsoft Press, 2001. ISBN 0-73561-485-7. This all-in-one reference is a compilation of technical documentation and valuable insider information that computer-support professionals and administrators can reference to install, customize, and support Windows XP.

 Microsoft Corporation. *Microsoft Windows 2000 Professional Resource Kit.* Redmond, WA: Microsoft Press, 2000. ISBN: 1-57610-808-2. This book reviews the core aspects of TCP/IP and the related protocol tools.

Search the Microsoft TechNet CD (or its online version through **www.microsoft.com**) and the *Windows 2000 Professional Resource Kit* CD using the keywords "RAS", "L2TP", "PPTP", "VPN", "ICF", and "ICS".

Sample Test

Question 1

You have a multiprooooor Windows XP Professional workstation. You are running a SQL Server database application on your server and a customized SQL client application on your workstation. You also run a custom Internet client application on your machine. You notice that performance sometimes is sluggish. You open Task Manger and see that one processor is being used much more than the other. What should you do to increase performance?

○ a. Set the processor affinity for the applications in Task Manager.

○ b. Add more RAM.

○ c. Increase the size of your pagefile.

○ d. Add another processor.

Question 2

You have a file that is encrypted. You want to use EFS file sharing to add one of your team members, Bob, to the file. How should you accomplish this?

○ a. You cannot. EFS does not support file sharing between multiple users on a single file.

○ b. You must place the users in a group first, and then you will have the opportunity to add Bob.

○ c. You first must encrypt the folder where the file is, and then you will be able to add Bob.

○ d. File sharing is enabled through a new button in the UI.

Question 3

Anne recently installed Windows XP onto a relatively small drive C, and is concerned about unnecessary use of storage space on drive C. Anne knows that the default document folder, My Documents, is on drive C, and she uses her computer extensively to create and edit digital photos, vector-based graphic art, and desktop publishing (DTP) files. Knowing that these types of documents can quickly consume a lot of disk storage space, she moves the data files to a different drive volume that has lots of available disk space. In addition, she creates a volume mount point on drive C under the My Documents folder called Art that references the new folder where she has moved all of the files. What should Anne do in order for this to be successful?

○ a. Anne should ensure that the host drive is formatted with NTFS.

○ b. Anne should ensure that the mounted drive is formatted with NTFS.

○ c. Anne should ensure that the mounted drive is on a dynamic disk.

○ d. All of the above.

○ e. None of the above.

Question 4

Bob is a member of the Sales group, a member of the Engineering group, and a member of the Marketing group. A server in the domain, SRV1, has a shared folder named STUFF with Allow Read NTFS permissions for the Sales group. Also on SRV1 is a shared folder named TECH with Allow Modify NTFS permissions for the Marketing group. The Engineering group needs access to both of these folders. Bob tries to create a file in the TECH folder but is denied access. What should you do to remedy the situation without giving Bob excessive permissions?

○ a. Make Bob a member of the Engineering group.

○ b. Make Bob a member of the Administrators group.

○ c. Remove Bob from the Marketing group.

○ d. Change the Deny Write permission for the Engineering group to Allow Modify on the TECH folder.

Question 5

You have 250 Windows XP Professional computers in various OUs in your domain. You have 100 remote Windows XP Professional computers that use VPN connections to connect to the corporate LAN. You are concerned about the security of the files in certain folders, so you set up a hidden share called SECRET$. In the folder is a file named Hrdays.txt. You want to monitor this file to prevent unauthorized changes with the least amount of administrative effort. What should you do?

- ○ a. Enable auditing and select Account Management.

- ○ b. Enable auditing and select Directory Service Access.

- ○ c. Enable auditing and select Object Access.

- ○ d. Use Network Monitor.

Question 6

John is the network administrator for ACME High, Inc., an international rope company. It has 1,500 print devices distributed throughout the enterprise. ACME High uses Internet Connection Sharing (ICS) in its company to provide Internet access to its users. John is having problems doing this with his Windows XP Professional workstation computers and enlists the help of Microsoft. The Microsoft technical support engineer tells John to enable the built-in support account. John does so and tries to use Remote Desktop. The Microsoft technical support engineer is still unable to connect to John's computer. What should John do next? [Check all correct answers]

- ❑ a. Edit the local policy setting in User Rights to enable Deny Access From Network.

- ❑ b. Edit the local policy setting in User Rights to enable Deny Log On Locally.

- ❑ c. Edit the local policy setting in User Rights to disable Deny Access From Network.

- ❑ d. Edit the local policy setting in User Rights to disable Deny Log On Locally.

Question 7

You are the administrator for a small office network of 15 workstations that participate in a workgroup. All the users are using Windows XP Professional computers. You share a printer and a volume on a Windows XP Professional computer for office documents. Intermittently, people are not able to print. How should you resolve the issue?

○ a. Install the printer on a Windows 2000 Server.

○ b. Install a printer pool.

○ c. Change the network protocol to NetBEUI.

○ d. Install Active Directory.

Question 8

You are the administrator of a medium-sized network. On a Windows XP Professional workstation that one of your users is assigned to, you need to modify the Boot.ini file and restart the computer starting only the essential services needed to boot. How would you accomplish this with the least amount of administrative effort?

○ a. Use SYSEDIT.

○ b. Use MSCONFIG.

○ c. Modify Boot.ini manually.

○ d. Use DXDIAG.

Question 9

You work for an international carpet company and are responsible for the network in the Latin American region. You need to create documents using both English and Spanish. How would you accomplish this with the least amount of administrative effort?

○ a. Install the Microsoft Select version of Windows XP Professional on all the client computers.

○ b. Install the Spanish version of Windows Office XP on all the client computers.

○ c. Click the Language icon in the system tray notification area and select Spanish.

○ d. Purchase Spanish-language keyboards for the client computers in the Latin American region.

Question 10

You are the administrator for a company that hires many employees who have accessibility issues. Many of the employees have problems holding down two keys at once. Which accessibility option should you enable?

○ a. High Contrast

○ b. FilterKeys

○ c. MouseKeys

○ d. StickyKeys

Question 11

You are the administrator of a medium-sized network. You use offline files on your laptop to help optimize your efficiency. You attempt to modify a document, but the document does not appear in your Offline Files folder. How should you resolve the issue with the least amount of administrative effort? [Check all correct answers]

❑ a. Select Manual Caching Of Documents.

❑ b. Select Automatic Caching Of Documents.

❑ c. Select Automatic Caching Of Programs And Documents.

❑ d. Copy all the files to your laptop and copy them back to the server.

❑ e. Open the file the next time you are connected to the server.

Question 12

You are the manager of a help desk team at a soft drink company. Your users use Windows 98 computers and participate in a Windows NT 4 Server domain. The company has decided to purchase new computers and adopt Windows XP Professional for the desktop users. Most of your users will require all of their settings from their old computers to be migrated to their new computers. What should you do to accomplish this task with the least amount of administrative effort?

○ a. Use the File And Settings Transfer Wizard.

○ b. Use the Active Directory Migration Tool.

○ c. Use the Windows Backup and Restore Wizard.

○ d. Use the Automated System Restore (ASR) utility with the Windows Backup program.

○ e. Copy all the files from the old computer to the server, and then copy them back to the new computer.

Question 13

You are installing a new device on your computer. You make a backup of the System State. After installing the device and rebooting, everything works as it should. Six months later, you notice that the manufacturer has updated the driver for the device. You download the new driver and select Install From This Location. After you reboot and log on, the device no longer works. What should you do to get the device to work again with the least amount of administrative effort?

○ a. Boot into Safe Mode, remove the driver, boot normally, and reinstall the previous driver.

○ b. Use the Driver Rollback feature.

○ c. Use the Last Known Good Configuration feature.

○ d. Use System Restore.

Question 14

You install security patches on your Windows XP Professional computer to prevent malicious users from attacking your system. After installing the patches and rebooting, you receive a series of checksum error messages. What tool should you use to help resolve this issue?

○ a. Hfnetchk.exe

○ b. Sigverif.exe

○ c. Eventtriggers.exe

○ d. Boot into Safe Mode

Question 15

You've just installed Windows XP Professional by accepting all the default settings. You want to be able to send and receive faxes from the fax modem installed on your Windows XP Professional computer. What do you need to do to set up this feature?

○ a. Double-click the Fax icon in the Printers And Faxes window and use the Fax Console to configure the Fax service.

○ b. Install a third-party fax program such as WinFax Pro.

○ c. First, open the Services Console, right-click the Fax service, and select Start. Next, double-click the Fax icon in the Printers And Faxes window and use the Fax Console to configure the Fax service.

○ d. Click Start|Control Panel|Add Or Remove Programs. Click Add/Remove Windows Components, select the Fax Services entry, click Next, and follow the on-screen instructions to complete the installation. Use the Fax Console to configure the Fax service.

Question 16

You are currently in an area where the power is not reliable. There are long periods of time when there is no electricity. You need your laptop computer to power down in a fashion that protects it from a serious power failure. You need to ensure that if you do power down, your computer is returned to its previous state as quickly as possible without losing any information. Which power option should you choose?

○ a. Standby

○ b. Hibernate

○ c. Shut Down

○ d. Restart

Question 17

You are the administrator for a law firm that has 30 users that use laptops with Windows XP Professional installed. One of the partners, Bob, uses a docking station to access network resources while at work. He calls you and reports that every time he boots up from home, he gets error messages concerning his network interface card (NIC). He does not receive those errors when he boots his computer at work. What should you do to resolve Bob's issue?

○ a. Use Hardware Profiles and create one profile that includes the drivers for the NIC and one profile that disables the drivers for the NIC.

○ b. Use Hardware Profiles and disable the NIC for Profile 1.

○ c. Have Bob boot into Safe Mode while at home.

○ d. Have Bob boot normally while at work, and boot into Safe Mode with Networking while at home.

Question 18

You've just performed a default installation of Internet Information Services (IIS) 5.1 on your Windows XP computer. You go to set up an FTP site for some users at your company by clicking Start|All Programs|Administrative Tools|Internet Information Services. In the Internet Information Services Console, you see the Default Web Site and the Default SMTP Virtual Server containers; however, no container is present for the Default FTP Site. What do you need to do to enable the FTP Server feature for Windows XP Professional?

○ a. Install Windows 2000 Server, because the FTP Server feature is not available under Windows XP Professional.

○ b. Click Start|Run, type in "Services.msc", click OK, and right-click the FTP Server service to start it and to set it to Automatic startup.

○ c. Click Start|Control Panel|Add Or Remove Programs. Click Add/Remove Windows Components, select the Internet Information Services (IIS) entry, and click Details. Mark the checkbox for File Transfer Protocol (FTP) Service, click OK, click Next, and follow the on-screen instructions to complete the installation.

○ d. Purchase and install the Plus! Pack for Windows XP or download and install the Windows XP Professional Resource Kit tools.

Question 19

You have a desktop with Windows XP Professional installed on it that contains three hard disks, and you want to ensure that you will be able to continue working if any one of the drives ceases to function properly. What should you do to accomplish this? [Check all correct answers]

❑ a. Convert from basic to dynamic disks.

❑ b. Implement disk spanning.

❑ c. Implement disk striping with parity.

❑ d. Implement disk mirroring.

❑ e. Format the disk and install Windows 2000 Server.

Question 20

You upgrade a Windows 98 computer with a single drive and single partition to Windows XP Professional, and you want to use the Encrypting File System (EFS). When you attempt to encrypt a folder, the option is not available. What should you do to accomplish this with the least amount of administrative effort?

○ a. Format the drive with the NTFS file system.

○ b. Convert the drive to the NTFS file system.

○ c. Install Windows 2000 Server.

○ d. Run the **CIPHER** command from the command prompt.

Question 21

You are the administrator for a banking company. Your network environment is currently supported by a Windows Active Directory domain with 300 Windows XP Professional workstations. Currently, the users save all of their documents and files in their personal folders on a file server named FSRVR1. You notice that drive space is becoming an issue on FSRVR1, and you decide to implement disk quotas. You give a certain user, User5, a quota of 20MB. Later, you look at his personal folder and see he is currently occupying 55MB of disk space. You check to see that disk quotas have been set up properly and enabled. You also verify that there is a quota entry for User5 and that the quota setting denies user access if the quota is exceeded. You verify that all the information is correct. What should you check next?

○ a. Check to see if User5 is a member of the Domain Administrators group.

○ b. Check to see if User5 is a member of the Server Operators group.

○ c. Check to see if the drive where the user's folders are located is formatted with NTFS.

○ d. Check to see if User5 is a member of the domain.

Question 22

You want to back up *only* your system files and create a floppy disk to recover your system in case of a failure, but when you start the Backup Or Restore Wizard, you do not have this option. What should you do to accomplish this with the least amount of administrative effort?

○ a. In the wizard, select All Information On This Computer.

○ b. In the wizard, select Let Me Choose.

○ c. Select Advanced Mode and select Automatic System Recovery.

○ d. In the wizard, select Everyone's Documents And Settings.

Question 23

You are the manager of application development for a custom software company. The developers' program builds (versions) are tested daily. The files of the old versions are backed up and stored to tape. One build caused a stop error screen. You need to restore the old build using the old files. Using the Windows Backup Or Restore Wizard, which restore option should you choose?

○ a. Do Not Replace The File On My Computer

○ b. Replace The File On Disk Only If The File On Disk Is Older

○ c. Always Replace The File On My Computer

○ d. None of the above

Question 24

You install an application on your Windows XP Professional that installs a new service. After installing the application and rebooting, you log on normally and begin working. Suddenly, your system becomes unstable and you receive a stop error. You investigate the nature of the error and discover that it is caused by a driver and a service that the application uses. You need to remove the driver and the service that is causing the stop error. What should you do to successfully remove the driver and service so that you can return the computer to its previous state with the least amount of administrative effort?

O a. Use the System Restore feature.

O b. Boot into the Recovery Console and remove the driver and the service.

O c. Boot into Safe Mode and remove the driver and the service.

O d. Boot into the Last Known Good Configuration.

Question 25

You are running two 16-bit applications, App16A.exe and App16B.exe. Your Windows XP Professional computer is also running two 32-bit applications, App32A.exe and App32B.exe. Each 16-bit application runs in its own memory space. You notice severe performance degradation on the system and you want to determine which application is causing the problem. Which tool is best suited to measure and monitor the operational efficiency of your system?

O a. Task Manager

O b. The Performance Logs And Alerts snap-in from the Performance Console

O c. The System Monitor snap-in from the Performance Console

O d. The Windows XP Event Log with auditing enabled for Process Tracking

Question 26

You are the network administrator for a state bank. Security is of the highest priority, so you want to ensure that unauthorized access is kept to a minimum. You implement System and Group Policy to ensure a standard environment for your users, who work with various client operating systems. Your remote users use Windows XP Professional on their laptops. These users do not always log on to the Windows 2000 domain you have set up. These remote users' computers contain highly confidential information, and you want to prevent them from copying to floppy. How should you accomplish this task?

- O a. Make a copy of the default hardware profile on all the laptops, and then change the hardware profile on all the laptops to disable the floppy drive. Then, delete the default hardware profile.

- O b. Create a group called Remote Users and then put it in an OU called Remote. Create a Group Policy that disables the floppy drives for users in the Remote OU.

- O c. Create a group called Remote Users and then create a System Policy that disables the floppy drive for everyone in the group.

- O d. Encrypt the remote users' hard drives.

Question 27

You are the network administrator for ACME Metals, Inc. and have 20 Windows 2000 Servers, 300 Windows 2000 Professional workstations, 50 Windows XP Professional workstations, and 150 Windows 98 computers. You have a single Windows 2000 Active Directory domain and implement roaming profiles. You have a drive on a server called FSRVR1 and designate it as X and create a folder for your users called USERS. You share the folder as USERS. You want to use GPOs to manage the roaming profiles. You create a policy and specify the target location as X:\folders. You receive an error message. What should you do?

- O a. Specify the target location as \\FSRVR1\users.

- O b. Share the USERS folder with the name of PROFILE.

- O c. Move the USERS folder to the SYSVOL drive and share it as %systemroot%\USERS.

- O d. Do nothing. Select OK and proceed.

Question 28

You are the system administrator and enterprise administrator for an engineering company. Your network is comprised of four Windows 2000 Active Directory domains. One of your assistants, Bob, is a domain administrator. Bob tries to log on to a remote Windows XP Professional computer, which is a member of the domain, using Remote Desktop but is unsuccessful. What should you do to ensure that Bob can log on using Remote Desktop without giving Bob unnecessary rights?

○ a. Remove and add Bob to the Domain Admins group.

○ b. Explicitly grant Bob's user account the ability to connect remotely.

○ c. Make Bob a member of the Enterprise Administrators group.

○ d. Give Bob the right to log on locally to the server.

Question 29

You are a sales representative for a garage door company. You use Windows 95 on your laptop, and use a dial-up connection to access your network via Remote Desktop to your Windows XP desktop computer at your office. You infrequently get disconnected from your RDP session with your Windows XP computer. You sometimes are not able to re-establish a connection. What should you do?

○ a. Disable APM on the laptop.

○ b. Upgrade your operating system on the laptop to Windows XP.

○ c. Disable PPP.

○ d. Change the network interface card.

Question 30

You have been recently hired as the lead help desk associate. The enterprise network has a Windows 2000 Active Directory domain, which has all new Windows XP Professional clients. You want to reduce the overall support costs, so you will use Remote Assistance to resolve many of the problem tickets that you will face in your company. What Remote Assistance options will your users have to use when they need to request assistance? [Check all correct answers]

- ❑ a. Email
- ❑ b. MSN Messenger
- ❑ c. Sending a file
- ❑ d. Internet Explorer

Question 31

As the lead help desk associate, you receive many trouble tickets in a day. As you are going through the tickets and open an invitation for help, you receive a message that the invitation has expired. The request came from an officer of the company and you need to help this person. How should you resolve this as quickly as possible?

- ○ a. Change the expiration time and connect to the remote computer.
- ○ b. Send a message to the officer to resend the invitation.
- ○ c. Connect to the remote computer via Remote Desktop, bypassing the security.
- ○ d. Change your system time and open the invitation again.

Question 32

You are the network administrator for a corporate network whose environment does not have an Internet connection. Your company's growth is demanding that you develop a way to assist them with user issues in an efficient manner. You would like to use Remote Assistance in conjunction with Windows Messenger to accomplish this task. What other service must be in place before your solution will function properly?

○ a. Exchange

○ b. DNS

◉ c. Microsoft .NET Passport

○ d. Remote Desktop

Question 33

You are the network administrator for a corporate network of three divisions, Marketing, Sales, and Engineering. You have a Windows 2000 domain with three child domains named after the divisions. Each division has a different configuration for its computers, and you create a template from which to create answer files, as well as multiple answer files for each division. You need to deploy 300 Windows XP Professional computers using Remote Installation Services (RIS), while ensuring that each answer file cannot be altered. What should you do to accomplish the task with the least amount of administrative effort?

○ a. Set NTFS permissions on the template to Everyone READ.

○ b. Set NTFS permissions on each SIF answer file to Everyone READ.

○ c. Set NTFS permissions on the \RemoteInstall directory to Everyone READ.

○ d. Set NTFS permissions on the %systemroot% directory to Everyone READ.

Question 34

You are the system administrator of a network that has a root Windows 2000 Active Directory domain with two child domains. You have several OUs with each domain. To help with the administration of the domains, you want to give Bob, one of your assistants, the ability to add computers, users, and groups to OUs. Bob later reports that he is unable to add computers to the OUs. What should you do to resolve this issue with the least amount of administrative effort and without giving Bob unnecessary rights?

- O a. Give Bob the Create All Child Objects permission in the Delegation of Control Wizard.
- O b. Make Bob a member of the Enterprise Administrators group.
- O c. Give Bob the Full Control permission in the Delegation of Control Wizard.
- O d. Make Bob a member of the Domain Administrators group.

Question 35

You are the IT manager for an automobile manufacturer that is opening a new branch in Phoenix. You want to use RIPrep and create an answer file. After running RIPrep, you want to create the answer file, as well as put the answer file in the correct location to ensure a successful unattended installation. What should you do?

- O a. Place the file in the Sysvol directory.
- O b. Place the answer file in the \RemoteInstall directory.
- O c. Place the answer file in the %systemroot%\system32 directory.
- O d. Do nothing.

Question 36

Your company has opened a new branch in New York. You have a need of purchasing 300 more computers. You use three different vendors, purchasing 100 computers from each. You image one system, run RIPrep, and then attempt to apply this image to the rest of the systems. When you do this, 200 machines get a stop error. What should you do to accomplish the task of imaging all 300 machines with the least amount of administrative effort?

○ a. Copy the Hal.dll file from the source machine and place it in the \i386 directory.

○ b. Run RIPrep on one machine per vendor and use the corresponding image on the target computers.

○ c. Run an unattended installation with a UDF file for all 300 computers.

○ d. Run an unattended installation with a UDF file for each vendor.

Question 37

You have 200 client computers that need Windows XP Professional and 20 applications. After installation of Windows XP Professional and the applications, you run RIPrep on the Windows XP Professional computer that contains two partitions, C and D. The applications reside on the D partition. When you attempt to run RIPrep and restore the image to the target computer, none of the applications are installed and you receive several error messages. How should you resolve this issue in the least amount of time?

○ a. On the source machine, reinstall the applications on the C partition, and then rerun RIPrep.

○ b. Run RIPrep on each partition individually.

○ c. On the target machines, create a D partition and install the applications.

○ d. Run an unattended installation with a UDF file.

Question 38

You work at an OEM called SBU Industries. For all computers that you sell, you use a SYSPREP image that has Windows XP Professional. This image is used on all computers and then shipped out. Customers are complaining about strange entries in the system log. What should you do to resolve the issue?

- ○ a. Run **Sysprep –reseal**.
- ○ b. Run **Sysprep –factory**.
- ○ c. Run **Sysprep –pnp**.
- ○ d. Run **Sysprep –quiet**.

Question 39

You are the lead IT associate in your company. You and your team have finally upgraded your network to a purely Windows 2000 environment. All file, DNS, DHCP, and WINS servers are running Windows 2000 Server. All applications and services have been upgraded to use only DNS name resolution. You have decommissioned all WINS servers. What should you do next to optimize the network?

- ○ a. Decommission your DNS servers.
- ○ b. Disable NetBIOS over TCP on your servers.
- ○ c. Decommission your DHCP servers.
- ○ d. Disable TCP/IP on your servers.

Question 40

You are the IT manager of an international plastics company. You have a team of 20 personnel, five of which are spread out over Latin America. Your assistant in Mexico, Tom, has a file server called Srv1 whose IP address is 206.109.180.10. Srv1 is relocated to Houston and a new IP address is assigned, which is 206.109.50.18. You manually change this information in DNS. Later, Tom reports that he cannot connect to Srv1. You check DNS and everything appears to be in order. What should you do next?

- ○ a. Run **IPCONFIG /renew** and then **IPCONFIG /release**.
- ○ b. Restart the DNS server.
- ○ c. Run **IPCONFIG /flushdns**.
- ○ d. Restart the DHCP server.

Question 41

You recently bought a retail copy of Windows XP Professional for your own personal home use. You enjoy using it and are learning new features. As you surf the Web, you notice that you have to authenticate and reauthenticate at several different sites. What can you do so that you might not have to authenticate and reauthenticate at different Web sites?

○ a. Enable cookies in your browser.

○ b. Sign up for .NET Passport services.

○ c. Disable cookies in your browser.

○ d. Set the security level for the Internet zone to Low.

Question 42

You want to host a family Web site from your home on your Windows XP Professional workstation, enabling your family to access the Web site and add content via FTP. You create the site, register its name, and enable Internet Connection Firewall (ICF). Later, you receive reports that your family can access the Web page without problem, but no one can upload their files. What can you do to resolve the issue? [Check all correct answers]

❑ a. Ensure that the FTP box on the Services tab of the Advanced Settings page of the ICF properties is checked and 20 is the number in the External Port box.

❑ b. Ensure that the FTP box on the Services tab of the Advanced Settings page of the ICF properties is cleared and 21 is the number in the Internal Port box.

❑ c. Ensure that the FTP box on the Services tab of the Advanced Settings page of the ICF properties is checked and 21 is the number in the Internal Port box.

❑ d. Ensure that the FTP box on the Services tab of the Advanced Settings page of the ICF properties is cleared and 20 is the number in the External Port box.

Question 43

You have a Windows XP Professional computer, XPM1, that is a member of the CORP.com domain. You want to use Internet Connection Sharing (ICS) on the computer to provide Internet access for your corporate clients. You also want to provide security, and thus decide to enable Internet Connection Firewall (ICF) to protect your network from hackers. You enable ICS, but cannot enable ICF. What should you do?

O a. Ensure that you are using a VPN connection for the ICS configuration.

O b. Ensure that the network bridge is established.

O c. Ensure that you are attempting to configure ICF on the proper interface.

O d. Remove XPM1 from the domain.

Question 44

You are the administrator for a national bank, and you will be installing 300 Windows XP Professional computers. During the installation, you want to ensure that you have the most current drivers and files available. Which of the following should you use to accomplish your task?

O a. Dynamic Update

O b. Windows Update

O c. Automatic Update

O d. **Winnt /update**

Question 45

You are migrating a user's settings from her Windows 98 computer to a new Windows XP computer. You want to use the User State Migration Tool to ensure the settings are migrated correctly. Which command should you use first?

O a. **Scanstate**

O b. **Loadstate**

O c. **Update**

O d. **Miguser**

Question 46

You are the administrator for a national bank and you have bought new Windows XP Professional computers for your department. You need to transfer data as well as other settings. You want to create a customized solution to migrate all users settings as quickly as possible with the least amount of administrative effort. What should you use?

- ○ a. ADMT
- ○ b. USMT
- ○ c. File and Settings Transfer Wizard
- ○ d. Lap Link

Question 47

You are the administrator for a national bank and your current protocol requires that you use Smart Cards for both local and remote user logons. You want the remote users to be able to use the Internet while connected to the corporate LAN. What must you do to ensure the successful connection of your clients? [Check all correct answers]

- ❑ a. Install a computer certificate on the remote access router.
- ❑ b. Configure remote access on the remote access router.
- ❑ c. Enable a Smart Card logon process for the domain.
- ❑ d. Enable the Extensible Authentication Protocol (EAP) and configure the Smart Card or other certificate (TLS) EAP type on the remote access router computer.

Question 48

You are the CIO of a startup Internet company. You want to provide VPN connectivity to your clients. You have strict requirements, which requires that both the IP header traffic and the packets are encrypted. You want to use L2TP with IPSec for the encryption method it offers. You have enabled RAS on a server in your Windows 2000 domain. You are concerned with security, so you enable NAT. When a client tries to connect, he receives the following error message: "The remote computer does not support the required data encryption type". What should you do to resolve the issue?

- ○ a. Remove NAT from your server.
- ○ b. Remove IPSec.
- ○ c. Change L2TP to PPTP.
- ○ d. Enable the Extensible Authentication Protocol (EAP).

Question 49

You want to ensure the correct protocols are being used in your VPN configuration. You are using IPSec for packet filtering, and you also require encrypted transmissions. What authentication protocol should you use?

- ○ a. PPTP
- ○ b. L2TP
- ○ c. EFS
- ○ d. EAP

Question 50

You are a Microsoft Certified Partner and you are concerned with Windows Product Activation. You change hardware frequently in your office. You want to be able to activate your copies of Windows XP Professional without having to call Microsoft frequently to activate the same copy because of the hardware changes. What should you do?

- ○ a. Do nothing. Use the Volume License Key that comes with your copy of the software.
- ○ b. Change only the RAM.
- ○ c. Make an image of the computer you will change, and then just reapply the image after the hardware change.
- ○ d. You must activate every time.

Answer Key

1.a	18. c	35. d
2.d	19. a, c, e	36. b
3.a	20. b	37. a
4.d	21. a	38. a
5.c	22. c	39. b
6.c, d	23. b	40. c
7.a	24. a	41. b
8.b	25. b	42. a, c
9.c	26. a	43. c
10. d	27. a	44. a
11. b, e	28. b	45. a
12. a	29. a	46. b
13. b	30. a, b, c	47. a, b, c, d
14. b	31. b	48. a
15. d	32. a	49. b
16. b	33. c	50. a
17. a	34. a	

Question 1

Answer a is correct. By setting the processor affinity for applications, you can increase performance by distributing processing load. Answer b is wrong because database applications are processor intensive more than they are memory intensive. Answer c is incorrect because increasing the size of your pagefile will not increase performance when it is indicated that lack of performance is due to processing power. Answer d is incorrect because processors must be put in pairs and Windows XP Professional only supports up to two processors.

Question 2

Answer d is correct. In Windows XP, EFS does support file sharing between multiple users on a single file. After selecting the Advanced Properties of an encrypted file, Bob may be added by selecting the Details button. Answer a is incorrect because EFS does support file sharing between multiple users on a single file. Answer b is incorrect because support for the use of groups on encrypted files is not provided in Windows XP. Answer c is incorrect because support for multiple users on folders is not provided in Windows XP.

Question 3

Answer a is correct. A volume mount point must be placed in any empty folder of the host NTFS volume. The volume must be formatted with NTFS. Answer b is incorrect because although the host volume must be formatted with NTFS, the volume to be mounted can be formatted in any Windows XP-accessible file system, including NTFS, FAT16, FAT32, CDFS, or UDF. Answer c is incorrect because a mounted drive can exist on either a dynamic disk or basic disk. Answer d is incorrect because answers b and c are incorrect. Answer e is incorrect because answer a is correct.

Question 4

Answer d is correct. Because Bob is a member of groups that have at least write permission to the folder, it must be that Bob has a Deny permission to the folder. Therefore, the permission should be changed to Modify. Answer a is incorrect because the Engineering group would grant no more rights to Bob's account. Answer b is incorrect because making Bob a member of the Administrators group would be conferring excessive rights to his account. Answer c is incorrect because removing his account would take rights away.

Question 5

Answer c is correct. Enabling auditing and selecting Object Access will log when a user tries to read or otherwise make changes to any object you select to audit. Answer a is incorrect because Account Management will monitor when a user account property changes and not when an object is accessed. Answer b is incorrect because Directory Service Access auditing will not inform you when a folder or file is accessed. Answer d is incorrect because Network Monitor will allow you to see packets on the network, but not allow you to see who is accessing a folder or file with the least amount of administrative effort.

Question 6

Answers c and d are correct. By default, the built-in support account is disabled and locked out of access to the local computer. The account must be enabled and allowed to connect to the computer across the network and given the right to log on locally to the computer.

Question 7

Answer a is correct. Windows XP Professional can accept only a maximum of 10 concurrent connections. In the scenario given, occasionally, too many people are trying to print and are not able to connect to the printer. You need to install a server. Answer b is incorrect because the same issue would be encountered with too many concurrent connections. Answer c is incorrect because NetBEUI is not a protocol offered natively on Windows XP Professional. Answer d is incorrect because Active Directory requires Windows 2000 Server or Windows .NET Server.

Question 8

Answer b is correct. MSCONFIG enables you to change the Boot.ini file and select which services you want to start from one window. Answer a is incorrect because SYSEDIT will not allow you to do either of the tasks. Answer c is incorrect because although modifying Boot.ini manually will accomplish what you need, it does not do it with the least amount of administrative effort. Answer d is incorrect because DXDIAG does not help you accomplish either task.

Question 9

Answer c is correct. Windows XP enables you to add support for languages without the need for installing language versions of the software. In Control Panel, click Regional Settings and add the languages desired. Answers a and b are incorrect because neither accomplishes the task with the least amount of administrative effort. Answer d is incorrect because simply connecting a foreign language keyboard will not add support for foreign languages.

Question 10

Answer d is correct. StickyKeys enables persons who have problems holding down two keys at once to perform this action by simply touching the specified key, and then the combination key that is desired. Answer a is incorrect because High Contrast is for persons who have sight disabilities. Answer b is incorrect because FilterKeys is an option that instructs the keyboard to ignore brief or repeated keystrokes, which helps people who have problems touching one key at a time. Answer c is incorrect because MouseKeys is an option to enable persons who have problems using a mouse or other pointing device to use the keyboard instead.

Question 11

Answers b and e are correct. Automatic Caching makes every file that someone opens from your shared folder available to them offline. However, this setting does not make every file in your shared folder available to them offline, only those files that are opened. Files that are not opened are not available offline. Therefore, you should open the files you desire the next time you are connected to the server. Answer a is incorrect because Manual Caching Of Documents provides offline access only to those files that someone using your shared folder specifically (manually) identifies. This caching option is ideal for a shared network folder containing files that are to be accessed and modified by several people. This is the default option when you set up a shared folder to be used offline. Answer c is incorrect because this option provides offline access to shared folders containing files that are not to be changed. This caching option is ideal for making files (DLL and EXE) available offline that are read, referenced, or run, but that are not changed in the process. Answer d is incorrect because it does not resolve the issue with the least amount of administrative effort.

Question 12

Answer a is correct. The File And Settings Transfer Wizard is useful in a corporate network environment for employees who get a new computer and need to migrate their own files and settings without the support of an IT department or help desk. Answer b is incorrect because the Active Directory Migration Tool (ADMT) is the tool that simplifies the process of migrating users, computers, and groups to new domains. It is not used to migrate files and desktop settings. Answer c is incorrect because although the files may be backed up, the setting will not be. Answer d is incorrect because the ASR utility is only for reinstalling Windows XP with all of its previous settings. Answer e is incorrect because it does not accomplish the task with the least amount of administrative effort.

Question 13

Answer b is correct. When you update a driver, a copy of the previous driver package is automatically saved in a special subdirectory of the system files. If the new driver does not work properly, you can restore the previous driver by accessing the Driver tab for the device in the Device Manager, and clicking Roll Back Driver. Driver Rollback permits only one level of rollback (only one prior driver version can be saved at a time); this feature is available for all device classes, except printers. Answer a is incorrect because it does not accomplish the task with the least amount of administrative effort. Answer c is incorrect because after you have successfully logged on, the Last Known Good Configuration no longer contains the previous configuration data. Using it would do no good. Answer d is incorrect because although you can accomplish the same result, it does not accomplish the task with the least amount of administrative effort—Rollback Driver is faster and easier.

Question 14

Answer b is correct. The Signature Verification Tool (Sigverif.exe) determines whether a file has been assigned a digital signature and whether that file has been modified after being assigned that digital signature. You should check the list of unsigned drivers, and then check if the driver manufacturer has an updated driver that is digitally signed. Answer a is incorrect because although you can use the Hfnetchk.exe tool to assess the patch status for the Windows XP operating system, it will not help resolve the issue of system instability. Answer c is incorrect because the Eventtriggers.exe utility causes an action to occur based on specific events logged by the Event Viewer, but this does not resolve the issue of system instability. Answer d is incorrect because although booting into Safe Mode may help in giving an environment in which to work, it does not help resolve the issue of system instability.

Question 15

Answer d is correct. The Fax service is not installed by default, as is the case with Windows 2000 Professional; you must install it separately. Answer a is incorrect because the Fax service is not installed by default. Answer b is incorrect because you do not need to purchase a third-party solution for faxing under Windows XP Professional. Answer c is incorrect because the Fax service is not installed by default; therefore, the Fax service is not present until you install it separately, or as an optional component during the Windows XP Professional installation routine.

Question 16

Answer b is correct. Although it takes longer to bring your computer out of Hibernate than out of Standby, you should put your computer into Hibernate mode. The Hibernate feature saves everything in memory onto disk, turns off your monitor and hard disk, and then turns off your computer. When you restart your computer, your desktop is restored exactly as you left it. Answer a is incorrect. Although Standby is particularly useful for conserving battery power in portable computers, Standby does not save your desktop state to disk; a power failure while on Standby can cause you to lose unsaved information. Answer c is incorrect because although the information is saved, it will not return you to the last state you were in when you shut down. Answer d is incorrect because a Restart is the same as a shutdown: essentially saving information, but not returning you to the last state you were in when you shut down.

Question 17

Answer a is correct. A hardware profile is a set of instructions that tells Windows which devices to start when you start your computer, or which settings to use for each device. By default, every device that is installed on your computer at the time you install Windows is enabled in the Profile 1 hardware profile. You would disable the NIC, create a profile, and name it something different, thus providing two profiles. Answer b is incorrect because by disabling the NIC for Profile 1, the computer would never be able to access network resources when the computer is using the docking station. Answer c is incorrect because booting into Safe Mode may disable other necessary drivers. Answer d is incorrect because booting into Safe Mode with Networking will cause the system to load the NIC driver, and that will cause the errors again.

Question 18

Answer c is correct. The FTP Server service is not installed by default when you install IIS 5.1. Answer a is incorrect because the FTP Server feature is available for Windows XP Professional. Answer b is incorrect because the FTP Server service is not installed by default when you install IIS 5.1, so the FTP service does not get installed by default, and therefore, it would not be listed as a currently installed service. Answer d is incorrect because the FTP Server service is not available in the Plus! Pack, nor in the Windows XP Resource Kit, because the Resource Kit for Windows XP Professional contains only documentation, not software utilities or add-ons.

Question 19

Answers a, c, and e are correct. Windows XP Professional does not support fault-tolerant volumes. You will need to format the disk, install Windows 2000 Server, convert the disks from basic to dynamic, and then implement disk striping with parity. Answer b is incorrect because disk spanning is not fault tolerant. Answer d is incorrect because disk mirroring is not available in Windows XP Professional, and it doesn't protect in the event that the third disk fails.

Question 20

Answer b is correct. Although Windows XP Professional supports EFS, EFS requires NTFS, and converting the partition to NTFS will accomplish the task. Answer a is incorrect because if you were to format the drive, you would lose all information contained on the drive. Answer c is incorrect because Windows XP Professional is already installed, and it is a more recent version of Windows than Windows 2000. Answer d is incorrect because the drive needs to have the NTFS file system, and running the **CIPHER** command will yield no results.

Question 21

Answer a is correct. Members of the Domain Administrators group, by default, have an unlimited quota. If User5 were a member of the Domain Administrators group, he would have an unlimited quota. Answer b is incorrect because had User5 been a member of the Server Operators group, the quota would have an effect on him. Answer c is incorrect because the ability to set quotas would not have been available under the FAT or FAT32 file system. Answer d is incorrect because making a quota entry for User5 would not have been possible if the user were not already a member of the domain.

Question 22

Answer c is correct. To back up *only* the system files and create a floppy disk to recover your system, you will need to select Advanced Mode from the Backup Or Restore Wizard window, and then select Automatic System Recovery (ASR). Answer a is incorrect because this option will back up *all* files on the computer, not just the system files. Answer b is incorrect because although you can back up just the system files, the option to create a recovery disk is not available. Answer d is incorrect because this option will just back up the Documents and Settings folders of all the users, not the system files. Nor will this option enable you to create a recovery disk.

Question 23

Answer b is correct. When restoring from a backup, the backup program checks for files with the same name. You must then choose what happens when the program encounters a file with the same name. You have three options: Do Not Replace The File On My Computer, Replace The File On Disk Only If The File On Disk Is Older, and Always Replace The File On My Computer. In this case, because the previous build worked, you should replace the file. Answer a is incorrect because you should replace whatever file(s) caused the system to become unstable. Answer c is incorrect because it is just for the current build that you want to replace the file(s). Answer d is incorrect because if you do not choose one of the three options, the restore process cannot proceed.

Question 24

Answer a is correct. System Restore automatically creates restore points every 24 hours, and every time that you install a new application. Answer b is incorrect because even though you can disable devices and services from the Recovery Console, doing so takes much more effort than simply performing a system restore. Answer c is incorrect for the reason that answer b is incorrect, because this also applies to Safe Mode. Answer d is incorrect because the existing settings become the Last Known Good Configuration after you successfully log on to the computer.

Question 25

Answer b is correct. The Performance Logs And Alerts snap-in enables you to track or chart specific system performance metrics over a period of time. Answer a is incorrect because the Task Manager displays only realtime performance data, and you cannot create a history file from Task Manager. Answer c is incorrect because System Monitor either displays system performance counters in realtime, or displays the results of a log file created by the Performance Logs And Alerts snap-in—it does not create a history file on its own. Answer d is incorrect because enabling auditing only enables you to track successes and/or failures of specific events—it does not track performance history using performance counters.

Question 26

Answer a is correct. By disabling the floppy in the hardware profile, you prevent your users from copying information to a floppy, and by deleting the default (or original) profile, the users do not have a choice of hardware profiles to choose from at bootup. Answer b is incorrect because the users do not always log on to the domain, and thus will not get the policy, and will not have access to their floppy drive. Answer c is incorrect because although System Policies are written to the Registry, they are designed for down-level clients such as Windows NT and 9X, not Windows 2000 or XP. There is no certainty that the Registry change will be consistent across platforms. Answer d is incorrect because the user will still have access to their floppy drive.

Question 27

Answer a is correct. The message that you would receive states that unless the target location is local to the user, the user will not receive the roaming profile. You should use the universal naming convention (UNC) format to specify the location. Answer b is incorrect because the name of the share will not ensure that users receive their roaming profile. Answer c is incorrect because the issue of the target folder still keeps users from accessing their roaming profiles. Answer d is incorrect because if you proceed through the message, the users' machines will look for the X:\users share. If it doesn't exist, the user will be given an error message that states their roaming profile cannot be located.

Question 28

Answer b is correct. The ability to connect remotely using Remote Desktop requires explicit permission. You must allow a user to connect remotely using Remote Desktop before they will be able to do so. Answer a is incorrect because putting Bob in the Domain Admins group will not ensure that Bob has permission to use Remote Desktop. Answer c is incorrect because it would give Bob unnecessary rights for the enterprise, and it would not ensure that he could use Remote Desktop. Answer d is incorrect because although Bob would have rights to log on locally, he still lacks permission to use Remote Desktop.

Question 29

Answer a is correct. This problem can occur because Remote Desktop was not designed to communicate with APM services. To work around this behavior, you should disable APM on the laptop. Answer b is incorrect because changing the operating system will not change the behavior of the Remote Desktop services. If the laptop is an older system, the hardware may be the limiting factor because it might only support APM. Answer c is incorrect because disabling PPP might prohibit the laptop from connecting to the network via dial-up. If you can't connect to the remote network, you will not be able to connect to the remote desktop. Answer d is incorrect because the problem is not NIC-related. Changing the NIC will result in having the same connectivity problem.

Question 30

Answers a, b, and c are correct. Remote Assistance enables a user to share control of his or her computer with someone on a network or the Internet. An administrator or friend can view the user's screen, and control the pointer and keyboard to help solve a technical problem. The fastest way to use Remote Assistance is via Windows Messenger. You can also initiate Remote Assistance sessions via email, by launching the email client directly from the Remote Assistance Invitation Wizard. Alternatively, you can fill out a form and save it as a file. The file can be emailed, shared, or hand-delivered to the desktop support personnel. Answer d is incorrect because you cannot send an invitation to someone for Remote Assistance through IE.

Question 31

Answer b is correct. After the invitation has expired, the request is void. The person who made the request must resend the invitation for assistance. Answer a is incorrect because after the invitation has expired, the request is void. You cannot change the expiration of an invitation. Answer c is incorrect because unless you have permission to connect to the remote computer, you will not be able to connect via Remote Desktop. Answer d is incorrect because this could cause other applications or invitations to behave incorrectly.

Question 32

Answer a is correct. With Exchange in place, you can establish the Instant Messaging service to function as your internal account service. This will allow communication internally, without having an Internet connection. Answer b is incorrect because DNS is not needed for Remote Assistance to work. Answer c is incorrect because this is only possible with an Internet connection in place. Answer d is incorrect because Remote Desktop is a feature of Windows XP and not a necessary service for Remote Assistance to function.

Question 33

Answer c is correct. The answer files are kept in the \RemoteInstall directory, and setting it to Everyone READ will ensure that none of it gets changed. Answer a is incorrect because although the template from which you make the answer files is read-only, it has no effect on the answer files that are created from it. You will need to change the permissions of the answer files themselves. Answer b is incorrect because not everyone should have Read access to all answer files. Answer d is incorrect because changing the permissions of the %systemroot% directory to Everyone READ could cause serious damage and problems to your system. The system itself will not be able to write to it, and your system may become unstable.

Question 34

Answer a is correct. Giving Bob the Create All Child Objects permission will give him the necessary rights to complete the task you gave him without giving him unnecessary rights. Answer b is incorrect because making Bob an Enterprise admin would definitely be giving him unnecessary rights. Answer c is incorrect because giving Bob Full Control permission in the Delegation of Control Wizard of an OU gives him too much latitude. All he needs to do is create computer objects and nothing more. Answer d is incorrect because making Bob a Domain administrator is giving him unnecessary rights.

Question 35

Answer d is correct. When the RIPrep Wizard is run, a new directory is created where the image file is uploaded, and the answer file is located there. Because this happens automatically, there is nothing you should do. Answer a is incorrect because moving the answer file will result in a failed installation, and placing it in the Sysvol directory would not help the installation. Answer b is incorrect because moving the answer file from its default location will result in a failed installation, and placing it in the \RemoteInstall directory for RIPrep would not suffice either. Answer c is incorrect because moving the file from its default location will result in a failed installation, and moving it into the system32 folder would not help the installation.

Question 36

Answer b is correct. Although RIPrep supports different hardware between the source computer used to create the RIPrep-based OS image and the destination computer that will install the image, the HAL must still be the same or a stop error will occur. Running RIPrep from each vendor's computer will ensure the proper HAL for the remaining installations. Answer a is incorrect because simply copying the Hal.dll file to the \i386 directory will result in the same problem. Answer c is incorrect because running an answer file with a UDF for all 300 computers would be time consuming and would not require the least amount of effort. Answer d is incorrect because only one UDF is needed for all computers.

Question 37

Answer a is correct. The RIPrep utility supports only a single disk with a single partition (C drive); therefore, the applications must be installed on the C partition. Answer b is incorrect because the RIPrep utility supports only a single disk with a single partition. Answer c is incorrect because this process would be very time consuming. Answer d is incorrect because it does not resolve the issue in the least amount of time.

Question 38

Answer a is correct. The Sysprep tool has new switches, one of them being –**reseal**. The –**reseal** switch clears the Event Viewer logs and prepares the computer for delivery to the customer. Answer b is incorrect because the –**factory** switch restarts the computer in factory mode, which allows the installation of additional drivers and applications after the reboot that follows Sysprep.exe. It will not clear the event log. Answer c is incorrect because the –**pnp** switch forces Plug and Play to refresh the next time that the computer is restarted. It will not clear the event log. Answer d is incorrect because the –**quiet** switch runs Sysprep without displaying the on-screen messages; it will not clear the event log.

Question 39

Answer b is correct. Because you no longer use NetBIOS name resolution in your environment, you should disable the NetBIOS binding for the WINS client (TCP/IP). Answer a is incorrect because Active Directory and the computers in the enterprise depend on DNS to function correctly. Disabling DNS will bring your network down. Answer c is incorrect because the network clients are using DHCP to obtain the IP address to communicate on the network.

Answer d is incorrect because TCP/IP is the protocol required for an Active Directory–based domain.

Question 40

Answer c is correct. Tom cannot connect to Srv1 because the information on his client contains cached information that is no longer valid. After he flushes this information and receives new information from the DNS server, he will be able to connect. Answer a is incorrect because this will release only IP information, not DNS cache information. Answer b is incorrect because the information is correct in DNS and the problem is with the client, not the DNS server. Answer d is incorrect because the issue is a name resolution issue and not an IP addressing issue.

Question 41

Answer b is correct. Microsoft Passport delivers the following two services: Passport Single Sign In and Passport Express Purchase. The Passport Single Sign In service offers an authentication service that allows Passport users to use a single username and password for authentication access to any Web site that employs Passport authentication. Answer a is incorrect because although cookies may help you log in to a site, you will still need to authenticate to the site when you return. Answer c is incorrect because disabling cookies will make it more difficult to authenticate with a site and will not fix the reauthentication issue. Answer d is incorrect because the security setting does not aid you in authenticating with a site, but may allow malicious users to abuse your system.

Question 42

Answers a and c are correct. Any service that you want to provide for remote clients must be enabled on the Services tab of the Advanced Setting page on the ICF VPN properties sheet. Both ports 20 and 21 need to be checked in order for the FTP communication to be successful. Answer b is incorrect because the FTP service option must be checked, not cleared. Answer d is incorrect because the option needs to be checked, not cleared.

Question 43

Answer c is correct. The public interface is the only interface that can be configured with ICF if you are using it in conjunction with ICS. Answer a is incorrect because either a VPN or dial-up connection is sufficient when using ICS. Answer b is incorrect because the network bridge would not solve this problem with regard to ICF not working. Answer c is incorrect because the computer can be in the domain and support both ICS and ICF.

Question 44

Answer a is correct. Dynamic Update ensures that the operating system files are up to date. Before the installation occurs, there needs to be a server configured with the latest updates from Microsoft's Web site. Answer b is incorrect because Windows Update contains compatibility updates, new device drivers, and other updates released for Windows XP Professional as they become available on the Windows Update Web site, not during installation. Answer c is incorrect because Automatic Update is an option for updating your computer without interrupting your Web experience. These downloads are throttled to minimize impact to network responsiveness, and are automatically resumed if the system is disconnected before an update is fully downloaded. After the update has been downloaded to the PC, the user can then choose to install it. This does not happen during installation. Answer d is incorrect because the **Winnt /update** command is used to slip-stream service packs into an installation of Windows XP. It does not ensure that the latest drivers are being installed.

Question 45

Answer a is correct. The User State Migration Tool consists of two executables (Scanstate.exe and Loadstate.exe) and four migration rule information files (Migapp.inf, Migsys.inf, Miguser.inf, and Sysfiles.inf). Scanstate.exe is the command that collects user data and settings. Answer b is incorrect because Loadstate.exe is used to deposit the information on the new Windows XP computer. Answer c is incorrect because it is not a part of the USMT, but rather the command for installing a service pack. Answer d is incorrect because it is one of the INF files used for the migration of the settings, not the command itself.

Question 46

Answer b is correct. The USMT is an excellent tool for customizing the migration of user settings in an efficient manner. With this option, you will be able to script the migration, as well as customize the migration files that determine which files, settings, and configurations are migrated. Answer a is incorrect because the Active Directory Migration Tool (ADMT) is the tool that simplifies the process of migrating users, computers, and groups to new domains. It is not used to migrate files and desktop settings. Answer c is incorrect because the File and Settings Transfer Wizard is useful in a corporate network environment for employees who get a new computer and need to migrate their own files and settings without the support of an IT department or help desk. Answer d is incorrect because it does not accomplish the task with the least amount of administrative effort.

Question 47

All answers are correct. Answer a is correct because you must install a computer certificate on the remote access router, because you are using Smart Cards. Answer b is correct because you must also configure remote access on the remote access router that remote clients can connect to. Answer c is correct because the remote clients need to be able to connect to the domain. Answer d is correct because EAP is the authentication protocol necessary for Smart Card use.

Question 48

Answer a is correct. IPSec does not work with NAT, and therefore, you will receive the error message. You will need to remove NAT. Answer b is incorrect because your requirements are that you have packet filtering; therefore, you must not remove IPSec. Answer c is incorrect because your requirements are that the IP headers be encrypted, and PPTP does not do this. Answer d is incorrect because EAP is the protocol used for Smart Cards.

Question 49

Answer b is correct. L2TP is an IETF draft specification for encapsulating and transmitting non-IP traffic through TCP/IP networks. L2TP uses IPSec for encrypted transmission. Answer a is incorrect because PPTP will not encrypt IP traffic. Answer c is incorrect because EFS (Encrypting File System) is used to encrypt files, not IP traffic. Answer d is incorrect because EAP is the authentication protocol for Smart Cards.

Question 50

Answer a is correct. Microsoft Certified Partners and CTECs receive a special Volume License Key (VLK) that enables them to activate a copy of the software as many times as needed, without having to call Microsoft. Only by using the VLK is this an option. Answer b is incorrect because it is not feasible to change only the RAM. One may have to change the hard drive or system board. Answer c is incorrect because a change in hardware may cause system instability if you make and try to apply an image on the machine. Answer d is incorrect because by using VLK, you will not have to do this.

Glossary

. . . .

A (address) resource record

A resource record used to map a Domain Name System (DNS) domain name to a host Internet Protocol (IP) address on the network.

Accelerated Graphics Port (AGP)

A new interface specification (released in August 1997) developed by Intel. AGP is based on the Peripheral Connection Interface (PCI), but is designed especially for the through put demands of 3D graphics. Rather than using the PCI bus for graphics data, AGP introduces a dedicated point-to-point channel so that the graphics controller can directly access main memory. The AGP channel is 32 bits wide and runs at 66MHz. This translates into a total bandwidth of 266Mbps, as opposed to the PCI bandwidth of 133Mbps. AGP also supports two optional faster modes, with throughputs of 533Mbps and 1.07Gbps. In addition, AGP allows 3D textures to be stored in main memory rather than in video memory. AGP has a few important system requirements: The chipset must support AGP, and the motherboard must be equipped with an AGP bus slot or must have an integrated AGP graphics system.

access control entry (ACE)

An element in an object's discretionary access control list (DACL). Each ACE controls or monitors access to an object by a specified trustee. An ACE is also an entry in an object's system access control list (SACL) that specifies the security events to be audited for a user or group.

account lockout

A Windows XP security feature that locks a user account if a certain number of failed logon attempts occur within a specified amount of time, based on security policy lockout settings. Locked accounts cannot log on.

Active Directory

The directory service included with Windows 2000 Server. It is based on the X.500 standards and those of its predecessor, the Lightweight Directory Access Protocol (LDAP). It stores information about objects on a network and makes this information available to users and network administrators. Active Directory gives network users access to permitted resources anywhere on the network using a single logon process. It provides network administrators with a hierarchical view of the network and a single point of administration for all network objects.

Active Directory Users and Computers snap-in

An administrative tool designed to perform daily Active Directory administration tasks. These tasks include creating, deleting, modifying, moving, and setting permissions on objects stored in the directory. These objects include organizational units (OUs), users, contacts, groups, computers, printers, and shared file objects.

Address Resolution Protocol (ARP)

A Transmission Control Protocol/ Internet Protocol (TCP/IP) protocol that translates an Internet Protocol (IP) address into a physical address, such as a Media Access Control (MAC) address (hardware address). A computer that wants to obtain a physical address sends an ARP broadcast request onto the TCP/IP network. The computer on the network that has the IP address in the request then replies with its physical hardware address.

Advanced Configuration and Power Interface (ACPI)

A power management specification developed by Intel, Microsoft, and Toshiba. ACPI enables Windows XP to control the amount of power given to each device attached to the computer. With ACPI, the operating system can turn off peripheral devices, such as CD-ROM players, when they are not in use. As another example, ACPI enables manufacturers to produce computers that automatically power up as soon as you touch the keyboard.

Advanced Power Management (APM)

An application programming interface (API) developed by Intel and Microsoft that enables developers to include power management in basic input/output systems (BIOSs). APM defines a layer between the hardware and the operating system that effectively shields programmers from hardware details. Advanced Configuration and Power Interface (ACPI) will gradually replace APM.

ARPANET

A large wide area network (WAN) created in the 1960s by the U.S. Department of Defense (DoD) Advanced Research Projects Agency for the free exchange of information between universities and research organizations.

Asynchronous Transfer Mode (ATM)

A networking technology that transfers data in cells (data packets of a fixed size). Cells used with ATM are relatively small compared to packets used with older technologies. The small, constant cell size enables ATM hardware to transmit video images, audio, and computer data over the same network as well as ensures that no single type of data consumes all of the connection's available bandwidth. Current implementations of ATM support data transfer rates from 25 to 622Mbps. Most Ethernet-based networks run at 100Mbps or below.

attribute

A single property that describes an object; for example, the make, model, or color that describes a car. In the context of directories, an attribute is the main component of an entry in a directory, such as an email address.

auditing

The process that tracks the activities of users by recording selected types of events in the security log of a server or workstation.

authentication ticket

A permission to access resources indirectly that a Kerberos Key Distribution Center (KDC) grants to clients and applications.

authorize

To register the Remote Installation Services (RIS) server or the Dynamic Host Configuration Protocol (DHCP) server with Active Directory.

Automatic Private IP Addressing (APIPA)

A client-side feature of Windows 98, 2000, and XP Dynamic Host Configuration Protocol (DHCP) clients. If the client's attempt to negotiate with a DHCP server fails, the client automatically receives an Internet Protocol (IP) address from the 169.254.0.0 Class B range.

Automatic update

A service that checks with the Windows Update Web site for critical updates and automates the process of downloading and installing the critical updates.

backup domain controller (BDC)

In Windows NT Server 4, a server that receives a copy of the domain's directory database (which contains all of the account and security policy information for the domain). BDCs can continue to participate in a Windows 2000 domain when the domain is configured in mixed mode.

Bandwidth Allocation Protocol (BAP)

A protocol that dynamically controls the use of Multilinked lines. BAP eliminates excess bandwidth by allocating lines only when they are required. You can control dynamic links with remote access policies, which are based on the percent of line utilization and the length of time the bandwidth is reduced.

baselining

The process of measuring system performance so that you can ascertain a standard or expected level of performance.

basic disk

A Windows XP term that indicates a physical disk, which can have primary and extended partitions. A basic disk can contain up to three primary partitions and one extended partition, or four primary partitions. A basic disk can also have a single extended partition with logical drives. You *cannot* extend a basic disk.

Basic Input/Output System (BIOS)

Built-in software that determines what a computer can do without accessing programs from a disk. On PCs, the BIOS contains all the code required to control the keyboard, display screen, disk drives, serial communications, and a number of miscellaneous functions. A BIOS that can handle Plug and Play devices is known as a Plug and Play BIOS. A Plug and Play BIOS is always implemented with flash memory rather than read-only memory (ROM). Windows XP benefits if your machine has the latest Advanced Configuration and Power Interface (ACPI)-compliant BIOS.

boot partition

The partition that contains the Windows XP operating system and its support files.

CD-R

A recordable CD-ROM technology using a disc that can be written only once.

CD-RW

A rewritable CD-ROM technology. CD-RW drives can also be used to write CD-R discs, and they can read CD-ROMs. Initially known as CD-E (for CD-Erasable), a CD-RW disc can be rewritten hundreds of times.

Challenge Handshake Authentication Protocol (CHAP)

An authentication protocol used by Microsoft Remote Access as well as network and dial-up connections. Using CHAP, a remote access client can send its authentication credentials to a remote access server in a secure form. Microsoft has created several variations of CHAP that are Windows-specific, such as Microsoft Challenge Handshake Authentication Protocol (MSCHAP) and MSCHAP 2.

client-side caching (CSC)

See *offline file*.

compression

The process of making individual files and folders occupy less disk space with the NT File System (NTFS) 5 file system in Windows XP. Compressed files can be read and written to by any Windows- or DOS-based program *without* having to be decompressed first. They decompress when opened, and recompress when closed. The NTFS 5 file system handles this entire process. Compression is simply a file attribute that you can apply to any file or folder stored on an NTFS 5 partition.

computer account

An account that a domain administrator creates and that uniquely identifies the computer on the domain. The Windows XP computer account matches the name of the computer that joins the domain.

container
An object in the directory that contains other objects.

counter
A metric that provides information about particular aspects of system performance.

daily backup
A backup of files that have changed today but that does not mark them as backed up.

Data Recovery Agent (DRA)
A Windows XP administrator who has been issued a public key certificate for the express purpose of recovering user-encrypted data files that have been encrypted with Encrypting File System (EFS). Data recovery refers to the process of decrypting a file without having the private key of the user who encrypted the file. A DRA may become necessary if a user loses his or her private key for decrypting files, or if a user leaves an organization without decrypting important files that other users need.

default gateway
An address that serves an important role in Transmission Control Protocol/Internet Protocol (TCP/IP) networking by providing a default route for TCP/IP hosts to use when communicating with other hosts on remote networks. A router (either a dedicated router or a computer that connects two or more network segments) generally acts as the default gateway for TCP/IP hosts. The router maintains its own routing table of other networks within an Internetwork. The routing table maps the routes required to reach the remote hosts that reside on those other networks.

Device Manager
The primary tool in Windows XP used to configure and manage hardware devices and their settings.

dial-up access
When a remote client uses the public telephone line or an integrated services digital network (ISDN) line to create a connection to a Windows XP remote access server.

differential backup
A backup that copies files created or changed since the last normal or incremental backup. It does *not* mark files as having been backed up (in other words, the archive attribute is not cleared). If you are performing a combination of normal and differential backups, restoring files and folders requires that you have the last normal backup as well as the last differential backup.

digital signature
The use of public key cryptography to authenticate the integrity and originator of a communication.

digital versatile disc or digital video disc (DVD)
A type of CD-ROM that holds a minimum of 4.7GB, enough for a full-length movie. The DVD specification supports discs with capacities from 4.7 to 17GB and access rates of 600Kbps to 1.3Mbps. One of the best

features of DVD drives is that they are backward compatible with CD-ROMs. This means that DVD players can play old CD-ROMs, CD-I discs, video CDs, and new DVD-ROMs. Newer DVD players can also read CD-R discs. DVD technology uses Moving Picture Experts Group (MPEG)-2 to compress video data.

Direct Memory Access (DMA)

A technique for transferring data from main memory to a device without passing it through the CPU. Computers that have DMA channels can transfer data to and from devices much more quickly than can computers without a DMA channel. This is useful for making quick backups and for realtime applications. Some expansion boards, such as CD-ROM cards, can access the computer's DMA channel. When you install the board, you must specify the DMA channel to be used, which sometimes involves setting a jumper or dual in-line package (DIP) switch.

discretionary access control list (DACL)

A list of access control entries (ACEs) that lets administrators set permissions for users and groups at the object and attribute levels. This list represents part of an object's security descriptor that allows or denies permissions to specific users and groups.

disk group

A Windows XP term for multiple dynamic disks that are managed as a collection. All dynamic disks in a

computer are members of the same disk group. Each disk in a disk group stores replicas of the same configuration data. This configuration data is stored in a 1MB region at the end of each dynamic disk.

Disk Management

A Windows XP MMC snap-in that you use to perform all disk maintenance tasks, such as formatting, creating partitions, deleting partitions, and converting a basic disk to a dynamic disk.

disk quota

A control used in Windows XP to limit the amount of hard disk space available for all users or an individual user. You can apply a quota on a per-user, per-volume basis only.

domain

The fundamental administrative unit of Active Directory. A domain stores information about objects in the domain's partition of Active Directory. You can give user and group accounts in a domain privileges and permissions to resources on any system that belongs to the domain.

domain controller

A computer running Windows 2000 Server that hosts Active Directory and manages user access to a network, which includes logging on, authentication, and access to the directory and shared resources.

domain forest

A collection of one or more Windows 2000 domains in a noncontiguous DNS namespace that share a common schema, configuration, and

Global Catalog and that are linked with two-way transitive trusts.

Domain Name System (DNS)
The standard by which hosts on the Internet have both domain name addresses (for example, rapport.com) and numerical Internet Protocol (IP) addresses (for example, 192.33.2.8). DNS is a service that you use primarily for resolving fully qualified domain names (FQDNs) to IP addresses.

domain tree
A set of domains that form a contiguous DNS namespace through a set of hierarchical relationships.

driver signing
A method for marking or identifying driver files that meet certain specifications or standards. Windows XP uses a driver signing process to make sure drivers have been certified to work correctly with the Windows Driver Model (WDM) in Windows XP.

DVD-R
A write-once optical disk used to master DVD-Video and DVD-ROM discs. DVD-Rs are the DVD counterpart to CD-Rs and use the same recording technology to "burn" the disc.

DVD-RAM
A rewritable DVD technology, best used for data storage. Recorded movies cannot be played on most consumer DVD players.

DVD-RW
A rewritable DVD technology. Information can be written and erased multiple times. DVD-RW primarily is used for movies and is compatible with most of the DVD players on the market.

DVD+RW
A rewritable DVD technology. Data can be written and erased multiple times. DVD+RW can be used for both data and movies and is compatible with most of the DVD players on the market.

dynamic disk
A physical disk in a Windows XP computer that does not use partitions or logical drives. It has dynamic volumes that you create using the Disk Management console. A dynamic disk can contain any of five types of volumes. In addition, you can extend a volume on a dynamic disk. Dynamic disks can contain an unlimited number of volumes, so you are not restricted to four volumes per disk as you are with a basic disk.

Dynamic Host Configuration Protocol (DHCP) server
A Windows 2000 server that dynamically assigns Internet Protocol (IP) addresses to clients. Along with the assignment of IP addresses, it can provide direction toward routers, Windows Internet Naming Service (WINS) servers, and Domain Name System (DNS) servers.

Dynamic Update
Works with Windows Update to download critical fixes and drivers needed during the Setup process. Dynamic Update provides important updates to files required for Setup to minimize difficulties during setup.

dynamic volume

The only type of volume you can create on dynamic disks. The five types of dynamic volumes are simple, spanned, mirrored, striped, and RAID-5. Only computers running Windows XP can directly access dynamic volumes. Windows XP Professional machines *cannot* host, but *can* access, mirrored and RAID-5 dynamic volumes that are on remote Windows 2000 servers.

emergency repair process (or repair process)

A feature that helps you repair problems with system files, your startup environment (if you have a dual-boot or multiple-boot system), and the partition boot sector on your boot volume. Before you use the emergency repair process to repair your system, you must create an Emergency Repair Disk (ERD). You can do this using the Backup utility. Even if you have not created an ERD, you can still try to use the emergency repair process; however, any changes you have made to your system (for example, service pack updates) may be lost and might need to be reinstalled.

Encrypting File System (EFS)

A subsystem of NT File System (NTFS) that uses public keys and private keys to provide encryption for files and folders on computers using Windows XP. Only the user who initially encrypted the file and a recovery agent can decrypt encrypted files and folders.

Extensible Authentication Protocol (EAP)

An extension of Point-to-Point Protocol (PPP) that provides remote access user authentication by means of other security devices. You may add support for a number of authentication schemes, including token cards; dial-up; the Kerberos v5 protocol; one-time passwords; and public key authentication using smart cards, certificates, and others. EAP works with dial-up, Point-to-Point Tunneling Protocol (PPTP), and Layer 2 Tunneling Protocol (L2TP) clients. EAP is a critical technology component for secure Virtual Private Networks (VPNs) because it offers more security against brute force or dictionary attacks (where all possible combinations of characters are attempted) and password guessing than other authentication methods, such as Challenge Handshake Authentication Protocol (CHAP).

fault tolerance

The ability of a computer or operating system to ensure data integrity when hardware failures occur. Within Windows 2000 Server, Advanced Server, and Datacenter Server, mirrored volumes and redundant array of independent disks (RAID)-5 volumes are fault tolerant.

file allocation table (FAT) or FAT16

A 16-bit table that many operating systems use to locate files on disk. The FAT keeps track of all the pieces of a file. The FAT file system for older versions of Windows 95 is called the virtual file allocation table (VFAT); the one for Windows 95

(OEM Service Release 2, or OSR 2) and 98 is called FAT32. Windows XP can use the FAT file system; however, it is not often used on Windows XP, 2000, and NT machines because of its larger cluster sizes and inability to scale to larger volume sizes. The FAT file system has no local security.

file allocation table (FAT32)

A newer, 32-bit version of FAT available in Windows 95 OEM Service Release (OSR) 2 and 98. FAT32 increases the number of bits used to address clusters and reduces the size of each cluster. The result is that it can support larger disks (up to 2TB) and provide better storage efficiency (less slack space) than the earlier version of FAT. The FAT32 file system has no local security. Windows XP can use and format partitions as FAT, FAT32, or NT File System (NTFS).

FireWire or Institute of Electrical and Electronics Engineers (IEEE) 1394

A new, very fast external bus standard that supports data transfer rates of up to 400Mbps. Products that support the 1394 standard go under different names, depending on the company. Apple originally developed the technology and uses the trademarked name FireWire. You can use a single 1394 port to connect up to 63 external devices. In addition to its high speed, 1394 supports time-dependent data, delivering data at a guaranteed rate. This makes it ideal for devices that need to transfer high levels of data in realtime, such as video devices. Although extremely

fast and flexible, 1394 is expensive. Like Universal Serial Bus (USB), 1394 supports both Plug and Play and hot plugging as well as provides power to peripheral devices. The main difference between 1394 and USB is that 1394 supports faster data transfer rates and is more expensive. For these reasons, it is used mostly for devices that require large through-puts, such as video cameras, whereas USB is used to connect most other peripheral devices.

forward lookup

In Domain Name System (DNS), a query process in which the friendly DNS domain name of a host computer is searched to find its Internet Protocol (IP) address.

forward lookup zone

A Domain Name System (DNS) zone that provides hostname to Transmission Control Protocol/Internet Protocol (TCP/IP) address resolution. In DNS Manager, forward lookup zones are based on DNS domain names and typically hold host (A) address resource records.

Frame Relay Permanent Virtual Circuit (PVC)

A protocol where messages are divided into packets before they are sent. Each packet is then transmitted individually and can even follow different routes to its destination. After all the packets that form a message arrive at the destination, they are recompiled into the original message. Several wide area network (WAN) protocols, including Frame

Relay, are based on packet-switching technologies. Ordinary telephone service is based on a circuit-switching technology where a dedicated line is allocated for transmission between two parties. Circuit switching is best suited for data that must be transmitted quickly and must arrive in the same order in which it is sent. Most realtime data, such as live audio and video, requires circuit-switching technology. Packet switching is more efficient and robust for data that can withstand some delays (latency) in transmission, such as email messages and Web content.

global group

A group that can be granted rights and permissions and can become a member of local groups in its own domain and trusting domains. However, a global group can contain user accounts from its own domain only. Global groups provide a way to create sets of users from inside the domain that are available for use both in and out of the domain.

Group Policy

The mechanism for managing change and configuration of systems, security, applications, and user environments in an Active Directory domain.

Group Policy Editor (GPE)

A Windows XP snap-in that enables customers to create custom profiles for groups of users and computers.

Group Policy Object (GPO)

An object created by the Group Policy Editor (GPE) snap-in to hold information about a specific group's association with selected directory objects, such as sites, domains, or organizational units (OUs).

Hardware Abstraction Layer (HAL)

A component of an operating system that functions something like an application programming interface (API). In strict technical architecture, HALs reside at the device level, a layer below the standard API level. HAL enables programmers to write applications and game titles with all the device-independent advantages of writing to an API, but without the large processing overhead that APIs normally demand.

hardware profile

A profile that stores configuration settings for a collection of devices and services. Windows XP can store different hardware profiles so that users' needs can be met even though their computer may frequently require different device and service settings depending on circumstances. The best example is a laptop or portable computer used in an office while in a docking station and then undocked so that the user can travel with it. The two environments do require different power management settings, possibly different network settings, and various other configuration changes.

Hash Message Authentication Code (HMAC) Message Digest 5 (MD5)

A hash algorithm that produces a 128-bit hash of the authenticated payload.

hibernation
A power option in Windows XP Professional portable computers that helps to conserve battery power. Hibernation is a complete power down while maintaining the state of open programs and connected hardware. When you bring your computer out of hibernation, your desktop is restored exactly as you left it, in less time than it takes for a complete system restart. However, it does take longer to bring your computer out of Hibernate mode than out of Standby mode. Put your computer in hibernation when you will be away from the computer for an extended time or overnight.

home directory
A location for a user or group of users to store files on a network server. This provides a central location for files that users can access and back up.

HOSTS file
A local text file in the same format as the 4.3 Berkeley Software Distribution (BSD) Unix /etc/hosts file. This file maps hostnames to Internet Protocol (IP) addresses. In Windows XP, this file is stored in the \%SystemRoot%\System32\Drivers\Etc folder.

incremental backup
A backup that backs up only those files created or changed since the last normal or incremental backup. It marks files as having been backed up (in other words, the archive attribute is cleared). If you use a combination of normal and incremental backups, you need to have the last normal backup set as well as all incremental backup sets to restore your data.

Infrared Data Association (IrDA) device
A device that exchanges data over infrared waves. Infrared technology lets devices "beam" information to each other in the same way that your remote control tells the TV to change the channel. You could, for example, beam a document to a printer or another computer instead of having to connect a cable. The IrDA standard has been widely adopted by PC and consumer electronics manufacturers. Windows XP supports the IrDA standard.

input locale
The specification of the language you want to type in.

input/output (I/O) port
Any socket in the back, front, or side of a computer that you use to connect to another piece of hardware.

integrated services digital network (ISDN)
An international communications standard for sending voice, video, and data over digital telephone lines or normal telephone wires. ISDN supports data transfer rates of 64Kbps. Most ISDN lines offered by telephone companies give you two lines at once, called B channels. You can use one line for voice and the other for data, or you can use both lines for data, giving you data rates of 128Kbps.

integrated zone storage
Storage of zone information in an Active Directory database rather than in a text file.

Internet Connection Firewall (ICF)

A built-in service that monitors all aspects of the traffic that crosses the network interface, which includes inspecting the source and destination addresses, for further control.

Internet Connection Sharing (ICS)

A feature that is intended for use in a small office or home office in which the network configuration and the Internet connection are managed by the computer running Windows XP where the shared connection resides. ICS can use a dial-up connection, such as modem or an integrated services digital network (ISDN) connection to the Internet, or it can use a dedicated connection such as a cable modem or digital subscriber line (DSL). It is assumed that the ICS computer is the only Internet connection, the only gateway to the Internet, and that it sets up all internal network addresses.

Internet Printing Protocol (IPP)

A standard that allows network clients the option of entering a Uniform Resource Locator (URL) to connect to network printers and manage their network print jobs using a Hypertext Transfer Protocol (HTTP) connection in a Web browser. In Windows XP, IPP is fully supported. The print server is either a Windows 2000 server running Internet Information Services (IIS) 5 or a Windows XP Professional system running Personal Web Server (PWS). PWS is the "junior" version of IIS. All shared IPP printers can be viewed at **http://***servername***/printers** (for example, **http://Server2/printers**).

Internet Protocol (IP)

One of the protocols of the Transmission Control Protocol/Internet Protocol (TCP/IP) suite. IP is responsible for determining if a packet is for the local network or a remote network. If the packet is for a remote network, IP finds a route for it.

Internet Protocol (IP) address

A 32-bit binary address used to identify a host's network and host ID. The network portion can contain either a network ID or a network ID and a subnet ID.

Internet Protocol Security (IPSec)

A Transmission Control Protocol/Internet Protocol (TCP/IP) security mechanism. IPSec provides machine-level authentication, as well as data encryption, for Virtual Private Network (VPN) connections that use Layer 2 Tunneling Protocol (L2TP). IPSec negotiates between your computer and its remote tunnel server before an L2TP connection is established, which secures both passwords and data.

Interrupt Request (IRQ)

A hardware line over which a device or devices can send interrupt signals to the microprocessor. When you add a new device to a PC, you sometimes need to set its IRQ number. IRQ conflicts used to be a common problem when you were adding expansion boards, but the Plug and Play and Advanced Configuration and Power Interface (ACPI) specifications have helped to remove this headache in many cases.

ipconfig
A command that enables you to view, renegotiate, and configure Internet Protocol (IP) address information for a Windows NT, 2000, or XP computer.

Kerberos v5
A distributed authentication and privacy protocol that protects information on a network between devices and enables Single Sign-On (SSO). Kerberos v5 is used in the Windows XP security model.

language group
A Regional Options configuration that allows you to type and read documents composed in languages of that group (for example, Western Europe and United States, Japanese, and Hebrew).

Last Known Good Configuration
Starts Windows XP using the Registry information that Windows saved at the last shutdown. Use this only in cases when you have incorrectly configured a device or driver. Last Known Good Configuration does not solve problems caused by corrupted or missing drivers or files. Also, you will lose any changes you made since the last successful startup.

Layer 2 Tunneling Protocol (L2TP)
An industry-standard Internet tunneling protocol. Unlike Point-to-Point Tunneling Protocol (PPTP), L2TP does not require Internet Protocol (IP) connectivity between the client workstation and the server. L2TP requires only that the tunnel medium provide packet-oriented point-to-point connectivity. You can use the protocol over media such as Asynchronous Transfer Mode (ATM), Frame Relay, and X.25. L2TP provides the same functionality as PPTP.

local group
A group account that is stored in the Security Accounts Manager (SAM) of a single system. You can give a local group access to resources only on that system.

local user
A user account that is stored in the Security Accounts Manager (SAM) of a single system. A local user can belong only to local groups on the same system and can be given access to resources only on that system.

logical drive
A simple volume or partition indicated by a drive letter that resides on a Windows XP basic disk.

logon script
A file that you can assign to user accounts. Typically a batch file, a logon script runs automatically every time the user logs on. You can use it to configure a user's working environment at every logon, and it allows an administrator to influence a user's environment without managing all aspects of it. You can assign a logon script to one or more user accounts.

Microsoft Challenge Handshake Authentication Protocol (MSCHAP) 1
A special version of Challenge Handshake Authentication Protocol (CHAP) that Microsoft uses. The encryption is still two-way and

consists of a challenge from the server to the client that is made up of a session ID. The client uses a Message Digest 4 (MD4) hash to return the username to the server.

Microsoft Management Console (MMC)

A set of Windows XP utilities that allow authorized administrators to manage the directory remotely. The MMC provides a framework for hosting administrative tools, called consoles.

mirrored volume

A fault-tolerant set of two physical disks that contain an exact replica of each other's data within the mirrored portion of each disk. It is supported only on Windows 2000 Server versions.

mixed-mode domain

A migration concept that provides maximum backward compatibility with earlier versions of Windows NT. In a mixed-mode domain, domain controllers that have been upgraded to Active Directory services allow servers running Windows NT versions 4 and earlier to exist within the domain.

mounted drive, mount point, or mounted volume

A pointer from one partition to another. Mounted drives are useful for increasing a drive's "size" without disturbing it. For example, you could create a mount point to drive E as C:\CompanyData. Doing so makes it seem that you have increased the size available on the C partition, specifically allowing you to store more data in C:\CompanyData than you would otherwise be able to.

Moving Picture Experts Group (MPEG)

A family of digital video compression standards and file formats. MPEG generally produces better-quality video than competing formats. MPEG files can be decoded by special hardware or by software. MPEG achieves a high compression rate by storing only the changes from one frame to another, instead of each entire frame. There are two major MPEG standards: MPEG-1 and MPEG-2. The MPEG-1 standard provides a video resolution of 352×240 at 30 frames per second (fps), which is video quality slightly below that of conventional VCR videos. A newer standard, MPEG-2, offers resolutions of 720×480 and 1,280×720 at 60 fps, with full CD-quality audio. This is sufficient for all the major TV standards, including NTSC and even HDTV. DVD-ROMs use MPEG-2. MPEG-2 can compress a two-hour video into a few gigabytes. Currently, work is being done on a new version of MPEG called MPEG-4 (there is no MPEG-3). MPEG-4 will be based on the QuickTime file format.

Multilink

An extension of Point-to-Point Protocol (PPP) that enables you to combine multiple physical connections between two points into a single logical connection. For example, you can combine two 33.6Kbps modems into one logical 67.2Kbps connection. The combined connections, called *bundles,* provide greater bandwidth than a single connection.

Multiple Processor Support (MPS)-compliant

Windows XP provides support for single or multiple CPUs. If you originally installed Windows XP on a computer with a single CPU, you must update the Hardware Abstraction Layer (HAL) on your computer so that it can recognize and use multiple CPUs.

name resolution

The process of translating a name into an Internet Protocol (IP) address. This could be either a fully qualified domain name (FQDN) or a NetBIOS name.

namespace

The method or conventions by which objects in a group of cooperating directories or databases are hierarchically structured and named.

native mode domain

A migration concept in which all domain controllers are running Windows 2000. The domain uses only Active Directory services multimaster replication between domain controllers, and no Windows NT domain controllers can participate in the domain through single-master replication.

network directory

A file or database from which users or applications can get reference information about objects on the network.

network interface card (NIC) or network adapter

A piece of computer hardware called an adapter card that physically connects a computer to a network cable.

normal backup

A backup that copies all files and marks those files as having been backed up (in other words, clears the archive attribute). It is the most complete form of backup.

NT File System (NTFS) 5

An advanced file system designed for use specifically within the Windows XP operating system. It supports file system recovery, extremely large storage media, and long file names.

NT File System (NTFS) permission

A rule associated with a folder, file, or printer to regulate which users can gain access to the object and in what manner. The object's owner allows or denies permissions. The most restrictive permissions take effect between share permissions and NTFS permissions on an object.

object

In the context of performance monitoring and optimization, a system component that has numerous counters associated with it. Objects include Processor, Memory, System, Logical Disk, and Pagefile.

offline file

A new feature of Windows XP that enables users to continue to work with network files and programs even when they are not connected to the network. When a network connection is restored or when users dock their mobile computers, any changes that were made while users were working offline are updated to the network. When more than one user on the network has made changes to the same file, users are given the option of saving their specific version of the file to the network, keeping the other version, or saving both.

Open Systems Interconnect (OSI) model
A layer architecture developed by the International Organization for Standardization (ISO) that standard-izes levels of service and types of interaction for computers that are exchanging information through a communications network. The OSI model separates computer-to-computer communications into seven layers or levels, each building upon the standards contained in the levels below it.

optimization
The process of tuning performance for a particular system component.

organizational unit (OU)
A type of container object used within the Lightweight Directory Access Protocol (LDAP)/X.500 information model to group other objects and classes together for easier administration.

Packet Internet Groper (Ping) utility
A utility that determines whether a specific Internet Protocol (IP) address for a network device is reachable from an individual computer. It works by sending a data packet to the specified

address and waiting for a reply. You use it to troubleshoot network connections in the Transmission Control Protocol/Internet Protocol (TCP/IP) network protocol.

paging file
Formerly called the swap file or virtual memory file, an extension of memory space stored on the disk drive as a kind of virtual memory.

partition
The information area beginning at a branch of a directory tree and continuing to the bottom of that tree and/or to the edges of new partitions controlled by subordinate Directory System Agents (DSAs).

Password Authentication Protocol (PAP)
The protocol that allows clear-text authentication.

Peripheral Connection Interface (PCI)
A local bus standard developed by Intel. Most modern PCs include a PCI bus in addition to a more general Industry Standard Architecture (ISA) expansion bus. Many analysts, however, believe that PCI will eventually replace ISA entirely. PCI is a 64-bit bus, though it is usually implemented as a 32-bit bus. It can run at clock speeds of 33 or 66MHz. Although Intel developed it, PCI is not tied to any particular family of microprocessors.

Personal Computer Memory Card International Association (PCMCIA)
An organization of some 500 companies that developed a standard for small, credit card–sized devices called PC Cards. Originally designed

for adding memory to portable computers, the PCMCIA standard has been expanded several times and is suitable for many types of devices. There are in fact three types of PCMCIA cards, along with three types of PC slots the cards fit into: Type I, II, and III, respectively.

Plug and Play

A standard developed by Microsoft, Intel, and other industry leaders to simplify the process of adding hardware to PCs by having the operating system automatically detect devices. The standard's intention is to conceal unpleasant details, such as Interrupt Requests (IRQs) and Direct Memory Access (DMA) channels, from people who want to add a new hardware device to their system. A Plug and Play monitor, for example, can communicate with both Windows XP and the graphics adapter to automatically set itself at the maximum refresh rate supported for a chosen resolution. Plug and Play compliance also ensures that devices will not be driven beyond their capabilities.

Point-to-Point Protocol (PPP)

A method of connecting a computer to a network or to the Internet. PPP is more stable than the older Serial Line Internet Protocol (SLIP) and provides error-checking features. Windows XP Professional is a PPP client when dialing into any network.

Point-to-Point Tunneling Protocol (PPTP)

A communication protocol that tunnels through another connection, encapsulating PPP packets. The encapsulated packets are Internet Protocol (IP) datagrams that can be transmitted over IP-based networks, such as the Internet.

policy

A configuration or setting that is specified for one or more systems or users. Policies are refreshed at startup, at logon, and after a refresh interval, so if a setting is manually changed, the policy refreshes the setting automatically. Policies provide for centralized management of change and configuration.

primary domain controller (PDC)

In a Windows NT Server 4 or earlier domain, the computer running Windows NT Server that authenticates domain logons and maintains the directory database for a domain. The PDC tracks changes made to accounts of all computers on a domain. It is the only computer to receive these changes directly. A domain has only one PDC.

primary master

An authoritative Domain Name System (DNS) server for a zone that you can use as a point of update for the zone. Only primary masters can be updated directly to process zone updates, which include adding, removing, or modifying resource records that are stored as zone data. Primary masters are also used as the first sources for replicating the zone to other DNS servers.

primary monitor

The monitor designated as the one that displays the logon dialog box when you start your computer. Most programs display their window on the primary monitor when you first open them. A Windows XP computer can support multiple monitors or displays.

privilege

The capability to perform a system behavior, such as changing the system time, backing up or restoring files, or formatting the hard drive. A privilege used to be, and often still is, referred to as a user right.

public key cryptography

An asymmetric encryption scheme that uses a pair of keys to code data. The public key encrypts data, and a corresponding secret key decrypts it. For digital signatures, the sender uses the private key to create a unique electronic number that can be read by anyone who has the corresponding public key, thus verifying that the message is truly from the sender.

Recovery Console

A command-line interface (CLI) that provides a limited set of administrative commands that are useful for repairing a computer. For example, you can use the Recovery Console to start and stop services, read and write data on a local drive (including drives formatted to use NT File System—NTFS), repair a master boot record (MBR), and format drives. You can start the Recovery Console from the Windows XP CD or by using the **winnt32.exe** command with the **/cmdcons** switch.

redundant array of independent disks (RAID)-5 (or striped set with parity) volume

A fault-tolerant collection of equal-sized partitions on at least three physical disks, where the data is striped and includes parity data. The parity data is used to help recover a member of the striped set if one of its members fails. Windows XP Professional cannot host a RAID-5 volume, but Windows 2000 Server versions can.

Remote Assistance

A built-in service that enables another user, typically a help desk or IT employee, to remotely help the end user with an issue that they are experiencing on their Windows XP Professional computer.

Remote Authentication Dial-In User Service (RADIUS)

A protocol used by Internet Authentication Services (IAS) to enable the communication of authentication, authorization, and accounting to the homogeneous and heterogeneous dial-up or Virtual Private Network (VPN) equipment in the enterprise.

Remote Desktop

A built-in service that enables you to access a session that is running on your computer while you are sitting at another computer. This will be extremely useful for employees who want to work from home, but need to access their computer at work.

Remote Installation Service (RIS)

An RIS server provides Windows XP Professional operating system image(s) that can be downloaded and installed by network clients using network adapters that comply with the Pre-Boot Execution Environment (PXE) boot read-only memory (ROM) specifications. RIS requires Active Directory, Dynamic Host Configuration Protocol (DHCP), and Domain Name System (DNS) to serve clients.

Removable Storage

Allows applications to access and share the same media resources. This service is used for managing removable media. Different types of media include floppy disks, Zip disks, CD-ROMs, CD-Rs, CD-RWs, DVD media, and tape backup devices. Some include removable hard drives as removable storage.

Resulting Set of Policies (RSoP)

A term for the resulting group policies that are applied to a computer and user. With multiple group policies at sites, domains, and OUs, it is very complex to determine the final, resulting policies that are applied.

reverse lookup zone

A Domain Name System (DNS) zone that provides Transmission Control Protocol/Internet Protocol (TCP/IP) address to hostname resolution.

route

A Windows XP command-line utility that manipulates Transmission Control Protocol/Internet Protocol (TCP/IP) routing tables for the local computer.

Safe Mode startup options

The options you get at startup when you press the F8 function key. Safe Mode helps you to diagnose problems. When started in Safe Mode, Windows XP uses only basic files and drivers (mouse, monitor, keyboard, mass storage, base video, and default system services, but no network connections). You can choose the Safe Mode With Networking option, which loads all of the previously listed files and drivers plus the essential services and drivers to start networking. Or, you can choose the Safe Mode With Command Prompt option, which is exactly the same as Safe Mode except that a command prompt is started instead of Windows XP. You can also choose Last Known Good Configuration, which starts your computer using the Registry information that Windows XP saved at the last shutdown. If a symptom does not reappear when you start in Safe Mode, you can eliminate the default settings and minimum device drivers as possible causes. If a newly added device or a changed driver is causing problems, you can use Safe Mode to remove the device or reverse the change. In some circumstances, such as when Windows system files required to start the system are corrupted or damaged, Safe Mode cannot help you. In this case, the Emergency Repair Disk (ERD) may be of use.

sampling (or update) interval

The frequency with which a performance counter is logged. A shorter interval provides more detailed information but generates a larger log.

scalability
A measure of how well a computer, service, or application can grow to meet increasing performance demands.

Security Accounts Manager (SAM)
The database of local user and local group accounts on a Windows 2000 member server or Windows XP Professional system.

Security Identifier (SID)
A unique number that represents a security principal, such as a user or group. You can change the name of a user or group account without affecting the account's permissions and privileges, because the SID is what is granted user rights and resource access.

Serial Line Internet Protocol (SLIP)
An older remote access communication protocol used in Windows XP for outbound communication only.

service (SRV) record
A resource record used in a zone to register and locate well-known Transmission Control Protocol/ Internet Protocol (TCP/IP) services. The SRV resource record is specified in Request for Comments (RFC) 2052 and is used in Windows 2000 or later to locate domain controllers for Active Directory Service.

Setup Manager
Used to create answer files for Windows XP unattended installations. Setup Manager can create answer files for unattended, Sysprep, or RIS installations.

share permission
A rule associated with a folder, to regulate which users can gain access to the object over the network and in what manner.

Shiva Password Authentication Protocol (SPAP)
A protocol that third-party clients and servers typically use. The encryption for the protocol is two-way, but it is not as good as that for Challenge Handshake Authentication Protocol (CHAP).

simple volume
In Windows XP, the disk space on a single physical disk. It can consist of a single area on a disk or multiple areas on the same disk that are linked together. You can extend a simple volume within the same disk or among multiple disks. If you extend a simple volume across multiple disks, it becomes a spanned volume.

slipstreaming
The process of integrating a Windows XP service pack into an existing Windows XP installation share. Subsequent installations of Windows XP will then include the service pack that you have slipstreamed into the installation share.

Smart Card
A credit card–sized device used to securely store public and private keys, passwords, and other types of personal information. To use a Smart Card, you need a Smart Card reader

attached to the computer and a personal identification number (PIN) for the Smart Card. In Windows XP, you can use Smart Cards to enable certificate-based authentication and Single Sign-On (SSO) to the enterprise.

Smart Card reader

A small external or internal device, or even a built-in slot, into which you insert a Smart Card so that it can be read.

spanned volume

In Windows XP, the disk space on more than one physical disk. You can add more space to a spanned volume by extending it at any time. In NT 4 and earlier, a spanned volume was called a volume set.

spooler service

The primary Windows XP service that controls printing functionality.

standard zone storage

Storage of zone information in a text file rather than in an Active Directory database.

Standby mode

A power-saving option in Windows XP. Your computer switches to a low-power state where devices, such as the monitor and hard disks, turn off and your computer uses less power. When you want to use the computer again, it comes out of Standby quickly, and your desktop is restored exactly as you left it. Standby is useful for conserving battery power in portable computers. Standby does not save your desktop state to disk; if you experi-

ence a power failure while on Standby, you can lose unsaved information. If there is an interruption in power, information in memory is lost.

static pool

A range of Internet Protocol (IP) addresses configured on the remote access server that enables the server to allocate IP addresses to the remote access clients.

striped volume

A volume that stores data in stripes on two or more physical disks. Data in a striped volume is allocated alternately and evenly (in stripes) to the disks of the striped volume. Striped volumes are *not* fault tolerant. Striped volumes can substantially improve the speed of access to your data on disk. Striped volumes with parity, also known as RAID-5 volumes, can be created *only* on Windows 2000 Server machines. In NT 4 and earlier, a striped volume was called a striped set.

subnet mask

A filter used to determine which network segment, or subnet, an Internet Protocol (IP) address belongs to. An IP address has two components: the network address and the host (computer name) address. For example, if the IP address 209.15.17.8 is part of a Class C network, the first three numbers (209.15.17) represent the Class C network address, and the last number (8) identifies a specific host (computer) on this network. By implementing subnetting, network administrators can further divide the host part of the address into two or more subnets.

Suspend mode

A deep-sleep power-saving option that still uses some power.

symmetric multiprocessing (SMP)

A computer architecture that provides fast performance by making multiple CPUs available to complete individual processes simultaneously (multiprocessing). Unlike with asymmetric processing, you can assign any idle processor any task as well as add additional CPUs to improve performance and handle increased loads. A variety of specialized operating systems and hardware arrangements support SMP. Specific applications can benefit from SMP if their code allows multithreading. SMP uses a single operating system and shares common memory and disk input/output (I/O) resources. Windows XP supports SMP.

Sysprep

A tool that prepares a Windows XP computer to be imaged using third-party disk image software. It does this by removing unique identifiers such as computer name and Security Identifiers (SIDs). Sysprep adds a service to the image that generates a unique local domain SID after the image has been applied.

system state

In Backup, a collection of system-specific data that you can back up and restore. For all Windows 2000 and XP operating systems, the system state data includes the Registry, the Component Object Model (COM)+ Class Registration database, and the system boot files. For Windows 2000 Server, the system state data also includes the Certificate Services database (if the server is operating as a certificate server). If the server is a domain controller, the system state data also includes the Active Directory directory services database and the Sysvol directory.

Sysvol

A shared directory that stores the server copy of the domain's public files, which are replicated among all domain controllers in the domain.

ticket

A feature of the Kerberos security model by which clients are granted access to objects and resources only indirectly, through services. Application servers use the service ticket to impersonate the client and look up its user or group Security Identifiers (SIDs).

tracert

A Windows XP command-line utility that follows that path of a data packet from a local computer to a host (computer) somewhere on the network (or Internetwork). It shows how many hops the packet requires to reach the host and how long each hop takes. You can use **tracert** to figure out where the longest delays are occurring for connecting to various computers.

universal group

A security or distribution group that you can use anywhere in the domain tree or forest. A universal group can have members from any Windows 2000 domain in the domain tree or forest. It can also include other universal groups, global groups, and accounts from any domain in the domain tree or forest. Universal groups can be members of domain local groups and other universal groups but cannot be members of global groups. Universal groups appear in the Global Catalog and should contain primarily global groups.

Universal Serial Bus (USB)

An external bus standard (released in 1996) that supports data transfer rates of 12Mbps. You can use a single USB port to connect up to 127 peripheral devices, such as mice, modems, and keyboards. USB also supports Plug and Play installation and hot plugging. It is expected to completely replace serial and parallel ports.

User Datagram Protocol (UDP)

A connectionless protocol that runs on top of Internet Protocol (IP) networks. Unlike Transmission Control Protocol/Internet Protocol (TCP/IP), UDP/IP provides very few error recovery services and does not guarantee delivery of data. UDP is a direct way to send and receive datagrams over an IP network. It's used primarily for sending broadcast messages over an IP network.

user locale

Controls the date, time, currency, and numbers on a per-user basis. These settings are used by all applications and can be configured via the Regional Options applet in the Control Panel folder.

user profile

The collection of desktop and environmental settings that define the work area of a local computer.

user right

See *privilege*.

User State Migration Tool (USMT)

A command-line interface set of tools that stores user data and settings for an upgrade or reinstallation of the computer. The tools include **scanstate** and **loadstate**, which extract the information and restore the information, respectively.

video adapter

The electronic component that generates the video signal sent through a cable to a video display. The video adapter is usually located on the computer's main system board or on an expansion board.

Virtual Private Network (VPN)

A private network of computers that is at least partially connected using public channels or lines, such as the Internet. A good example would be a private-office local area network (LAN) that enables users to log in remotely over the Internet (an open, public system). VPNs use encryption and secure protocols like Point-to-Point Tunneling Protocol (PPTP) and Layer 2 Tunneling Protocol (L2TP) to ensure that unauthorized parties do not intercept data transmissions.

Volume Shadow Copy Technology (VSCT)

A volume that represents a duplicate of the original volume taken at the time the copy began.

Windows Backup

A Windows XP utility that helps you plan for and recover from data loss by enabling you to create backup copies of data as well as restore files, folders, and system state data (which includes the Registry) manually or on a schedule. The Windows XP Backup program enables you to back up data to a variety of media types, not just tape.

Windows Installer Packages

Files with the .msi extension that install applications. These files contain summary and installation instructions as well as the actual installation files. You can install Windows Installer Packages locally or remotely through Group Policies.

Windows Internet Naming Service (WINS)

A service that dynamically maps NetBIOS names to Internet Protocol (IP) addresses.

Windows Management Instrumentation (WMI)

An initiative supported in Windows XP that establishes architecture to support the management of an enterprise across the Internet. WMI offers universal access to management information for enterprises by providing a consistent view of the managed environment. This management uniformity enables you to manage your entire business rather than just its components. You can obtain more detailed information regarding the WMI Software Development Kit (SDK) from the Microsoft Developer Network (MSDN).

Windows Messenger

The new application built into the OS that allows for chatting, notifications, voice communication, file transfer, and sharing of applications.

Windows or Win32 Driver Model (WDM)

A 32-bit layered architecture for device drivers; it allows for drivers that Windows XP, 2000, NT, and 98 can use. It provides common input/output (I/O) services that all operating systems understand. It also supports Plug and Play; Universal Serial Bus (USB); Institute of Electrical and Electronics Engineers (IEEE) 1394 bus; and various devices, including input, communication, imaging, and digital versatile disc or digital video disc (DVD) devices.

Windows Update

Offers device driver support that supplements the extensive library of drivers available on the installation CD. Windows Update is an online extension, providing a central location for product enhancements.

winnt32 /cmdcons

The command and switch used to install the Recovery Console onto a

Windows XP computer. This command uses **winnt32** on the installation media, or in the distribution source.

workgroup

A peer-to-peer network in which user accounts are decentralized and stored on each individual system.

X.25 Virtual Circuit (VC)

A connection between two devices that acts as though it's a direct connection although it may physically take different routes. X.25 connections involve at least two hosts in a packet-switching network. With X.25 VCs, two hosts can communicate as though they have a dedicated connection, although the data packets might actually travel very different routes before arriving at their destinations. VCs can be either permanent or temporary.

ZAP

A file that you use to allow applications without an MSI file to be deployed via Group Policy.

zone

In Domain Name System (DNS) standards, the namespace partition formed by each domain within the global namespace or within an enterprise namespace. Each zone is controlled by an authoritative DNS server, or in the case of Active Directory services, by a group of domain controllers.

zone transfer

Copying of Domain Name System (DNS) database information from one DNS server to another.

Index